THE ENGLISH LANGUAGE
ITS BEAUTY AND USE

General Editors

J. M. PARRISH, M.A. (Oxon,)
JOHN R. CROSSLAND, F.R.G.S.

A Midſommer nights dreame.

As it hath beene ſundry times pub-
lickely acted, by the *Right honoura*
ble, the Lord Chamberlaine hrs
ſeruants.

Written by William Shakeſpeare.

¶ Imprinted at London, for *Thomas Fiſher*, and are to
be ſoulde at his ſhoppe, at the Signe of the White Hart,
in *Fleetestreete.* 1600.

"WRITTEN BY WILLIAM SHAKESPEARE."
The title-page to "A Midſommer nights dreame," first edition.

THE
ENGLISH LANGUAGE
ITS BEAUTY AND USE

ENGLISH LITERATURE
LANGUAGE: JOURNALISM

Advisory Editor

PROF. LASCELLES ABERCROMBIE, M.A.,
Litt.D., D.Lit., *Goldsmiths' Reader in English,*
University of Oxford. Lately Hildred Carlile
Professor of English Literature, University
of London.

Edited by

J. M. PARRISH, M.A. (Oxon.)
R. D. COOLE, B.A. (Oxon.)

ODHAMS PRESS LIMITED
LONG ACRE, LONDON, W.C.2

INTRODUCTION

LITERATURE—indeed, all art—is splendidly rebellious. It will never lie meekly in the compartments the critic makes for it. Literature is not poetry, plus drama, plus novel, plus essay; the compartments are not water-tight: a play may be at the same time the very finest poetry—Shakespeare's best work fused both together; a novel that had no poetry in it would be drab stuff, for the novelist reflects life, and poetry is inextricably interwoven with life. No, literature is not the sum total of its different mediums; it will not be confined; it overflows our classifications, and, bearing onwards, falls into its own forms; the critic labours after, marking its course as best he can.

Yet the arrangement of literature into various kinds, though it can never be adequate, is essential if we are to obtain the necessary framework for the increase of our pleasure in reading. By making divisions in literature—poetry, prose; novel, short story; drama, narrative—we form as it were a trellis-work in our minds, a frame on which literature may grow, gracing our leisure hours, blossoming amongst the worries and depression of the work-a-day world. In this way we have a place prepared for beauty. That is the purpose of all criticism, and its sole justification; its aim should be to help us appreciate art; criticism should explain, not destroy; and a critic should teach and assist, not rant and bewilder.

The Editors of this book have planned it as an assistance to literary appreciation, as a guide through the wide, fragrant expanses of Literature. Each article takes one kind of literature for its province, and explains, without entering into controversy and without confusing detail, what to look for, how best to appreciate it. Unnecessary elaboration has been avoided, for the Editors believe that the best framework is the simplest.

If the articles succeed in sending the reader to roam for himself in what Keats called the " Realms of Gold," then the Editors will be amply justified. The articles are not intended to form a rigid sequence to which the reader must adhere. Literature has no fixed starting-point. True, poetry was written before novels were, but nothing prevents the student of literature from starting with the novel and working back to the foundations of creative writings, to the old epics and ballads. *One should start reading where one's main interests lie.* Guides to the greatest creative works in literature, as well as to the pronouncements of famous critics, will be found at the end of each article.

HOW THE BOOK IS PLANNED

The book is divided into two parts. The object of the first part we have outlined above. The second part is concerned with the craft of writing as it comes into the province and the activities of the ordinary professional men or women who do not aim primarily at writing masterpieces, but who appreciate the practical value of being able to express themselves in correct English, clearly, forcefully, with the minimum of wastage. Such an ability may well be called " The Craft of the Written Word." There is as much satisfaction in expressing oneself well, be it in a letter, a newspaper article, a debate, or even in a diary, as a carpenter finds in fitting together a perfect desk or chair.

Words, sentences, articles—these are the subjects of the second half of the book. Beginning with the smallest units —English words—tracing their history and going into their etymology, the authors of the various articles pass progressively through the craft of fitting the words together in a sentence (the grammar of language) to the craft of constructing articles and stories, or journalism. These articles in the second part deal also with the opportunities of turning the craft of writing to profit ; with what to write and where to submit it.

To be able to appreciate the best creative writing of all time ; to be able oneself to write in such a way as to experience the pleasure that always comes from a worthwhile thing well done, these are faculties that any one should be glad to acquire. It is the aim of the Editors of this book to make possible for every reader during spare hours this double pleasure ; and, further, they have attempted to arrange the facilities in such a way that they shall be at once scholarly and interesting, pleasantly acquirable and of lasting value ; they have tried to give a comprehensive, living introduction to a subject that is co-extensive with all the ages.

CONTENTS

CONTENTS

"READING MAKETH A FULL MAN"

by GEOFFREY CRUMP, M.A.(Cantab.)

IN an entertaining little book, entitled *Literary Taste*, Arnold Bennett wrote these words : " The average person is bound to have read somewhere that the style of Sir Thomas Browne is unsurpassed in English literature. One day he sees outside a book-shop a copy of the *Religio Medici*, and he buys it by way of a mild experiment. He does not expect to be enchanted by it ; a profound instinct tells him that Sir Thomas Browne is ' not his line ' ; and in the result he is even less enchanted than he expected to be. He reads the introduction, and he glances at the first page or two of the work. He sees nothing but words. The work makes no appeal to him whatever. He puts the book away. If Sir Thomas Browne is mentioned, he will say : ' Oh yes, very fine ! ' with a feeling of pride that he has at all events bought and inspected Sir Thomas Browne. But deep in his heart is a suspicion that people who get enthusiastic about Sir Thomas Browne are vain and conceited poseurs." Many of us can sympathise with this. Genuine lovers of literature have never been numerous, but at the present time there is probably more interest in books than ever before, and that interest is increasing. Few, however, have the time, or the knowledge, to find the books they want ; and haphazard incursions into the works of celebrated writers are likely, as Arnold Bennett has pointed out, to prove discouraging.

The purpose of this book is to furnish a guide for those who want to read the best books, but do not know where to find them. It is, moreover, a guide to those who want to read primarily for pleasure, not for study. The first thing to do, therefore, is to examine this belief that what is commonly called " literature " is dull.

THE ESSENCE OF ALL LITERATURE

LITERATURE is a record of the experience and imagination of mankind. It might fairly be described as " life on paper." Elsewhere in the same book Arnold Bennett said that " the makers of literature are those who have felt and seen the interestingness of the universe,"—that is to say, of life. "Whatsoever," as Sir Arthur Quiller-Couch says, "engages man's activity of soul or body, may be deemed the subject of literature, and is transformed into literature by the process of recording it in memorable speech." The propositions of Euclid, the lyrics of Shelley, the learned dissertations of Bacon, the whimsical musings of Charles Lamb, all share this distinction, and it is a distinction that can be appreciated by any moderately experienced reader ; it is easy to tell whether a book "engages man's activity of soul or body," and whether it is "recorded in memorable speech." If it fulfils these conditions it cannot be dull.

"Interestingness" is the basic condition of the existence of literature ; books that cease to be interesting are soon forgotten. Life interests us through our emotions and through our intellects, and so do the writers of books—the poets, by appealing to the emotions, by exciting feelings of pity, sadness, delight, wonder, awe, or enthusiasm, the prose-writers by appealing to the intellectual faculties of reason, curiosity, and wit. Human interests are of course numerous and diverse, and a book that interests one reader may irritate another. But the supreme test of the value of a book to the reader is that it should interest him ; if it does not, it is of no use to him, though it may be the most famous book in the world. "Literature" may be taken to mean that body of recorded experience that interests enough people to keep it alive. There is nothing in the ranks of literature that has not a reason for being there, and there is something there for every one. What we need is first to know what there is, and where to find what we want ; secondly, to give the books that we try a fair chance ; and thirdly, to sharpen our judgment so that we can recognise the best. If these conditions are fulfilled, literature becomes one of the most precious enrichments of life ; and it is to further that end that this book is designed.

DESIRES THAT FIND FULFILMENT IN BOOKS

THE spirit of man desires truth, goodness, and beauty, and it is to books that we turn most of all to satisfy these needs. Perhaps it is the greatest value of literature that it purifies, and to some degree satisfies, these elemental cravings. Literature is the recorded experience, intellectual and moral and emotional, of the human race ; and by assimilating this experience we come to recognise and value these three qualities for their own sake (not, for instance, honesty because it is the best policy, or goodness because it will purchase eternal salvation, or beauty because it happens to be rare or expensive). The instinct for truth, the desire for knowledge, drives every one to books at some time or another. All the knowledge in the world is stored in books, and not in learned volumes only. We can find out as much about life from the imaginative writer as from the scientist or the historian. Both kinds of writer have their faces turned towards the truth ; the man of learning sees truth as a mighty pile of facts looming through the fog of imagination, but the man of letters, being primarily an artist, sees truth as an unscalable mountain of imagination, obscured by a mist of facts.

Our instinct for goodness, or in other words our interest in moral values, is also largely directed to books. We are all of us concerned with the problem of good and evil, though that does not imply that we find ourselves greatly interested in moral treatises and so-called " improving " books. The intensive study of morals is not popular ; yet it is true that morals are the concern, often the principal concern, of writers on almost every subject. Philosophy, religion, good and evil, social behaviour, human relationships, the laws of nature, are the chief preoccupation of our greatest writers—poets, prose writers, and dramatists alike. To many this is the main interest of literature. " Poets," said Shelley, " are the unacknowledged legislators of the world." Literature, however, is not merely a mine of information ; it is an art. It captures the interest not only by what is said, but by the way in which it is said ; for great books appeal to the intellect through the emotions, by embodying fine thought in beautiful form. All effective pieces of writing are works of art, and the more we read, the more we come to demand, not only interest, but symmetry of form, and language that is pleasing and memorable.

THE GOLDEN GIFT OF LAUGHTER

To these three qualities, information, moral interest, and competent execution, a fourth may be added—namely, laughter. Laughter may spring either from the brain or from the heart ; it may be provoked either by wit or by humour. The best comic writers succeed in blending the two, but the distinction is clear if we compare, say, the comedy of Oscar Wilde with that of Shakespeare. Wilde's brilliant and absurd dialogue would be funny whoever spoke it, and we remember his epigrams independently of their context. But Shakespeare's comic characters, although they say amusing things, are enjoyed and remembered for what they are rather than for what they say. There is no lack of wit amongst English writers, but the English pride themselves on possessing a sense of humour that is peculiarly their own, and certainly it is one of the greatest glories of our literature. Foreigners say that it is a myth, and indeed it is almost impossible to analyse and explain. It is perhaps a certain quality of critical yet sympathetic awareness of the peculiarities that make every human being interesting as an individual. But definitions are dangerous ; and those who read Chaucer, Shakespeare, Mr. Pepys, Jane Austen, or Dickens, not to mention scores of less famous writers, cannot fail to be aware of this element in their work. Matthew Arnold said that the outstanding characteristic of the best English poetry was its " high seriousness," and it is perhaps because this is balanced by such a keen sense of fun in other kinds of writing that the reputation of English literature stands so high.

We are grateful to an author who makes us laugh, and we are grateful to an author who makes us think, or wonder at his skill. But writers who aim at one of these qualities only can seldom sustain much interest. A book that tries solely to be funny generally ends by being as dreary as a recital of dry facts, a moral dissertation, or a mere wallowing in words. But the greatest books—such as the Bible, the plays of Shakespeare, the works of Swift, Hardy, or Bernard Shaw —combine most of these four qualities, if not all, to a high degree, and give the reader that feeling of satisfaction which is experienced only in the masterpieces of literature.

MANIFOLD ADVENTURES

Books have been written about every conceivable subject, and in every conceivable form. " Literature " implies principally books of the imaginative kind, such as novels, short stories, plays, and poetry of all sorts. But there are also works of history, biography, travel, criticism, philosophy, and every department of specialised knowledge ; these, if " recorded in memorable speech," are a part of our literary heritage, and to some people a more interesting part than imaginative literature. There are also the newspapers. The daily papers and other periodicals cannot be classed as literature, but the best of them merit more respect than they generally receive. Journalism differs from literature in kind, but not in degree. Literature is experience of permanent interest recorded in memorable form. Journalism, however, as the word implies, deals with affairs of the day ; it is a record in vivid form of matters of immediate interest, and is not intended to have lasting qualities. Such writing demands very high abilities ; it is only because bad journalism is not infrequent that the journalist is often spoken of as an inferior kind of writer. A good journalist must be an accomplished writer, but though he writes of what concerns us closely, it concerns us only temporarily. To-day's newspaper lights tomorrow's fire ; but *Hamlet* will never be forgotten.

HOW TO SATISFY OUR NEEDS IN LITERATURE

Books differ from one another not only in kind, but in the individual methods and characteristics of their authors. A book may be a novel, a biography, or a history ; it may be written in verse or in prose ; and, independently of this, it may or may not be rightly described as " poetry." For poetry is not a formal distinction ; any writing can be justly called poetry if it is the expression of thought that is imaginative and impassioned, rather than reasoned and logical. But, in addition to all this, the attitude of the writer may be serious or farcical, sentimental or satirical, realistic or romantic. It may be said that we read to find either an interpretation of life, or an escape from it. Which of these we get depends not so much upon the kind of book that we choose, as upon the attitude and method of the writer ; and it is as well to know in advance which we want, and where it is to be found.

Style has been well defined as the impact of personality upon the spirit of the age. It is this spirit of the age that we are apt to overlook in reading books of the past. Shakespeare's genius is indeed " not of an age, but for all time," but he wrote for the England of Elizabeth and James I., and not for us ; therefore the more we can read and watch his plays through the eyes of his public, the better we shall appreciate his genius. Malory, Chaucer, Herrick, Dr. Johnson, and Lamb, were all men whose personality so shines through their writings that they soon become real people to their readers ; but they are far more real if we know how they dressed, whom they knew and what their houses and music and theatres and cities were like. The man who wants to get the most out of books gradually builds up a historical background, a perspective, into which he can fit all that he knows, not only of literature, but of politics, science, music, architecture, or whatever happens to engage his particular interest.

A good plan is to have a rough idea of a succession of great writers, around whom others can be grouped. For example, there is little to interest the general reader before Chaucer, and he died in 1400. The fifteenth century, too, is a dull one for literature. After the Renaissance there are more books to read. Spenser was contemporary with Queen Elizabeth ; Shakespeare began writing about 1590, and died in 1616. Milton was eight when Shakespeare died, and outlived the Puritan régime for fourteen years after the Restoration in 1660. Dryden, the foremost Restoration writer, died in 1700. The eighteenth century, the Age of Good Sense, is represented by Pope and Dr. Johnson, and saw the birth of the novel. Then, towards the end of the century, came the Romantic Movement—Wordsworth, Scott, Shelley, Byron, and Keats—until, after the Napoleonic wars, life and literature settled down to the England of Queen Victoria, Tennyson and Dickens. Meredith, Hardy and Galsworthy in fiction, and Swinburne, Kipling and Masefield in poetry, bring us to our own times. Into such a scheme, which can be memorised with little trouble, it is easy to fit other knowledge that we acquire and other writers whom we get to know. Thus the past becomes real, and literature a living force.

THE AUTHOR AND THE AUDIENCE

BOOKS will not deliver up their treasures without some co-operation on the part of the reader. It has already been pointed out, for instance, that every book must have its limitations, and we must recognise those limitations. It is of no use to complain that an elegy is too solemn, or a farce too frivolous, or an epic too long. These are inherent qualities of those kinds of writing, and we cannot blame the authors if we do not happen to like them. Again, most books are written for readers of a certain period or of certain fairly limited tastes. One reader may dislike very long novels ; but that gives him no just cause of complaint against eighteenth century novelists, who wrote for a public that did like them. Another may find Chaucer's language difficult, Milton's theology intolerable, Congreve's plots indelicate. But these books were not written for us, and they were suited in all respects to the age in which they were written. It is often forgotten that we do not read the work of famous writers such as these (the "classics," as they are called) *because* they are old, *because* they were written for bygone ages, but in spite of this fact. We read them, if we do, because their authors were men of such pre-eminent genius that they had something to say to all mankind that we cannot afford to miss, and in spite of the obstacles that their antiquity necessarily imposes. Each has survived because of some inherent excellence ; but if we find that excellence too difficult to appreciate, the fault lies with us, and not with the author.

"IMAGINATION BODIES FORTH THE FORMS OF THINGS UNKNOWN"

BESIDES requiring such reasonable allowances to be made, books demand to be read in a reasonable manner. It is not sufficient merely to read the words in a book. If a book is to be fairly treated, it must be read with attention and imagination, and it should be thought about afterwards. Moreover, a book must have a fair trial. There is such a vast quantity of literature that no one can hope to read more than a little of it, so that it is obviously wise to read only those books that interest us. But unless we do more than glance at a few pages, unless we read enough, and with sufficient concentration, to understand what the writer is getting at, we have not given the book a fair chance, and we may have missed an experience of great delight and value.

Those who enjoy books most are those who cultivate the active use of their imaginations. All the books worth reading demand an effort of the imagination, and the best books are those which make this effort an enjoyable and fruitful one— which, in the words of Coleridge, " force a willing suspension of disbelief." To get all that may be got out of books we must train ourselves to hear, see, and feel all that the author describes, so vividly that we remember it as we remember an actual experience. An habitual reader of plays rapidly learns to do this. A novel tells us almost everything ; all we have to do is to visualise what we are told. But in a play where description is practically excluded, the reader generally has to supply his own conception of the setting and the movements and appearance of the actors. Any one who knows how to get the best out of a novel or a play can describe, at any point he may have reached, exactly the scene that is in his mind's eye—the position of people in a room, their clothes, and so on. In reading poetry, particularly, all the senses must be imaginatively alert, especially the sense of hearing. Not only is the poet constantly appealing, through the imagination, to the eye, the ear, and all our feelings, as well as to the intellect, but poetry must be heard, in the " mind's ear," so to speak, or it never exists for the reader at all. Poetry is articulate music, and depends very largely upon the *sound* of what is written. It is not always possible to read poetry aloud, as it should be read, but to read it without hearing the sound of it in the imagination is not to understand it, not even to know it ; it is merely to find out what it is about, as if one were to read the title under a picture without bothering to look at the picture itself.

THE RIGHT APPROACH TO BOOKS

IT can be readily seen that such a habit of reading, either in poetry or prose, demands not only alert imagination, but concentration, both mental and emotional. Those who read fast never attain it, nor is it likely to be achieved if the wireless is turned on as soon as a book is opened. Moreover, a lover of books has not finished with a book when he reaches the end. He ponders over it, often re-reads it, and, if he is lucky enough to have friends who share his tastes, he discusses it with others. An attitude of this kind is an active, not a passive one, and therefore may not find favour with every one. But it is the only reasonable attitude to adopt. It is intellectually dishonest to read to save ourselves the trouble of thinking ; we should read in order to think, in order to set our own reason and imagination working. Reading is not a relaxation for tired minds—bodies, perhaps, but not minds. A tired mind needs physical exercise, a tired body needs mental exercise. We read in order to live more fully, and consequently we should read the writings of those who are wiser, wittier, and more lovable than ourselves, so that we may increase our stock of wisdom, wit, and love. We should accord to books at least the same attention, respect, and politeness that we should accord to their writers if they were speaking to us in person.

If we are going to limit ourselves to books that we find on examination to be worth reading (and this is a wise precaution), we must have some means of judging what is worth reading and what is not. In these days an enormous mass of printed matter is thrust before us, and we can only hope to derive pleasure and profit from our reading if we refuse consistently to bother about a large proportion of it, and if we disbelieve a great deal of what we are asked to believe. This critical, almost sceptical, attitude to the printed word is nearly as important as the habit of attention. Most people are deplorably ready to accept the printed word with unquestioning respect ; for a thing is really no more likely to be true or venerable because it is printed instead of spoken. There is no reason for believing that Miss X's novel is the outstanding success of the season because her publishers say so. It is the natural thing for them to say ; but all the other publishers who make similar claims cannot be right—yet we allow their statements to influence us. Those who treat the printed word in this way are allowing their individual judgment, their intellectual conscience, to be overcome by the insidious power of mass-suggestion, and this suggestion is not confined to advertisements, or to the public Press. We should never be over-awed by a writer's reputation, or prejudiced by the opinions of others ; our opinion is our own, and it is the sole judge of the value of any book to ourselves.

HOW TO GET AT GRIPS WITH BOOKS

OPINION, however, is of very little use to us, or to any one else, unless it is based on reasoned judgment and experience. Taste, in literature as in anything else, is bred by enthusiasm out of experience. Those who do not care about a thing do not bother whether it is good or bad, but every man is increasingly particular about what he delights in— he demands higher and higher standards of excellence, and is never satisfied unless he has the best that can be obtained. This is the only kind of criticism that is worth having ; there is a spurious kind, based on the standards of others, but genuine, living criticism springs from the knowledge born of an eager desire for the best. A man who is an enthusiatic motorist soon becomes, through his experience, an expert on the relative merits of different cars. So it is with books. The more we care, and the more we read, the more determined we become to confine ourselves to the best that can be found. But that is not enough. The motorist knows what to look for when he is estimating the merits of a new car, and the reader must know what to look for in a book. Thus, before passing judgment on a book of any kind, it is well to ask oneself the following questions:

> *What was the writer trying to do ?*
> *Was it worth while ?*
> *How far did he succeed ?*
> *If he did succeed, how ?   If not, why not ?*

Criticism that is based on these principles will not be uniform, because the answers must depend upon opinion and experience, but it will at all events be thoughtful and reasoned. An unsatisfactory answer to any of the first three questions is sufficient to deter us from persevering with a book. If we cannot determine the purpose of a book, what is being explained, or argued, or attacked ; if we cannot grasp the plot of a play, or understand the dialogue or the characters in a novel ; if we do not know whether we are meant to laugh, or cry, or shudder, or wonder at a poem ; if we are uncertain of any of these things, the book is of no use to us.

Again, if we understand the purpose of the book, but are totally out of sympathy with it ; or if we find that the author is unequal to his task, we are not likely to waste our time over it. The last two questions on the list are not essential to an estimate of the book, but they complete the initial process. Every one likes to be able to support his opinions. Moreover, just as the motoring expert can tell you not only that one car can go fifteen miles an hour faster than another, but can also tell you why, so the literary enthusiast is sure to follow up his admiration with determination to know how the result that he admires is obtained. If our opinion is supplemented with some degree of technical analysis, we shall ensure that our criticism is not based, as criticism so often is, principally on emotion and prejudice.

SINCERITY THE TEST OF MERIT

SINCERITY is a cardinal test of merit. If any hint of insincerity can be detected in a book, if once we suspect that the author is laughing at us, pretending to know what he does not know, or believe what he does not believe, pretending to be serious when he does not care, or funny when he is not amused—we lose faith in him, and all that he writes is suspect. And sincerity is no less necessary in the reader. We must be sincere in our likes and dislikes, and we must keep our values clear. It is foolish to call a book a good book because it flatters our prejudices, or a book bad because we dislike incidents or characters in it. A book may be well written, yet unpleasant; full of information, yet dull; passionately conceived, yet quite unimpressive. " Good " and " bad " are futile categories. A book has meant little to us unless we can explain clearly whether or not it interests us, and why.

Those who read little are not particular about the manner in which a book is written, so long as they are interested in the matter. As we read more, we come to demand, not only that what we read should interest us, but that it should be written in the best possible way. This demand will lead us inevitably to the great masters. It is wise to read modern authors ; their troubles and joys and interests and language are closest to our own. But, like a violinist and his instrument, or a golfer and his clubs, as our familiarity increases, we demand better workmanship, and we find ourselves turning to those who have written best in all ages—from Masefield to Chaucer, from Marjorie Bowen to Scott and Malory, and from Bernard Shaw to Shakespeare.

" Studies," said Bacon, " serve for delight." This is the first and great reward of reading, and to the man who reads for delight all the other things shall be added. It is because we think of the reading of famous books as a duty, and not as a pleasure, that we so seldom approach the classics with the same gusto with which we approach a monthly magazine. We determine, perhaps, to read Gibbon's *Decline and Fall of the Roman Empire*. We proceed to do so, and we say to ourselves : " This is doing me good ; I shall be proud of having read this." But we continually glance to see how many more pages there are. We do not read it in the small hours, and keep exclaiming : " Well, I must read one more chapter before I go to bed." No ; we make little rules about reading it regularly, and we always break those rules. The trouble is that the whole thing is being approached in the wrong spirit. What matters is not knowledge, but taste. To have read a book is nothing, to have understood it and enjoyed it, everything. As Ruskin said, " A man's character is formed, and can be judged, not by what he knows, but by

what he likes." The end of reading is not knowledge—
rather the wisdom that comes of knowledge. A well-
informed man is really no more admirable than a well-fed
one, unless his knowledge is put to use.

Besides pleasure and wisdom, there are many other rewards
of reading, if books are read in the attentive and critical spirit
that has been suggested. The habit of concentration and
disciplined thought, and the sharpening of the judgment
and sense of values that result from such an attitude of mind,
not only enrich the whole of life, but are of immense practical
value in all our activities. Familarity with the best books,
too, cannot fail to improve our powers of expression ; for
by appreciating how the greatest writers (both ancient and
modern) have expressed themselves, we learn to handle
language more effectively in both speech and writing. These,
and many others, are the practical rewards of a love of
literature.

ONE JOY THAT ONLY BOOKS CAN GIVE

BUT there remains one joy that only books can give, and
that is perhaps the most valuable of all, especially for
those who live restricted lives. Few of us can have all the
actual experiences that we should like to have. Work, lack
of money, responsibilities—these things narrow our lives ;
and even if we have the means to go where we like and do
what we will, we can only go to a tithe of the places, and meet
a fraction of the people, that we can read about : and none
of us can step back into the past. We can never meet Falstaff
or Sam Weller or Mr. Pepys ; we can never hear Milton or
Chaucer talk, or go with Ben Jonson to the Mermaid Tavern.
But we can meet all these people in books. We read to enlarge
our circle of friends, to increase the range of our emotions
and ideas, to escape from our own dullness, to get the other
fellow's point of view, to add to our knowledge of men,
countries, science, and politics, to outgrow our own opinions ;
we read to become troubled, amused, astonished, thrilled,
delighted. Talk and travel as we will, we can live only one
life ourselves ; but with the aid of books and nothing else
but our imagination, we can live thousands of lives in any
age and any country, with as much pleasure and as much
pain as we experience in our own lives. In short, to quote
Bacon once more, " Reading maketh a full man."

Sir John Falstaff : most convivial character in literature.

THE NOVEL : A MIRROR HELD TO LIFE

by B. E. SEARS, B.A.(Oxon)

MILTON once said that books were as lively and as vigorously productive as fabulous dragon's teeth. This remark is particularly true of the modern novel. Novels are written and published to-day at such a rate that even if a man read three novels every day he could not keep abreast of the stream of contemporary work. Such wealth of material at once makes selection imperative and very difficult. Choice must be made since it is no longer possible to read every novel as it comes from the press, but how shall we choose ? If we are merely seeking a few hours' entertainment the problem can be solved easily. Most newspapers and periodicals have a book column which tells in outline the stories of the more prominent new novels and divides them up into novels of mystery, detection, romance, travel, so that the reader has little trouble in finding something to suit his mood. The problem is more complicated when we consider the novel as a serious form of art or think it valuable because it reflects contemporary life and sometimes shows the trend of modern thought. The critics do not agree, and they are frequently mistaken. Novels which were enthusiastically read and praised in 1920 are now forgotten ; others, neglected then, are to-day claimed as masterpieces. However carefully we form our judgments we cannot be sure time will not prove us wrong.

But this is no modern difficulty. At the end of the eighteenth century, when it was still possible to read every novel as it appeared, there was a tremendous vogue for *The Castle of Otranto*, an early thriller. Scott praised it extravagantly, and at Cambridge it so affected the Dons that they wept. Gray, the poet, says that he and his friends were almost afraid to go to bed at night after reading it. Yet to-day it is read only for its historical importance. Its obvious mysteries make the reader laugh rather than cry, and no one would call it a first-class novel. On the other hand, Jane Austen's novels written forty years later were at first rejected by the publishers. To-day they are read and re-read and are placed among

24

the finest English novels. Contemporary novels are not the only ones subject to changes in taste. The Victorians admired Scott more than Fielding, but many people now prefer Fielding to Scott, and even to Dickens. Opinions vary more widely concerning contemporary writers, but even on the classics they are not always unanimous.

There is thus no final infallible test by which we can tell whether a novel is good or bad. A novel which is a work of art cannot be examined, tested, and judged with the accurate precision possible for a motor-car or a roll of cloth. For a work of art, novel, poem, picture, or symphony is neither independent and self-contained nor a dead machine. A work of art is peculiar in this : until it is read, heard, or seen it is non-existent. The moment it is appreciated it leaps into life and at once gives life. So a novel, until it is read, is nothing. The reader brings it to life as Prince Charming revived Sleeping Beauty. Once read, the novel lives in the reader and in this way some of its quality depends upon the reader.

THE TEST OF A GOOD NOVEL

THUS we can say the only test of a novel is its value to the reader. A novel which pleases a man is a good novel for him. If the immediate pleasure, instead of fading, deepens and grows with time, the reader may say with assurance he has found a good novel. If he is thus affected by a novel which has delighted people over a long period—fifty or a hundred years or more—he can be sure he has found a true classic.

Since the novel is not self-contained but depends on the reader for its life, it cannot be judged solely by its technique. A novel may be a convenient length, its plot may be well-constructed, its characters nicely observed, its style exquisite, yet it will fail to be a good novel if the reader does not enjoy it. But, just as most people do not appreciate oysters the first time they eat them, so the taste for novels is a cultivated one. The more we know about the novel, the more novels we read and examine, the more discriminating our taste becomes, until we find ourselves appreciating books which, when we began novel reading, bored us extremely in spite of their good reputation. For this reason every reader of novels eventually finds himself asking : " What then *is* a novel ? What is the proper scope and subject of a novel ? How does the novelist succeed in giving me this pleasure ? "

WHAT IS A NOVEL ?

D H. LAWRENCE wrote enthusiastically : " Oh, give me the •novel ! Let me hear what the novel has to say." The novel has everything to say. It is a story in prose of varying length about a character, or characters, and events in connection with them. The story at once gives it licence as wide as the earth and leagues beyond it. The novel can be a quiet story about village tea-parties, or one about wrecks and desert islands ; it can be a study of character or a study of manners ; it can be told in a hundred ways. The novelist can even turn round inside his novel to be a prophet, a humorist, a scientist, and a first-rate story-teller all in one, as H. G. Wells was in *The War in the Air*. There are so few restrictions that the novelist can shape his story to his heart's content. The novel can be made as large as life and as full as life, and consequently it serves as a social mirror, reflecting the social history and the character of every age in which it has been written.

With the exception of the short story, the novel is the youngest of the literary forms in English. From its beginnings it has always been popular, if not always in favour with the authorities, and consequently in arrangement and subject matter it has been influenced in no small degree by popular taste. The result is that the novel enjoys a wide freedom and even to-day cannot be said to be governed by any definable clear-cut rules.

THE NOVELIST'S FLEXIBLE TECHNIQUE

THIS freedom is at once noticeable in its length. A novelist can have as many or as few chapters as he pleases, and the chapters can be long or short. Joseph Hergesheimer, an American writer, has only ten chapters in *Java Head*. Tolstoi generally gives many very short chapters. If one chapter is of especial interest to the writer he can make it as long as he pleases, or even turn an exciting incident into seven chapters on end, as Norman Douglas does in *South Wind*. A modern novel usually contains between seventy and eighty thousand words. The Victorian novel in three volumes, the " three-decker " as it is called, was three times as long as this ; yet even to-day it is not unusual for an established novelist to write a book containing one hundred and fifty thousand words. Aldous Huxley's *Point Counterpoint*, for instance, is very long for a modern novel, while Gerald Bullett's *The Quick and the Dead*, is about half the usual length. Galsworthy's *Forsyte Saga*, which moves slowly through a sequence of several books telling at leisure the history of one family through generations, is perhaps the longest English modern novel.

The novel is not only free as regards length, but its story may be told in many ways. It gives a generous chance for narrative, description, and conversation. This second freedom is best realised by comparison with the drama, a literary form which is limited to conversation and monologue. In a play the number of acts may vary, but the action can be advanced only by means of conversation between people.

The author cannot intrude himself in person, either to explain the characters' remarks, or to express his private opinion on their actions. But in a novel, subject to his discretion and the patience of his readers, he may do almost anything he likes.

THE EFFORTLESS MANNER OF STEVENSON

THE most natural way of presenting a story is to tell it ; and the simplest way of telling a story is by narration. The reader listens while the novelist relates what happens. R. L. Stevenson's *Treasure Island* is a good example of straightforward, swift narrative. The story is told throughout by Jim, so the reader sees everything from one point of view only. He naturally identifies himself with Jim and shares all his adventures. Jim's last words, in their dramatic simplicity, show how effectively narrative can be used by an experienced author. He says, " Oxen and wain-ropes would not bring me back again to that accursed island ; and the worst dreams that ever I have are when I hear the surf booming about its coasts, or start upright in bed, with the sharp voice of Captain Flint still ringing in my ears : ' Pieces of eight, pieces of eight.' "

To make his tale more convincing, the novelist may dramatise the narrative by putting it into direct speech, but he is freer than the dramatist because he may also comment on what his characters say. A chapter in Mary Webb's *House in Dormer Forest* shows how a skilful writer can do this to advantage. She describes the family at Dormer House, after supper. In the room are Mrs. Velindre, her daughter and son-in-law, Mr. and Mrs. Darke, her grandchildren

Amber, Ruby, and Peter, and a distant relative, Catherine.
The situation is explained dramatically by actual remarks.
We learn that Jaspar, the elder son, is expected home from
college in disgrace. The conversation shows which members
of the family are friendly and which are hostile towards
Jaspar. As the gig arrives outside the door with Jaspar
inside, we know what every one thinks of him and exactly
how they will greet him.

THE ART OF USING BACKGROUND

THE novelist can produce some of his most profound
effects by description. The opening to Thomas Hardy's
Return of the Native is a classic example of this. He devotes
the first chapter entirely to a description of Egdon Heath.
We see it for the first time on a November afternoon, with
its titanic form, " which seems to wait for something."
Human characters are secondary in importance and so are not
introduced until the second chapter, and even then they
appear on the Heath. The story tells the romance of Clym
Yeobright, who has renounced a promising career in Paris
because he cannot live happily away from the Heath, and of
Eustacia Vye, who hates the Heath and longs to escape from
it. The Heath shapes the destinies of the characters and gives
them their significance. In the end " its fearful gloom and
loneliness " cause the heroine's death. The Heath dominates
the book ; it would be impossible to tell the story without
giving a full description of it.

Besides enlivening his story by conversation and description,
the novelist is at liberty to retire in person, as a dramatist
does. May Sinclair in *The Tree of Heaven* gives a brilliant
modern example of the way in which the story may be rendered by the characters. You never think of the author in
person, any more than you expect the dramatist to walk on
to the stage to explain the action. In some novels, however,
the novelist makes a personal appearance and, in so doing,
risks much on the chance of adding intimacy to the book.
He may tell the story in the first person, and thus take you
into his personal confidence about the characters and the
situation. If he has something urgent he feels he must say
to his readers, he may do so in detached paragraphs that
stand quite apart from the story. More daring still, he may
hold up the plot while he speaks directly to the reader.
Trollope does this in *Barchester Towers*, in order to apologise

Egdon Heath, which dominates Hardy's " Return of the Native."

because Belinda, the heroine, slaps a man in the face. Nashe, an early writer, goes further still and stays the plot to comment on himself. He cannot go on till he has remarked most happily to the reader, " Here let me triumph a while and ruminate a line or two on the excellence of my wit," and he is so delightful about it that you agree. Lyly, one of his contemporaries, refuses point blank to say what happens to his heroine in *Euphues*, and concludes : " What end came of her, seeing it is nothing incident to the history of Euphues, it were superfluous to insert, and so incredible that all women would rather wonder at than believe in."

There are thus no hard and fast rules for the novel. Everything depends on the author's ability, charm, and sense of proportion. Where these fail the freedom which is the novelist's privilege causes his downfall. His descriptions are drawn out to tedious lengths ; his plots are so involved no one can understand them ; his explanations and interruptions break the thread of the story without adequate compensation. His novels then cease to please and become " bad novels."

HOW THE STORY IS UNFOLDED : THE PLOT

MORE than three hundred years have passed since Englishmen first attempted to write a story in prose. During those years many experiments have been made to find the most effective way of telling the story, and although no final result has been reached, the novel is now a recognised artistic form and as such has certain characteristics which make it different from other artistic forms. The first of these is the story itself—that is, the plot.

A plot is the plan of action in which the particular events with which the novel deals are set forth. It must have a beginning and an end, and during its course tell about the character or the incident with which the events are concerned. It is very easy to begin a plot. Any one can begin to tell of something which has happened. But it is one of the hardest things in the world to begin so effectively that the particular moment takes fire and has the reader willing to follow up hill and down dale. It is equally difficult to end a plot well. It cannot stop suddenly with a jerk, unless the novelist feels that his only course is to stop and run away. Nashe, after greatly enjoying the plot of *The Unfortunate Traveller*, feels the worry of an ending. He says to the reader, hoping for the best, " This tale must sometime or other give up the ghost."

A good plot requires as much skill as a well-made piece of furniture. The whole must give a complete shape so that each episode is necessary, or it will lop like a chair with a spar missing. It must have a chief interest, such as the life of one special important character, or the account of one central adventure towards which other incidents lead. The main interest is presented at the beginning. It claims attention so vividly that you are ready for the action from the first moment, and this action continues to a conclusion so natural and inevitable that you feel there could be no other ending. Episodes on the way are not mere diversion. They help to explain the main plot, or provide excitement which directly advances the story.

A bad plot is the contrary of all this. The attention is not centred on the main interest, so that in the beginning the reader does not know his direction. As he continues, he finds either that he is not progressing, or that there seems to be no special reason for the direction taken. A bad plot leads to no conclusion, or to one that seems imposed. It may be strong, but then it is not in harmony with the natural actions of the characters. Or it may be weak because the characters do not advance the action, but stray about dissipating the main interest. A bad plot always results when the novelist loses his first intention ; for, as we have shown, a novel needs design, just as much as a piece of furniture.

THE TWO KINDS OF PLOT

PLOTS, whether well shaped or loose in construction, are roughly of two kinds : Those made by the narration of successive events and those that spring from the characters of the people portrayed. Plots which deal with the active movement of events are found pre-eminently in the adventure novel. Here the action is sensational, and in the stress of it there is no time to wonder too much about individuals. Characters are there, and lively too, but you push forward cheek by jowl with them towards the next event, which is the vital thing. The chapter headings alone in Jules Verne's *Secret of the Island* are sufficient to show the heat of the moment. Here are three at random : " Death of Captain Nemo," " Sinking of the Nautilus," " Listening to the rumbling of the Volcano." The concluding chapters follow one another in a rush, bringing a sail in sight at the eleventh hour.

Plots of action are not always hair-raising. A plot dealing with wandering adventurers—a picaresque plot—like that of *Don Quixote*, has action dispersed in many directions, and sometimes lasting for years. In Dickens's *David Copperfield*, alongside the tragedy of Little Em'ly's ruin, there is another very different event, the humorous slow wooing of Peggotty by Barkis. It is even possible to have a plot of action so quiet that one of the most exciting events is the sucking of an orange behind a screen. This happens in *Cranford*, Mrs. Gaskell's novel, which tells of the happenings in an old-fashioned village. Here, when the cat swallows the lace, the crisis is as thrilling as a catastrophe at sea.

The kind of plot which springs directly from character can also contain vivid dramatic action. In Henry James's novels, characters decide and cause plenty of events. Kate O'Brien's character novel, *Without My Cloak*, has at moments a most riotous movement. Catherine, one of the most attractive women in modern romances, decides, at one point in the story, to run away to London. But the interest is in Catherine's decision to do this rather than in the commotion which results. That commotion is foreign to her, yet she causes it, because she happens to be that particular person Catherine. And so the plot continues, in quiet days or rousing ones, exactly as the characters grow in experience and order their action.

The character plot may contain plenty of action, but more frequently it has very little. Sometimes the action is so slight that there is almost no plot left. In Peacock's novels the interest is in the humorous way people behave when, occasionally, they do act. The Squire in *Headlong Hall* decides to move, but our interest is confined to the exciting way he does it. "He bursts from room to room like a cracker." Henry James's *Golden Bowl* is a classic example of action so restrained as to be almost motionless.

With modern writers who stress character above all, the result is a special kind of psychological novel in which there is hardly a stir of action. The novelist sets out to show the state of the characters' minds. Rex Stout in *How Like a God* does allow his hero to walk upstairs, but this is, physically, all that happens. The rest of the plot consists of the hero's private history which he recollects as he climbs the stairs. By the time he has come to the top, the reader has learned all about his past. Virginia Woolf's novels are entirely concerned with the states of mind of her characters. The events which give rise to the situation belong mostly to the past, and are recalled by the characters. The intensity of the plot is sustained by concentration on the points of view of the people and by analysing their thoughts. A plot of psychological action can be as thrilling as the plot of a detective novel.

PEOPLING THE PAGES WITH CHARACTERS WHO LIVE

THE plot is only one of the essential characteristics of a novel. A well-made plot is not by itself enough to ensure a good novel. This is well illustrated by the ordinary feuilleton of the daily newspaper where incident is handled with skill and ingenuity but with small regard for character. Meredith's *Egoist*, with its excellent plot, is appreciated less than Cervantes's *Don Quixote* with its loose, rambling construction. Dickens's novels have plots which would have shapes like contour maps if we tried to pencil every direction taken from the opening chapter. These novels have weak plots but give lasting pleasure because their authors knew the secret of creating unforgettable people. Peggotty, Little Nell, Oliver take our imagination by storm and hold us captive for ever. This is the second essential characteristic of a novel, that it should tell us about people or things which are alive, which have character.

Novel people may be any kind from kings to chimney sweeps, from squirrels to fairies. But they must be alive. However fantastic a world they are in, we must feel bound to believe in them. Robinson Crusoe delivers sermons on his desert island. We should not expect in the ordinary way to hear a sermon in such a place, but we do expect to hear one from a man like Crusoe. He gives us one, and would do so if he were at the North Pole. This means that whatever his situation his behaviour in it would be consistent with his own character. As long as the people are alive and consistent (that is, true to themselves), they may perform the most astonishing feats. Thus, in David Garnett's *Lady into Fox*, a beautiful woman changes into a vixen and yet we do not protest, because she is real and so is the vixen.

The novelist creates his people by drawing them either from the outside or from the inside, though sometimes he

2

combines the two methods. The author may give life to his creatures by describing their outward appearance. Then the reality of the character depends on the author's powers of observation and selection and the vividness with which he can describe. Conrad opens *Lord Jim* with Jim staring us in the face in the first paragraph. We get a " close-up " of his person, as on a film.

> " He was an inch, perhaps two, under six feet, powerfully built, and he advanced straight at you with a slight stoop of the shoulders, head forward, and a fixed from-under stare which made you think of a charging bull. His voice was deep, loud, and his manner displayed a kind of dogged self-assertion which had nothing aggressive in it. It seemed a necessity, and it was directed apparently as much at himself as at anybody else. He was spotlessly neat, apparelled in immaculate white from shoes to hat, and in the various Eastern ports where he got his living as ship-chandler's water-clerk he was very popular."

This method often tempts a novelist to give too many details. He is free to give as many as he pleases, even to the number of buttons on a glove, but the art of creating character by description is *to* give significant details. Conrad makes us see Jim vividly and also feel his presence, because he does not confuse the picture with too many lines.

THE ART OF CARICATURE

THIS necessity for selection may lead the author to select so severely that instead of a portrait he presents us with a caricature. He chooses two or three details—a pair of startling eyebrows, a long nose, a dismal voice—gives them a grotesque name and says no more. This can be effective when it is well done. Dickens illustrates it at its best and worst. He sometimes uses it lazily as with the fat boy in *Pickwick Papers*. It is amusing to see the fat boy asleep on his first appearance, but Dickens shows him in this state so often, that when he does rouse into activity, he seems too absurd to be real. A more revealing use of caricature is seen in *Great Expectations*. Mr. Wemmick, the shy clerk, is made as vivid as the fat boy by an exaggerated humorous description on his first appearance. But Dickens does not merely strike an attitude with him and keep repeating it. We visit Mr. Wemmick's home and even Pip gasps at the revelation of his friend in the home circle. Mr. Wemmick is no longer a city clerk, with a " mouth as tight as a pillar-box." He is still presented in caricature but we see him differently as a son, making " a haystack of buttered toast " for his father, and also as a suitor, sharing a glass with Miss Spiffkins, who, with her tight waist and prim manner, is a caricature of all the old maids of the world. Mr. Wemmick's habit of addressing his old father as " The Aged " or " Aged P." (short for " aged parent ") shows how a character may be created by a single phrase.

THE NOVELIST BECOMES MORE SUBTLE

IN the early days of the novel the characters were always drawn from outside. The reader was told what the hero looked like, what he did, and what he thought; but he was not shown how the hero's mind worked. We never over-hear Tom Jones thinking aloud. But gradually the novelist became more subtle. He began to penetrate inside his characters, to identify himself with them and then to draw us a picture not of Tom Jones but of the world seen through Tom Jones's eyes. This method of characterisation is favoured especially by modern novelists. James Joyce in *Ulysses* tells us nothing. He does not describe Stephen Daedalus or Leopold and Marion Bloom. They are revealed to us—if we can under-stand the revelation—by their thoughts which are given in full. But unedited thoughts are only intelligible to the thinker, the psycho-analyst, and perhaps, to a reader who is prepared to take a great deal of trouble. Consequently *Ulysses* is a very difficult book read more by writers than by readers.

HOW THE SPELL IS WOVEN : STYLE AND HUMOUR

A GOOD novelist is a wizard. Before the fascinated eyes of our imagination he conjures up scenes, people, episodes which live longer than the cleverest of men. Part of his magic lies in the people and episodes themselves; but almost his most potent spell is the way he presents his story, the very words in which he tells it and the atmosphere they create. This manner of telling is called style and is the third characteristic of the novel, not so essential as plot and character but still indispensable in a novel which is to give lasting pleasure.

" Style," said Buffon, " is the man," which is a concise way of saying that the manner of writing is inseparable from the writer. Applied to novel-writing it means that style is the individual way the author tells his story. Just as no two people talk or move exactly in the same way, so no two authors have exactly the same style. A good style is one which is natural to the character of the author and adequate to the purpose he has in hand. Jane Austen is regarded as a great stylist because her particular manner of writing is in perfect harmony both with her own character and with the matter she wishes to present. And she says of style : " No, I must keep to my own style, and go in my own way. I am convinced that I should totally fail in any other." Style, to be good, must be in the first place true, and in the second, adequate. It must be true in the sense that it is expressive of the individual and not merely imitative. It must be adequate in the sense that it fits the subject and does not appear pompous or undignified. Some people are simple by nature, and others as naturally complex. Good style for the simple person will be writing simple in form and construction. Good style for the complex person will naturally be elaborate and may even be involved. John Bunyan was a beautiful stylist, and his style is simple in the extreme. Henry James was an exquisite stylist, and his style is highly ornate and complex. Both are good because they are true and because the different styles are adequate to the authors' intentions. *Gulliver's Travels* and *Tristram Shandy* show how magnificent may be the result if the style is natural to the man employing it. Style in writing is what expression is to the human face : it is most pleasing when it is most truly characteristic.

HUMOUR BRINGS JOY TO THE NOVEL

IT is not necessary to have humour in the novel, any more than it is necessary to have it to keep alive. The world does continue quite steadily if we miss noticing its funny sides. In some novels we never stop to wonder why it is not there. D. H. Lawrence seldom introduces humour, and yet his *Sons and Lovers* is one of the best modern novels. In Richardson's *Clarissa Harlowe*, however, we do feel that humour is absent and sigh occasionally for Clarissa to laugh about her broken heart instead of describing its injured state so often to her friend.

There is no clear definition of humour in a novel, and not

a single rule about the introduction of it. It is used as the novelists decide for themselves, but many of them feel like Jane Austen, who says that if she had to keep on writing and never relax into laughter at herself or other people she would be hanged before the end of the first chapter. Humour is one of the joys in a novel, and it is not often lacking in the English novel. Some novels are called humorous novels because they set out with no other purpose in the world but to make us laugh, and the more we guffaw, and the more our ribs ache, the greater is the success of the novel. P. G. Wodehouse's novels are typical of this kind. In the *Jeeves* books, Bertie Wooster is the type of perfect idiot who does obvious things which go wrong. If he sees a bucket in front of him we know he will fall over it ; if there is water inside the bucket, it is sure to splash him. The humour arises because we laugh at Bertie Wooster either because he says silly things or because the situation he is in makes him look such a fool. It is a quick, easily roused laugh, because nothing is easier than to think we are normal ourselves and see another person being ridiculous. But the intentionally humorous book is not often successful. The duty to laugh removes all desire to do so. Consequently, humour enchants us most when it is incidental to a serious book.

A good laugh does not always mean that we are laughing at other people. There is a more subtle kind of humour. The scene may still be an absurd one in which a rough and tumble humour provokes a broad grin, but the laugh may be introduced purposely to bring urgent relief at a tense moment in the plot. In Rose Macaulay's novel, *They Were Defeated*, the book opens with a harvest festival service in progress. Parson Herrick has just been most vehement. The congregation is feeling the strain when suddenly a sucking pig begins to eat the vegetables near the pulpit. Before it is removed from the scene, both the reader and the congregation have relaxed into a good laugh, and feel the easier for it. Mary Webb's use of humour for relief serves a further purpose of satire. In *Gone to Earth*, Edward feels he has succeeded in improving Hazel's mind and asks in a rather condescending tone what her father is doing. Hazel answers with a good broad " Guzzling, I expect." It is a wonderful comment on Edward's correct English.

Some comedy arouses another kind of laugh which Meredith calls thoughtful laughter. This depends chiefly upon character. In *David Copperfield*, Peggotty's buttons burst when she hugs David, but we are warmed more with sympathy towards Peggotty than with joy at the rolling buttons. In *Great Expectations*, Dickens shows in one short scene the quick interplay of humour, irony, burlesque, and satire. Pip has come into a fortune, and therefore goes to Mr. Trabb the tailor in order to celebrate the event with new clothes. Mr. Trabb at first barely nods and continues to eat. Dickens caricatures the scene, as Mr. Trabb busily slices his hot roll into three feather beds and slips butter in between the blankets. The moment Mr. Trabb realises Pip is rich, the vein becomes ironical. He hardly stops to wipe his fingers on the tablecloth before calling Pip " My dear Sir ! " Later Pip walks out in his new clothes. It is a delightful moment. He feels they give him an importance far above Trabb's boy who must now only look at him and not dare to speak. Pip steadily snubs him as they meet outside, until at last Trabb's boy seizes the chance for burlesque and swaggers in front of Pip, saying : " Don't know yah, don't know yah, 'pon my soul, don't know yah ! "

THE FIRST ENGLISH NOVELISTS

FROM the vantage point of the twentieth century it is easy to describe the characteristics of the novel-form. So many novels have been written in the last two or three hundred years that we have rich material on which to base conclusions. To-day we can say the novel has three essential characteristics : plot, character-drawing, style. But in the days of Defoe, Richardson, and Fielding the novel form was in the making. The novel did not in fact exist as a recognised literary form like the drama, and most of the early novelists wrote novels by accident. *The Pilgrim's Progress* was intended by Bunyan to be a religious allegory, and Fielding's *Joseph Andrews* was meant in the beginning to be a parody. During the eighteenth century people first began to take an interest in the novel as such. Great writers experimented with it and gradually it came to be recognised as a new *genre*. A knowledge of how this happened is indispensable if we are to understand and appreciate fully the work of novel writers in our own day. The story is fascinating, especially when it is told of the English novel, which has a greater tradition than the novel in any other language.

The earliest English books which we now consider as experimental novels were written during the sixteenth century in the days of Queen Elizabeth. But impulses towards the novel were felt before this, in the fourteenth century. After the Crusades had stimulated adventure and opened the magic of the East, people felt the next best thing to going there was to hear about it. Long metrical romances telling of Christian knights exploring remote lands were accepted as eagerly as thrillers are now. But gradually these became boring, for they rambled tediously and the knights were all so equally gallant and successful, the heroines all so beautiful and good, they could with difficulty be told apart.

Chaucer was the first to rebel against these tales of monotonous virtue by creating human beings who were capable of faults. In his long poem, *Troilus and Cressida*, he gives the first hint of the novel by his deliberate study of character. Its plot, set in the legendary years of the Trojan Wars, requires as many pinches of salt as the usual romance of the time and could not be used in a novel as it stands ; but few novelists have given more brilliant characterisation. Chaucer shows the different points of view of the lovers, Troilus and Cressida, and by giving them interplay anticipates the modern novel by six centuries. Pandorus, Cressida's uncle, even dares tell Troilus he is boring when he mopes. Never before had a hero been full-blooded enough to be spoken to like this. Pandorus has only to cough discreetly before an interview which requires tact with his niece, and we feel here is some one we know now and for ever. In *The Canterbury Tales*, which are stories, some long, some short, told in verse, Chaucer again shows us he has matter that would serve for a novel. Long before Canterbury is reached we know the pilgrims' clothes, manners, and opinions, and each pilgrim stands out vividly as an independent character. The host at the outset poses as a blustering man of authority, but later he swears by his wife's favourite oath, a most shrewd observation.

Chaucer was the first to give an air of reality to English story-telling by his introduction of complete human beings into stories. Not until the eighteenth century were writers again sufficiently trustful and observant to be as successful with characterisation. Meanwhile other impulses helped towards the evolution of the novel. There were the *Jest Books*, the popular collections of jokes which the Elizabethans loved. Gradually these jokes came to be attributed to one person, who, by being held responsible for them, gave a certain unity to the book. In the same way the picaresque or adventure novel, introduced during the sixteenth century from Spain, had one hero for its series of adventures and this further influenced the sustaining of interest in one long tale.

ONE OF THE EARLIEST BEST-SELLERS

IN 1579 Lyly's *Euphues* was published. It marks the first conscious attempt at a novel in England. Robert Greene's *Pandosto*, Sidney's *Arcadia*, Lodge's *Rosalynde*, Nashe's *Unfortunate Traveller*, and Deloney's *Jack of Newberie*, followed, and were all gay experiments in a form which was new and therefore exciting. *Euphues* was as popular in its day as a best-seller is now. The story is obviously impossible and badly managed. It tells of the courtship of Lucilla by Euphues and two other suitors, but the romance is tedious. It is written in balanced sentences, most carefully built up and contrasted, which drag the story slowly along. When there is a chance for pace, Euphues himself holds up the movement by writing letters to his friends. The public, however, loved the style, and were content to revel in it quite apart from the plot. In addition they did not mind the badly managed story because there was other entertainment. Euphues is a trying young man, one of the worst examples of feeble characterisation, but he knows about magic and fills his letters with the stories of toads, scorpions, and magic beasts. It is pleasant even to-day to be told that " he who playeth upon a tabor may, while that music continueth, stand upon a tiger in perfect safety."

Sidney's *Arcadia* is a tedious romance, parts of it are overcrowded and others drawn out, but again the Elizabethans were content with the exquisite sound of the words, and occasionally one finds with delight vivid homely details even though the characters are handicapped with names like Gynecia and Parthenieia. Nashe's *Unfortunate Traveller* tells the many adventures of Jack Wilton. There is little unity to them, but they have a wonderful bustling vigour, and though Nashe rightly feels his plot is presented badly, there is really no need for him to say : " You would have laughed your face and knees together if you had been there," because the word pictures are so vivid you are already present. Deloney's *Jack of Newberie*, more than any other early novel, shows hints of realism. He tells of the lives of everyday London cobblers, and writes with his eye on the object.

Judged by standards of to-day, these early writers produced clumsy novels. To enjoy them the reader must be prepared first to work hard. The plots are best summarised by Philautus, one of the suitors in *Euphues*. He says : " In faith thou hast told a long story : the beginning I have forgotten, the middle I understood not, and the end hangeth not together." If the reader is willing to accept the standards of their day and read these novels in order to enjoy the personal introduction they give to the author (who is always present as an inexhaustible host) he will be rewarded ; but it is left to more experienced writers to bring unity to the novel.

THE NOVEL TAKES SHAPE

DURING the early seventeenth century Overbury and Earle indirectly encouraged the growth of the novel by writing character studies. They made studies of particular social types and wrote about these in simple language. One example is *A Faire and Happy Milkmaid* by Overbury. These character sketches are still-life portraits never seen in movement, but they are important as showing early attempts at psychological interpretation.

Bunyan (1628–1688) unconsciously brought the art of pure story-telling to the novel. His *Pilgrim's Progress* is one of the finest early novels, though it was in fact written as a spiritual allegory. It has a thrilling romantic plot, real human characters, and a simple, lively style. Bunyan himself was telling a story for the moral lessons behind it, but he gets carried away with fervour so that the moral is forgotten by the reader in the exciting action. You do not feel that Christian has escaped from a spiritual Slough of Despond so much as from a real bog which sticks to his shoes. Bunyan is only interested in Christian and the other characters according to their religious convictions ; but for the reader, these people are actual individuals. He writes, like Chaucer, from personal observation and a real experience of life, and the homely details he gives so earnestly in order to bring realism into religion make his story one of the most vivid in literature. His other spiritual allegory, *The Holy War*, is also an exciting novel. The battles are described so vividly that we forget what they stand for and begin taking sides. Bunyan would have been shocked at our doing this. His purpose was to convince sinners, but unconsciously he engrosses the reader in the way every great novelist does so that he leaves him with a fuller experience of life. With this the reader can certainly combat the devil better, and so, in the end, Bunyan gets his wish.

Daniel Defoe (1659 ?–1731) tells a story as well as Bunyan does, but he intends to do so, and thus takes a conscious step forward in the history of the novel. Defoe did not begin writing till he was nearly sixty, and some of his minor works are badly constructed, rambling tales. In *Robinson Crusoe*, his masterpiece, he deliberately tried to shape his work into respectable form. He tells a story of strange adventure, but uses every device to make the strange events read like a real history. He intends to give thrills, but these are to be taken seriously in order that the novel shall not be dismissed as mere fiction. For years people believed that a man called Robinson Crusoe was born in 1632 in the city of York, and that he left England to make a fortune in Africa. From the moment Crusoe sails from London, breathless experiences are related in a purposely flat style designed to keep the reader from doubting the actual truth of the tale. The plot is simple and dramatic. Crusoe's feelings are described in such natural and intimate detail that we feel we could have found them out for ourselves.

THE NOVEL ACHIEVES FAME

BY the early eighteenth century the novel had gained much by Bunyan's fervent narrative power and Defoe's sense of biographical reality. The next contribution came from Addison and Steele, the essayists, when they created Sir Roger de Coverley and the other members of the Spectator Club. Sir Roger is the type of the " good old English country gentleman," but he is also a real human person made of flesh and blood and as different from Overbury's still-life figures as a waxwork from its living counterpart. If the essays were put together they would make something very like a novel. After Sir Roger the way was prepared and in the second quarter of the eighteenth century the novel in the hands of Richardson, Fielding, Smollett, and Sterne took definite shape and became the literary equal of poetry and the darma.

Samuel Richardson, who did not begin writing till he was over fifty, is the next novelist of importance after Defoe.

His three novels, *Pamela*, *Clarissa Harlowe*, and *Sir Charles Grandison*, were immediately popular at home and abroad, and yet when he began to write his first book he did not realise it was going to be a novel. In 1739 he had been requested by a firm of London publishers to write for them a " little volume of letters, in a common style, on such subjects as might be of use to those country readers as were unable to indite for themselves." Richardson asked the publishers if they would allow him to tell country readers how they should " think " and " act," as well as " indite." The publishers agreed, and instead of a " model letter-writer," he produced *Pamela, or Virtue Rewarded*, a long novel written in letter form.

His chief contributions to the novel were, first, this introduction of the letter form, which was imitated by later writers and still has vogue in modern fiction, and secondly, his particular sentimental treatment of the heroine. This feeling for sentiment made him universally popular with the middle-class woman ; it also influenced his French contemporaries. People were a-tiptoe for something new, and although Richardson's treatment gave no permanent shape to the novel his writing was vivid and intense, and his characters, especially the women, were described in a new and more sympathetic way. *Pamela*, his first novel, appeared in 1740 and completely won the heart of the public. It tells the story of a servant girl who finally marries and reforms the master who has previously tried to seduce her. She relates her experiences in letters to her parents, who answer with good advice only. This is a slow and cumbersome method of advancing the action and would not be tolerated to-day, but it enables the reader to understand and appreciate Pamela's personality, and thus for the first time to share in a heroine's intimate feelings and reactions.

BID FOR THE WOMAN READER

IN his second novel, *Clarissa Harlowe*, published in 1748, Richardson tells the story of a rich and well-born girl who is infatuated by Lovelace, a handsome and witty but morally worthless young-man-about-town. Unable to reclaim him, she refuses his offer of marriage and finally dies of grief. Her cousin avenges her wrongs in a duel. Clarissa, although handicapped by excessive sentiment, is one of the most attractive heroines in fiction, and this story is Richardson's

best work. In spite of Clarissa's fate, however, he had succeeded in making the figure of Lovelace so dazzling to his
sentimental female public that he felt he must in some way
try to readjust its perverted scale of values. He therefore
published in 1753 *Sir Charles Grandison* in which, for the
first time, his hero really is a hero. Grandison is a man of
unimpeachable character, successful in all he undertakes,
and is loved by two beautiful girls, one Italian and one
English. He marries the latter; but even this does not
prevent Richardson's last (and longest) novel from being
also his most tiring. This is chiefly because he is trying to
depict a purely imaginary character in, and for, a society of
unimaginable perfection.

Richardson's novels were written to please and instruct
women. They met with overwhelming success because they
flattered. They showed woman to herself as she would like
to be: a beautiful creature of tender heart, perfect morals,
and saintly character. They also put her into her favourite
rôle of the martyr patiently suffering incredible wrongs at
the hands of that monster—man. Reading the pitiful story
of Clarissa, every woman felt her heart moved in sympathy.
She dissolved in tears and knew herself—as she had always
suspected—a woman of sentiment. But her illusions were
soon to be shattered—naturally, by a man.

Pamela created a sensation in literary London. The
book was read and eagerly discussed in the clubs, coffee-
houses, and other places where men met. Among Richardson's hostile critics was a barrister and writer of plays—Henry
Fielding. Fielding saw through Pamela's namby-pamby
virtue, and to show how ridiculous she was, set out to parody
her in his first published novel, *The History of the Adventures
of Joseph Andrews and his friend Mr. Abraham Adams*. The
form of the parody was borrowed from Cervantes's *Don
Quixote*. Joseph Andrews, brother of Pamela, was to be
laughed at in a series of absurd adventures connected with
one another only by the presence of the hero in each. The
story begins as its author intended. Joseph is tempted by
his mistress and coyly resists her overtures, thus repeating
Pamela's behaviour with her master. But as soon as the
characters are in motion the parody is forgotten, and the
novel moves with an epic stride to a theme of comedy. The
characters revolve round Adams, a poor and worthy parson,
and are always vividly alive even if not always strictly virtuous.

This is where Fielding breaks new ground as a novelist. He did not set out like Richardson with an axe to grind—that is, a public to instruct. His aim was to represent life as he saw it, and with his robust sense of reality and a broad acceptance of humanity in all its phases he succeeded superbly.

THE GAY IMPERFECTION OF TOM JONES

BUT it is with his next book, his third novel, that Fielding takes his place among the greatest novelists. To the writing of *Tom Jones* Fielding brought the technical skill acquired from his play-writing and a wide experience of life gained partly from his duties as a magistrate. *Tom Jones* is the story of a young man, generous-hearted, kindly, well-intentioned, but with the faults of his youth and hot-blooded nature. He is continually falling into scrapes which bring him into disfavour with his benefactor, Mr. Allworthy, but the reader is shown and made to feel that in spite of his lapses from strict morality Tom Jones is a fine man in the making and one infinitely to be preferred to the mean-spirited, crafty, but impeccable Blifil.

In this novel Fielding presents his story with a gentle penetrating irony which keeps the characters in proportion. The men are neither villains nor saints, but human ; even Sophia Western, one of the most amiable women in fiction, is shown to have her foibles. In the story itself, which is constructed as soundly as a good play, no one is taken too seriously. But Fielding realised that in thus daring to portray human imperfections with sympathy he might be misunderstood and accused of condoning immorality. Accordingly, at intervals throughout the book he inserted short chapters in which he speaks direct to the reader, explaining clearly his own motives and those of his characters. As he says, the reader is at liberty to skip these lectures if he is so minded, and consequently they need not interfere with the plot.

In his fourth and last novel, *Amelia*, Fielding abandoned this device, perhaps because, in spite of it, he had still not escaped the anger of the moralists. In technique this novel is his best. The plot is carefully thought out and deftly executed. Amelia is thought by many to be the portrait of the woman every man would have to be his wife if he could. But although it has great charm, this novel does not speak so directly to our sympathies as *Tom Jones*, the first immortal novel in English.

Fielding is unique among eighteenth-century novelists in his command of plot and understanding of character. But he was not alone in writing novels which to this day continue to be read and enjoyed. Tobias Smollett (1721–1771) did not advance the construction of the novel but increased the popularity of the adventure story which has little or no plot. This form of adventure novel continued for over fifty years after Smollett's death and was used by Dickens in depicting the merry bustling life of the traveller in coaching days. Smollett wrote of adventure from his own travels and, since he was himself a doctor and had been a surgeon's mate on a man-of-war, is particularly successful in describing the lives of medical men. He lived for a time in the West Indies and was thus able to give realistic studies of strange foreign people observed in their own surroundings. Smollett discarded Richardson's tedious moralising and allowed his characters their own standards of living. *Roderick Random* is the story of an unscrupulous Scot and his life at sea, told with crude realism. *Peregrine Pickle* is an exciting story of a wastrel heir. Smollett's best novel is his last, *Humphrey Clinker*, written in letter form by the characters; it shows a gentler humour than appeared in his earlier work, and depicts the manners and customs of the day in England and Scotland. Smollett's people give the stay-at-home reader a less insular view of life and set him on a vagabond trail of buffeting adventure and tawdry ribaldry.

INTRODUCING MY UNCLE TOBY

LAWRENCE STERNE (1713–1768) was a country parson who wanted to increase his meagre stipend. So he decided to write a novel of pure manners and to continue writing it in parts as long as the public showed willingness to buy them. The result was *Tristram Shandy*, the most formless and yet one of the greatest novels. Defying all convention, particularly the code of reticence upon matters relating to sex, Sterne allowed his whimsical humour to play upon almost anything which came into his head that might somehow be related to a hero writing in the first person. Sentiment and sensitivity are the secrets of *Tristram Shandy*. Sterne's sensitivity kept him humorous; his sentiment kept him human. So, by an unexampled process, he built up a domestic scene in which the principal characters, Tristram's father, Uncle Toby, Corporal Trim, and Widow Wadman, find their places among the immortals of fiction. Sterne is the complete master of the inferential style. He dissertates, satirises, nods, winks, and gesticulates in a more lively manner than any author in the world. He is a true descendant of one of Shakespeare's fools—a Touchstone of literature, or, as he styles himself in *The Sentimental Journey*, poor Yorick, the King's jester. But beneath the bubbling wit and continuous merriment lies a humanity which rounds his characters into life. Sterne took Richardson's recipe and added humour and philosophy to it ; and he showed how plain narrative might be completely dispensed with if only some device for retaining the reader's attention were found. He discovered this in his own wit. *Tristram Shandy* is the perfect example of a novel which lives entirely upon its author's wits.

The minor novelists of this period can now only be obtained in original editions. Mrs. Manley and Mrs. Heywood achieved some popularity by libellous books which are only of interest to-day as showing the entrance of the married woman into fiction. Fanny Burney, however, with *Evelina*, provides a landmark. *Evelina* is the story of a girl of high birth brought up by her guardian. She is introduced into society and visits a family of " vulgar " cousins in London. Finally she marries Lord Orville. Fanny Burney, the " pet " of Dr. Johnson, was experimenting. She realised that Richardson, Fielding, and Smollett had taken their paths, and says with a delightful courage : " Let us not spend time in trying to do what has already been done excellently. Let us give our attention to different phases of life and new aspects of men and women." The result is a lively picture of home life, a subject not treated by novelists before.

THE NEW AGE OF ROMANCE

TOM JONES, published in 1749, brought the novel fame and necessitated its acceptance as a definite literary form. Critics in future might argue about details, about the ability of this novelist and that, but they would have to agree that there was a technique of novel-writing as distinct as that of play-writing, although less circumscribed. The further story of the development of the novel, therefore, tells more of changing subjects and methods of approach than of advances in form and technique.

The Vicar of Wakefield was the last novel of repute in the

Fielding tradition. When it was published in 1766 the novel describing real people and everyday life had already gone out of fashion, for in 1764 a tale of horror and bloodshed which we should now call a thriller had taken literary England by storm. Horace Walpole's *The Castle of Otranto* marks the beginning of a romantic movement in the novel. Walpole realised that it was a new venture, and said : " I have not written the book for the present age which will endure nothing but cold common sense." The public, however, were willing enough for a change. For some time there had been a revival of interest in the past. People admired Gothic architecture because it was exciting, and they tried to build houses and plan gardens in shapes equally fantastic. The novel complied with the new taste by offering strange thrills. The public was tired of Richardson's heroines, who sighed so often and lived in a world which could easily be recognised ; they even wanted a change from the healthy bustle of Fielding's cheerful world. *The Castle of Otranto* provided it. It was the first amateur thriller and set the fashion for many more.

A STORY OF HORROR, MYSTERY, AND DEATH

TO-DAY *The Castle of Otranto* has lost its sensational power. It is out of date in its methods as compared with the accomplished skill of Edgar Wallace. If read at all it is for the fascination of watching the author prepare his magic behind the scenes and the pleasure of hearing vivid description. Walpole tells a story, but it is an involved mediæval legend of a prince killed on his wedding day by an enormous helmet which falls and crushes him. His father persecutes the bride, and she escapes him through subterranean passages in the castle. The chief attention is given to the castle, a romantic Gothic castle, with towers, battlements, cloisters, trap-doors, and galleries, which are mentioned at every opportunity. Such things were new to the public, and they read of them with eyes open in amazement.

It was only necessary for a character to find a trap-door and the effect was complete. Walpole's readers did not mind the constant interference of a ghost in the plot, or object to the rather material horrors. Manfred's grandfather was an impressive ghost in their eyes when he uttered a deep sigh and heaved an actual breast. Once, at a critical moment, three drops of blood fall from the nose of a statue. They

were accepted without dispute. A modern reader would
not pass this. In addition, Walpole deliberately introduced
homely scenes in the middle of the horrors, in order to make
the unusual atmosphere seem more real. These domestic
scenes are, however, so convincing that no one would really
be afraid to explore the castle even at midnight. The hero
would be rather a shock to meet because he is so melancholy ;
but the servants, Diego and Jacques, tumble about and
shout aloud when they see a strange hand appear, so that the
reader feels more inclined to go and have a look than to
hide in terror. Bianca, another servant at the castle, is a
wonderful creation. We cannot possibly feel terrified by her
voice exclaiming : " Oh ! the hand ! the giant ! the hand !
support me ! I am terrified out of my senses ! I will not
sleep in the castle to-night," when she adds most thought-
fully, " My things can come after me to-morrow."

Such crudities would be impossible in a modern mystery
story, but *The Castle of Otranto* is an important landmark.
With its romantic hero, its castle, and its deliberate atmosphere of dread, it created the taste for a new chivalric novel,
and its conventions were useful to later writers. Both Scott
and Jane Austen, two of the greatest novelists, derived something from Walpole's contribution to the novel. *The Castle
of Otranto* was soon followed by many minor novels which
supplied horrors in plenty. Clara Reeve's *Old English Baron*
imitated Walpole's book. Mrs. Radcliffe wrote a number of
thrillers, of which *The Mysteries of Udolpho* was the most
popular. The book is interesting to-day chiefly because it
shows Mrs. Radcliffe's private opinion of ghosts. She feels
she ought to give an explanation for their existence, and
make their appearance in her plot respectable. Matthew
Lewis in his *Monk* has no such scruples and fills his story
with ghosts. All these novels were very popular for a time,
but they were not of lasting importance. Continuous
sensation became finally as monotonous as everyday events
had seemed. Gradually a reaction came, but novelists
turned their energies into a new field all the fresher for a
sojourn among horrors.

Maria Edgeworth was one of the first to rebel against the
horror-story. She had read Mrs. Radcliffe eagerly at school,
and when she was young could tell stories after that lady's
own heart. One of her early villains has a mask " made
from the skin of a dead man's hand." But she outgrew this

taste, and her sense of humour came to the rescue. *Scenes of Irish Life* and *Castle Rackrent* are her best known books. *Castle Rackrent* is an excellent novel about four generations of an Irish family, told from the point of view of an old servant. Once more the normal world was restored to the novel, and Maria Edgeworth's lively humour made it a very attractive one.

THE DAZZLING COLOURS OF SCOTT

SCOTT benefited both from Horace Walpole and Maria Edgeworth. He admired *The Castle of Otranto* very much, and found it far more thrilling than we do to-day. As a direct result he felt inspired to introduce mystery into his novels ; but he gave it a wider treatment than Walpole had done. Scott created the vast historical novel and in this an enthralling mystery is only one of many elements. Walpole further influenced him in the realistic treatment of servants : Scott introduces them with the same purpose of giving comic relief. On the other hand, Maria Edgeworth's living picture of Irish life moved Scott to do the same kind of thing for Scotland. In 1814 he published his first novel, *Waverley*, a tale of Scottish life.

Once more the public were ready for the different kind of story which *Waverley* offered. It was so popular that Scott continued writing romances for some time at the rate of two a year and made fifteen hundred pounds a year from them. He had been renowned as a story-teller at school and now, in *Waverley*, romance appeared as never before. The public still had its thrills as in the description of the last Jacobite insurrection, but the studies of Scottish character and the description of Scottish scenery were new. Here were real places and people again, but now seen in most exciting situations. *Waverley* was followed by a series of romances dealing with Scotland. *Guy Mannering*, *The Antiquary*, *Rob Roy*, and *The Heart of Midlothian* are perhaps the best known. In 1819 Scott took the times of Cœur de Lion for the subject of *Ivanhoe*, and from that date until he published his last novel in 1831 he changed his historical setting with astonishing skill. In all, he wrote thirty-four novels, each a masterpiece of its kind. His reputation grew almost daily until his novels were as eagerly awaited in France and Germany as in Edinburgh and London. It is difficult to assess the value of the novels. Some people rank the Scottish novels highest; others *Kenilworth* with its brilliance and pathos; others *Quentin Durward* with its thrilling foreign adventures. It is easy to find some character here, some brilliant picture or moving tragedy there which brings the conviction this must be his best novel.

Faults also are easy to point out. The early novels are well planned, as witness the compact and swiftly moving *Legend of Montrose*, but later, when Scott was in debt and had to write fast to make money, the quality of his work suffered. *Redgauntlet*, one of the late books, is typical in its looseness of construction and flagging invention. He himself realised that his plots were sometimes faulty. But whatever he lacks in this direction is made up for by his magnificent power of description both of incident and landscape. His characters are great historical and romantic figures, though not psychologically realised. But there is always warmth and intimacy in his presentation of peasants and simple folk, just as there is in his descriptions of the wild grandeur of the Scottish countryside. Scott immortalised his country in literature.

THE POLITE WORLD OF JANE AUSTEN

HORACE WALPOLE, who inspired Scott to take the horror novel and widen it into a great historical romance, inspired Jane Austen to laugh over the mysteries of his imitators, and in revolt, to create an exquisite realistic novel, in which the chief events are tea parties, balls, social visits, engagements, and marriages. Jane Austen wrote only six novels altogether. In comparison with the number Scott produced, *Northanger Abbey, Sense and Sensibility, Pride and Prejudice, Mansfield Park, Emma*, and *Persuasion* seem very few. And in all of them there is not one romantic character. The first, *Northanger Abbey*, ridicules the extravagant atmosphere of Mrs. Radcliffe's stories; Catherine, the young heroine, tries in vain to find a mystery in a secret chest at the abbey where she visits. Most of the characters are fairly prosperous middle-class people. Jane Austen said of her work: " Three or four families in a country village is the only field to work on." She allowed herself no scope for the exhilarating sweep of scenery Scott gives. Her characters do not even admire Nature.

Scott, however, was himself so enthralled by her work that he said: " I have just finished reading *Pride and Pre-*

judice for the third time." *Pride and Prejudice* is Jane
Austen's best book. The story tells of a heroine, Elizabeth
Bennet, who refuses to marry a very rich suitor because of
his disrespect to her family, and of Elizabeth's sisters Jane,
Kitty, and Lydia. The characters are so vivid and the
dialogue is so true that the reader has the sensation of being
present at every scene and of being drawn into actual touch
with the intimate lives of the characters. Jane Austen tells
with penetrating irony of the jealousies, snobbery, and affec-
tations of her small society; we laugh quietly, but most
completely. She gives us plenty of common sense, but we
get a renewed zest for life from it. Her style is modest but
exact. Words are carefully chosen, so that the weight of
each adjective is felt. All the time there is the same careful
balance. Her books have been called " little bits of ivory
two inches wide." Jane Austen showed how the novel, by
taking everyday happenings and realising them intensely,
could give the most humdrum life a universal significance.

THE GOLDEN AGE OF THE NOVEL
I. 1837—1880

THE death of Scott in 1832 marks the end of an era. As
the nineteenth century proceeds through the Victorian
Age towards our own time England changes and the novel,
life's looking-glass, faithfully reflects the change. Between
1830 and 1900 the population of England, as a direct result
of the Industrial Revolution, was more than doubled. At
first the mass of the people lived under conditions so brutally
degraded no thoughts could be spared for anything beside
food and work. But improvement was inevitable because
starved, embittered workers are good for nothing. Soon
Factory Laws were passed, the Corn Laws repealed, making
food cheap and plentiful, and gradually education spread,
at first by the efforts of the Churches and private enterprise,
but finally by Government decree.

The result to literature was a far larger public than it had
ever known, but a public with diminished discrimination.
People who could only just read and write could not appreciate
beauty of literary forms and style. The demand was rather
for entertainment of a crude sensational kind. Of the
existing literary forms the novel was the one best fitted to
supply this demand, and accordingly it rose on a wave of

popularity to a position similar to, but perhaps even more powerful than that enjoyed by the drama in the days of Shakespeare. The condition of its popularity, however, meant that the novel must change. It had to please its public, that is, reflect the taste of its public; but since a large proportion of that public had no understanding of literature many of the multitude of novels written between 1840 and our own day cannot claim to be literature. They do not please a public of educated taste even at the first reading and no one reads them twice.

Nevertheless, apart from these novels made for the moment, the novel which offered far more than an evening's entertainment also received a strong impetus from the new popularity, so that soon many more novels of real merit and lasting interest were written than any one person could hope to read. Among the Victorians, early and late, we can acquaint ourselves with the work of the immortals, but the rest we must of necessity leave to scholars.

JOHN BULL IN HIS SHIRT SLEEVES

THE first and probably the greatest Victorian novelist is Charles Dickens. He represents the real democratisation of literature in which the novel has played so important a part. A child of poor parents (his father was imprisoned for debt), with scanty education, he had read to advantage the rambling tales of Smollett, and with a taste for romance suffered the bitterness of social inferiority. His novels reflect these impressions. Dickens combined realism and romance with a sense of humour and a wide humanity. In these characteristics he is English of the English. *Pickwick Papers* is really a humorous study of John Bull at his ease. *Nicholas Nickleby* and *Oliver Twist* are social studies humanised. Dickens loved life and was determined to portray it as he saw it, in all its diversity, its comedy, its pathos, its cruelty, and its opportunity for chivalry. He was essentially a great humanist. He believed in the goodness of ordinary human nature and upheld it against the oppressions and the tyrannies of his day. He loved the common people and filled his novels with full-length portraits of them. He drew humble folk, not as the members of a social class, but as individuals whose personal fortunes are our concern. Sam Weller is a typical ostler, but he is magnificently himself. Dickens possessed the art of taking his characters out of the masses and yet of identifying them with exact particularity, consequently he met with the popularity at the outset of his career which he has retained to this day. His greatness lay in his power to perceive significance in the ordinary man and woman.

In form his novels are loose and rather sprawling. His method is to gather together people from different walks of life and see what happens to them. Swift, dramatic plot is foreign to his love of social reactions, and the only novel of rapid movement he wrote is *A Tale of Two Cities*. There the urge of events in the French Revolution contends with Dickens's fondness for an English woman and her father caught in the tide. But this novel is the least characteristic of all his works. *David Copperfield*, an autobiography, shows him at his best and simplest; the story meanders along like a south country stream. *Nicholas Nickleby*, *The Old Curiosity Shop*, *Little Dorrit*, and *Oliver Twist* are pictures of the humble lives of good people suffering and triumphing over some form of social oppression. As he grew older Dickens extended his range, and in *Martin Chuzzlewit*, *Bleak House*, and *Dombey and Son* he shows how the middle-class people of his day maintained their human and religious existence in the face of the threats of industrialism.

THE SECRET OF DICKENS'S POPULARITY

DICKENS'S novels instantly gripped the popular imagination. During his lifetime he was hailed all over the world as the greatest English writer alive, the only man comparable to Shakespeare. His popularity continues to this day. Every town in England has its Dickens Society. In America and on the Continent his novels are read by every school child. But critics have not been lacking. No one can deny his power of vivid portraiture and of being intensely interesting, but it has been pointed out that he did not escape either the price of his popularity or the defects of his own gifts.

Perhaps the worst sin of which he is accused is intellectual dishonesty. His public wanted entertainment; it did not object to weeping over Little Nell or shuddering at the wickedness of Quilp, but it would not tolerate suffering and evil winning in the end. So Dickens was obliged to end all his novels happily and to see to it that righteousness triumphed in the long run. He had to describe life, not as he knew it to be but as his public desired. In the same way he was forced to make his heroes and heroines conform to the accepted standards of behaviour. They might be sorely tempted, might indeed commit sins society could condone, but they must never be shown capable of real lapses from virtue. Thus Pip in *Great Expectations* is shown guilty of extravagance and snobbishness, but he never puts himself outside the social pale. Tom Jones would not have been tolerated by Dickens's public.

The novels also have artistic flaws. Sometimes they are melodramatic, often they are over-sentimental ; the character-drawing is on occasion so hasty that it becomes rough cari-cature. These weaknesses spring from a lack of self-criticism. Dickens represents the new democratic generation. Like the poet Whitman in America he is the articulate voice of democracy. Like Whitman he had little appreciation of the forms and manners of achieved art. His novels sprawled, for one reason because they were written in serial form and published in monthly parts ; but any rigidity of form would have been fatal to Dickens's genius, which was essentially generous. He brought to the novel the sense of richness and plenty just because he was ready and able to bring everybody into it. His discursiveness, his fantastic humour, his rather maudlin sentiment, and his love of the grotesque are all typical of the weaknesses common to people of newly achieved consciousness. But in spite of their faults his novels remain among the most easily read and most fasci-nating in English.

VIRTUE UNREWARDED IN "VANITY FAIR"

DICKENS has often been compared with Thackeray who was his great rival at this period, and there are still eager claims for the supremacy of each. In 1848 Thackeray was considered the greatest living writer, though for fifteen years he had written without recognition. It was not until he was thirty-six that his first mature work, *Vanity Fair*, brought him fame. His first book, *The Paris Sketch Book*, consists of reprints of his work as Paris correspondent to various newspapers. It is unequal, and so is the *Collection of Tales* which followed. Both volumes show traces of hasty writing, but have an exuberant vivacity and humour. *Vanity Fair*, his greatest novel, was issued in monthly parts and was followed by the series of great novels *Pendennis, Esmond,*

The Newcomes, and *The Virginians*. His books have been called gigantic essays.

Vanity Fair is a brilliant satirical comedy. Intended as a challenge, it throws down the glove by calling itself a *Novel without a Hero*. Thackeray turned to Fielding for inspiration and attempted, as he says, " to give scenes of all sorts, in which the fool and the rogue, the weak and the brave, single-eye and double-face play their parts, as in the world of all of us." The story is concerned with the social success of a brilliant adventuress, Becky Sharp. Her adventures form the main action of the comedy. With her wiles she succeeds in life most triumphantly, but Amelia, the virtuous woman, fails. *Pendennis* is another novel which paints life realistically. In this novel Thackeray revived the letter-form and wrote in an intimate and exciting style some of his own experiences under the name of Arthur Pendennis. In *Esmond* Thackeray gives a vivid historical romance set in the reign of Queen Anne. Henry Esmond tells the story in autobiographical form, and the re-creation of the atmosphere of the period is so natural that one feels Thackeray is describing his own day.

HOW THACKERAY CONTRASTS WITH DICKENS

As a novelist Thackeray undoubtedly shows more technical accomplishment than Dickens, but his vision of life is narrower. In treating his subjects Thackeray was influenced, as was Dickens, by the caricaturists of the day. Thackeray can caricature as effectively as Dickens. In *Major Gahagan* he describes the Major as though he had an eye on the absurd figure such a man would make in the illustration of a magazine. The Major uses bullet paper for his letters, a gunpowder barrel for his writing-desk, and keeps a lit candle close to some powder under his bed.

Dickens and Thackeray were both conscious in their novels of the social evils of their times. Their attitude in commenting on life reveals a significant contrast. Thackeray's early life was passed in easy conditions. He was well educated and of good family. He satirises the society which he knows with a critical aloof irony. Dickens gives the humours of low life with a rough and tumble vigour. We feel he turns his characters round to face us before he gives a description. Thackeray is never boisterous even in his indignation. Dickens is optimistic. He could describe the terrible atmo-

Mr. Micawber : one of Dickens's liveliest characters.

sphere of prison life, in *Little Dorrit*, and enter fully into the well-fed content of a Christmas party in *Pickwick Papers* without any sense of the incongruous. Thackeray was more depressed by the wickedness in life. He leaves on the reader an impression of permanent disillusionment. He is reflective and stays his story for comment. His characters are self-critical and their inner motives are exposed. In *Vanity Fair* he set out with an earnest moral aim. Becky Sharp illustrates the text " all is vanity " by succeeding in life when she ought to fail. Yet she is real. We do not feel she is an illustration of a text, but that she is a living person. Both Dickens and Thackeray present life without attempting to define it. They present the social scene and leave its interpretation to their followers.

THE STARK GENIUS OF EMILY BRONTË

IF Jane Austen's stories were the almost perfect antitheses of Scott's, *Wuthering Heights*, the single novel of Emily Brontë, was certainly the polar opposite of Thackeray's work. His voice is the voice of the town, and echoes about the fashionable clubs and drawing-rooms of Victorian London. Hers, emerging from a remote parsonage on the Yorkshire moors, has the magnetic quality of oracle and portent—a note beyond the ordinary sounds of life, but informed with a wild authenticity. This sense of power that must be potent—must find its object and there utter itself completely and be spent—is at the very core of Emily Brontë's work, as it was of her life.

Wuthering Heights is a story of wild love and wild hate ; of souls caught and racked in what Blake truly described as the " torments of love and jealousy." But it is not (as it has been called) a nightmare or a phantasmagoria because the souls themselves are capable of great suffering, and that makes them great souls. To share in the suffering of great souls is to have one's own soul educated. The Greeks called this process *Catharsis*, or purification by means of pity and terror. *Wuthering Heights* is more akin to a Greek tragedy than almost any other piece of English literature, and few can read this story without experiencing a catharsis in themselves. The elemental power which streamed through Emily and wrought this one image, unique in the history of the novel, was diffused through the rest of the Brontë family, and in Charlotte again expressed itself in fiction. Charlotte's novels, *Villette*, *Shirley*, and *Jane Eyre* are human studies of passionate and sensitive young womanhood. For these her own and her sister's lives had provided the pattern. *Shirley*, who is drawn from Emily, contains satirical portraits of various members of the limited moorland society, and is Charlotte Brontë's most objective work. In the other novels her own feelings sometimes ran away with her pen and produced scenes and characters (notably that of the fierce and gloomy but magnetic Mr. Rochester of *Jane Eyre*) which are obviously the creations of phantasy. But when she speaks simply and from the heart there is no resisting her, and her power of describing scenery and conveying atmosphere sometimes rivals that of Emily, who had the poet's vision.

THE JOLLY FRANKNESS OF TROLLOPE

SINCE the World War the literary reputations of the Victorian Novelists have undergone revaluation. Dickens and Thackeray stand high, but not so high as once they did. Emily Brontë has outstripped them both and also passed her sister, Charlotte, who was for a long time better known. The novelist who has gained most from the change in values is Anthony Trollope. Trollope was a post-office official whose work took him about the country. In this way he gained much of the experience out of which he fashioned the novels known as *The Barchester Series*. Trollope was a most prolific writer who poured out words, his critics declared, as machines pour out sausages. His work was at first well received, but possibly because he was too frank about the ease with which he could write he fell out of favour towards the end of his life and his novels were long unread.

Trollope was distinguished from his contemporaries by his truthfulness. He was honest about himself, his work, and his world. In his novels he wrote of men and women as he really knew them, not as they like to imagine themselves. An age which preferred plaster saints to fallible human beings did not appreciate him, but to-day his rough downright frankness is winning him a larger audience. His best novel is *Barchester Towers*, in which he describes the everyday events in a small cathedral town. His skill in laughing at the absurdities of curates has been compared not unfavourably with Jane Austen's.

THE GOLDEN AGE OF THE NOVEL
II. 1880—1914

BETWEEN 1837 and 1882 when Trollope died, many more enjoyable novels were written than could be discussed in anything less than a full-sized history. George Eliot's *Mill on the Floss*, *Silas Marner*, and *Adam Bede* are still widely read. Mrs. Gaskell's *Cranford* has a secure niche in the hearts of all lovers of literature. Charles and Henry Kingsley, George Borrow, Charles Reade, and a score of others reward attention. But these writers did well what the giants did better, so that their work, delightful though it is, is inevitably overshadowed.

The group of novelists next to be considered rounded off the century in a blaze of glory which has lasted almost to our own time. Most of them were very young men when Dickens died in 1870. Some of them, such as H. G. Wells, are still writing, while others have died only within the last few years. When we read the work of these writers and those who follow them we cannot be sure that our appreciation will be endorsed by later generations. They are too near us to be seen in perspective. Some of the older among them, such as Meredith and Hardy, write of problems swept away by the War so that their novels have temporarily lost something of their force. More modern writers are perhaps credited with greater powers than they in fact possess because they write of life as we are experiencing it and their problems are vital to us.

CONTINENTAL INFLUENCE FREES THE NOVEL

BETWEEN 1880 and 1914 the English novel changed fundamentally owing to the influence exerted by the translation of continental novels. Until this time novelists had been content to tell of people living within the accepted structure of English society. They had been occupied in observing, perhaps laughing at, the foibles of individual men and women, and in imagining their adventures in situations romantic, fantastic, or everyday. Dickens and some of his contemporaries, such as Charles Kingsley and Reade, turned their attention to the more startling inequalities industrial England endured and helped to rouse public opinion against them. But even Dickens did not carry his criticism beyond superficialities ; he did not venture to criticise the very stuff and fabric of society. French and Russian novelists, on the contrary, wrote freely on any subject ; they were not bound by the reticences and discretions which hampered English writers. Russia and France had nothing like the famous " British Constitution." Their social institutions had been shaken by too many violent upheavals to appear sacred, so these could be and frequently were questioned without profanity.

When between 1885 and 1900 the work of Tolstoi, Dostoievsky, Balzac, Flaubert, and Zola became known in England it opened a new world, preparing the way for an English " novel of ideas." From this time the English novel began to fight for intellectual freedom with the result that to-day, as we know, almost nothing is excluded from its province. Any attempt to assign the responsibility for this new development to particular novels must fail. The nature and extent of the change can be best realised by first reading Dickens and then comparing his novels with Thomas Hardy's and with these foreign novels : Tolstoi's *War and Peace* and *Anna Karenina* ; Dostoievsky's *Crime and Punishment* and *The Idiot* ; Flaubert's *Madame Bovary*.

THE SOCIAL COMEDY AMUSES A POET

MEREDITH was the novelist to succeed to the position held by Dickens and Thackeray. Meredith was essentially a philosopher. As a novelist he is the social commentator who is most at home in places where economic security gives people time to think their own thoughts. In the thoughts and feelings of well-bred people Meredith discovers social comedy. Proud, sensitive, an aristocrat by nature, though not by birth, Meredith sees life in the terms of the ascending effort which the recently discovered theory of natural selection imposed upon the progressively-minded men of his day.

Meredith believed in hard thinking, and his severely intellectual and often tortuous style betrays his taste. Wit, satire, and irony are always at his back, and in *The Egoist* especially he makes use of all three with splendid effect. But he has also great tenderness. The quality lies hidden for the most part beneath a stoic philosophy, but it shines out with lyric fervour in the early *Richard Feverel* and the later *Diana of the Crossways*. In *Evan Harrington*, his easiest novel, he laughs gently at himself and draws an amusing picture of his remarkable father. Meredith reflected in his novels all the best elements of the wealthy governing classes in the 'nineties, when England's imperial glory was at its zenith. His popularity has waned since his death, but Meredith was a poet and his fame has only begun.

DARK TALES OF DESTINY AND FATE

THOMAS HARDY, the other great novelist of the period, offers a sharp contrast. He, too, is a philosopher, but his philosophy is one of endurance rather than of hope. Nature is unutterably beautiful to Hardy : yet at the same time " red in tooth and claw." And Nature is dominant. The people of Hardy's country are embedded in the landscape. They are the peasantry of his beloved Wessex, simple men and women, with passionate hearts and kindly instincts, but their lives are victimised by inauspicious Fate and they die as the cattle die—by chance or caprice. Hardy is oppressed by Destiny. He knows the sweetness of life, the purity of early love, the lyric splendour of which Nature is capable, and all the pleasures native to traditional English life. But he also knows the ardours and endurances which humble folk must suffer. He knows that virtue is seldom rewarded, that hypocrisy wears a smiling face, and that injustice is done to innocence in the name of law. Against these he protests, calling upon our human pity.

Tess of the D'Urbervilles is a terrible story of the treatment met by a simple country girl who has ignorantly violated the social code of her time. *Jude the Obscure* is an even darker tale of a young man thirsty for learning but denied by poverty, and of a young woman, Sue, who breaks herself in resisting the demands of the rôle then considered inevitable for a woman. These two novels, both in choice of subject and in the dark, fatalistic philosophy with which the stories are worked out, clearly show the Russian influence at work. They aroused a storm of protest and controversy because they criticised the accepted ideas on marriage and the relations between men and women. This subject had hitherto been taboo in literature and Hardy was thus guilty of great daring when he described Tess, in spite of her illegitimate child, as " a pure woman." The moralists raged but Hardy won, so that, by the turn of the century, problems of sex could be treated in novels almost as freely as they are to-day.

Of Hardy's other novels, *The Mayor of Casterbridge* is

growing in popularity and threatens to displace *Tess* and *Jude*. *The Return of the Native* stands out for its superb description of Egdon Heath. *Under the Greenwood Tree* and *Far from the Madding Crowd* are idylls of romance narrated with exquisite realism and fidelity. Hardy's greatness as a novelist is shown by the stark simplicity with which he achieves his object. His plots are straightforward, his characters unsophisticated, and his manner simple and dignified; yet with the crudest materials he can convey the sense of tragic inevitability. The action of his figures is seen silhouetted against the bright canvas of complacent Nature, or in relief against her darkness. The characters move compelled by powers too great for human perception, to destinies which only Time can decide. Man is pigmy; but Destiny is a presence felt. Could it be that Hardy's prophetic soul was dimly aware of the coming cataclysm of the World War? Were his novels in the sum a foreshadowing of the tragedy which closed his era?

CHAMPION OF DEMOCRACY : H. G. WELLS

H. G. WELLS is an author of such comprehensiveness that he is almost impossible to place. He has written a cycling story, *The Wheels of Chance*, and a complete *History of the World*. His main interests lie not in literature but in applied science, sociology, and politics. He has written a great many novels, however, because the novel-form provided him with the ideal means of making the world listen to his ideas. *The War in the Air* is a successful anticipation of events ; *Anne Veronica* and *The New Machiavelli* well reveal Wells's philosophy of life. His later books grow further away from literature, tending to become sociological treatises.

H. G. Wells's literary reputation will probably rest on his earlier novels, which are humorous studies of middle-class domesticity. *Love and Mr. Lewisham*, the immortal *Kipps*, and the incomparable *History of Mr. Polly* are his most enjoyable novels. In them Wells is at his most exuberant ease and his sociological sense becomes effervescent. *Tono Bungay* is a witty satire on the power of advertisement, and affords some scathing comment on modern commercialism. The social reformer is seldom absent from his novels. He is the novelist of changing times anticipating the changes and wondering, in a rather brusque manner, why, with the scientific knowledge at its disposal, mankind is so slow to change its ways.

Arnold Bennett was a writer as prolific as Wells, and nearly as versatile. He wrote, as he frankly said, to make money, and succeeded in achieving this aim and more besides. He not only became a " best-seller, ' but at least one of his novels, *The Old Wives' Tale*, promises to become a classic. Bennett owed much to French example, and learned from it the precepts of objective truth. An unsophisticated man of very wide sympathies, he excels in his acute power of observation. The whole social scene is his province and he observes it with such precision and fine proportion that his work has more than photographic veracity. Emotionally his work is limited. The sequel to *Clayhanger* and *Hilda Lessways* fails for want of emotional depth. But Bennett produced one masterpiece : *The Old Wives' Tale*. Bennett was a writer of amazing industry. Besides his novels he wrote a number of successful plays, and was a tireless essayist. Throughout his life he remained a simple middle-class provincial man. When wealth came to him he wrote of wealth with naive admiration. His later novels show some falling off, but *Riceyman Steps* is notable.

THE SWAN SONG OF THE VICTORIAN AGE

PERHAPS no novelist since Dickens has enjoyed so high a reputation, especially abroad, as John Galsworthy. Towards the end of his life he was to some extent eclipsed at home, and to-day he is possibly under-rated, but in France and Germany his work is still eagerly read and appreciated. His public in England has decreased because many of the problems which interested him have gone out of date, while it is yet too soon for any universal quality his work may possess to be perceived. On the Continent his novels rank high because they give a careful, detailed, and full picture of English life and a society now almost passed away. Galsworthy interprets the English spirit and explains with understanding the much misrepresented ideal of the " English Gentleman," both the natural one and the synthetic product of the public schools and the older universities. Englishmen of every type are mysteries to foreigners and consequently Galsworthy's novels have a fascination for them we cannot share.

The prose epic, *The Forsyte Saga*, is Galsworthy's greatest work, and the one by which he is best known. In this he tells the story of one family, the Forsytes, through four generations, and so is able to show in perspective the influences which have been at work on the structure of society from the end of the nineteenth century until after the World War. When the story begins Galsworthy is in sympathy with the younger generation, but as it draws nearer our own time it passes its author, leaving him slightly hurt and bewildered by a generation he tried, but failed, to understand. For this reason he is more successful with his portraits of Old Jolyon Forsyte and his son, Soames, than he is with Soames's daughter, Fleur, and her husband. Galsworthy has been reproached with superficiality and lack of penetration. The charge is perhaps justified in his later work, but the first books of the Saga show him a true artist.

At the end of the nineteenth century more talented men and women were writing novels than at any previous period. It is no longer possible to read a few outstanding works and feel nothing of importance has been neglected. Names crowd into the memory of authors who, each in his way, have contributed something of value to the development of the novel. Samuel Butler with *The Way of All Flesh*, George Moore with *Esther Waters*, Stevenson with *Dr. Jekyll and Mr. Hyde*, Isaac Zangwill with *The Children of the Ghetto*, Sir James Barrie with *The Little Minister*, have all produced novels of the first order. Injustice is unavoidable when selection is made ; nevertheless, three other novelists of this period seem to claim individual mention.

GISSING'S NEW NOTE OF REALISM

THE first of these is George Gissing, who, under the influence of Zola, was one of the first to bring the new realism to the English novel. This realism which has since found its culmination in Theodore Dreiser's *American Tragedy* consists in revealing the drab, ugly sides of everyday life in all their hideous boredom. Writers of this school do not paint crime and immorality in lurid, wickedly attractive colours, but show them as the outcome of grey desperation. Gissing, who was a scholar and a man of sensitive culture, was early forced into circumstances of hardship and poverty, and his real tales of the squalor attendant upon poverty in our great cities were written from bitter experience. *New Grub Street* is a tale of sordid journalism. *Demos, Born in*

3

Exile, and *Thyrza* are all novels showing human beings struggling to wrest a tolerable existence from a mechanised society.

At the other end of the social scale was Henry James, a novelist who was essentially an artist, fascinated by the subtleties and refinements of cultured society. James was an intellectualist who inherited a taste for the abstruse, and his style is often quoted as showing the limit of intelligible super-subtlety. His novels, however, well repay the pains required to read them, and *The Tragic Muse*, *Roderick Hudson*, *The Sacred Fount*, and *The Ambassadors* are characteristic. *What Maisie Knew* is an acute analysis of the adolescent mind.

Joseph Conrad has points of comparison with Henry James ; but with Conrad the psychological motive is more obvious and his passion for analysis less insistent. Conrad wrote of the sea, which he loved, and is at his best when it is most troublesome to man. But although he wrote in the romantic vein, Conrad was not so much interested in events as in the psychological reactions to them of his deeply-seen people and in their psychological reactions to one another. Caught between admiration for the obvious virtues and a disinterested desire to understand human nature, his novels have a hybrid character and are not wholly successful. But *Lord Jim* is a fine study, and *The Nigger of the Narcissus* a piece of very vivid writing. *Almayer's Folly* and *Tales of Unrest* are also good reading. *Victory*, a late work, shows how he sometimes beat his emotions into a state of unreal feverishness.

HOW MODERN WRITERS ARE CHANGING THE NOVEL

THE World War forms a barrier at which the attempt to assess the permanence of individual novels and novelists must be relinquished. When the significance of that disaster to western civilisation has itself been assessed, the world will be in a position to take stock of its literary assets and discover the modern novelists of permanent value. We shall then find out whose work was following the lines of life and whose was merely reflective of some passing phase. At present the essential perspective is lacking. Opinions regarding the comparative importance of contemporaries must be mere opinions based upon personal hopes, fears, and tastes, all of which time may well belie. As in the past, novelists who now seem to us all important may appear as merely the last flames of a dying fire, while novelists whose names are now barely known will be found to have lit candles that will stand in the wind.

But, although individual assessments are impossible, tendencies may be indicated. The age is scientific and materialistic. The upward rise on the graph of scientific knowledge becomes almost vertical at the beginning of the twentieth century; and this knowledge is not only of the external world. Science begins to explore the caverns of the mind and to touch upon ground hitherto regarded as the preserve of religion and art. Modern psychology begins to unfold a new page of human history—one of vital importance to the novelist. The bald explanations of human conduct which satisfied our forbears no longer suffice for those who see in glimpses the workings of the unconscious. The novelist has to find a new perspective and take a fresh look at his subject. The necessity to do this has resulted in the modern psychological novel. James Joyce, Dorothy Richardson, Virginia Woolf, Gertrude Stein, and their followers, are not, as might be thought, merely placing human nature upon the dissecting table for the purpose of gratifying a morbid taste. They are endeavouring to see human beings and their relation to life more closely and more truly in the light of increased knowledge. The ultimate value of their work may be small, but it forms an essential link in the necessary assimilative process. Their intense interest in psychology is itself a sign of their sensitivity to the movement of life, and their responsiveness to one of its deep tremors.

The psychological novel and the " novel of ideas," of which Aldous Huxley's *Point Counterpoint* is the best example, owe much to French influence, and in particular to Marcel Proust's *Remembrance of Things Past* and André Gide's *The Counterfeiters*. These two novels have been excellently translated into English and should be read by every one who is interested in the modern novel. But neither they nor their English followers are easy to read. They repay trouble, because they make an unforgettable impression on the mind and open up long vistas of new ideas. But it must be admitted that they do not appeal to a wide public and are in no sense popular. This is perhaps their weakness, for the very greatest art has something to say to every one.

For this reason it may be that those critics are right who claim D. H. Lawrence as the only modern novelist of genius. Lawrence's work has excited more controversy than that of any other writer since Flaubert, partly because he has allowed his fine imagination to penetrate further than any one else has dared into the relationships between men and women, but also because he has an unequalled power of vivid writing. Lawrence had the artist's passion for truth ; he turned his face from nothing, but ventured to the core of existence. His work has faults : he exaggerates ; he loses his sense of proportion ; he allows his ideas to carry him away so that he forgets momentarily to be an artist and just rants ; he is sometimes submerged in bitterness. But still his work has a power and beauty which can be felt by every reader.

Lawrence's most widely-read book in England is *Sons and Lovers*, in which he describes the subtle relations vibrating between Paul Morel and his mother and the women he tries hard to love. *Women in Love* reveals Lawrence's mature philosophy of life, a philosophy which found its simplest, most artistic expression in his banned novel, *Lady Chatterly's Lover*. *The Man Who Died*, one of his latest works, shows a strong tendency towards mysticism. In all Lawrence's books there are passages of remarkable beauty.

CONTEMPORARY NOVELS WHICH RESPECT TRADITION

IN the hands of Joyce, Huxley, Mrs. Woolf, and D. H. Lawrence the novel has changed in subject matter, method of approach, and form. These novelists analyse and interpret rather than construct and describe, and are more preoccupied with motive and personality than with action and character. Consequently they care less about the construction of their plots and sometimes try to dispense with a plot altogether. The characters carry most of the weight in their books ; action is shown as meaningless, unless considered in the light of intention.

But apart from these, the pioneers among contemporary novelists, there are many writers whose work, following the older tradition, is wholly delightful and is indeed preferred by a large section of the public. May Sinclair, Compton Mackenzie, Sheila Kaye-Smith, Hugh Walpole, Margaret Kennedy, Clemence Dane, Mary Webb, with Sinclair Lewis, Thornton Wilder, and Ernest Hemingway in America are

D. H. Lawrence : the century's most controversial novelist.

only a few among the authors of modern novels likely to endure. J. B. Priestley's *The Good Companions* has a wide appeal for its lively pictures of English country life and because it tells of people who, in a time of peculiar stress, can still take life lightly.

THE SECRET OF THE DETECTIVE NOVEL

IN the psychological novel, character is all-important, and the plot is often neglected; but there is another very successful type of modern novel, in which everything depends on the plot. In a detective story, Sherlock Holmes, Poirot, Father Brown, or Peter Wimsey may add charm and interest, but if the plot is not faultless, if it is not thought out along strictly mathematical lines, the story fails. One reason for this may lie in the fact that the first and still the greatest writers of detective fiction—E. A. Poe and Conan Doyle—expressed themselves mostly in the short story, not in the novel. A second and more potent reason is that the detective story is concerned with the solution of a problem. The detective novel has been despised by some critics because it deals in crime and panders to a vicious taste for sensation. But the real interest in stories of horror and mystery is not in the dark deeds performed, but in the abstruse problem of finding the guilty person. If this were not so, crime stories would pile murder on murder in the manner of the Elizabethan melodramas; but, in fact, a detective novel which reeks overmuch of blood is not often successful.

A good plot is the sheet-anchor of the detective novel. Edgar Wallace owed his unprecedented success to his genius for constructing plots which puzzled the reader's ingenuity to solve but which were capable of a fair solution in the end. Writers as talented as G. K. Chesterton or Agatha Christie may widen the scope of the detective novel by attempting psychological interpretation of the criminal, by character-drawing as brilliant as that of Father Brown, or by writing in polished, gently ironical English. But Edgar Wallace has proved conclusively that the only essential quality of this type of novel is sound construction.

WHY THE "BEST-SELLER" SELLS

WE have now seen that the modern novel can be roughly divided into categories, as the psychological novel, the "novel of ideas," the traditional novel, and the novel of crime and detection. But these categories do not cover all the kinds of modern novels. There are, for instance, the War novels. Of these there is little to be said. They were wrung out of terrible experiences which found, of necessity, bitter and troubled expression. Many of them are already forgotten and few have any permanent value. Their subject is special-ised, and they cannot be said to have shown the way to new developments in form.

A more disturbing problem is presented by the novels of such best-sellers as Ethel M. Dell and Elinor Glyn. Here the critics fall between two stools. They cannot whole-heartedly praise, but they dare not decry too lustily for fear of being called " highbrow." Moreover, they cannot deny that works which please so many people must have some quality to recommend them. One reason for the popularity of novels of this kind is that they are written for and enjoyed by women ; men very seldom like them. They satisfy an urgent need by supplying emotional colour to women whose lives are cast in dull, narrow circumstances. A second reason for their wide appeal is that, as Gerald Gould says in his book *The English Novel of To-day*, they tell a story with considerable narrative skill.

But, in spite of their immediate success, these novels fail eventually because they gain all their effect by appealing direct to the sensations. They please at first and so, at first, are good. But the pleasure is not lasting, and the ability to give lasting pleasure is the test of a good novel.

PATHWAYS INTO THE WORLD OF FICTION

" BEGIN at the beginning," said the King in *Alice*, " go on to the end and then stop." Although we have followed this advice in discussing the novel the reader who is not already acquainted with seventeenth- and eighteenth-century literature will be wise to do the exact opposite when selecting a course of novel-reading. The best approach to the novel, as to most forms of literature, is through the finest work of contemporary writers. Thus an interesting and illuminating course of novel-reading would begin with D. H. Lawrence's *Sons and Lovers*, and would include Hardy's *Mayor of Casterbridge* and *Tess of the D'Urbervilles*, Emily Brontë's *Wuthering Heights*, Sir Walter Scott's *Heart of Midlothian* or *Waverley*, and then the work of the eighteenth-century novelists, Fielding, Sterne, Smollett, Richardson, in that order.

An alternative course for those whose main interests lie in science, politics, or sociology, would start with H. G. Wells's *Tono Bungay* or *Joan and Peter*, and go on to Arnold Bennett's *Old Wives' Tale*, Samuel Butler's *Way of All Flesh*, Trollope's *Barchester Towers*, Charles Dickens's *Nicholas Nickleby*, Jane Austen's *Pride and Prejudice*, and end with Smollett's *Roderick Random*, and Fielding's *Tom Jones*.

Readers who want to know more about the work of writers mentioned in the section on the novel and to go more fully into questions of form and technique, are recommended to read E. M. Forster's *Aspects of the Novel* (Arnold) and J. B. Priestley's little book entitled *The English Novel* (Benn).

THE SHORT STORY : A MINIATURE PAINTED WITH WORDS

by J. M. HALFORD, B.A.(Lond.)

ALTHOUGH there never was an age when literary traditions were not in the melting-pot—for it is only by
recasting itself in the contemporary mould that literature keeps alive—the cult of the short story, as opposed to
the story which is short, is something more than a swing of
the pendulum ; it is a portent. The story which is short
is as old as speech itself, but it survives to-day chiefly in the
regard of magazine editors. On the other hand the short
story as a form of expression with its own aims, existing in
its own right, is to all intents and purposes the invention of
the nineteenth century, and it may well be that its greatest
achievements are yet to come. Certainly it has an immediacy
of effect unmatched by any other literary medium which is
primarily concerned with the relationship of human beings
both to each other and to the vaster, impersonal forces of
the world as a whole ; and in the hands of such masters as
Poe, Maupassant, and Tchekov it has attained the perfect
harmony of form, content, manner, and intention, characteristic of great art.

WHAT IS A SHORT STORY ?

THE mention of these names, all great in the history of the
short story yet each representative of different aims and
different achievements, is a reminder that, despite a great
deal of theorising and speculation to the contrary, the short
story conforms to no rules except the artistic necessity of
unity. It can begin anywhere and end nowhere ; it need
not be short—Henry James's *The Turn of the Screw*, which
is commonly classified as a short story, is forty thousand words
long—and it certainly need not conform to the conventional
idea of a story as a narrative with a plot. The only rule
for the short story is that, within the limits of its conception,
it must be an organic whole. Poe, in a review of Hawthorne's
Tales, explicitly declared that " in the whole composition
there should be no one word written, of which the tendency,
direct or indirect, is not to the one pre-established design " ;

73

and although neither he nor anybody else has ever obeyed this ruling literally, the principle is sound. It is the recognition of what he called, in the course of the same review, " the immense force derivable from *totality*." To make the reader aware of this force is the prime aim of all short stories written with a conscious artistic purpose ; and it is the necessity of achieving " totality " that demands on the part of the writer a highly developed sense of form, so that the body and end of a short story may be, as R. L. Stevenson declared they should be, " bone of the bone and blood of the blood of the beginning."

Although it is clear that conformity with these standards demands a relatively high degree of technical skill, this is not in itself sufficient to explain why unity of impression should be preferred to the cumulative effect of the novel ; why, in fact, the short story is " modern." To understand how the short story has come to enjoy a position in literature almost equal in prestige and popularity to that of the novel, it is essential to know something about its evolution and to see what short-story writers are trying to do.

NEW WAYS WITH OLD THEMES

THERE is no avoiding the conclusion that theories as to how a story should be told and what it should tell have rather a pretentious air in face of the fact that story-telling is one of the oldest of human activities. Indeed, all the stories in the world have already been told. There is no such thing as a new plot : there are only new ways of handling an old one. This is the purpose and essential character of literature : to re-interpret the eternal truths in the light of contemporary experience. For, although human nature does not change, its complexes do. The ordinary man of to-day is at once very like and very unlike all the ordinary men who have preceded him ; alike in his instinctive human qualities, unlike in the mental outlook imposed upon him by the ever-changing social conditions which make up his environment.

It is for this reason that the characteristic medium of expression changes from age to age ; for the medium of expression— the epic, the drama, the novel—is simply the formula, as it were, which is understood by the greatest number of people at a particular time. In the fourteenth century, for example, the only people likely to understand any kind of literary formula were the elite, for only the elite could read. Consequently Chaucer, whose superb gifts of humour, insight, and verbal felicity would have placed him in the front rank however he chose to write, turned naturally to narrative poetry as the only medium likely to satisfy a sophisticated demand for manner as well as matter : the demand that a thing should be not only worth saying but also well said.

In the sixteenth century the appeal of literature was suddenly broadened and given new life by the development of the theatre. The Elizabethan drama, in its bewildering mixture of crudity and poetic splendour, was the response to the demand of a naïvely imaginative audience for the dramatic presentation of history, legend, and romance. Later, when the theatres were closed, and afterwards at the Restoration, the drama lost its " common touch," and a gradually increasing reading public turned to the novel because it seemed to give a truer and more embracing picture of life as it is lived by ordinary people.

The novel's popularity has continued to grow, but there are signs that its long innings may be drawing to a close. It is true that more novels are being written now than ever before, but they are none of them taken so seriously as they were even thirty years ago. There is a growing suspicion that no very extraordinary gifts are required to do something that so many people can do well. But something more than this is responsible for the novel's diminishing status. It is not so much that it is easy to write as that it seems to be losing its grip on reality.

Life to-day is more complex than it was. The industrial revolution brought about an economically and intellectually interdependent world and at the same time greatly increased the scope and variety of human activity. This means that not only is it impossible to write comprehensively, as Jane Austen could, about one minute corner of life regardless of the affairs of the world at large, but that it is equally impossible to cram an all-embracing panorama of human life on to one canvas. This double difficulty is further complicated by the fact that men have increased in self-knowledge and are no longer satisfied with black and white delineations of character. It is recognised that human beings are neither good nor bad, but mixtures, and inconsistent mixtures at that ; and on analysis their behaviour resolves itself into a series of impulses whose origin is frequently so obscure that more interest attaches to the causes of behaviour than to behaviour itself.

HOW THE SHORT STORY DIFFERS FROM THE NOVEL

BUT, in spite of James Joyce's magnificent attempt in *Ulysses*, the task of describing the behaviour and motives of even one character through the course of a single day remains a superhuman one. It is, moreover, open to the valid objection that the resulting novel is almost unintelligible except to the psycho-analyst or to the reader equipped with the specific knowledge and experience of the author. Faced with these handicaps, writers are more and more adopting the contrary method. Instead of trying to put everything in they leave nearly everything out. Instead of attempting to create character they confine themselves to the analysis of a situation, perhaps including, though not necessarily, its causes and repercussions. In short, they aim not at giving a composite picture of reality, but at illuminating the whole problem of existence in a single comprehensive flash.

The short story has evolved as a conscious art form, because it is especially well adapted to further this aim. To begin with, from the mere fact that it can be read at a sitting, it impresses itself on the mind of the reader as a unified conception in a way that the novel cannot. Secondly, it does not concern itself with the development of character but with what really amounts to a bundle of impulses existing at a particular moment. The persons in a short story cannot grow in the same way that the persons in a novel are expected to grow, nor are they rounded. They are shown at the beginning of the story to possess certain characteristics and these they usually keep to the end. But any other traits they may happen to possess which are not essential to the theme are excluded. In Maupassant's masterpiece, *The Necklace*, the events of five years are compassed in as many pages. Had this story been told in the form of a novel, the descent of Mathilde and her husband from genteel to grinding poverty could have been elaborated with a wealth of detail ; but the tragic climax would have been too sudden, out of all proportion to the body of the narrative leading up to it. Proportion is, indeed, the hallmark of the good short story, and cannot fail to be present if the story has unity of purpose and construction. This is the one law of a short story : it should say all that needs to be said to illuminate its underlying idea ; no more and no less. Apart from this, the short story knows no limitations of structure or of theme.

THE FAR-DOWN ROOTS OF THE SHORT STORY

BEFORE the nineteenth century, short-story writing was not a conscious art. If an author wrote a short story it was rather by accident than by design. An anecdote grew longer than he expected or a romance shorter. Before the novel form became to some extent standardised, it was not unusual for several complete short stories to be incorporated in one novel. The earliest short stories in English prose are two of Chaucer's *Canterbury Tales*, the *Tale of Melibee*, told by Chaucer himself, and the *Parson's Tale*. Of these, the first was an experiment, the second a translation. During the Elizabethan period, which was rich in every kind of literature, the short story in the guise of the *novella* served mainly to provide the dramatists with material for their plots.

During the seventeenth and eighteenth centuries the development of periodical literature quickened interest in the short story by providing a consistent outlet for it. Addison and Steele in the *Spectator*, Johnson in the *Rambler*, and Goldsmith in the *Bee*, all exercised their talents in short narrative, and the Coverley papers, at least, are widely read and loved still. Sterne placed his pathetic *Story of Lefevre* in the middle of *Tristram Shandy*, but it is complete in itself, and can legitimately be regarded both in structure and conception as a short story ; it is indeed an interesting early example of the conscious use of the short story for a specific artistic purpose. By the end of the eighteenth century the magazine was firmly established as a literary medium, and the development of the short story was greatly facilitated by the rapid growth of the magazine habit.

But it was in America that the magazine first proved the forcing-ground of the new art. While Scott, Southey, Miss Edgeworth, and Hannah More were all experimenting sporadically in the medium of the short tale, on the other side of the water Washington Irving and, after him, Hawthorne were systematically responding to the new demand for literature that could be read at a sitting and at the same time satisfy the artistic canons of coherence and unity.

Irving, literary compeer of Addison and Steele, was fundamentally an essayist, and his *Sketch-Book*, as its name implies, was little more than a series of elaborated word pictures. Hawthorne, on the other hand, aimed, not at diffusion, but at concentration upon a single situation. He substituted suggestion for detail, subjective analysis for pictorial effect, and has been considered by many to be the founder of the modern short story. Certainly he was the first to give it that unity of impression which is now its distinguishing characteristic.

To Edgar Allan Poe, however, belongs the credit of having been the first to feel the new demands of his age, to forecast the new art and to formulate its laws. Something of this must be ascribed to the fact that Poe was for long a magazine editor, but more to an abnormally concentrated power of imagination subserved by a passion for form. Hence his finest efforts as, for example, *The Black Cat. The Fall of the House of Usher* and *William Wilson* are models of action proceeding to an inevitable end, with every sentence, practically every word, contributing to the final development. Nevertheless it must be recognised that his range was a narrow one. The shadow of death looms over all his stories, and although there is in them something more than pure horror, the less good among them tend to be *tours de force* rather than literary achievements of the highest order. Technically his stories are brilliant, but some of them owe more to invention than to the dual faculty of observation and sensibility which reveals a new meaning in the normal and humdrum.

POE DEFINES THE NEW ART

THIS much admitted, Poe remains unsurpassed in the evocation of the mystery whose hold over the mind is the terror of the irrational and the inexplicable. He, above all other authors, has the gift of rousing terror, not of the ghosts, the blood, and the clanking chains of the *Udolpho* school, but of the spiritual forces that penetrate the imperfect armour of the flesh. In his own life he knew the inhumanity and madness of existence, and from bitter experience learnt to describe in vivid language the workings of those weird powers which terrify the very souls of men.

Poe was the first to consider the short story as a separate literary form and to give it prestige. His concentration on the abnormal, gloomy aspects of life, added to his natural genius, gave his work a distinction which soon won him recognition both in America and in Europe. Since his death, his influence has touched almost every outstanding writer of short stories in both continents.

But in addition to his preoccupation with horror and death,

Poe was deeply interested in abstruse problems such as the decoding of ciphers and the unravelling of mysteries. Combined with his brilliant analytical ability and great literary skill, this interest led him to become the founder of the modern detective story. Between 1840 and 1845 he wrote five detective stories : *The Murders in the Rue Morgue*, *The Purloined Letter*, *The Mystery of Marie Roget*, all three of which deal with the exploits of the French detective Auguste Dupin, *Thou Art the Man*, and *The Gold Bug*, which is often regarded as his finest mystery story. The most remarkable thing about these tales is that they contain practically all the technical ingenuities his successors have been able to discover. At best there are only about half a dozen methods of fooling the reader, and the germ of most of them is to be found in Poe. Moreover it is to the eccentric Dupin and his unnamed chronicler we owe the long and still increasing line of detectives and their biographers whose crowning glory is the immortal Sherlock Holmes and Dr. Watson.

The detective story has evolved a highly perfected technique, and at its best is a model of construction combined with considerable charm of presentation. It was about forty years, however, before Poe's most important innovation— the detective with a distinctive personality—bore fruit in its original short story form. The vogue for crime fiction started earlier, with the novels of Emile Gaboriau, in France, and of Wilkie Collins in England ; but it was not until 1887, with the electrifying success of Conan Doyle's *A Study in Scarlet*, that the detective story achieved the full measure of that popularity which it has never since lost. *A Study in Scarlet* was a novel ; but it is now probably less well known than the series of Sherlock Holmes stories which followed it and made the fortune of the *Strand Magazine*. In his handling of the new medium Conan Doyle's chief merit was a crispness and polish which a host of followers and imitators have not been able to dim. Holmes is the first and greatest of modern detectives. After him the best-loved is perhaps Mr. Chesterton's Father Brown, but for ingenuity and omniscience, Austin Freeman's Dr. Thorndyke deserves to be singled out from a host of colleagues too numerous to name and among whom selection would be invidious.

Although Holmes and his successors have been at their best in small doses, the short story of detection is, to-day, tending to suffer from the restriction of length imposed upon

it by the requirements of its chief market, the magazine.
The first writers of detective stories could afford to be prodigal
with their plots, because the field was a new one and the
audience more eager than critical. But within recent years
competition has become so keen and readers so expert at
the game that the time and ingenuity required for the finding
and working out of a new plot is no longer proportionate to
the remuneration to be derived from the few thousand words
into which it has to be compressed. The result is that the
magazine no longer provides a satisfactory outlet for original
work. Writers reserve their good plots for novels, and the
short story of detection is declining into a mechanical affair
which is told in brief, simply because it is not worth
expanding.

THE INFLUENCE OF THE MAGAZINE

SOMETHING of this same process has influenced the development of what, for want of a better term, is usually called
the literary short story. The Victorians wrote for magazines
with the enthusiasm, the excitement almost, that new movements, new outlets for expression, arouse in original minds ;
but their technique has become stereotyped through continual
imitation, and to-day the writer who refuses to conform to
the established pattern has to find his market elsewhere.
This is a tendency whose influence on the short story as an
art form must be recognised as revolutionary. For just as it is
the virtue of the sonnet that it conforms to a pre-ordained
pattern, and of the drama that it is expressed within the
arbitrary divisions of a limited number of acts, so, too, it
was the virtue of the short story in its initial stages that it
performed its function in obedience to the technical demands
of the medium in which it was intended to appear ; that
is to say, the magazine. The rapidly increasing class of short
stories which have no natural home is, in fact, in something
of the same predicament as those admirable plays whose
only defect is that they cannot be acted.

There is thus an important technical difference between
the best short stories of to-day and those of the nineteenth
century ; and there is an equally important difference of
inspiration. Generally speaking, the prevailing influence of
the nineteenth century was that of the French *conte*, while
that of the twentieth century is the more formless Russian
short story. The reason for this is not hard to discover.
In England, if not in America, the short story did not come

The " inimitable Holmes " : fiction's most famous detective.

into its own until the eighties. The mid-nineteenth century was the age of the novel, and although the great novelists wrote short stories on occasion they were inclined to look upon them as a pleasant relaxation from the more exacting and important business of writing novels. Moreover, great novelists rarely find themselves at home in the technique of the short story. But whether it was that the novelists could not write short stories, or that they were not interested in writing them, it is certain that the short story did not come to maturity in England until the established order, which had once seemed as fixed and immutable as a decree of Nature, began to show signs of breaking up. With the development of a social conscience, Maupassant's remorselessness and his artistic apprehension of the significantly little, became the model for every writer who acknowledged the necessity of looking life in the face. Later on, as existence became increasingly unsatisfactory, the dreariness, stagnation, and apathetic pessimism expressed by Tchekov and the Russians seized hold of a generation no longer content with the completeness which, though it may be true to art, is not true to life.

THE LAST OF THE GREAT ROMANTICS

THERE is thus, despite the charm of a beautiful prose style, an almost archaic quality about the short stories of Stevenson ; archaic from the standpoint not only of to-day, but of his immediate successors. For Stevenson, " mentally half a Frenchman ; in tastes, habits, and prepossessions almost wholly French," as his stepson wrote of him, was born too soon, as Thackeray was born too soon, for the audience that would have sympathised with and understood his outlook on life. Unlike Thackeray, however, he took refuge in romance and fantasy. His first published story, *A Lodging for the Night*, which appeared in *Temple Bar* in 1877, dealt with an episode in the life of the mediæval French poet Villon. It was followed by others which likewise owed their inspiration to the past, by fantastic inventions such as the stories which make up the *New Arabian Nights*, and by grim conceptions such as *Thrawn Janet* and *Markheim*, rendered still more grim by an underlying hint of human cruelty and superstition. But there is nothing of contemporary significance in these stories, nothing forged out of the impact of life on a creative imagination. Stevenson was more interested in art than in life. He was a writing animal, but his imaginative work, both in the genre of the novel and the short story, lacks the prime virtue of vitality ; and although he was one of the first writers in England to endow the short story with an existence in its own right, the full possibilities of the innovation remained unrealised until Rudyard Kipling's volume of Indian stories, *Plain Tales from the Hills*, burst upon an astonished world in 1887.

It is Kipling's supreme achievement, which neither familiarity nor imitation has been able to stale, that at one bound, and at the very outset of his career, he brought the short story out of the domain of the mysterious and the fanciful into a world of colour, movement, and passion, of speaking men and women, of fresh air and the open day. Something of this he owes to the fortunate accident of his Indian background ; but the gods who gave him a subject to his hand also endowed him with the superb gifts for narrative, dialogue, and description, which have placed him in the front rank of the world's story tellers. His work is unequal, and frequently disfigured by stylistic mannerisms and technical crudities which would have been the downfall of a lesser writer. On the other hand, he has a singularly fertile imagination combined with unusually developed powers of observation. In matter and spirit, if not in method, Mr. Kipling is wholly original. It is impossible here to do full justice to his range and variety, but mention must be made of the soldier-cycle which gave the world the immortal Private Terence Mulvaney ; the stories of childhood, and of the lives of British officials in India, of which the beautifully realised *Without Benefit of Clergy* is perhaps the best known ; the sensitive handling of the things of the spirit as in *They* and *The Brushwood Boy*, probably his two most famous stories ; the vivid re-creation of history in *Puck of Pook's Hill* and *Rewards and Fairies* ; and the inspired beast-tales of the two *Jungle Books*, which many critics regard as his finest work.

For tautness of construction and brevity of statement Kipling remains, despite his numerous imitators, an un-challenged master of the English short story. His influence has been great not only in the realm of technique but also, and perhaps more importantly, in the widening of the scope of the short story to include the interpretation of contemporary life. The inspiration of his success was in large part responsible for the great vogue which the short story enjoyed in the 'nineties, when a host of magazines—*The National Observer*, *The Fortnightly Review*, *Macmillan's*, *Longman's*, *The Yellow Book*, *The New Review*—gave unrivalled opportunities to the bright young men of the period. George Gissing, Joseph Conrad, Jerome K. Jerome, Kenneth Grahame, George Moore, Frank Harris, Hubert Crackanthorpe, and, among the living, Sir James Barrie, H. G. Wells, and W. W. Jacobs, are only a few of the talented writers who seized eagerly on this new form of literary expression. The work of Jacobs is especially noteworthy for raciness of dialogue. His skill in the portrayal of humble life is not always given the praise it deserves.

THE HOMELY TOUCH OF O. HENRY

KIPLING's influence was as great in America as in England, perhaps, in some ways, even greater. He himself owed something to Bret Harte, whose *Luck of Roaring Camp*, remarkable for a novel combination of sentimentality, local colour, and romance, unified by a sense of form inspired by Poe, is a landmark in the history of the American short story. In return, he taught the Americans that technical efficiency which is their chief virtue ; or, as the saying goes, " There is only one Kipling, and O. Henry is his prophet." Whether O. Henry is America's greatest writer of short stories is a matter of dispute. There are those who would reserve that title for Henry James, whose subtle and impressionistic studies of situations brought the short story to the highest peak of artistry it has yet achieved, although they devitalised it to some extent in the process. Others, again, prefer the finished and powerful psychological stories of Ambrose Bierce.

But O. Henry is the guiding spirit of the contemporary short story in America, and it is estimated that about ninety per cent. of the short stories that are being written in the United States to-day are imitations of his work. From Kipling he learned the bad trick of intruding his personality into the story ; but he was one of the ablest spinners of plots who ever lived, and combined this gift with an amazing vocabulary of colloquialisms and slang, and a sympathetic knowledge of many sides of life and many kinds of people. His virtues and defects are well shown in the little sketch of a shop-girl, a type he excelled in depicting, called *An*

Unfinished Story. Equally famous are *A Municipal Report*, *The Furnished Room*, and, perhaps most of all, *The Gifts of the Magi*. The simple themes of these stories, despite the trick device of the surprise ending, are treated with the economy, directness, and sympathy which indicate the master hand.

THE REVOLT OF THE MODERNS

THE technical efficiency which the short story attained by the beginning of the twentieth century has had the inevitable result. On the one hand it has led to conventionality of theme and construction, and on the other it has caused the revolt, both in method and in substance, expressed in the work of such individual artists as Katherine Mansfield and A. E. Coppard. It is true that a great many gifted writers have been able to conform to the conventional standards without cheapening their art, and the work of Stacy Aumonier in particular deserves to be remembered for the sincerity and brilliant narrative skill which went to its making.

Among living writers, Somerset Maugham is notable for gifts of style, constructive ability, and a matured point of view which distinguishes everything he writes. But it is none the less true that much exciting and significant work is no longer easily available. Indeed, in their way, the short stories of Katherine Mansfield mark an epoch as distinctly as those of Kipling. She was greatly influenced by Tchekov. Her best and most subtle achievements are probably revealed in the exquisitely conceived interplay of human thought and feeling of *Je Ne Parle Pas Français*, and *The Daughters of the Late Colonel*.

SOME FINE EXAMPLES OF THE SHORT STORY

"OF making many books there is no end," said the Preacher, and the remark might truthfully be applied to the short story to-day. There are thousands of good short stories to choose from and a course of reading must therefore be arbitrarily selected from among the best, with a view to providing a criterion to test other stories which may subsequently be read.

An interesting and valuable course of further short-story reading would begin with Conan Doyle's *Adventures of Sherlock Holmes*, and go on to compare these with G. K.

Chesterton's *Innocence of Father Brown* and E. A. Poe's *Tales of Mystery and Imagination*, especially the story entitled *The Gold Bug*. There would follow Rudyard Kipling's *The Courting of Dinah Shad* (*Life's Handicap*), R. L. Stevenson's stories in *The New Arabian Nights* and *The Merry Men*, and then, by way of contrast, Katherine Mansfield's *Garden Party* and James Joyce's *Dubliners*.

The most useful collections of short stories are *Great Short Stories of the World* edited by Clark and Lieber (Heinemann), *Great Short Stories of Detection, Mystery, and Horror*, two series, edited with a brilliant introduction by Dorothy L. Sayers (Gollancz), and the volumes edited annually by Edward O'Brien entitled *The Best English Short Stories* and *The Best American Short Stories* (Cape).

There is no standard English work on short-story writing, but there are three accepted classics by American writers : *The Philosophy of Composition* and *Nathaniel Hawthorne* by Edgar Allan Poe, and Brander Mathews' *Philosophy of the Short Story*.

ENGLISH PROSE : THE LANGUAGE OF ORDINARY LIFE

by SYLVIA NORTON, B.A.(Oxon)

"WHAT is prose?" we may ask, when we consider that the novel and newspaper we are reading, the speech we have just heard on the wireless, and the injunction to " pass right down the car please ! " are all prose. Molière in *Le Bourgeois Gentilhomme* makes his M. Jourdain demand " neither prose nor verse " for the letter which the Master of Philosophy is to compose for him ; when he learns that he has been speaking prose for forty years his astonishment is great. Although we may not be under the same misapprehension as M. Jourdain, yet we may ask ourselves how much we know about prose and attempt some definition.

Prose is the natural language of man as opposed to verse, which takes the form of some definite scheme of rhythm and sometimes rhyme. Verse is said to be the older, rhyme being used as an aid to memory. We see this tendency at work in traditional sayings such as " Change n'er a clout till May be out," and " Red sky at morning, the shepherd's warning." Prose is the language in which we ordinarily speak and write. It consists of words and their arrangement, and it is the individual choice of words and their order which constitutes style. Just as an apple varies in kind and in quality, so does prose, and it should be almost as easy to recognise good prose as to tell a good apple, for there are definite standards by which we may judge either to be good, bad, or indifferent. Again, of prose as of apples, there are many kinds, and the choice of one rather than another is, in the usual way, a matter for individual taste. This, however, with one reservation—and a very important one : just as a dessert apple is useless for baking, and *vice versa*, so the style must be suited to the writer's matter.

GROWTH AND FLOWERING OF THE LANGUAGE

MODERN English may appear to be a simple language with few restrictions, but this apparent simplicity has been achieved only by the natural growth of the language through the centuries. Our grammar is easy in comparison with

German or French, but if we take an English sentence and examine each word, we gain some idea of the many and varied sources of our vocabulary.

The history of the language is the history of the land. We have only to look back upon the greatest events in our history to learn how English began, how it grew to be the language we know, and, if we are sufficiently interested in such things, we can watch it grow, judging by modern tendencies what will be the English of to-morrow. The Saxon invasion gave us the bedrock of the language, for it is from this Germanic tongue that modern English is descended. The first great change was due to the settlement of the Danes in England in the ninth century; they gave us the names of everyday things, and words relating to war and the navy. From them we took our pronouns *They*, *Them*, *Their*, in place of the Saxon ones, and in the fifteenth century we find Caxton wondering whether to print the Old English word *Ey* or the Scandinavian word *Egg*. The Norman Conquest was a far bigger landmark than the Scandinavian. The Normans were the ruling class, their tongue became the official speech, and we find a fourteenth-century prose writer complaining that children learn to speak French before they know their mother tongue.

Feudalism came from France, giving us such words as *vassal*. To the Normans, too, we owe our law terms : *prison*, *male*, *heir ;* our military words : *defend*, *army ;* words connected with religion : *virtue*, *charity ;* with hunting, cooking, gaming, and dress. Just as French is the language of the upper classes in Belgium as opposed to Flemish, the peasants' tongue, so it stood in relation to Old English. In *Ivanhoe* Scott makes the Saxon swineherd and another argue over the new-fangled terms *Mutton* and *Beef* which have been introduced for *Sheep* and *Oxen* when killed for food. The Revival of Learning is the next milestone ; the new interest in art and literature which awoke in France and Italy in the Middle Ages came into England as early as the fourteenth century, bringing Latin and Greek words into our vocabulary and influencing our sentence structure.

HOW TO RECOGNISE GOOD PROSE

LITERARY prose is the subject of this section ; here we are not concerned with the language of colloquial speech which is so very different from the written word. There are many ways of writing the same thing, and the writer must choose the kind of prose most suited to what he has to say. In judging whether prose is good or bad, we first decide if the style is suited to the subject; for example, a business letter in the elaborate style of Meredith would be as bad as *Treasure Island* in the stately manner of Dr. Johnson. When we have made up our minds that theme and treatment are in harmony, we next ask ourselves what impressions the prose makes upon us. Are the descriptions in the *Pilgrim's Progress* beautiful? Is Captain Silver of *Treasure Island* sinister? Is the anecdote in *Pickwick* of Mr. Winkle on the ice funny? It is easy to tell what kind of impression the author is seeking to create, but a great deal harder to discover why he fails or succeeds. The sound of the words, the way they are arranged, small words in short, sharp-sounding sentences to convey fear or suspense, big words in long rhythmical sentences for descriptions of peaceful country scenes; these are some of the means at the author's disposal. The style of the " Penny Dreadful " and the cheaper magazine story we can recognise as bad prose by any of these tests which we have applied to classic writers.

"THE RIGHT WORD IN THE RIGHT PLACE"

THE prose writer with a good style pays attention to choice of words and their arrangement in order to achieve the right expression of his thought. He seeks to put " the right word in the right place," and in doing this, he obtains beauty of expression, that is, style; he writes good prose. The purist or the writer who insists too strongly on classical and pedantically correct expression, is in danger of robbing the language of its vitality. He neglects the law that the controlling force, the genius of the language, is determined by the popular will, and that it cannot be governed altogether by lures.

When we read a piece of prose we may find that although we can clearly see what impression the author is trying to convey, his work, in fact, has a different effect. He may attempt to make us sad but only succeed in making us merry. He may aim at being dignified and serious, but only manage to appear ridiculous. The cause lies in some lack of harmony between the thought and its expression. If we examine prose of this kind, we shall nearly always find the author guilty of tricks of style such as " the purple patch," exaggeration, the over-ornate and journalese.

EARLY ENGLISH PROSE : THE CHRONICLE AND KING ALFRED

OUR earliest prose consists of a small collection of Old English manuscripts of which the Anglo-Saxon Chronicle, dating from about the eighth century A.D., comes first. In this, every outstanding event was set down, so that it forms an invaluable storehouse for the student of Anglo-Saxon history. To the general reader it is not only unintelligible owing to the great changes which have since taken place in our language, it is also rather dull. The first English prose writer of interest to us to-day is King Alfred. Most of his work consists of translations from the Latin, but he interspersed his translations with thoughts of his own which reveal him to us as a remarkably enlightened man and king, and one who longed ardently to improve the culture of his people. His work can be read and enjoyed in translation, but he wrote in Anglo-Saxon, which, although it is the basis of modern English, is as different from it as German or Latin.

It is not until the fifteenth century that with Sir Thomas Malory's translation of the *Morte d'Arthur* we have a prose work of the first order, easily understood by any modern reader who is prepared to take a little trouble in looking up unusual words. By this time Anglo-Saxon had undergone so many alterations at the hands of the Danes and Normans that from middle English it had become early modern English.

The introduction of printing in the fifteenth century takes us a long way on from the days when King Alfred referred to the three copies of the Bible in all England. The monasteries now began their collections of books, and literature flourished. It was at this time that Malory brought all the many age-old tales of Arthur together and made a book which should be a delight to any reader. The beauty of the chivalric idea and the simple narrative in which the tales are unfolded make it one of the permanent things in literature. The story of the Holy Grail, all the colour and mysticism of that age of chivalry, of " battles long ago " have made one of the rarest books in our tongue.

The *Morte d'Arthur* stands alone among early English prose works. After its printed publication about 1485, there is nothing comparable to it to claim our attention until, nearly a hundred years later, we reach the days of Queen Elizabeth. The age of Elizabeth was the age of romance. The national consciousness was increasing ; the exploits of Raleigh and Drake, and the discoveries in science and letters, were all one with the temper of the age. A courtier of Queen Elizabeth might write sonnets to his lady—the sonnet was a new form of verse from Italy—or go in search of Spanish gold, for the delight of fresh experience in every field was the quintessence of sixteenth-century England.

THE GALLANT SPIRIT OF SIR PHILIP SIDNEY

SIR PHILIP SIDNEY was most representative of his age by virtue of that gallant spirit in which he gained distinction as courtier, soldier, scholar, and not least as poet. His prose works, the *Arcadia*, a romance, and the *Defense of Poesie*, are essentially the prose of a poet. The *Defense* is one of the loveliest writings in praise of poetry and ranks with the *Essays* of Shelley and Francis Thompson. Sidney's prose is full of metaphor ; he talks of " the speaking picture of Poetry," and again, " the poet has all, from Dante's heaven to his hell, under the authority of his pen." Lovely as his writing is, it is essentially poetic prose, and he sways the emotions rather than the intellect by an imaginative appeal. The style of the *Arcadia* is much more involved than that of the *Defense*, and it is here that we see the need for a simpler, more direct, prose for the telling of a story than that of the Elizabethans.

Lyly's *Euphues*, sometimes said to be the first English novel, shows us more clearly still that a language so weighed down with classical allusion, rhetorical question, and antithesis is no fit medium for narrative, despite the fact that Lyly had set out with the idea of improving English prose. Of the Elizabethans, Bacon was the first to break away from this elaborate writing, though he delights in Latin quotation and his *Essays* are riddled with tags, not always correctly quoted. Montaigne was his master, and possibly the French passion for form did something towards clarifying Bacon's thought. He is fond of classical allusion and carefully balanced phrases, but his sentences are short and his imagery is not laboured like Lyly's.

THE MAJESTIC PROSE OF THE BIBLE

THE *Authorised Version of the Bible* is generally said to be the first English prose classic, as it is the greatest. There were several early translations ; Bede put the Gospel of St.

John into Old English, Wycliffe made a translation, but our greatest debt is to Tyndale and Coverdale, and the Authorised Version of 1611 is in essentials that of Tyndale. Since the whole Bible deals with man's relation to God and the Universe, it must appeal to every one alike, and when we consider how this theme is treated, with what passion and poetry, we may realise why it is the greatest book in the world. The Hebrew imagination is that of the poet. The language is essentially concrete, and as there are no words in Hebrew for abstract ideas, these must be expressed in symbol. Thus expressions such as " The Cedar of Lebanon," or " Wine and oil," are used to signify the majesty and providence of God. Since the sense of the Bible demanded urgent expression, the writers practised the utmost economy of style ; there was no room for any writing descriptive or otherwise, which might be spared from the account. This is seen in the unadorned narrative of the Parable of the Prodigal Son, where no irrelevant detail is included, and in the simplicity of statements such as : " And God said ' Let there be Light and there was Light,' " and again, " Jesus wept."

The translators, always sensible of their high calling and conscious that they must make the Bible accessible to everybody, translated literally, adding nothing, but working to preserve the original. Coverdale indeed introduced some of our most beautiful words : " loving kindness " and " tender mercy," which are the most literal rendering of the Hebrew, but neither he nor Tyndale presumed to tamper with the original.

The Bible has been more studied and quoted in England than in any other country, and its influence both upon the substance and upon the manner of our literature has been tremendous. Within a comparatively short time of its publication, the custom arose of reading aloud passages from " the good book " in church, home, and school. From their earliest years children were accustomed to hear its fine rhythms, droned out, it may be, in a dreary monotone, but nevertheless spoken aloud every day. The influence thus unconsciously exerted on the formation of a prose style in even the least gifted writer is incalculable. In our greatest authors the result has been an unrivalled beauty and grandeur of expression, combined with a weight and dignity of thought. Men such as Bunyan and Carlyle who, in their youth, had no other book to read, profited more from this one teacher than perhaps later writers gain from all the libraries at their disposal.

PROSE RICH IN IMAGERY : MILTON, BURTON, BROWNE

MILTON's prose at its best, like Sidney's, is the prose of a poet, but of a poet who has studied the Bible closely, and has also steeped himself in Greek and Latin. In the *Areopagitica* (a plea for uncensored printing) there is imagery worthy of the author of *Paradise Lost*. Speaking of England, he says : " Methinks I see in my mind a noble and puissant nation rousing herself like a strong man after sleep and shaking her invincible locks. Methinks I see her as an eagle mewing her mighty youth, and kindling her undazzled eyes at the full midday beam ; purging and unscaling her long-abused sight at the fountain itself of heavenly radiance ; while the whole noise of timorous and flocking birds, with those also that love the twilight, flutter about, amazed at what she means, and in their envious gabble would prog-nosticate a year of sects and schisms." The grand and statuesque inspire his metaphor here as in verse, and his sense of rhythm makes his prose at times lyrical, as when he asks : " And who shall silence all the airs and madrigals that whisper softness in chambers . . . ? "

But in spite of superb passages such as these, much of Milton's prose is difficult and uninteresting reading. Most of it consists of pamphlets which are nothing but treatises on Church matters of the day, written in long, winding sentences with many subordinate clauses, a Latin form utterly unsuited to English. Long words abound, and there are many coined from the Latin, such as *inquisiturient, matricu-lated, confutant, connivant, oscitant*. The love of rhetoric adds weight to invective, but often dulls the edge of argument, and Biblical and classical allusion so remote as to escape any but the most scholarly makes for a prose which is likely to be neglected except by the student.

The seventeenth century was rich in scholars. Whereas the Elizabethans were interested in their own discoveries, the masque from Italy, the morris dance, as much as the voyages of Hakluyt and Frobisher, men like Robert Burton, Sir Thomas Browne, and Jeremy Taylor dwelt upon the thoughts and fashions of the Ancients, preferring the old world to the new. Burton in the *Anatomy of Melancholy* set out to give a history of melancholy in its fullest sense.

It will be remembered that the Greek theory of the humours reached this country from the great Arabian schools of medicine in the eleventh and twelfth centuries and influenced many authors, notably Ben Jonson, as we see in his play, *Every Man in his Humour*. According to this theory the human body was said to contain four humours ; blood, phlegm, yellow bile, and black bile (melancholy). A superabundance of any one of these was held to be bad. Although Burton was said to be " very merrie, facete, and juvenile," an excess of the fourth humour seemed to him to be the lot of the majority of mankind, and accordingly he set out to make a study of it. He was learned and an omnivorous reader, and like his great contemporary, Sir Thomas Browne, versed in medicine as well as literature.

Perhaps the chief merits of the *Anatomy* are its human interest together with the wealth of quaint story and instance. We read enthralled of " the country fellow that had four knives in his belly with other baggage," of the young maid in Amatus Lusitanus that " would wash her hair in the heat of the day," and so on. The *Anatomy* is a book to browse in, a little library in itself. It has been as much loved as perhaps any book in English with the exception of Boswell's *Life of Johnson*. Johnson himself, who counted indolence as one of his worst vices, paid it the high tribute of declaring that it " was the only book that ever drew him out of bed an hour sooner than he would otherwise have got up." If other recommendation is needed, it is to be found in Lamb's *Essays of Elia* (*Mackery End in Hertfordshire*) where Lamb describes himself " hanging over (for the thousandth time) some passage in old Burton." It was Lamb, amongst others in the nineteenth century, who revived interest in Burton, Sir Thomas Browne, and their contemporaries.

THE SONOROUS LANGUAGE OF A SCHOLAR PHYSICIAN

Sir THOMAS BROWNE was possibly the greatest of the group of writers, including Burton and Taylor, known as the Antiquaries. A doctor in Norwich, he combined, like Burton, the interests of literature and medicine. In his *Religo Medici*, his best known work, he set out to clear his profession from the ancient stigma of irreligion to which Chaucer amongst others alludes. Browne's deep religious faith and mysticism shine through all his writings. He says : " We carry with us the wonders we seek without us : there is all Africa and her prodigies in us." His faith was simple, as we see from his belief in witchcraft ; he declares that it is a riddle to him how any one can doubt the existence of witches. It is Browne's whimsical manner of argument which makes for a great deal of his charm. The style of *Religio Medici*, *Urn Burial*, and Browne's other writings is typical of his age. Biblical and classical allusion, balanced sentences, Latin quotations, give the prose a grandeur, a rhetorical roll unmatched in later centuries but unsuited to the exact expression of clear thought. The prose typical of the seventeenth century is not so much the limpid prose of the *Bible* and *The Pilgrim's Progress* as the melodious prose-poetry of *Urn Burial*.

In spite of its funereal title, *Urn Burial* is not gloomy ; it is imbued rather with the sad and gentle beauty of autumn. Passages such as the following linger in the memory long after their context is forgotten :

> " But the iniquity of oblivion blindely scattereth her poppy, and deals with the memory of men without distinction to merit of perpetuity. Who can but pity the founder of the Pyramids ? *Herostratus* lives that burnt the Temple of *Diana*, he is almost lost that built it ; Time hath spared the Epitaph of Adrian's horse, confounded that of himself. In vain we compute our felicities by the advantage of our good names, since bad have equall durations ; and *Thersites* is like to live as long as *Agamemnon*, Who knows whether the best of men be known ? or whether there be not more remarkable persons forgot, then any that stand remembred in the known account of time ? Without the favour of the everlasting register, the first man had been as unknown as the last, and *Methuselahs* long life had been his only Chronicle."

IZAAC WALTON had many of the characteristics of his age ; a devout faith, a reverence for antiquity, a love of learning, but to these he added a delight in country things which was practically unknown to his contemporaries. Unlike the *Anatomy* and *Religio Medici*, the *Compleat Angler* has always been a favourite book with many different kinds of readers. The simple way in which it is written, and the dialogue form which makes concentration so easy, have ensured a wide reading. Above and beyond the question of style, the charm ot Walton's personality is evident in every phrase. We go with him, almost hand in hand, on " a fine fresh May morning," through the pleasant fields of Hertfordshire, along the river bank, listening to the strangest fishing stories we have ever heard, part fact, part folk lore. We may learn much of the simple faith and ancient learning, and around and about us are the sights and smells of the English countryside. Now we are told what holy Mr. Herbert says of such days and flowers, or how to take the chavender or chubb, or that a learned physician tells us of a people that once a year turn wolves, partly in shape and partly in condition. The prose flows like one of Walton's silver streams through a most pleasant land. Walton's *Lives*, though not ranking with the *Compleat Angler*, are full of interest, particularly the *Life of Donne*, and any one who loves the author of *Death, be not proud*, and *The Ecstasy* should read it.

EXUBERANCE GIVES WAY TO CLARITY : THE BIRTH OF MODERN PROSE

WITH one or two outstanding exceptions, such as the Bible and Sir Philip Sidney's *Defense of Poesie*, all the greatest works in English prose written before about 1660 are distinguished by a gorgeousness and elaboration of style entirely unsuited to the varied ends prose now has to serve. The seventeenth century was an age of great prose, but a poetic, imaginative prose as far removed from the ordinary language of conversation or even letter-writing as the poetry of *Paradise Lost*. After the Restoration, with the advent of Dryden and Bunyan, English prose put off its silks and satins, as it were, changed to serge and tweeds, and showed itself ready, at last, for the serious business of exact expression.

Among the many reasons for this important revolution, perhaps the most influential was the growth of that rationalism which, refusing to be bound by faith, insists on the right of the individual mind to criticise and examine the world for itself. The interest in science revealed strongly in the work of Francis Bacon, shining fitfully in the writings of Sir Thomas Browne, gathered force throughout the seventeenth century until it resulted in the foundation of the Royal Society to foster research, and to make known to the people the discoveries of the scientists.

But the language of Browne and Burton was not well

fitted to describe chemical experiments with clearness and accuracy. With the rise of popular interest in science, it was inevitably superseded, at first by a plain style, sometimes colloquial to the point of vulgarity, later by the dignified, straightforward, pointed prose of the eighteenth century.

The new prose was not confined to scientific and practical writings. It won approval from poet, dramatist, critic, and reader alike ; in the hands of such masters as Dryden, Bunyan, Swift, with Fielding, Sterne, and Smollett among the novelists, it soon achieved glories as great in their way as those of the older style.

THE FATHERS OF MODERN PROSE : DRYDEN AND BUNYAN

UNTIL the age of Dryden, prose had not been regarded as the equal of verse as a means of literary expression, and it was Dryden amongst others who did away with the disparity. Dryden in his *Essays* and *Prefaces* shows the lucid, direct writing of the new age at its best. He achieved the mastery of prose with the famous *Essay of Dramatic Poesy* which he began about 1665. The style consists of short, well-balanced sentences ; there is restraint, precision, lucidity, a tone of friendly intercourse with the reader, an ease which never becomes familiarity, a dignity which is never pompous. This essay and the *Preface to the Fables*, published in 1700, are perhaps the chief of his prose works.

Dryden came of a good family. He belonged to the fashionable London society of his day and held an honoured and secure position in literature. The man who shares with him the distinction of being the founder of modern English prose, could lay claim to neither breeding nor education. John Bunyan was of lowly birth ; he is known to have lived as a tinker and wandering preacher, and his most famous work, *The Pilgrim's Progress*, was written in Bedford Gaol. In spite of this, his work has exercised a deep and wide influence on English thought and expression, and there are people who rank *The Pilgrim's Progress* as second only to the Bible and the Prayer Book.

THE GOLDEN AGE OF PROSE : JONATHAN SWIFT

THE eighteenth century is known as the Age of Reason, because more weight was given to the testimony of the intellect than to that of the emotions. The easier ways of communication, the life of the town with its coffee houses

4

and assembly rooms and the first clubs, gave us a public who were eager for the novel and the journal. From such beginnings as the Elizabethan romance the novel grew until we have Fielding, Smollett, Sterne, Defoe, and Richardson. Fashion and the talk of the town were recorded by Addison and Steele in the *Spectator*, which marks the beginning of journalism. Twice as much was written as before, and the influence upon prose was naturally great ; it became more adaptable and equally suited to the breathless narrative of Defoe's *Moll Flanders* or the entertaining letters of Horace Walpole.

Swift was the first and perhaps greatest prose writer of the new century. His prose is some of the finest in the language. It is clear and pointed, and therefore most easy to read. He never uses a word too many or, conversely, a word too few. He seems to be able always to say exactly what he wants and he has no tricks of style. It is generally agreed that his prose was much influenced by that of Sir William Temple, his patron and a prose writer of standing. *Gulliver's Travels*, one of the greatest political satires and yet one of the best children's books, shows Swift's style at its best ; here it is like a diamond for point and brilliance. *The Tale of a Tub*, *The Journal to Stella*, and *The Battle of the Books*, are all magnificent prose. When he wishes, Swift can conjure up the most vivid picture without any recourse to fine writing. This is well shown in his description of Virgil in *The Battle of the Books* : " On the left wing of the horse, Virgil appeared in shining armour completely fitted to his body ; he was mounted on a dapple grey steed ; the slowness of his pace was an effect of the highest mettle and vigour." Any reader of the *Aeneid* will at once cry : " There is Virgil ! "

"THE GREAT LEXICOGRAPHER" : DOCTOR JOHNSON

ONE might say of Johnson that he was born and brought up in a bookshop. He read omnivorously, and mixed almost entirely with men of letters and those whose interests lay in books and the conversations of the club and coffee-house. He was a dictator in letters ; questions of literature or morality were referred to him, and his pronouncements were final. When asked whether an author should write for money, he answered : " Sir, none but a fool ever wrote except for money." His downright, equable mind was typical of the Age of Reason, and it was these qualities,

The Fight with Apollyon : a Scene from " Pilgrim's Progress."

allied to his attractive and vigorous personality, which established him as a literary authority. His style shows the influence of Latin diction, and he loved long words, but it is
the balance of thought which makes for his balance of sentence
and, at best, results in a concentrated and precise style. The
Letter to Lord Chesterfield is perhaps the finest example of
Johnson's prose. His writing at its worst, or *Johnsonese*,
as it has been termed, becomes pompous, as when he says :
" The proverbial oracles of our parsimonious ancestors have
informed us that the fatal waste of our fortune is by small
expenses, by the profusion of sums too little singly to alarm
our caution, and which we never suffer ourselves to consider
together." Nevertheless, he did much to discipline prose,
handing on his love of order to the younger generation, so
that the writers in the second half of the century owed him
much. That his authority was still great in the nineteenth
century we know from *Vanity Fair*, where Miss Pinkerton,
commending his famous dictionary to her pupils, refers to
him with awe as " the great lexicographer."

Edmund Burke was a friend of Johnson and came under
his influence. His prose is that of the day, the latter half
of the eighteenth century, as regards idiom and structure.
It is removed from the direct conversational prose of Dryden
and Swift by changed social circumstances ; it has more
dignity, weight, and conventional elegance, and for these
Burke was indebted to Johnson. It is most important to
remember that Burke was first of all an orator, and that
in the composition of his speeches he is thinking not of his
reader, but of his audience. He had a passionate temperament, his imagination was readily fired by the wrongs of
others, and he chose a diction which would, by its very
sound, convey his feeling. His vivid imagery is reminiscent
of Milton, Browne, Taylor, Clarendon, though his prose is
never that of the poet since there is no lyrical note. This
is clearly seen by comparing one of his speeches on the
Warren Hastings Trial or the French Revolution, or America
with the *Areopagitica*, or with the romantic prose of Wordsworth and Coleridge, Carlyle, and Ruskin.

PROSE VEINED WITH POETRY : KEATS AND CARLYLE

WITH the nineteenth century Romantic Revival and return
to Nature, imagination and emotion prevailed over
" good sense " and " reason," and the change was quickly

felt in prose. The age was rich in poets whose prose was of a very high order, as for example, Wordsworth and Coleridge, Shelley and, later, Francis Thompson. With these Keats can compete, and indeed many would hold that in his *Letters* he excels them all. The Lake poets and Shelley wrote about poetry, its philosophical conception and theories of diction. Keats does the same, but he traces the growth of his own genius in relation to his poetic ideals. His development can be realised as much from the *Letters* as from the poems. For beauty of image these letters compare favourably with the prose of any of the poets and offer an intimate survey of Keats's mind from the time when he was sensible of his poetic vocation until the close of his life. They record his feeling and thought with regard to poetry and the many and varied influences which played upon his mind. Here is Keats's passion for beauty, " the shapes of things, their colours, lights and shades, changes, surprises," his yearning for knowledge, " which is needful to thinking people, it takes away the heat and fever, and helps by widening speculation to ease the Burden of the Mystery."

This period is so rich in prose that there is room here only for the bare mention of many great names. We must pass over De Quincey, whose romantic prose, as in the *Mail Coach* and the *Opium Eater*, is infused with the imaginative quality of a dream consciousness ; Lamb, with his gentle, whimsical *Elia* ; Hazlitt, whose high spirits and easy-flowing style in *My first acquaintance with the Poets* belie his assurance that he found writing so hard.

Carlyle's prose is so individual as to be unlike that of anyone else. His thought, feeling, and imagination are alike violent, and the forcefulness of his style is born of the essential quality of his mind. His writing gives one the impression of a coloured cinematograph, for vivid scenes flash in swift succession. When his imagination, fired by political or social ideas, is at white heat, he gives us such memorable pictures as the flight to Varennes in the *History of the French Revolution*.

However much we may admire Carlyle, we must admit that he is not easy reading ; his sentences are jerked out, words tumble one after another ; this sentence is typical of his style : " Surely also, in some place not of honour, stands or sprawls up querulous, that he too, though short, may see,— one squalidest bleared mortal, redolent of soot and horse dung : Jean Paul Marat of Neuchâtel." Ruskin is always associated in our minds with Carlyle as far as ideas are concerned, but he was not much influenced as regards style. The essential differences in the prose of the two men is shown by comparing Ruskin's chapter on *The Nature of Gothic* in the *Stones of Venice* with Carlyle's *On Labour*.

THE GAY SPIRIT OF STEVENSON

STEVENSON frankly admitted that he had modelled his style on that of the best authors. In his essay, *A College Magazine*, which appears in the collection entitled *Memories and Portraits*, he said : " I have played the sedulous ape to Hazlitt, to Lamb, to Wordsworth, to Sir Thomas Browne, to Defoe, to Hawthorne, to Montaigne, to Baudelaire, and to Oberman. . . . That, like it or not, is the way to learn to write." Whether as the result of this careful study, or a natural feeling for style, possibly a fusion of the two, the result was fortunate. The vigour of his mind, the spirit of romance and adventure which inspired such different books as *Treasure Island* and *Travels with a Donkey* prevented his writing even in the earlier essays from being that of the author who is too self-conscious in the matter of style.

Pater's prose is so much the outcome of his philosophy that it is imperative to examine his doctrine. He believed that amongst the " changes and chances " of the world the only stability lay in Art for Art's sake ; life he held to be a series of moments, and its aims to make the moment as exquisite as possible. This theory caused him to handle prose with the same meticulous care as a jeweller touches the mechanism of a watch. The result is beautiful but brilliant, with the hothouse beauty of an orchid. Pater was not a little afraid of rough winds ; for him art was " not only an interpretation of life, but an escape from it," and this approach makes for a feeling of impending decay in his work and the sense that his prose is overlaboured. *Marius the Epicurean* is a fine romantic novel ; the *Renaissance Studies* and the *Child in the House* are to be recommended. Here are colour, romance, Roman philosophy, and Italian art portrayed with an exquisite pen akin to that of George Moore.

The æsthetic movement of which Pater and Oscar Wilde were representative each in his way has been called " the perfumed dusk of the nineties." This epigram has survived because " dusk " is apt for the atmosphere of shadow and unreality, so is " perfumed " for the predominance of sensuous beauty of the most exotic kind. Wilde is extravagant in his choice of image and phrase; metaphors taken from pomegranates, poppies, turquoise, and jasper adorn his prose to the point of making it appear like a woman who is wearing too many jewels. In his later work, however, this quality is not so evident, and *De Profundis* has a simple grandeur both of thought and of style.

PROSE AT THE DAWN OF THE TWENTIETH CENTURY

THE twentieth century saw a large increase in the number of first-class authors, and they all brought their contribution to prose. Hardy wrote a fine unpretentious style, the beauty of which is most apparent, either when he is describing some moment of tense drama, as, for example, when Tess goes to the scaffold, or some country scene such as the opening of *Under the Greenwood Tree*. Kipling wrote a narrative prose which is of its kind unsurpassed, and the descriptive passages in *Kim*, particularly the chapter where Kim and his Llama reached the Himalayas, are superb. One could multiply instances of fine prose from novelists and others; Galsworthy's *Indian Summer of a Forsyte* and Walpole's descriptions of Cumberland in the *Rogue Herries* trilogy are only two of the many. Amongst the wealth of writers in the early twentieth century, W. H. Hudson stands apart by virtue of the quality of his mind. He was happiest in the virgin forests of Patagonia, alone with " those vanished scenes, those rushy and flowery meres with their varied and multitudinous wild life, the cloud of shining wings, the heart-enlivening wild cries " (*Far Away and Long Ago*). He had something of Wordsworth's nature mysticism, and of Gilbert White's naturalist genius, and this rare combination makes his books unique. Of his prose Conrad said : " One can't tell how this fellow gets his effects : he writes as the grass grows."

That extraordinary creative vitality which made Lawrence a force in literature, which spent itself in human relationship, and in the attempt to find some way of living to meet his needs and what he felt to be the needs of his contemporaries, informs his prose. He has something in common with Hudson, the love of Nature at her most elemental. It is interesting to compare Lawrence's description of the Australian bush in *Kangaroo* with that of the forest in Hudson's *Green Mansions*. There the affinity ends, however, for Lawrence was less of a mystic than Hudson, and his interest in human nature was foreign to Hudson. Lawrence's prose is very uneven. At times he gives us descriptive passage of the greatest distinction, such as the descriptions of flowers in *Sons and Lovers*, the scene in *Women in Love* where the lovers watch the cats, much of the writing in the *White Peacock*, where the fever of high summer is so wonderfully suggested, and in numerous letters from Italy and Germany. On the other hand, his torrential vitality often lacks restraint, making his prose abrupt, distorted, and confused. Lawrence is not at his best in passages such as this : " Even the athletic young man that wanted to be approved of. Even he. He had not much true spunk. But what was he feeling now ? Unless, of course, he had got into business and was successfully coining money. That seemed to be the only safety-valve : success in money-making. But how many men were successful, now ? "

MODERN EXPERIMENTS IN ENGLISH PROSE

L AWRENCE bridges the gulf between pre-war and post-war writers. We are conscious, more in the *Letters* than in his novels, of the restless spirit of war-time which, pressing in on him, joins forces with the fever of his own genius to drive him further to challenge the old ideals and search for new ones. After the World War the changes in social and economic life found their counterpart in literature. A shifting of values meant the overthrow of certain traditions.

The philosophers of new schools of thought have found their disciples amongst men of letters, and everywhere we see the new ideas, revealed especially in a tendency to experiment. We have been experimenting with prose since Elizabethan days, but in no age has this tendency been so strong as in our own. The Time Philosophy is one of the twentieth-century ideas which has exerted most influence on writing. The purely physical time theory of Einstein, Bergson's philosophical conception of the duration of time (the psychological aspect of time, in conjunction with the theory of timelessness) have left their mark on both matter and form, particularly in the case of the novel. Roughly the effect in literature of the study of the Time Philosophy has been for writers to assume that we can, if we will, transcend our human conditions as regards time, impossible though that may be for practical purposes, such as catching a train. So it is that James Joyce, who heads the list of those who have experimented with subject-matter and form, confines the action of *Ulysses* to one day, and in *The Portrait of the Artist as a Young Man* he writes : " So timeless seemed the grey, warm air, so fluid and impersonal his own mood, that all ages were as one to him." Joyce's public is necessarily limited by difficulties of style, as much as by the nature of his subject-matter. He has, however, been widely read by literary people, and his influence on the moderns has been considerable.

In the writings of Virginia Woolf, for instance, the affinity with Joyce is very strongly marked. Like him, she takes the time-limit of one day for her novels *Mrs. Dalloway* and *To the Lighthouse*, and her method of describing everything " from the inside out," as Wyndham Lewis terms it in *Time and the Western Man*, is the psychological approach of Joyce, though it is not easy to see where the influence of Joyce ends and that of Proust begins. *Swann's Way*, the English translation of Proust's masterpiece, has had a very great influence on contemporary prose, and no one owes him more than Virginia Woolf. Like him, she takes a small canvas and makes her subject live by a wealth of significant detail, the light and shade of her painting. Like a flower under the microscope she shows us some moment in perfect proportion, but the structure revealed in such detail that common experience recognises its truth ; the description of the dinner-party in *To the Lighthouse* is an admirable example. She writes in a subjective manner, for she gets right into the minds of her characters, and subjects and incidents are significant only as they inspire the thoughts and feelings of her people.

This method makes for a special kind of descriptive prose. In *To the Lighthouse* Mrs. Ramsay calls her daughter from her easel to ask her whether the guests have returned. It is not the question but the psychological effect of it which is significant, and calls for such analytical description. " The words seemed to be dropped into a well, where, if the waters were clear they were also so extraordinarily distorting that, even as they descended, one saw them twisting about to make Heaven knows what patterns on the floor of the child's mind."

An experiment such as *The Waves*, however interesting in

form, gives us nothing in the same class as the skating scene in *Orlando*, or the brilliant description of the thieves' den in Whitechapel in *Flush*, where everything—sights, smells, impressions—is described from the dog's point of view.

EDITH SITWELL'S BRIGHT PATCHWORK

EDITH SITWELL has also experimented in prose, though not to the same extent as Virginia Woolf. In that intimate yet scholarly criticism in which she excels, her writing is succinct, direct, and vivid. As in her verse, she is fond of expressing one sensuous impression in terms of another, as when she says : " The sound is thick, gross, and blind as stupidity itself." This method gives her great descriptive power, although it is easy to see that it might become a trick of style. Another of her characteristics is the tendency to coin composite adjectives, as when she speaks of " the air-born lightness of the Zambra Dance," and " the water-smooth beauty of Annus Mirabilis." Her love of strange, fantastic beauty ; bright-coloured cockatoos, rare Eastern silks, and so forth, goads her into making great lists of them through sheer delight in the music of their names.

Gertrude Stein and James Joyce have experimented in prose to such an extent that it is permissible to wonder whether they are not experimenting for experiment's sake. In Gertrude Stein's *Composition as Explanation*, for example, with its repetition and extraordinary syntax, it is difficult to see the value of a passage such as this : " There is singularly nothing that makes a difference a difference in beginning and in the middle and in ending except that each generation has something different at which they are looking."

WHAT TO READ NEXT IN ENGLISH PROSE

PROSE is a means of expression, not an end in itself ; therefore he who reads prose must at the same time be reading a novel, an essay, a sermon or some other form of literature. Prose is best approached either through fiction or through newspapers and periodicals. The courses of reading recommended at the end of the sections on the novel and the short story will give those interested in prose an introduction to and a liking for well-written English. The same end can alternatively be achieved by making a habit of reading the third leading article in *The Times* or the literary

Virginia Woolf's " Flush " sees the dog's point of view.

column on the back page of the *Manchester Guardian*. In this way readers will make the acquaintance of many styles of English prose and, by deciding which they prefer, will form their own tastes. They will then be in a position to begin the course of reading suggested for the essay, confident of enjoyment and profit.

For detailed analysis of the prose of individual writers, readers are referred to the suggestions following the section on criticism. A short general review of English prose is given by Arthur Clutton-Brock's essay, *Defects of English Prose*, in the anthology *Essays and Essayists* (Nelson), edited by Sir Henry Newbolt.

"ESSAIES—THAT IS, DISPERSED MEDITATIONS"[1]

by F. W. BATESON, B.A., B.Litt.(Oxon)

THE essay is one of the youngest, perhaps *the* youngest, of the literary forms. It is three hundred and sixty-odd years old. Its inventor was Michel de Montaigne, a French nobleman of the sixteenth century, who has recorded both the time when and the place where he wrote his first essay. The time was the month of March, 1571 (a few weeks before Shakespeare's seventh birthday), and the place was " the second story of the old tower of the castle of Montaigne, in a study to which the philosopher withdrew, surrounded by his books, close to his chapel, sheltered from the excesses of the fatiguing world."

Montaigne was one of those enchanting people, like our own Pepys, who are interested in everything. A raging and insatiable curiosity possessed him. His writings are one long eager " Why ? " There was literally nothing that he was not inquisitive about—from the band round the belly that his doctors recommended against sea-sickness to such grave problems as " Whence this custom ariseth, to bless and say God help to those that sneeze ? " But Montaigne's curiosity, though always intense, was always short-lived. He was one of the world's smatterers, a picker-up of unconsidered trifles, who skimmed the surface of a hundred subjects and never got to the bottom of one. There were a great many things that he knew a little about, but the only topic on which he was an expert was—himself. And so when Montaigne came to put his experiences and observations into writing the result was not a book in the ordinary sense at all. It was too disconnected, too trivial, too personal for that. A book that is worth the name is an orderly affair, whether it is a fictitious narrative or a philosophical discourse. But Montaigne's writings are a rag-bag into which he poured the chips and shavings of scores of books. They are specimens, fragments, casual notes, and isolated chapters of the books he never wrote—or, to use his own word, *essais* (trials).

[1] Francis Bacon.

"IT IS MYSELF I PORTRAY"

MONTAIGNE'S *Essais* are, both in name and in fact, the first essays. There had never been anything remotely resembling them before. But the stuff out of which they are made—day-dreams, whims, fantastic speculations, trivial observations, and odds and ends of learning—is of course as old as mankind. Montaigne's originality did not consist in thinking things that no one had thought, but in recording things that no one had thought it worth while to record. He was interested in everything impartially and the zest of his interest communicated itself to his writings. The little things that most of us are half ashamed of, our tricks of speech, our mannerisms, our secret ignobilities, were just as important to him as the big things. His shamelessness is his fortune. Literature has always been unduly dominated by the Superman—the sublime thinker, the heroic actor, the tragic lover, the Plato, the Achilles, the Romeo. Montaigne put the Superman in his place. Montaigne's hero was the average man, *l'homme moyen sensuel*, that fascinating and complicated compound of little hypocrisies and generosities that he recognised in the retired magistrate of Perigueux who was himself. "It is myself," he begins by warning his reader, "I portray."

THE ENDURING CORE OF HUMAN NATURE

THE world, which is lazy and self-centred, has never ceased to be grateful to Montaigne. Life is short—and books are long. But the essay is neither too long nor too short. It is as long as a twopenny bus-ride and it is as short as a solitary meal ; it accompanies the smoker through his pipe ; it is finished before the bedside candle is out. And the essayist's subject is the one subject that is always certain to enthral even the dullest and the most altruistic of us—ourselves. It is of course true that human nature is the ultimate subject of all literature. (That is what Matthew Arnold meant when he called poetry a "criticism of life.") But the essayist is the only writer who is content to take human nature as he finds it. The others, the poets and preachers, the novelists and satirists, are secretly dissatisfied, one and all, with what Wordsworth has called "human nature's daily food." They demand a rarer diet. The poet wants to spiritualise you, the preacher to improve you, and the novelist to make you more exciting. The satirist, with the blazing eyes, is angry with you because you will not conform to his ideals.

The essayist is more tolerant. He will share your aspirations, and he will sympathise with you when you fail to live up to them. He does not expect too much. You are what you are, sensible and kindly perhaps, but forgetful and unimaginative. And nothing, not even falling in love or the experience of a religious conversion or the rites of psychoanalysis, is going to alter you very much one way or the other. Your hair will go white and your skin will break into wrinkles, but the man or woman inside you, your inner self, is not going to change. You will get more cunning and more confident as you grow older, but the important things about you, the things that make you what you are, will always remain the same. You can never escape from yourself until you die.

It is this sobering philosophy that the essayist teaches. But, though he will not let you blink this horrid truth, he is really more concerned to offer you certain consolations. Why, after all, should you wish to change yourself? Are you not noble in reason, infinite in faculty, in form and moving express and admirable, in action like an angel, the beauty of the world, the paragon of animals? Hamlet's temperament was not that of an essayist, far from it, but his " What a piece of work is man ! " is a splendid summary of the essayist's creed.

The essayist is a believer in man. He is a humanist. To those who, like Shelley, see in man a potential angel, or, like D. H. Lawrence, a fallen animal, the essayist retorts that it is better to be a man than an angel or an animal. The cure for our discontents is to be *more* human, *more* manly. *Homo sum*, the old Latin poet wrote, *nihil humanum alienum mihi puto*. I am a man, the essayist would agree, and the proper study of mankind is man. Aldous Huxley, one of the cleverest of contemporary essayists, has called one of his collections *Proper Studies*. But all essays are proper studies.

For human nature in the long run is more interesting, more attractive, and more satisfying to the essayist than anything that has ever been or ever can be proposed as a substitute for it. That is the challenge he makes the world. If you subscribe to its truth you will read and enjoy the essayists to whom you are now to be introduced. You are an essayist in embryo yourself. But if you deny it, if you are an explorer of other worlds and terrestrial Paradises, you will be wasting your time. The essay is not everybody's meat.

A NATIVE GROWTH OF THE ENGLISH MIND

THE essay, in spite of Montaigne, is the peculiar glory not of French but of English literature. Montaigne was not only the first but, for all practical purposes, the last French essayist. His followers, Pascal, La Bruyère and La Rochefoucauld, developed a parallel form, the *pensée* or aphorism, that was better suited than the wavering outlines of the essay to the clear-cut and logical genius of France. The English, on the other hand, less methodical and less anxious to press everything into the strait-waistcoat of a definition, found in the essay, almost from the first, a *genre* that has proved curiously congenial to the national temperament. The frankness and unpretentiousness of Montaigne were qualities that are characteristically English, and when the *Essais* were " done into English," in a brilliant if at times fantastically inaccurate version, by John Florio in 1603, English literature was only reclaiming what was really her own. The essay is the way in which an Englishman naturally expresses himself.

There are essays of a sort, brilliant essays, imbedded in the narrative poems of Chaucer, and Caxton's inimitable *Prologues* and *Epilogues* are only essays in disguise. But before Montaigne there was no recognised mould into which writings of this kind could be poured. They had to survive as best they could as digressions in, or introductions to, longer works. Montaigne provided the essayist with the pretext and the formula to exist in his own right. The history of the English essay from the time of Florio's translation is the record of the avidity with which the opportunity was grasped. For the essay has come to be the most English of all the different ways of writing. It is the quality of Englishness, that paradoxical mixture of poetry with common sense and obstinacy with gentleness which insists on recurring in these islands, that gives the essay its peculiar flavour. All the great essayists possess it, even Frenchmen like Anatole France and Germans like Heine. (A piquant illustration of the invincible Englishness of the essay is that the French and German words for the essayist—*l'essayiste, der Essayist* —are taken straight from the English. The thing was so English that the name had to be English too.)

A study of the essay is something more, therefore, than the

investigation of a particular way of putting words on to paper. It is the study of a manner of thinking, a philosophy of conduct. The essay is the English contribution not only to the literature of the world but to the life of the world. You will never surprise the reserved and inarticulate Englishman out of the whole of his secret, but you will come nearer to it in his essays than anywhere else. The essay is the Englishman thinking aloud.

FRANCIS BACON : THE FIRST ENGLISH ESSAYIST

THE first English essayist is Bacon, the first edition of whose *Essays* was published in 1597, only five years after Montaigne's death. But Bacon, who " wrote of science like a Lord Chancellor," is only chronologically the first English essayist. He had not the true essayist's temperament or style. " Reading," he wrote in one of those tremendous sentences of his that seem to be cut in iron, " maketh a full man ; Conference a ready man ; and Writing an exact man ; and therefore, if a man write little he had need have a great memory ; if he confer little he had need have a present wit ; and if he read little he had need have much cunning, to seem to know that he doth not."

Writing made Bacon an exact man. He knew exactly what he wanted to say and he said it in exactly the way he intended. But exactness is the essay's deadliest enemy. An essay is by definition a trial, an experiment, a tentative groping for truths whose wings we may brush but that we can never quite capture. Bacon was too clever and too confident. He had an explanation for everything. His wisdom is a worldly wisdom that only reaches the gross exteriors of things and leaves out the imponderables and the fine shades that are the essayist's real prey. It is impossible not to admire Bacon's *Essays*. They have a sonorous eloquence veined with poetry that is above praise and almost explains why Shakespeare's plays have been fathered on him, but they are not essays at all except in name. The first genuine English essayist was a much humbler person, though a more attractive personality.

A LOVER OF " LITTLE THINGS " : ABRAHAM COWLEY

" WHO now reads Cowley ? " Pope was able to ask only seventy years after Abraham Cowley's death. And the answer, both then and now, must be " Very few." But

Cowley is an essayist and a poet worth knowing. A gentle, retiring creature naturally, whose greatest happiness was to sit and bask in the sun, he was caught up, like the rest of his contemporaries, in the maelstrom of the Civil War, in which he acquitted himself with distinction on the Royalist side. But the court and the camp were not his choice and he escaped from them as soon as he was able. The *Several Discourses by way of Essays, in Verse and Prose*—first published in 1668, but written earlier—are the record of the sense of relief and exhilaration that he felt when he was at last his own master and could retire into the country and vegetate. The titles of his essays tell their own story—*Of Liberty, Of Solitude, Of Obscurity, Of Agriculture, The Garden, The Country Life*. "I never had any other desire so strong," he writes, "and so like to covetousness as that one which I have had always, that I might be master at last of a small house and large garden." A modest ambition, but it was not achieved until the very end of his life. "I still stick," he complained to Evelyn the diarist, "in the inn of a hired house and garden, among weeds and rubbish, and without that pleasantest work of human industry the improvement of something which we call—not very properly, but yet we call—our own."

Cowley is a real essayist, a true follower of the "Sieur de Montagn," whom he quotes in the essay *Of Greatness*, because he strikes the personal note. In this he is the antithesis of Bacon who, except indirectly, does not portray himself in his writings at all. Cowley, on the other hand, whatever the subject he is discoursing upon, is always reverting to himself. But it is with humility, without ostentation, without forcing himself upon his reader. "There may be perhaps some village in Scotland or Ireland," he writes, "where I might be a great man, and in that case I should be like Cæsar—you would wonder how Cæsar and I should be like one another in anything—and choose rather to be the first man of the village than second at Rome." He is almost apologising, you see, for the intrusion of insignificant Mr. Cowley in such exalted company.

But the apology was unnecessary. Cowley's best essay is *Of Myself*, and the best passages in the other essays are those in which he turns to illustrate his theme by a personal reference. Here is one example from *Of Greatness* : "I confess I love littleness almost in all things. A little convenient estate, a little cheerful house, a little company, and a very little feast, and if I were ever to fall in love again (which is a great passion, and therefore I hope I have done with it) it would be, I think, with prettiness rather than with majestical beauty." And here is a longer passage, a particularly charming one, from *Of Myself* :

> " I believe I can tell the particular little chance that filled my head first with such chimes of verse as have never since left ringing there. For I remember, when I began to read, and to take some pleasure in it, there was wont to lie in my mother's parlour (I know not by what accident, for she herself never in her life read any book but of devotion), but there was wont to lie Spenser's works. This I happened to fall upon and was infinitely delighted with the stories of the knights and giants and monsters and brave houses which I found everywhere there, though my understanding had little to do with all this, and by degrees with the tinkling of the rhyme and the dance of the numbers, so that I think I had read him all over before I was twelve years old."

THE FATHERS OF THE ENGLISH ESSAY

COWLEY'S essays had a small success when they were published after his death, but the essay did not come into its own as a literary form, as a rival of the poem and the play, until the beginning of the eighteenth century. Addison and Steele are the real fathers of the English essay. They made it popular and they made it respected. After them it was no longer possible to overlook the essay or to pooh-pooh it as a mere *parvenu* in the society of letters. The best of Addison's essays are perfect of their kind. They do something that could not be done in any other way either in poetry or in prose.

Addison and Steele were the inventors of the *periodical* essay. *The Tatler* and *The Spectator*, in which all their best essays were printed, were newspapers that came out three times and six times a week respectively, but the contents of each issue instead of being items of news was a single essay by either Addison or Steele, or occasionally by one of their friends. (Swift, for example, contributed several papers to *The Tatler*.) They were dashed off, therefore, on the spur of the moment and are naturally more unequal than the leisurely compositions of Bacon and Cowley. The level of

The Spectator especially is extraordinarily high considering the circumstances in which it was written, but no one in his senses would sit down and read the whole of it or of *The Tatler*. They should be dipped into or read in selections. Three or four essays by Steele and ten or twenty by Addison are all that any one except the expert need be expected to be familiar with. If you like them you can read on, but *The Spectator* is not every one's taste. A great many of the essays are rather more solemn and didactic than we are accustomed to nowadays, and the lighter moments are mainly satirical. A little of Addison's playful and almost caressing satire can be very enjoyable, but it becomes wearisome as page follows page and the raillery of extinct fashions and forgotten affectation continues.

SIR ROGER DE COVERLEY

ADDISON and Steele achieved their masterpiece in the series of essays in *The Spectator* that are concerned with Sir Roger de Coverley. The Worcestershire baronet is one of the most delightful figures in English literature. We are introduced to him in his country house by Addison, in No. 106, and Steele completes the picture in No. 107. No. 108 (by Addison) is devoted to Sir Roger's friend and neighbour, the incomparable Will Wimble—who " hunts a pack of dogs better than any man in the country and is very famous for finding out a hare." The next number, on the family portraits of the de Coverleys, was by Steele, and in No. 112, Addison accompanies Sir Roger to church—where he " will suffer nobody to sleep in it besides himself. For if by chance he has been surprised into a short nap at sermon, upon recovering out of it he stands up and looks about him, and if he sees anybody else nodding, either wakes them himself or sends his servant." No. 113, by Steele and one of the best of the series, is devoted, in a mixed spirit of sympathy and fun, to Sir Roger's disappointment in love.

It was a widow, a fascinating and heartless creature, who had been his undoing. " After she had done speaking to me," he confides, " she put her hand to her bosom and adjusted her tucker. Then she cast her eyes a little down upon my beholding her too earnestly. They say she sings excellently ; her voice in ordinary speech has something in it inexpressibly sweet. You must know I dined with her at a public table the day after I first saw her, and she helped

Sir Roger de Coverley visits his tenants.

me to some tansy in the eye of all the gentlemen in the country. She has certainly the finest hand of any woman in the world."

A later series, all by Addison, brings Sir Roger to London, and we accompany him to Westminster Abbey, to the theatre, and on the river, until, finally, in a letter from the butler, we hear that the old baronet has breathed his last. "We were once," the butler writes, "in great hope of his recovery, upon a kind message that was sent him from the widow lady whom he had made love to the forty last years of his life. But this only proved a lightening before death. He has bequeathed to this lady, as a token of his love, a great pearl necklace and a couple of silver bracelets set with jewels which belonged to my good old Lady his mother."

A LEARNED AND A LIVELY PEN

DR. JOHNSON and Goldsmith are the best of Addison and Steele's immediate followers. *The Rambler* and *The Idler* are full of Johnson's characteristic good sense, and the style, though not without its absurdities, is also not without vigour and a certain monumental beauty. "The graces of writing and conversation," we read in No. 14 of *The Rambler*, "are of different kinds." Johnson certainly talks a great deal better in Boswell's pages than he ever wrote. But he wrote well enough, and his essays are quite as good, really, as Goldsmith's livelier but superficial *Citizen of the World*. Goldsmith, according to Garrick, "wrote like an angel and talked like poor Poll." *She Stoops to Conquer* and *The Vicar of Wakefield* are angelic, but I cannot help wondering if Garrick had read Goldsmith's essays. I have heard poor Poll chattering in more than one of them. The best of them are the series in the *Citizen of the World*, of which the delicious Beau Tibbs is the hero.

WILLIAM HAZLITT : MAN OF ENTHUSIASMS

THE world of Addison and Steele, and of Johnson and Goldsmith, is a foreign country to most of us. A tour in it can be very exhilarating, but we cannot live there. The people are too different from us. They look at things from another angle ; it is difficult for us either to laugh with them or to be serious with them. But the world of the nineteenth century, the world of essayists like Lamb and Hazlitt, is our world. We feel at home again. These are writers who speak the language we speak and who are interested in the things that interest us. Their essays could be printed in our magazines and newspapers, and we should never know that the authors had been dead and buried a hundred years or more.

Hazlitt, indeed, is more alive to-day than he ever was. In the best of his essays he seems to be speaking directly to us over the gulf of the years and appealing to us against his own time. *You* will understand me, he seems to be saying, *you* will do me justice. It is Hazlitt's sincerity, the fire of conviction that burns in him, that is so winning. We believe him implicitly. His loves and his hatreds are genuine. He really felt like that; he did not assume the feeling, as Stevenson often did, in order to write an essay about it. And on the whole we share his likes and dislikes.

" I never was in a better place," he begins one essay, " or humour than I am at present for writing. I have a partridge getting ready for my supper, my fire is blazing on the hearth, the air is mild for the season of the year, I have had but a slight fit of indigestion to-day (the only thing that makes me abhor myself), I have three hours good before me." We agree with him at once. If we had to write an essay ourselves—as (who knows ?) we may one day have to—we should choose just such a moment as Hazlitt's. A whiff of the partridge cooking coming under the door would encourage us to persevere, and, if we found ourselves without ideas, we would stare into the fire until we found them in the red coals. And it is the same with Hazlitt's hatreds. " A lady," he writes, " the other day, could not refrain from expressing her surprise to a friend, who said he had been reading *Delphine*. She asked if it had not been published some time back ? " How he hated that lady ! But we know her just as well as Hazlitt did, we meet her at every other tea-party, and we loathe her with just his inextinguishable loathing.

Hazlitt's likes and dislikes were clear-cut and intense. When he hated he hated with passionate venom ; when he loved he loved with an enthusiastic ardour that is irresistible. And what a strange and motley company his loves were ! A game of fives, a country walk, Richard Wilson's paintings, a boxing-match, Fielding's novels ! Hazlitt is the most infectious writer in the whole of English literature. It is impossible not to fall in with his enthusiasms. When he

has praised a picture there is nothing to do but go and see it.
When he praises a book it must be bought. When he de-
scribes a friend of his we want to meet him. In the essay
On the Conversation of Authors he writes :

> "There was L. himself, the most delightful, the
> most provoking, the most witty and sensible of men.
> He always made the best pun, and the best remark
> in the course of the evening. His serious conversa-
> tion, like his serious writing, is his best. No one
> ever stammered out such fine, piquant, deep, eloquent
> things in half a dozen half-sentences as he does. His
> jests scald like tears, and he probes a question with a
> play upon words. What a keen, laughing, hair-
> brained vein of home-felt truth ! What choice venom !
> How often did we cut into the haunch of letters, while
> we discussed the haunch of mutton on the table !
> How we skimmed the cream of criticism ! How we got
> into the heart of controversy ! How we picked out
> the marrow of authors ! "

An immortal conversation ! And we can reconstruct it.
For, if Hazlitt's essays provide one side of it, the other side
is provided by the essays of " L." For " L." was, of course,
no other than Charles Lamb, the greatest, except for Hazlitt
himself—some would say greater even than Hazlitt—of all
the English essayists.

THE ESSAYIST OF MANY MOODS

LAMB once called his essays " a sort of unlicked, incondite
things—villainously pranked out in an affected array of
antique modes and phrases," and the overstatement possesses
a kernel of truth. Lamb's style is not as good as Hazlitt's.
The old authors of the seventeenth century, Burton, Fuller,
and Sir Thomas Browne, whose folios were always in his
hands, and whose phrases were never out of his mouth,
stand between us and him. We cannot hear Lamb's own
voice for theirs. The charm that he exercised in conversation, of which Hazlitt is only one of many witnesses, does
not quite carry over into his writings. There is always an
element of artificiality, of preciosity even, in his essays.
They do not ring quite true.

But if Lamb is not a perfect essayist, he is a very good
essayist. Take this as a specimen of his quality :

" All this time sat upon the edge of the deck quite a different character. It was a lad, apparently very poor, very infirm, and very patient. His eye was ever on the sea, with a smile : and, if he caught now and then some snatches of these wild legends, it was by accident, and they seemed not to concern him. The waves to him whispered more pleasant stories. He was as one, being with us, but not of us. He heard the bell of dinner ring without stirring ; and when some of us pulled out our private stores—our cold meat and our salads—he produced none, and seemed to want none. Only a solitary biscuit he had laid in ; provision for the one or two days and nights, to which these vessels then were oftentimes obliged to prolong their voyage. Upon a nearer acquaintance with him, which he seemed neither to court nor decline, we learned that he was going to Margate, with the hope of being admitted into the Infirmary there for sea-bathing. His disease was a scrofula, which appeared to have eaten all over him. He expressed great hopes of a cure ; and when we asked him, whether he had any friends where he was going, he replied, ' he *had* no friends.' "

The tender pathos of a passage such as this is the quality in which Lamb excels. It recurs in such masterpieces as *Old China, Mackery End, Christ's Hospital Thirty-five Years Ago*, and, loveliest of all, *Dream Children*. But Lamb is an essayist of many moods. He has his satirical moments, as in *The Old and New Schoolmaster* and *A Bachelor's Complaint of the Behaviour of Married People*. He can be simply and gaily absurd, as in *All Fools' Day* and *Popular Fallacies.* And he is always a brilliant portrait-painter—witness Samuel Salt and Lovell in *The Old Benchers of the Inner Temple*, George Dyer in *Oxford in the Vacation*, and, above all, the heroic and indomitable Sarah Battle.

THE ESSAY TO-DAY

LAMB and Hazlitt are incomparably the best, but they are not the only essayists of the nineteenth century. Their contemporaries, Leigh Hunt and De Quincey, are very fine, too, and R. L. Stevenson, though he won his real triumphs elsewhere, was an essayist of quality. But these writers, delightful though they can be, did not add anything new to the essay. The *form* stagnated in their hands. It was not until the very end of the century, with Max Beerbohm and G. K. Chesterton, that a new note was struck.

Beerbohm has introduced himself, a debonair and unobtruding figure, into several of his essays and caricatures, and into at least one of his short stories. (It was in the presence of the young Max, just down from Oxford, that Enoch Soames sold his soul to the devil.) But he remains persistently in the background. He is the chorus, not the protagonist in his writings. " My life," he has said, " (though to me it has been, and is, extremely interesting) is without a single point of general interest." And so there is no autobiography in his essays. What he contributes to the essay is a novel point of view and a malicious, twinkling, all-observing eye.

THE QUINTESSENCE OF MAXISM

THE best of Beerbohm's essays are in the collections entitled *Works* (1896) and *And Even Now* (1920). *More* (1899) is not so fresh and well written as *Works*, and prolongs the fun of its predecessor, that of an impudent, adolescent sophistication, without elaborating or improving it. *Yet Again* (1909) is a book full of good ideas, rather than a good book. It is better, though, than *More*, and one or two of the essays, that *On Shakespeare's Birthday*, for instance, are among Mr. Beerbohm's best. But it is to the raffish impertinences of *Works* and the matured and mellow wit of *And Even Now* that the true Beerbohmite returns. There we have the quintessence of Maxism—a suave and imperturbable epicureanism imbedded in an impeccable style. If I were compelled to choose the two best essays Beerbohm has written, I would take one from *Works*, perhaps " Dandies and Dandies," which, beginning with Brummel, is a complete and devastatingly witty analysis of *le dandysme* of the nineteenth century—and for the other that exquisite reminiscential vignette of Swinburne's later years, " No. 2 The Pines," from *And Even Now*.

G. K. CHESTERTON : LOGICIAN OF THE ILLOGICAL

G. K. CHESTERTON is unique among contemporary essayists in possessing a consistent and articulate philosophy. He has condensed his credo into the statement that " life is not only a pleasure, but a kind of eccentric privilege," and the whole of his writings may be considered an elaborate commentary upon this epigram. It means, put more simply, that Chesterton has been attempting to recapture the point of view of the child. He is the logician of the illogical. He has given a metaphysical basis to the old fairy stories of Grimm and Perrault. He has justified the cosmos of Wonderland. He is the apologist of the Great Gromboolian Plain. It is true, Mr. Chesterton argues, that bean-stalks are frequently not more than a few feet high. But is that any reason why Jack's bean-stalk should not climb into the skies ? Is it impossible to imagine a bean-stalk five miles high ? Of course not, Mr. Chesterton replies, every nursery in England has done it.

G. K. Chesterton's metaphysics are delightful. They enable him to enter into our modern world *sub persona infantis* and to see old controversies from new angles. But they are not the whole of his equipment as an essayist. Mr. Chesterton is the owner of a grotesque sense of humour, which expresses itself in shameless puns and comically unexpected illustrations. And his jokes, generally good in themselves, are always heightened by the air of solemnity with which he introduces them. In one of the essays he has interrupted a serious discussion of optimism and pessimism with the remark that he discovers " a sort of allegorical truth " in " the mysterious but suggestive definition said to have been given by a little girl : ' An optimist is a man who looks after your eyes, and a pessimist is a man who looks after your feet.' " The quotation is from *Orthodoxy*, one of the most ambitious of Chesterton's collections of essays because it develops, with a considerable degree of success, a continuous argument. But *Orthodoxy* is not Chesterton's best book. The collected essays that deserve that title best are probably *Tremendous Trifles* and *A Miscellany of Men*. They can be recommended with absolute confidence to the incipient Chestertonian.

THE SOCIAL HANDSHAKE OF PRIESTLEY

G. K. CHESTERTON and Max Beerbohm are the best of the older living essayists. But they made their names and formed their styles before the cataclysm of 1914. They are survivors from that giant race before the flood, the Edwardians, which is already becoming mythical. J. B. Priestley and Aldous Huxley, on the other hand, with whom we must conclude this survey of the English essay, are post-war. They are our own contemporaries, and they represent the best that has been done in the field of the essay in the course of the ten years 1924 to 1934.

Priestley's novel, *The Good Companions*, alternated between moods of jovial humour and poetic sentiment. There is the same dichotomy in his essays. In his jovial mood Priestley reveals himself as a shrewd and companionable observer of our foibles. He is an apotheosis of the uncles of our childhood, always patting us on the back or digging us in the ribs. Our secret sorrows are open books to him. In an essay *On Haberdashers* he shares with us the agonies of buying a new hat. In *Song* he divines our unwhispered ambitions. He, too, has the irrational conviction we all have that we can sing :

> " We know that Art could do much for us, but, at the same time, we are convinced that Nature, in her own kindly fashion, has carried us a great way upon the road. It is not that we want to be singers, but that we are singers by nature and have simply not chosen either to make a business or even a hobby of song.
>
> ' I do but sing because I must,
> And pipe but as the linnets sing '
>
> we cry with Tennyson ; only most of our piping is done not in public but in strict privacy ; indeed, to be brief and perhaps brutal, in the bath-room."

But there is a poetic as well as a prosaic Mr. Priestley. It is the poet in him, indeed, that gives his essays their peculiar distinction. The poetic Mr. Priestley is a sort of divine simpleton, a modern Don Quixote, all innocence and unsophistication, who looks out on the world with clear and incredulous eyes. He walks up and down London in a dream. It is all a mirage, much too wonderful to be true. Dixie, in *I for One* (the best of his collections of essays), is a gem of whimsical poetry. But one can imagine what the prosaic Mr. Priestley would have made of it. How he would have chuckled at the inanity of the Dixie songs ! What remorseless fun he would have made of those triumphs of vulgarity ! But with the poetic Mr. Priestley even the cotton fields and Uncle Joe and the roses round the door turn to favour and to prettiness. Is not this a delicious piece of anthropology ?

> " It seems that, at the beginning of last century, a certain slave-holder called Dixie removed his slaves

from Manhattan Island to the Southern States, where the poor creatures fared much worse. They began to sigh for their old home, which they called Dixie's Land. Gradually, as time went on, the old folks, telling their tales, lost sight of reality, and the credulous, imaginative younger generations added their share of myth, until Dixie's Land became one of the Delectable Kingdoms, a land of milk and honey, the land of Beulah, ' where the sun shineth night and day.' It became Dixie. Thus, to the great list, Hesperian Fields, Fortunate Islands, Tir-na-nog—the Land of the Living, the Island of the Seven Cities, the Isles of the Blest, the Isle of Avalon, and I know not how many more—to this great list another name was added. Another quaint shape suddenly appeared on that map which I have called the map of moonshine, though I believe it to be more significant, perhaps closer to essential reality, than those maps, so cocksure in their bright blues and pinks, that we receive from the hands of cartographers. After all, moonshine endures, and will outlast all your Gas Light and Coke Companies."

It is obvious that Priestley is a stylist. But his style is of a very different kind from your common-or-garden essayist. He hates, he tells us, " ' snip-snap ' that takes a breath every other moment, avoids conjunctions, and achieves a mechanical, rattling effect, coming to the ear like the noise of a machine gun." J. B. Priestley's prose is the leisurely meditative and weighty prose that one associates with the seventeenth century, though it is sometimes, like that prose, too self-conscious, too indifferent to the art that conceals art, and too indulgent to the *bravura* that revels in its own strength.

ALDOUS HUXLEY : ESSAYIST IN SPITE OF HIMSELF

ALDOUS HUXLEY, an undoubted essayist by temperament, is an essayist almost in spite of himself. The reader of his very entertaining novels will remember how often he brings the plot to a standstill to permit one of his puppets to soliloquise in what are, in all but name, admirable essays. Mr. Scogan, in *Chrome Yellow*, and Mr. Cardan in *Those Barren Leaves*, are only the most hardened offenders. Occasionally too, as in the analysis of bores in the opening pages of *Two or Three Graces*, Huxley drops all pretence of writing a novel, and we get an essay from him in his own person. But the remarkable thing is that these divagations, which would be intolerable in another novelist, are not only inoffensive but are actually the tit-bits of the novels. For Huxley, though a novelist of talent, is an essayist of genius.

On the Margin is probably the best of Huxley's collections of essays. The book begins, in an essay on the Shelley centenary of some years back, by contrasting the stuffiness of our celebrations with the fun the Italians got out of the six-hundredth anniversary of Dante's death about the same time. In England we had to be content with speeches and sermons and the unveiling of statues. In Italy they had military reviews and *maifestazioni sportive*—football matches, hill-climbs, and bicycle races. Huxley's comment is well worth reading, for it illustrates his witty, careful prose and the indignation and sincerity that give his essays their unique air of distinction.

It is, above all, the intensity of Huxley's bitterness that is so impressive. The despairs and humiliations that the War forced upon every sensitive person seem to have been concentrated and exaggerated in him. He has become the point of focus, as it were, of the disillusionment of a whole generation. And this emotional background, perhaps because his reticence is as marked as his sincerity, has given his writings a firmness of outline that is not common in contemporary literature. The supple, incisive strength of his prose is more reminiscent of Voltaire. It cannot be entirely a coincidence that the best of all his essays, a kind of *confessio fidei* for our time, should be *On Re-reading " Candide."*

SOME FINE COLLECTIONS OF ESSAYS

THE essay, as it is concerned with human nature itself, is modern in appeal, regardless of the date when it was written. Consequently, he who sets out for the first time to make the acquaintance of the essayists may either begin with a contemporary author, such as G. K. Chesterton or Hilaire Belloc, and work backwards to Montaigne, or he may choose to start with Lamb or Hazlitt, go forward to contemporary writers and then return to Addison, Bacon, and Montaigne.

Whichever route is chosen, the most convenient way to reach it is by a good anthology of essays. Two collections which begin with the earliest writers and include essays by

Aldous Huxley : talented novelist and essayist of genius.

Edward Thomas, G. K. Chesterton, and Hilaire Belloc are *A Century of English Essays* (Everyman), edited by Ernest Rhys, and *Essays and Essayists* (Nelson), edited by Sir Henry Newbolt. A good anthology of the contemporary essay is in the *World's Classics* series (Oxford University Press), edited by H. S. Milford, and entitled *Modern English Essays*. The series *Essays of To-day and Yesterday* (Harrap) includes selections from Philip Guedalla, Alice Meynell, A. C. Benson, J. B. Priestley, C. E. Montagu and others, and is especially valuable because it provides introductions and bibliographies.

Those who are interested in the development of the essay are referred to Professor Hugh Walker's *Essays and Essayists* in the series entitled *Channels of English Literature* (Dent), edited by Oliphant Smeaton.

POETRY : THE FLOWER AND FRAGRANCY OF HUMAN EXPERIENCE

by PAUL CHADBURN, B.A., B.Litt.(Oxon)

A TRAVELLER in post-war Serbia, passing through a small village near nowhere in particular, stopped to find out what a group of persons which had collected in the market-place was doing. He saw on approaching that in the centre of the group, the object of its attention, was a man with a one-string fiddle. The fellow was evidently entertaining the people with a kind of tale, accompanying it upon his instrument. Peasants, children, storekeepers, idling gossips, courting couples were listening enthralled. The traveller, though he did not understand Serbian, was able fairly accurately to trace the progress of the recital on their faces. Though the fiddle-bow sawed placidly over the one string, the tale seemed to touch more chords of emotion than is customary in old Serbian songs. There was tragedy in it, for a tear rolled off the end of a stout woman's chin on to her apron ; and moments of tense excitement, in one of which a gap-toothed ancient dropped his pipe clattering on the ground ; and some comedy, for the entertainer was an excellent mime ; and incidents of love found shining response in the dark eyes of the village belle.

Supposing the tale to be some national epic that had been handed down from mouth to mouth through centuries, the traveller asked a German-speaking butcher in the audience what had been the subject that moved the villagers so visibly, hazarding at the same time a parallel with the Nibelungenlied of the Germans. The butcher, a stolid man, replied that he did not know anything about the Nibelungenlied, but the man with the fiddle was recounting the story of his own adventures, in marriage, in war, in prison, in love, and in his cups. The minstrel was blind, the butcher added, and had to earn his living somehow.

THE STIRRING STORIES OF THE ANCIENT BARDS

THERE have been many thousands of critics who have written many million words about poetry, who have talked about it and about mincing distinctions fine, soaring

5

up as high and probing down as deep as metaphysics and psycho-analysis will take them ; yet none, probably, ever came closer remarking the nature of poetry than did the traveller in Serbia. He heard the rhythmic, repetitive flow of sound ; he saw it stimulating response in the people's emotions, stirring their imaginations, as the tale found contact in their own experience ; he saw poetry in its primitive function, when cinemas, theatres, books were not yet, entertaining the listeners as a tale, moving them with its crude music.

He understood poetry as it was before being refined and polished and written down, when it spoke directly to the emotions, directly through the ear ; before, on the one hand, it had attained to the grandeur of *Paradise Lost*, but, on the other hand, before it had become emasculate, either simulating passion, or eschewing passion altogether, caught up in an intellectual labyrinth, inviting the reader there without a guiding thread. He heard poetry before it had become a grandee with a noble heritage, when it was a handy man, more of a craftsman than an artist, its business taking it from the king's court to the village street ; when it went among all and sundry, hawking a more heroic world to those who knew no more of life than a bean field and a cottage hearth, a field to hoe and a dinner to cook.

The function of poetry remains. It must still to-day present a more heroic world—yet heroic not in the sense that it falsifies life, but in the sense that it fulfils life, bringing to concrete expression what was previously but vaguely felt, deepening experience, charming the whole man to life, awaking potentialities, equipping the spirit with the weapons of Blake's invocation :

> Bring me my bow of burning gold !
> Bring me my arrows of desire !
> Bring me my spear ! O clouds unfold !
> Bring me my chariot of fire !

Poetry evolves with life, refining its expression as our experiences become more varied, yet the poet to-day must induce a corresponding response from the modern, urbanised man as did that fiddling Serbian " Gouslar " from the primitive villagers. And that is the problem of the modern poet.

HOW TO RECOGNISE A GOOD POEM

How can a good poem be distinguished from a bad one ? Only by taste, and taste comes through reading and experience. We must understand a poem before we can judge it ; and before we can understand it we must have prepared a place in our minds—or it may be in the heart or the imagination, or all together—to receive the experience expressed. Appreciation of poetry begins with response in the reader. If the writer cannot evoke this, one of the alternatives must be true : either he cannot communicate his experience and is no poet, or the reader, through lack of experience or unfamiliarity with the poetic medium, is himself at fault. Poetry is " the blossom and the fragrancy of all human knowledge, human thoughts, human passions " and a man must have reached a certain stage of culture before poetry will begin to affect him at all. The more variously and intensely one has experienced life—though this does not mean after the fashion of the hero in the novelette, " going everywhere and doing everything "—the more poetry will one be able to appreciate ; conversely, the more one brings poetry to the illumination and enrichment of life, the more intensely will one live.

A great mistake in education even to-day is that poetry is put before us in schools—and sometimes not only put before us, but crammed most roughly into us—which we have not yet the stomachs, as it were, to digest, much less to appreciate. Some of us came instinctively at school to substitute the word *rep.* (an abbreviation of *repetition*) for poetry ; it was something to vomit forth by the line—frequently as a punishment. No wonder we abandoned it as soon as we were able. It would have been better had we been left to find it out for ourselves, rejecting what we could not possibly understand at that time. It would have been easier then, step by step, as our experience grew, to have returned to poetry and made our appreciation as individual as our lives, fashioning both together. It is better that a child should be put in the way of mere jingles which it can understand than confronted with a masterpiece which presents a blank to its understanding.

" I know what I like, but I don't know—and I don't care—why," is the philosophy of the ruminating ox. The intelligent person does question why from the moment he begins to take notice of things ; and when, if ever, his interest is awakened in poetry, he will naturally wish to know the different kinds of poetry, its various forms, something about the great poets' lives and what the critics have written.

SOURCES OF POETRY THAT ARE STRANGELY DIVERSE

THERE are two kinds of person whose attitude one towards the other might be summed up in the words of one of Dickens's female characters : " I despise him and I pity his ignorance." In their extreme examples the two kinds might meet in Whitehall—only while the representative of the one kind would be sitting at his desk, quietly, efficiently, unquestioningly carrying out orders from above, breathing in sustenance from established authority, his opposite would be in a cellar underneath, intent to blow up Whitehall and all it stands for. Either of these two kinds of man may occasionally, as circumstances dictate, become a poet. Then the first kind will be dubbed by the critics a classicist : that is to say, a poet who employs conventional verse forms, whose subjects have stood the test of general approval—he will be a poet, in short, who takes both the matter and form of his poetry from outside ; a poet who does not question the established order of things. The other, the romantic, takes his subject from inside—in fact, his ego is his subject ; its discontents, its loneliness, its aspirations towards a better dispensation, its revolt against an unsympathetic society.

Classicism and romanticism are terms which serve to denote a predominating tendency in an age or in an individual ; yet all poets have something of both kinds in them, and the greatest poet of all, Shakespeare, effects such an equipoise that he eludes classification by either term.

THE MANY FORMS OF POETIC EXPRESSION

POETRY is not exclusive as some æsthetes would make out. It has in its time put itself to many uses ; it has been an entertainer, providing the theatre with plays, and before that, castle halls and the countryside with stirring tales ; it has been an instructor with text-book and rod, laying down precept upon precept, line upon line, and castigating the abuses of an age with satire. And besides these three types —narrative, dramatic, and didactic and satirical poetry— there is lyrical poetry, or the spontaneous song. This fourth type, of equal antiquity with the others, is pure poetry.

That is to say, that while poetry *served* to entertain, to teach, and to correct, while it entered these spheres in the course, as it were, of its professional career, its exclusive domain where no other medium—not the prose play, the essay, the novel, the popular treatise, the cinema—may intrude, is the lyric.

Since poetry is conditioned by the times, it may yet express itself in popular drama, as it did in the Elizabethan age ; events may occur productive of another great epic like the *Chanson de Roland* ; there seems no reason why a great satirical poem should not be written to-day—in fact, considerable cause for it to be written. Yet it must be acknowledged that genuine poetry, with the invasion of its other spheres by new modes of expression, tends to-day to express itself more frequently in the lyrical type.

The rudely scanned tale of the Serbian wandering minstrel was an early kind of narrative poetry. This kind consists of a recital of loosely connected adventures. Alliteration—similarity of vowel sound within the line—and a rough rhythm served to set up the necessary beat ; and the scantiness of music in the language was frequently supplemented by an instrument.

Another type of narrative poetry is the ballad. This tells a tale in a manner more vivid, episodic, and direct than the former kind. There is a dramatic unity condensing it ; it presents one incident, generally a tragic one. The unity and the dramatic effect is often increased by a phrase repeated in each stanza.

A third sort of narrative poem is the epic. This, a detailed account of heroic battle in verse, is a rare kind. The framework is large ; to fill it in figures are required of mythical or semi-mythical proportions ; heroes there must be and faiths and loyalties which would appear incongruous in most settings, most of all modern ones. Epics belong to the ingenuous ages, to the first dawn of a civilisation ; they are closely related to the early ballads, from a fusion of which some believe them to have been composed. Though Milton's *Paradise Lost* is generally described as an epic, it is very far removed from the *Iliad* of Homer or the *Chanson de Roland*. Later ages have amused themselves by composing burlesque epics, obtaining an effect by recounting trivial events in the grand manner. Pope's *Rape of the Lock* is the most famous poem of this sort. Pope was also the chief exponent of didactic and satirical poetry. The first aims to instruct the age through poetical precept, the second to correct it through poetical criticism or ridicule.

MOMENTS OF VISION VOICED IN SONG

THE lyric is the poetical expression of a mood ; a lark's flight upwards and its song. It may be an ode, it may be cadenced poetry without metre or rhyme—it is a song all the same, an ecstasy of flight, momentary as moods are, as moments of vision. No poet could keep it up long. Some persons, indeed, among them the American poet and critic, Edgar Allan Poe, have maintained that this is the only kind of poetry, that anything prolonged must inevitably sink to a lower plane. This is not altogether true, though ; there is in a long poem such as *Paradise Lost* a harmony of part answering to part and note to note which fulfils the poetic conception of the whole, elevating it to the highest realms of poetry.

Some of the finest English lyrical poetry has expressed itself in the ode. This is a poem—in its finest English examples—which, besides being the expression of a mood or a moment of vision, is toned with some philosophical concept or reflection which requires graver, slower movement interrupting the sharp flight of lyrical impulse. The best English odes have not only a keen, soaring ecstasy, but a serene contemplative splendour too, as Wordsworth's *Ode on the Intimations of Immortality*. The ode, which was taken from the classical poets of Greece and Rome, has not in English poetry preserved its original strict form. English poetry cannot be restrained within classical bounds, and " ode " has come to mean not so much a form, as a kind of lyrical poetry.

PASSION AND PATTERN : THE DIFFERENCE BETWEEN POETRY AND VERSE

THE form of poetry is dictated by the poetic impulse ; is inseparable from it. The difference between poetry and verse is that with the latter the form is imposed from without, words being turned as elegantly within it as taste, wit, learning, grace, and every attribute save only the poetic impulse can devise. The more complicated the form, the less likely is deep emotion to express itself in it. The purest poetry is generally the simplest in expression. But if the form is simple, this does not mean that it is easy to employ. The more artificial aids one uses, the more artful systems of rhymes, rhythms, alliterations (which may be sophisticated as well as primitive), the more easily is one able to persuade oneself—and possibly others too—that it is not prose one is writing. The two forms which appear to be the most simple of all, but which are, in fact, the most difficult to employ successfully, are cadenced poetry and blank verse.

Cadenced poetry (sometimes miscalled " free verse ") has been frequently misunderstood, though twentieth-century poets—especially in America—have done much to bring it back into repute and dispel the illusion that poetry must be metrical, that is, divided into a set number of feet with the stress falling regularly. The form of cadenced poetry has no objective existence like that of metrical poetry ; it is peculiar to every subject expressed by it ; its rhythm is the rhythm of a stream flowing over its bed, its stresses as the jutting stones.

A good explanation of cadenced verse is given in a manifesto of a group of English and American poets writing just previous to the War. " We attach the term," they write, " to all that increasing amount of writing whose cadence is more marked, more definite, and closer knit than that of prose, but which is not so violently nor so obviously accented as the so-called ' regular verse.' " It is a mistake to suppose that cadenced verse is modern. It is at least as old as metrical verse and has been constantly employed in English poetry, though not so copiously as metrical verse. The following stanza by W. E. Henley is in cadenced verse :

So be my passing !
My task accomplished and the long day done,
My wages taken and in my heart
Some late lark singing,
Let me be gathered to the quiet west,
The sundown splendid and serene,
Death.

THE SHAPES INTO WHICH OUR POETRY FALLS

IN metrical poetry the line is composed upon an objective system of scansion. The poet, as we have said, does not choose this deliberately, but his poetic experience flows into one of a number of established forms, whichever one may best express it. The line most frequently used in English poetry contains five feet of two syllables, the second being stressed (the iambic pentameter). This may be rhymed with the next succeeding line (heroic couplet) or it may be un-rhymed (blank verse) ; and there are many other rhyme arrangements of which the most notable is the Spenserian stanza used in *The Faërie Queen*. The metrical line may, of course, be composed of any reasonable number of feet—three to six is the normal range—and analysis will yield all kinds of other variations too, which may be found in any manual of prosody. H. W. Fowler's *Modern English Usage* furnishes as succinct an account as any under the entry *Technical Terms*.

Metrical poetry is not only distinguished according to line, but according to the arrangement of lines within the stanza and stanzas within the poem. Many of the more complicated of these forms derive from France and Italy and, however well adapted for foreign languages, are more likely to produce verse in English than poetry ; in English they do not suggest themselves as a medium for expressing deep poetic experience. Of these complicated forms only the sonnet has constantly furnished a medium for the purest English poetry since the form was first introduced into England in the sixteenth century.

The ballade (not to be confused with the old English ballad, which is a kind, not a form, of poetry) is an exceedingly difficult form, as the entire poem, consisting of twenty-eight lines, or more, must be composed on three or four rhymes. Rossetti's translation of Villon's *Ballade des dames du temps jadis* is a modified ballade with a fresh set of rhymes to each verse. The form was popular in the 'nineties.

CHAUCER : THE GOOD COMPANION

THE essence of life which is the inspiration of poetry flows continually through all civilised peoples, as it flows through all civilised persons. Poetry is latent everywhere. Then, suddenly, in some nation, in classical Greece, Rome, or renaissance Italy, it bursts forth. The poetic impulse working upon the stream of human experience is like the mills beside the Nile which convey water over the land, fertilising it. So does poetry enrich a civilisation, entering back into the people's consciousness whence it arose, rejoining the essence of life, mingling inseparably with it. When the bright stream has fallen back from the minds of Sappho, Catullus, Dante, subsequent poets, perhaps in other lands, in France or England, take it up and transmute it afresh.

Moses, when he led Israel out of Egypt, is said to have carried with him a branch of the vine, as Noah took a sprig with him in the ark. The wine that Solomon drank in Palestine had all the suns of Egypt in it. So with poetry ; it is conveyed from land to land, but its essence is the original essence, the pulsing flood of human experience. When friction had ceased between Saxon and Norman in England, when a literary expression had been forged out of the fusion of the two languages, a man arose who diverted the western tradition of poetry into England and started a native tradition unparalleled in any other civilisation.

A heterogeneous collection of persons bound for Canterbury on pilgrimage met one spring day six hundred years ago at the Tabard Inn, Southwark, the point of departure. Among them was a burly, merry-eyed, but rather pensive man, a mixture of the *bon viveur* and the scholar ; unobtrusive and unassuming. No highbrow, but such as the miller, the cook, and the shipman could ride with in undisturbed levity. Yet a reserved man too, often lost in abstraction, as though, in the words of the innkeeper, who was evidently uninterested in the immaterial, he were watching the ground for sight of a hare. This man was Chaucer, with the exception only of Shakespeare, of all English poets the one with the deepest and widest understanding of his fellows, the shrewdest, most humorous observation of them.

Chaucer, pre-eminently, was able to look at life " steadily and as a whole " ; he saw it all—beauty and ugliness, nobility and villainy, the humour and the pathos ; he wore no spectacles tinted rose or yellow ; he was no æsthete, no exquisite versifier, no mystic or dyspeptic poet ; first and above all he was a man, a very English man. His idea of happiness —had he ever troubled about definitions—might well have been " to live throughout the whole range of one's faculties and sensibilities." He had his position in society, not as a poet, but as a state official ; nor did he devote all his spare time to study and to the writing of poetry. " When the month of May is come," he said, "and I hear the birds sing, and see the flowers springing up, farewell then to my book and to my devotion (to reading)."

THE GREATEST PORTRAIT GALLERY IN POETRY

We left the pilgrims at the Tabard in order that we might consider the only one of them whose likeness is not to be found in the most famous portrait gallery in English poetry —*The Prologue* to the *Canterbury Tales*. All English society is there, the types that are in Shakespeare, Fielding, Dickens, Hardy, as they are still to-day, though the advance of civilisation has smoothed out the rugged proportions somewhat. There goes riding the English gentleman, the " vary parfit gentil knight." There is the Wife of Bath, a full-blooded, generous creature, five times married. As the Clerke of Oxenford personifies the poet's love of the intellectual life, and the country parson stands for his veneration for morality, simplicity, and truth, so the Wife of Bath is the incarnation of another tenet of Chaucer's creed ; the joyous acceptance of the physical life.

Although Chaucer's satire, mellowed by fellowship with all kinds and conditions of men, is never bitter, although he laughs and does not sneer, no trait of vanity, hypocrisy, pettiness escapes him, no human foible—be it the Summoner's garrulity in the Latin tongue (of which he knew but a few poor phrases) after he had fuddled himself with wine, or the pretentions to gentility of the nun, who " at mete wel y-taught . . . leet no morsel from hir lippes fall, ne wette hir fingres in hir sauce depe." Nor does he spare himself, but records how the host rallied him on his waist measurement : " He (Chaucer) in the waast is shape as wel as I ; this were no popet in an arm t' enbrace." There could be no surer proof of Chaucer's humanity than this.

THE MUSE THAT SLEPT FOR A HUNDRED YEARS

After Chaucer a dark period supervened in English poetry. It was as though chanticleer had made a mistake about the dawn, for more than a hundred years elapsed before the Elizabethan awakening. During that time, however, enlightenment was coming in other ways. Classical literature which had lain unregarded for so many centuries flooded into the west ; it " rose like a shining cloud on the horizon of a world dark with monkish superstition and narrow-mindedness." Equally important for poetry was the invention of the printing press. Literature, preserved hitherto

" To Canterbury they wend " : *Chaucer's Pilgrims.*

in manuscript and accessible only to a few men of learning, could be enjoyed by all educated people.

Prior to the invention, popular poetry had perforce been composed for the ear ; it had been preserved passing from memory to memory and was in consequence rudely rhythmical rather than metrical. The printing press made it possible to introduce a refinement into English poetry which it lacked, to make an instrument fitted to produce that veritable diapason of notes sounded by the later Elizabethan and Caroline poets.

While the Renaissance was still preparing, in the dark preceding the Elizabethan dawn, a single poet stepped forth in England (in Scotland the times were not so lean : William Dunbar was writing and a number of other poets) and castigated the corruption of the age. John Skelton is an anomaly ; the ugly duckling of English poetry, he might be called. Though Skelton was not without fame in his own day, succeeding generations looked upon him as an uncouth, negligible rhymster, unworthy the critic's notice, and even painful to it. Then at last, five hundred years after his birth, his poetry was discovered and acclaimed by a generation—that which had gone through the World War—in whose consciousness Skelton's bitter rage found response.

Skelton is sour, realistic, wilfully rugged ; his short lines rush along to a rattle of rough rhyme. His poem *The Tunnyng of Elynour Rummynge* is like a scene depicted by Rowlandson, the eighteenth-century caricaturist ; no gross detail is spared. But there is humour and close observation of life in it. Skelton can also write with a curious quaint tenderness, as in his elegy upon Philip Sparrow.

POETRY UNDER A COURTLY INFLUENCE

TWO poets heralded the Tudor Age—Henry Howard, Earl of Surrey, and Sir Thomas Wyatt. They were men who had travelled extensively on the continent and who had learnt much from the elegance of foreign models. They brought a courtly refinement into English poetry. Their theme was most frequently love, their treatment of it gallant and sophisticated. It was chamber music they played, sweet, slender, exquisite. Surrey it was who first used blank verse in English, establishing a medium which Marlowe was later to employ in drama. There is a story about Surrey that he was arrested for shooting bolts from a cross-bow into the windows of sleeping burghers. When questioned about this, he replied he had thought it fit to warn complacent citizens of the divine wrath to come if they did not mend their ways.

Surrey and Wyatt were the most notable contributors to *Tottel's Miscellany*, an anthology of contemporary lyrics which appeared in 1557. With the publication of this collection English poetry entered upon a course of splendour and profusion which has continued, with periodic abatement, to the present day.

While the Elizabethan seamen were sailing out in search of new conquests and new continents ; while the lyricists —many of them soldiers—were composing their courtly songs with the facility born of the exuberant vitality of the age, Edmund Spenser was exploring continents of a very different kind and writing his stanzas in a manner all his own. As Chaucer is a poet of this world, counting nothing in everyday life too insignificant for his tale, so Spenser is a poet of the world of the imagination, a poet of fairyland. It has been said of him that " the love of beauty, not of truth, is the moving spring and guiding principle of his mind and imagination." His fancy travelled among the regions of the old romances, and the sensuous apprehension of his language charmed the radiance of pure poetic life into places that would, but for him, have remained for ever desolate realms of superstition, cluttered up with a jumble of antiquated myth and legend.

SPENSER'S WORLD OF SOFT ENCHANTMENT

WE do not read *The Faërie Queen* for its allegory—a veritable maze in which the same characters symbolise different qualities and represent different historical personages from book to book ; we read it, in the words of another poet, Leigh Hunt :

> . . . do we wish, out of the common sun,
> To lay a wounded heart in leafy rest,
> And dream of things far off and healing.

We read Spenser for the sweet, subtle harmonies of his stanzas, for the vivid imagery and rich colouring of his language ; we read him so that our imagination may dwell among his scenes, may loiter in the Bower of Bliss or be witness of the procession of the seven deadly sins. If " **very**

few and very weary, are those who are in at the death of the
Blatant Beast " (the last episode in the huge unfinished
romance), there are many who return to Spenser again and
again, for he has the power to bring to life, in all minds that
will submit themselves to his magic, the fabric of a vision
most men have left behind in their childhood, a vision which
may be baseless in the sense that subsequent experience has
put foundations elsewhere, but which for all that is as real
as any of those dreams of national conquest that sent Spenser's
contemporaries forth across the seas.

GENIUS THAT DEFIES DEFINITION

IN Shakespeare all poetic experience before and after him
seems to have been resumed and recreated with a round-
ness and finality placing him beyond classification. The
world is there, and who should classify the world who knows
no others ?   Shakespeare has flowed into his subjects and
characters, identifying himself with them so completely in
their myriad variety, so far transcending any one type of
experience, that he seems to be equal with Nature itself.
This is not the place to speak of him as a dramatist, working
in the medium where his genius found its complete mature
expression ; where there is no chord of the human emotions
he has not touched, no secret place of the heart he has not
revealed ; where the language is as rich, as colourful, and
as various as the thought, a vocabulary seemingly limitless
in its resources, as perfectly expressive of Lear thundering
back the storm as of Ariel's delicate singing.

For some time, as the poetic profusion of the Elizabethans
underwent the scrutiny of eighteenth-century classical taste,
Shakespeare's sonnets and narrative poems (*Venus and Adonis*,
The Rape of Lucrece), together with the lyrical fragments
collected under the title of *The Passionate Pilgrim* (only two
of which are certainly Shakespeare's) were considered very
small beer.   One editor wrote in a preface to *The Works* :
" We have not reprinted the sonnets, etc., of Shakespeare
because the strongest act of Parliament that could be framed
would fail to compel readers into their service.   Had Shakespeare produced no other works than these, his name would
have reached us with as little celebrity as time has conferred
on that of Thomas Watson, an older and much more elegant
sonneteer."

Though Shakespeare's sonnets are unequal, taken together

they represent the finest collection in the language. The identity of the " fair youth " who inspired one series and of the " dark lady " to whom the rest were written will never be known. There may have been a number of fair youths and several dark women. The identities are unimportant. What is important is the spiritual biography emerging from the poems. There is revealed in them—though one must juggle with the order, for they are not all arranged chronologically—a voyage of the soul, the soul of a man possessed of a power of intellect and a depth of passion that were afterwards to express themselves in such tragedies as Lear and Othello.

The sonnets are no elegant compositions of a young gallant or an old rhymster ; they really are " passions," as an affected contemporary called the affected productions of Thomas Watson ; passions at grips with an intellect which will accept them only when they are directed towards ideal beauty. The same conflict brought to birth the superb imagery of *Venus and Adonis*, a poem that for vigour of language and vividness of pictorial representation has few equals. There is such close-packed, such rich imagery in it that the imagination labours to apprehend the rapid sequence. The combat between intellect and passion never ceases in these poems—*The Passionate Pilgrim* might well have served as title to them all. Not until Shakespeare wrote his plays, perhaps, did the restless contention cease ; when he became identified completely with his creation.

CONFLICT BETWEEN PAGAN AND SPIRITUAL BEAUTY

THE note of passion, comparatively rare in English poetry, is heard also in John Donne, Shakespeare's junior by nine years. Donne's conflict was essentially the same as Shakespeare's ; it was a conflict between a pagan insistence of the senses to realise physical beauty and an equally strong aspiration of the spirit beyond such a fulfilment, towards ideal beauty. Donne sought the resolution of his problem in the Church. The young courtier, who had brought in his first poems such a depth of intellect to bear upon the senses' riot, became in middle age Dean of Saint Paul's. Sermons and religious poems took the place of love poetry. But the struggle was never quieted.

In the twentieth century T. S. Eliot, whose poetical

development bears some affinity with that of Donne, has written of him :

> Donne, I suppose, was such another
> Who found no substitute for sense . . .

All his life Donne was striving to discover that substitute. The nearest he attained to a conception of love satisfying to both sides of his nature is expressed in his most famous poem, *The Ecstasy*. Two lovers are reclining on a bank of violets. The platonic communion of their souls is described :

> And whilst our souls negotiate there,
> We like sepulchral statues lay ;
> All day, the same our postures were,
> And we said nothing, all the day.

But the poet suggests finally that this is not enough, that unless the soul is released through the senses, it must remain languishing like a great prince in prison :

> So must pure lovers' souls descend
> To affections and to faculties,
> Which sense may reach and apprehend,
> Else a great prince in prison lies.

AN AGE RICH IN POETIC GENIUS

THE hundred years from the middle of the sixteenth century to the Restoration in 1660 represent the golden age of English poetry. The lives of Spenser, Shakespeare, Milton fall within these years. And even without their names the achievement of a host of other poets would make the period outstanding. The first fifty years—the Elizabethan heyday —was an age turned outwards towards the discovery of new land and the rediscovery of old learning. The Elizabethans had little time for introspection. Only the thought of death disturbed them. But they conceived death as no more than the blank reverse of bright life—a pagan conception. The seventeenth century brought civil, religious war to England. The Puritan conscience assailed the libertinism—as much in thought as in morals—of the age ; faith unsheathed a flaming sword ; the kingdom of the spirit declared war on materialism. But the poetic impulse was not checked by the political and religious upheaval ; it was directed into fresh channels.

The Elizabethans may have composed their best things, if not over, at least after capons and ale at the Mermaid tavern. Ben Jonson, that tun-bellied poet, according to a contemporary would go to the tavern, afterwards sweat and sleep off his surfeit, and then to work. Not so such religious poets as Vaughan, Crashaw, Traherne, and Herbert; after fasts and macerations they may have sung, after vigils and mystic abstractions, weakening the flesh and awakening the spirit.

Milton became blind, yet his imagination ranged in realms of more dazzling day than his eyes had ever known. The essence of light and the essence of music seem to merge into a single splendour in his poetry. If there is in Milton none of Chaucer's or of Shakespeare's humanity; little of the earthy element; no passion; there is perfect harmony which, in the words of Campion:

> . . . still moves delight,
> Like clear springs renew'd by flowing,
> Ever perfect, ever in them-
> Selves eternal.

His words move, jocosely or gravely, fretting as it were, a cerulean clearness with their radiance. Tennyson, a " great meterer " himself, sounds tinny in comparison with Milton.

The creator of *Paradise Lost* was not an original thinker. Though Milton is careful to preserve just proportions in his great theme, co-ordinating each part to artistic rightness, yet his tragedy of the fall of man has not the organic complete-ness of *Othello*, for instance, but an imposed one which does not emerge inevitably from the action. Milton was a classicist in that he took over generally accepted doctrine (the Puritan reformer in him represents another side of his conservatism); and in his language, purged of the redundancies of Elizabethan exuberance, shorn clean with the subject, Milton is a classicist too. Intellectually Milton does not question; he passes over the problems of predestination and free will inherent in his theme. Raphael is his spokesman—and that of classicism—when he answers Adam's question about God and the universe:

> . . . Heaven is for thee too high
> To know what passes there. Be lowly wise:
> Think only what concerns thee and thy being.

This is the very sense of Pope's decree voicing the eighteenth-century ideal:

> Know then thyself, presume not God to scan;
> The proper study of mankind is man.

Milton, therefore, in language and thought is a herald of the century to come. Yet he is no less a romantic; his Satan, expelled from the classical heaven, was later to arise, at the beginning of the nineteenth century, as the patron fiend of the romantics, the archetype of their ideal. In Shakespeare romantic and classicist are so fused that neither can be distinguished; in Milton both are clearly perceptible, the entire theme of *Paradise Lost*, in effect, resolving itself into a war between the principles of order and revolt. Milton's Satan is the real hero of *Paradise Lost*, the only human figure in the poem. Unconsciously, it may be, Milton sympathised with him in his revolt, investing him with lordly lineaments while the other fiends are mere monsters; Satan stands out advantageously, even in contrast with the heavenly choir. His refusal to serve under an authority " upheld by old repute, consent, or custom " emerges as more admirable than the acquiescence of the conforming angels, for Milton was at war within himself, and his heart and head never came to terms.

POETRY SHAPED BY ART AND REASON

O Gracious God ! how far have we
Profaned the heavenly gift of Poesy !
Made prostitute and profligate the Muse,
Debased to each obscene and impious use . .

So wrote John Dryden of the state of poetry at the restoration of King Charles the Second. "The steaming ordures " of the stage of that time have become a byword ; the poetic impulse which had flamed so splendidly during the first years of the century glowed feebly indeed. John Wilmot, Earl of Rochester, of whom the story goes that he was drunk for the greater part of his adult life—he died in his early thirties —among many merely witty, and frequently filthy, verses, wrote a few very fine poems. But the redeeming figure of the Restoration is John Dryden. He carried on the torch of poetry—but he trimmed it not a little. The " dower of lights and fires " of his predecessors became something of a drawing-room chandelier when Dryden handed it over to the Augustans (the writers of Queen Anne's reign).

Dryden was the first great arbiter of taste in English poetry. He sat in his coffee-house and laid down the law—and the law, salutary in many ways, was a classical one. Dryden brought poetry to a sober measure. He was obedient to the counsel of Milton's Raphael and thrust romantic Satan effectively behind him. He imposed French restraint on English poetic exuberance and ushered in the age of reason. Apart from his achievements as a critic, Dryden wrote the best satirical poetry that has ever been written in English— not excluding that of Pope. What Marlowe's blank verse is to Milton's, Dryden's satirical heroic verse is to that of Pope. Dryden's couplet, if it is more unruly, if the lines do not pace together so easily, has more mettle in it than Pope's ; it has more of the " bound and high curvet of Mars' manly steed."

RULES OF NEATNESS MADE FOR POETS

EIGHTEENTH-CENTURY poetry was composed according to carefully established canons of taste. It is polished, predominantly intellectual, positive, and definite. There was a fixed mould for poetry, the heroic couplet, a form which was found best suited to express certain sentiments common to and appreciated by a society to which " enthusiasm " was anathema and all vagueness, which believed in an ordered state of things built up as clear defined as the facade of a Queen Anne mansion ; a society which did not seek to know what was not plainly ascertainable by the sober processes of the intellect ; that had use for nature, human as well as inanimate, only when it was trimmed and trellised and elegantly shaped by art. And " elegant " was the term of approbation : a garden, a house, a poem, and a man were all, if approved by eighteenth-century taste, " elegant." There was no place for those who broke off at a tangent from the ambit of prescribed experience. It was an age in literature of condensation and epigram, of neatness and utility.

The eighteenth century, therefore, was not likely to produce adventurers into the depths of the soul or the high realms of the imagination. It produced as its representative literary figure Pope, a poet who has prescribed definitely for the middle region of human experience, for all that which comes within the scope of the intellectually definable. The romantics, a hundred years later, in natural revolt against the limitations of the eighteenth-century ideal and the tyranny exercised over poetry by the heroic couplet, and the Victorians after them, would have none of Pope ; he was not recognised by them among the great English poets. After the War the pendulum swung back again and the classical love of order and precision received merited respect ; eighteenth-century clarity came as a needful corrective to the fuddled obscurity of much post-war verse.

THE BENEVOLENT DESPOTISM OF POPE

POPE is as much a poet of the contingencies in the everyday life of a well-educated Englishman as Chaucer is the poet of the highways and byways of England itself, its scenes and characters. No poet except Shakespeare has given so many phrases to the language as Pope, for no other poet has given so many happy definitions to the subjects of everyday civilised conversation. No one has ever defined man himself more neatly :

> Created half to rise, and half to fall ;
> Great lord of all things, yet a prey to all ;
> Sole judge of truth, in endless error hurled :
> The glory, jest, and riddle of the world.

In his *Essay on Criticism* is to be found almost everything there is to be told about the craft of good writing ; those inevitable couplets, polished to a degree of excellence bewildering to any one who has tried to write them, not only perfectly explain, but perfectly illustrate the poetic craft :

> The sound must seem an echo to the sense.
> Soft is the strain when zephyr gently blows,
> And the smooth stream in smoother numbers flows ;
> But when loud surges lash the sounding shore,
> The hoarse, rough verse should like the torrent roar . . .

Politics, ethics, philosophy, Pope brings them all to his measure ; if much escapes him, if he has no falcon on his fist to soar beyond the reaches of the intellect, what he has caught he has dressed as no other poet has done—in England, at least. He has competed with and equalled the French where they have placed their pride ; in clarity and precision, in the neat formulæ of reason.

The wonderful instrument Pope perfected was not employed by him only for purposes of polite precept ; it was deadly in his hand as an offensive weapon against his enemies, real or imaginary. A wizened, sickly, hump-backed man, he was morbidly sensitive, forever suspecting affront. Women seem to have annoyed him considerably, judging from his characters of the sex. But poetasters, critics, and booksellers annoyed him more. He composed about these persons, it is thought on the suggestion of Swift, a burlesque epic poem, *The Dunciad*.

WISTFUL CHARM AND GENIAL WIT

THE representative figures of eighteenth-century poetry all employed the heroic couplet in their more ambitious poems. After Pope, Goldsmith used the form in his two long poems, *The Traveller* and *The Deserted Village*, infusing it with a certain wistful charm and genial wit unknown to his predecessor. Johnson, elaborating it to the ultimate point of artificiality, swelling it out to dropsical fullness with his pontifical antitheses, composed in the couplet medium his *London* and *The Vanity of Human Wishes*. Yet throughout the vogue of this classical poetry, undertones are detected of another kind. The Countess of Winchelsea wrote in the full rigour of the Augustan age these lines :

> In the Muses' paths I stray ;
> Among their groves and by their sacred springs
> My hand delights to trace unusual things,
> And deviates from the known and common way :
>   Nor will in fading silks compose
>   Faintly the inimitable rose,
> Fill up an ill-drawn bird, or paint on glass
> The Sovereign's blurred and undistinguished face,
> The threatening angel, and the speaking ass.

Later in the century a distinct, though comparatively genteel, breakaway towards Nature occurred. The Scottish poet, Thomson, wrote his *Seasons* in blank verse ; Collins composed his beautiful *Ode to Evening*. At the same time this slight restlessness within the limitations of the century's ideal was evidenced by an awakened interest in the past. Bishop Percy's *Reliques of Ancient English Poetry* were published. A gothic gloom overmantled the verse of some poets ; spleen—that gentlemanly eighteenth-century affliction—began to exhibit a tendency towards the romantic symptom, melancholy. Chatterton, after he had perpetrated his literary fraud, pretending to have discovered the poems of a fifteenth-century English monk, committed suicide in an attic ; Gray frequented churchyards and wrote his *Elegy*. Heresy was about, stalking at large—alone. The rise of the individual was imminent.

A POET WHO PRESUMED TO SCAN THE HEAVENS

" KNOW then thyself, presume not God to scan." One poet in the eighteenth century did so presume. To a certain extent the life of William Blake bears out Pope's injunction. Dazzled by his scrutiny of splendour beyond the world, Blake eventually lost the power to communicate his vision ; though he still wrote poetry, his *Prophetic Books*, which he averred were comparable to Milton, must forever be sealed books to the commonalty. Yet Pope's neat precept could not serve for such a poet as Blake. If, in his *Prophetic Books*, he fell irretrievably deep into a vague world of symbols, he had darted back before that to communicate such radiant truth that only after the World War helped clear away the clutter and sediment of ages of false feeling and murky thinking did the full meaning of his cry begin to penetrate the minds of Englishmen. Yet so direct is Blake's vision, rending so cleanly through conventional conceptions of the world, that even now it is not always easy to follow his meaning ; his vision is so lucid that it sometimes seems obscure.

Blake is a humanist ; if he presumes to scan God, it is in man he sees Him first. He saw the potentialities for happiness in the body and in the soul of man. In contrast with his vision he saw with the more bitterness the miserable disfigurations of the ideal, noting in every face he passed "marks of weakness, marks of woe." Blake hated with as fierce a hatred as Pope had wasted on his petty critics, brutality and lechery and sneering doubt and timorousness. But he does not destroy. He affirms. Like a morning trumpet, clear and confident, his poems ring out, summoning men away from their sordid, complacent pursuits, away from the " dark, satanic mills," to fulfil their natures, to become men. However much one may appreciate conventional eighteenth-century poetry, in the refulgence of Blake's vision it fades from the mind, as when one has looked at the sun, houses and hedgerows are momentarily blotted from sight.

POETRY CLOSE TO LIFE ITSELF

CONTEMPORANEOUSLY with Blake in England, there was living across the border another humanist poet, Robert Burns. But the two men had nothing else in common. Not for Burns the mystic's vision. He had no ideal of human life, but from his own experience he knew very well what it contained. Life and poetry have seldom been so close together as they are in Burns; his poems are spontaneous comments on everyday experiences; he is melancholy, gay, satirical, tender, as the mood takes him. Wordsworth said poetry was "emotion recollected in tranquillity," and so, no doubt, it was with him. But one imagines Burns was seldom tranquil. He does not seem to have that period of gestation between experience and expression which is the privilege of more sedentary poets. In this he is like French Villon, the "sad, bad, glad, mad" poet.

Yet Burns's facility does not come from a superficial brush against life. He experienced life more intensely than most poets have done; he knew the lessons of Don Juanism—how much better than Don Juan (in Byron) himself:

> I waive the quantum of the sin,
> The hazard of concealing:
> But, O, it hardens all within
> And petrifies the feeling.

He had the rare faculty of living fully, the faculty that puts bone and muscle and blood into his poetry, that places him in the company of Chaucer and Shakespeare.

Burns found in his native dialect a perfect medium; the vivid, bright, direct, homely expressions fairly dance to his measure; they have no languid Latin graces; they are male words, brisk and hardy. They serve him equally well over a wide range; the love song, the patriotic poem, the verse tale, the *genre* picture in the Hogarth style (*The Merry Beggars*), satire. Burns excels in all kinds (leaving his standard only when he writes in "the King's English"), but that which chiefly distinguishes his poetry is its humanity salted with humour. He writes as a man of men and the places dear to men's hearts, be they meadows in the gloaming or tavern firesides at night. He has no philosophical conception of man's mystic union with Nature, nor does he abstract Nature as something apart, unworthy of the poet's notice. Burns sings of Nature as any ploughman might had he Burns's gift, as a larger room where man goes "to his work and to his labour until the evening"; as a setting to his activities, a couch for his loves and a covering for his bones at last.

THE ROMANTIC POETS

WHILE Crabbe, who has been dubbed " Pope in home-spuns," was still reaming out heroic couplets in his country vicarage, two young men were walking among the Somersetshire hills discussing the theory of poetry. One of them, a hale-looking, long-legged, rather rustic man, strode on in silence except for an occasional request that his companion should repeat his remark. The companion, a shorter, thick-set man with a very large head and a strange mixture of the intellectual and the sensualist in his features, zig-zagged his way from side to side of the path, talking continuously, now about Kant's theory of knowledge, now about the Greek dramatists, now about Shakespeare. This was Coleridge, the most brilliant man of the nineteenth century, a genius given, unfortunately for poetry, to indolence and opium, who has left only fragments to posterity : two fine poems, *Kubla Khan* and *The Ancient Mariner*, and scraps of critical writings, jottings for lectures, which were to have composed an extensive system of criticism, the most ambitious ever attempted. Yet little as that remarkable intellect in its restless zigzags from subject to subject ever directly achieved, on the productions of others it had an incalculable influence. Coleridge was the brain behind the romantic revolt against the eighteenth century ; though the romantic manifesto—the preface to the *Lyrical Ballads*, published in 1798—was written by Wordsworth, there can be no doubt that Coleridge's conversation largely inspired it.

POETRY AND EVERYDAY LANGUAGE

THE famous preface contends that poetic diction should be natural, that it should come nearer the everyday speech of the people than did that of the eighteenth century. Compared with the course which English poetry was to take from this time, the contention is mild. Nor was it in fact consistently put into practice. The diction of the best romantic poetry is as remote from common speech as the refined expression of Pope's school. Wordsworth, more by accident than design perhaps, has some examples of his theory. " I do not doubt that it may safely be affirmed," he writes in the preface, " that there neither is, nor can be, any essential difference between the language of prose and metrical composition." He afterwards produced the following—though in metrical lines : " One adequate support for the calamities of mortal life exists, one only—an assured belief that the procession of our fate, howe'er sad or disturbed, is ordered by a being of infinite benevolence and power, whose everlasting purposes embrace all accidents, converting them to good." The only feature here which is poetical is the omission of the " v " in however.

The achievement of the *Lyrical Ballads*—which, besides poems by Wordsworth, contained *The Ancient Mariner*—was best stated later by Coleridge. He said, in effect, that the volume proved both how a supernatural subject (that of Coleridge's famous ballad) cou d be made acceptable to the imagination through a natural, simple diction, and how everyday subjects, such as Wordsworth's, could, by a similar sincere treatment, be elevated to high imaginative art.

A POET OF TRANQUIL LAKES AND RUGGED HILLS

THE French poet, Baudelaire, said of Victor Hugo that he was an inspired cabbage; Matthew Arnold more reverently said of Wordsworth : " It might seem that nature not only gave him the matter for his poem, but wrote the poem for him." Wordsworth, who with the exception of Keats is the greatest poet of the nineteenth century, seemed to lack a critical faculty. He wrote steadily for sixty years, producing the purest poetry and the drabbest doggerel indifferently, showing a personal preference not infrequently for the doggerel. Much has been written of Wordsworth's philosophy, consisting in his belief in a kind of mystic identification of man with Nature, but in fact it is far less Wordsworth's philosophy than his pure poetic vision that is important. His best poetry expresses those moments, rare in life, when there comes upon the " inward eye " what may strike one as a momentary recollection of beauty which was once familiar ; or it may come upon one as the intimation of felicity beyond the ken of the everyday self, to be enjoyed hereafter perhaps. With Wordsworth the momentary contact of the essential self, the spirit—or call it what you will—was with inanimate Nature ; he felt spirit answering to spirit in those moments and all his best poetry records them :

> Hence, in a season of calm weather
> Though inland far we be,
> Our Souls have sight of that immortal sea
> Which brought us hither.

The resurrection of Nature from an inanimate to an animate state was but one of the achievements of this new romantic school. Eighteenth-century poetry had been social, urban, moving among people. Wordsworth begins a famous poem with this line : " I wander'd lonely as a cloud." This was the second tenet of the romantic creed. The romantics lauded loneliness ; because social consciousness had been uppermost so long, they were inclined to shout up the rights of the ego with the gusto of what would to-day be called an inferiority complex. They were revolutionaries to a man. But the French Revolution was a peg for their theories rather than a pivot for their verse. They were ready to champion any revolt that was about—with more poetic fervour, perhaps, than political judgment. They were in revolt, so all revolutionaries must be in the right. The romantics were out (with Milton's Satan at their head and Coleridge directing them from the base) to overset the authority " upheld by old repute, consent, or custom." They were justified in their onslaught, for the romantic revival would never have taken place had not the eighteenth-century standards outworn their use.

If Coleridge was the general directing the romantic campaign, then the dashing lieutenant with the ladies' favours, the Young Lochinvar, was Lord Byron. Byron took his training with the enemy ; some of his first—and best—poetry derives directly from the eighteenth century. His satire, *English Bards and Scottish Reviewers*, composed in heroic couplets against the Edinburgh critics, is as good as anything he wrote, and better than most. But the bulk of his poetry brings out all that is worst in the romantic movement ; a theatrical " satanism," bemoaning a soul that has revolted and is for ever damned ; the despair ; all the clap-trap appurtenances—gloom and horror and debauch with its saintly attendant, Purity, personified in an unattainable young maiden. All this was wretched stuff and very popular in its day. Yet Byron had better poetry in him ; he has passion, and in his satires, in parts of *Don Juan* and occasionally in *Childe Harold*, it finds fine expression. But in his love poems, unlike Donne or Shakespeare, Byron could not bring the raging conflict within him to truce ; he could only present the antagonists, saint and sinner. He was either stickily sentimental or callowly cynical.

LINES THAT DO NOT PASS THE TEST

SHELLEY is a poet who has aroused a great deal of contro-versy. Those critics who advocate sobriety and precision, in short, restraint, in poetry have censored him severely. Perhaps the classical attitude towards romantic poetry can be illustrated best by analysing four lines of Shelley from the standards of this classical school. If the reader does not agree, as probably he will not, then let him explain why.

> The One remains, the many fade and pass ;
> Heaven's lamp for ever shines, earth's shadows flee ;
> Life like a dome of many coloured glass
> Stains the white radiance of eternity.

These lines were composed by Shelley. They have been highly praised, and some have gone so far as to describe them as the finest lines in English poetry. People who go in for picking out best lines cannot be competent to judge poetry. Poetry, when it has been distinguished from verse, is either good or bad. If it is good—that is to say, if it is real poetry—then there is no standard by which one poem in the first class can be established as superior to another in the same class. The above lines, however, do not fall within this order of poetry. They do not pass the test.

What is bad poetry ? It is not, as has already been explained, verse, which is deliberate metrical composition. Bad poetry may well be poured out—as the song of Shelley's own skylark—" in profuse strains of unpremeditated art." Yet it is bad because, though it may sound fine on a first reading, stirring deep thoughts and bringing into existence images vaguely splendid, it is not exact ; its metaphors slop loose over inaccurate observations ; it is fabricated almost entirely from the fancy. Though Shakespeare's language is, perhaps, more richly packed with metaphor than that of any other English poet, the images are made up of minute, exact observation. His passages teem with everyday things. And this is why they satisfy the imagination, because there is a substructure of concrete, precise facts.

Let us look into the last two lines of this passage in Shelley which has been so much praised. What do they mean ? For poetry, if it is to be good, must reveal more meaning, more truth at subsequent readings than it does at first. It must not evaporate on intensive scrutiny. This passage, which starts as a simile and ends as a metaphor, seeks to present to the imagination life in relation to eternity. The simile chosen for life is a " dome of many coloured glass " —well, such a structure is conceivable—though, instead of staining any radiance, it would probably be much stained itself before long by the weather. Now for the metaphor— " the white radiance of eternity." If the whole image is to satisfy the imagination, if it is to be precise and meaningful, there must be a definite, observable resemblance connecting the " white radiance " against which the " many coloured dome " is set with some effect of the sun. For only through such a resemblance can the mind grasp the image at all. But the sun makes no such effect in the sky ; there is no diffusion of white radiance. And even if there were, the metaphor would have been badly chosen, for the sun is not a symbol for eternity, but, on the contrary, used often as a symbol for time. Shelley, instead of giving to " airy nothing a local habitation and a name," has brought, in this instance, local habitations, dubiously existent to begin with, to airy nothing-ness. He has not crystallised what was abstract and general in a particular, vivid instance.

Unfortunately Shelley is frequently guilty of such inaccuracy, a failing common among the romantics, who were inclined to leave the earth altogether and scorn the poet's first lesson —the study of Man and the material world he lives in. Yet it would be misleading to say Shelley did not write any fine poetry. His odes, particularly the *Ode to a Skylark* and the *Ode to the West Wind*, and his best lyrics will always be read with delight, especially by adolescents.

POETS WHO FORSOOK THE EARTH

THE tendency of the romantics was to leap over everyday life, the facts one meets with first of all, the human things. They incline to believe that, being poets, they are angels— or, at least, that they need not bother about anything below a thousand feet. They aspire to be larks that do not rise from the ground but are for ever " at Heaven's gate." Keats is an exception. He was familiar with the earth and loved it, and he loved human nature even more : " Scenery is fine," he wrote, " but human nature is finer." Keats started properly ; he was first and foremost a man. If he sang of " the viewless wings of poesy," it was not before he had acknowledged " Flora and the country green, dance and

Provençal song and sunburnt mirth." Keats took his departure from the senses ; he was a pagan, a lover of good
cheer, and of all the beauty which sensual apprehension can
bring to the mind. Not that he stopped at this ; he knew the
ecstasy of the farthest flights of the imagination. Keats is
in the tradition of Chaucer, Spenser, Shakespeare, Milton ;
he makes a natural fifth to them. It is significant that one
can read Keats without thinking of the romantics, as an
individual, apart from any movement. He is a poet, not a
Don Juan or a revolutionary spirit. As with Spenser, Keats's
aim was always beauty. No one shall deny that he splendidly
achieved it.

WHAT WAS WRONG WITH VICTORIAN POETS ?

WHAT was the matter with the Victorians ? The matter
was that they were inflated. Material prosperity bloated
them out to a florid complacency. The stuffing was cant.
Moralising, poetical bombast, sentimentality—they crammed
all this into their poetry. At the time, the bad was taken
with the good—frequently it was taken for the good. The
fraud has been looked into now, thoroughly, by Lytton
Strachey, and his followers. Yet, when the pretensions have
been taken from the Victorians, when the awesome sanctity
has left those bearded, solemn figures, sitting in their gloomy
studies, milling out their daily quota of verses, it would be
foolish to deny the remaining greatness. In the words of
one of them :

> Though much is taken, much abides ; and tho'
> We are not now the strength that in old days
> Moved earth and heaven : that which we are, we are . . .

The fine frenzy of the romantics sobered after the pre-
mature deaths of Byron, Keats, and Shelley and after Wordsworth had left the ranks to become a prosy poet laureate.
The Victorians were far too satisfied with the world in which
they lived to be revolutionaries ; they were placid reformers
rather. The French Revolution had proved a flash in the
pan, British industry was booming after the depression
following the Napoleonic wars ; the poet could sit back and
write about chivalric love ; he could search for a subject
which promised to furnish spectacular poetic treatment.

Thus a tendency set in to write about " some nebulous lost love " or to go in for " sentimental transcriptions of foreign or domestic tales." The poetic impulse was still vigorous, but poetry tended to spread itself out over " poetical " subjects which by virtue of their romantic nature did duty when inspiration failed—as it could not help but do with poets who produced verse in such quantities.

Both Tennyson and Browning in their different ways enlarged the stream of English poetry, the former widening it, introducing many formal refinements, the latter deepening it. Browning's province was psychological drama. Whereas Chaucer wrote of human life as expressed exteriorly in action, Browning records the tracings upon the soul. Novelists by his time had got to work in earnest, and though there was as yet no psycho-analysis, they had extended man's awareness of himself considerably ; so it came about that the novel which had developed out of poetic narrative reacted on poetry. The play was also a prime influence. Many of Browning's lyrics—not to mention his longer poems—might be poetic abstracts of novels, or soliloquies of actors and actresses. After the insistent personal note in the poetry of the romantics this dramatic type of poetry, in which the poet enters into the minds of a variety of characters, comes as a distinct relief.

It is seldom that any one appreciates both Tennyson and Browning at the same period of his development. Tennyson naturally comes first with his Lydian airs and romantic themes. For mastery over his medium, for ease and grace of execution in all types and forms of verse, Tennyson is second only to Milton. His lines flow with exquisite harmony in all measures ; he expresses more by mere sound than any other poet has been able to convey in this manner. Tennyson was the more easily able to achieve this as his meaning is rarely deep. He was no profound thinker, like Donne or Browning ; he never attained the keen, bright purity of the very finest lyrical poetry, that of Shakespeare and Blake and the religious poets of the seventeenth century. Tennyson has not the gift of ecstatic vision ; instead he has a sweetness which sometimes cloys rather. His narrative poems, though they contain noble passages, suffer through the unreality of his characters, if so they may be called ; and the themes are too remote. Tennyson in the choice of his subjects seemed to believe that distance lends enchantment to the view. But after some decades have removed his scenes still farther, they tend to melt in a mist of mere phrases ; the voices fade to the " murmur of innumerable bees."

THE SUBTLETY AND DRAMA OF MEREDITH

MEREDITH wrote in the genre of Browning. His sonnet sequence, *Modern Love*, is in fact an analytical novel in verse, its chapters condensed to separate sonnets. The sequence is jointed very subtly together, and one cannot, as in most sequences, take the parts separately. In this, Meredith's sequence differs from that of Rossetti, whose *House of Life* is a sonnet collection structurally more akin to Shakespeare's sequence ; it is a spiritual autobiography extending over a certain period of life. Meredith's sequence is dramatic ; Rossetti's is lyrical. Meredith's poetry is close-knit and sinewy with thought, its music only emerges fully when the sense has been grasped ; Rossetti's is predominantly musical.

Meredith, like Browning, is a poet for mature years. He is a poet who grew up into a man—a fact worth remarking, for it is surprising how many poets have either never reached the adult stage or, having attained it, have ceased writing poetry. There is an island of Never Never Boys in poetry. Swinburne was one of them. His pan pipes were Peter Pan pipes, and that pagan side of him represented in *Poems and Ballads* (first series) represents the bookish boy turned truant. But the Victorian verities, those grave schoolmasters, were constantly there for him, unquestioned masters ; while lilting out his most daring lines he has always a glance of pleasurable anxiety towards them. The part of Swinburne's work which is " naughty " is all part of the fifth form rebellion that culminated in the 'nineties with Oscar Wilde and Aubrey Beardsley. Swinburne grew up to be a sixth form boy, a very learned scholar with an extensive knowledge of literatures in many tongues. He wrote ballades, ballads, rondeaus ; he reintroduced classical and mediæval themes into poetry and made some exquisite translations. His chief failing is indulgence in sound effects for their own sake.

EXPERIMENTS OF A POET AND PRIEST

AS Blake in the eighteenth century struck a note which startles us to-day with its modernity, so in the late Victorian period, when the great poets of that time were serenely pursuing their allotted courses, one man, a Roman Catholic priest, was experimenting, in manuscript obscurity, with a new poetic expression altogether ; he was forty years ahead of his age. Gerard Manley Hopkins was contemporary at Oxford with Robert Bridges, but when Bridges—who was far from being a " popular " poet—was elevated in the course of time to the poet laureateship, Hopkins, who had then been dead some twenty years, was unknown as a poet to all but a few friends ; no volume of his poems had been published. Post-war poets made all kinds of experiments, trying to evolve some new expression, determined at all costs to break with the Victorian tradition. Hopkins forty years before them had already done it. Since his poems were published posthumously in 1927 his renown has steadily increased.

His experiments with metre have been written about and sometimes imitated. In fact, he did not experiment with metre to such an extent as Robert Bridges did. Hopkins's rhythmic peculiarities form but a small part of his contribution to poetry. No traditions of poetic diction awed him. He needed kaleidoscopic effects ; he shook, shifted, and sifted the vocabulary until he got them. He needed a speed, a tumbling rush of bright colours, a sensuous richness exceeding anything in Spenser or Keats. The effect of his poetry is something like that of an impressionist picture painted in dabs of colour. Hopkins sees directly with the eye, before the intellect has brought sensuous perceptions to perspective. His poems—save for a few early ones in another manner— are short, intense, vivid. He can trace the flight of a bird and record the notes of its song as no poet has ever been able ; he can catch the multiple movements and colours in Nature ; he is the poet of " pied beauty."

POETS WHO CHALLENGED THE GODS OF THEIR AGE

WHILE Wordsworth was still living, a very old man in his Grasmere cottage, a boy called Thomas Hardy in a Dorset cottage may well have been reading the *Lyrical Ballads*, that volume which had struck out for simplicity in poetry. In the half-century intervening great changes had come over English poetry : it had freed itself from the narrow bounds of the heroic couplet ; it had left elegant gardens to wander at large among natural scenery, acquiring a closer fellowship with Nature than it had ever known ; it had had its Ulysses period—" always roaming with a hungry heart " in foreign lands and former times ; then it had, as it were, settled down, with honours thick upon it, rich, rather florid, showing an inclination towards corpulence; it repeatedly affirmed that God was in His heaven and all was well with the world, but at considerably more length and more sententiously than the little lyric by Browning.

Though Hardy was a Victorian—the last of the great Victorians—he doubted their gods. Hardy's conception of the world as a scene of mutually destructive human destinies working always towards each other's rencounter and annihilation; his idea of God as *metteur en scène* of the grisly show, Himself at a loss for the ultimate reason of it all, is better known from his novels than his poetry. His poetry is tinged with the same pessimism, however. His dramatic lyrics seem to express an intuition of the ironic and tragic in life which he elaborated in his novels. Sometimes he writes of Nature; his fields and hills and the beasts that inhabit them are generally sad counsellors. There is always the thought, implied or stated, of successive generations of men passing away unheeded before the indifferent spectators of man's brief sojourn: hills, trees, fields.

Yet despite his pessimism, there is in Hardy's poems a virility, an affirmation of life, though it be so " beset round with dismal stories ; " the gods may mock, yet Hardy can write such lines as these :

> Let it befall that one shall call
> " Soul, I have need of thee ! "
> What then ? Joy-jaunts, impassioned flings,
>   Love and its ecstasy,
> Will always have been great things,
>   Great things to me !

And it was left to Hardy to write the one fine poem upon the outbreak of war in 1914 (*Men Who March Away*).

Hardy's poems are simply, almost roughly, constructed. Perhaps because he too was born among peasants, his poetry has a Wordsworthian simplicity about it. The remote, romantic themes and the learned, polished metres are not for him. His subjects are the Wessex folk and the Wessex fields and hills. Hardy called poetry home from regions where it had strayed too long, where it was inclined to become unreal and academic. He confined his poetry to moments of vision, to the human heart and the English scene.

This work of simplifying poetry was continued by A. E.

6

Housman whose small volume of lyrics, *The Shropshire Lad*, profoundly influenced the generation of poets who wrote from the turn into the twentieth century until the World War. Housman, too, localised his poetry, confining it to one county. His poetry is easy, limpid, flawless ; it has a classical finality. His themes are the ageless ones : friendship, love, death. Tragedy is for ever darkening his vision. Time with its ironic transpositions is always upon the tracks of his Lad ; there is a skeleton lurking somewhere at all his wakes.

POETRY UNDER PROSPERITY'S INFLUENCE

THE phrase " Georgian Poetry " was first employed to describe an anthology of contemporary poetry which appeared in 1911. The Georgians are those poets who, about the time of the accession of George the Fifth, were recognised by public taste as distinguished moderns. Therefore, although Robert Bridges was middle-aged at the time of Queen Victoria's death, and Kipling was writing his poetry when Rupert Brooke was still in the cradle, all these may be termed Georgians. On the other hand, Hopkins, a chronological contemporary of Bridges to the year, may not so be termed, for had one of his poems been included in that 1911 anthology, there would have been a public outcry against its compilers. Nor would T. S. Eliot be referred to as a Georgian, although he was born the year after Brooke. The Georgians are defined by the taste which approved them in a certain year.

So-called Georgian poetry constitutes a kind of Indian summer after the serene Victorian period. The Georgian era when all has been said will probably stand out as a very fine one, distinguished primarily for its lyrical quality. Yet though it produced many notes, these have not the " first fine careless rapture " of Elizabethan lyrics ; nor have they the deep, clear tone of seventeenth-century religious poetry. The Georgians have not the ardour of the romantics, nor the staying power of the Victorians. They have a wide range, facility, and sweetness, yet they lack dynamic force ; they lack depth. They are like sons of famous fathers, subdued by paternal renown. They are not so much struggling to find a new expression as making variations upon the old. The Georgians are the good children of the preceding generation, those who did not rebel. Those who did rebel were unfortunate enough to lose the initiative of assault in the general annihilation effected by the World War. It achieved their purpose of iconoclasm and left them virtually mute.

A POET OF THE EMPIRE

GOD was still in his heaven for the Georgians, and times were prosperous for Great Britain ; none was more aware of this, nor expressed it better than Kipling. He became the poet of Empire, a good theme but one beset with all the dangers of jingoism. His well-known *Recessional* hymn, even while it condemns, assumes a barbarian creed :

> God of our fathers, known of old,
> Lord of our far-flung battle-line . . .

It takes it for granted that British armies are the Almighty's storm troops. Kipling is better in the fanciful, half-playful mood. Another Georgian poet who is known chiefly for his patriotic verses, but who writes more genuine poetry when he leaves the subject of service to an Empire ideal, is Sir Henry Newbolt, who has composed some first-class lyrics. Patriotic verse of the type written by Kipling and Newbolt has a tendency to lose its inspiring quality in the ears of another generation and acquire an ironic note.

A number of young English poets—brought up, no doubt, to the notes of Henley's anthology, *Lyra Heroica*—were either killed during the World War or died while it was going on. Rupert Brooke possessed facility and a rich store of imagery gleaned from the Elizabethan dramatists. He was brilliant, but his brilliance was that of public sentiment reflected by a gifted literary mind rather than the clear radiance of poetic vision.

James Elroy Flecker was a more original poet. Though his poems are usually romantic—*The Golden Journey to Samarkand*, the prologue to his Eastern play, *Hassan*, might serve as a general title to them all—he is less oracular than Tennyson, less copious and more self-critical.

Edward Thomas was killed at the front in 1917. He is a poet of the English countryside and his later lyrics are among the best in the language. There is nothing finer of its kind than his poem *The Trumpet*.

The two poets killed in the War who perhaps showed the greatest promise of later development—for both were very young—are Wilfred Owen and Charles Hamilton Sorley.

The former's War poems, disillusioned and tragic with an undertone of half-strangled tenderness, are the best records of the poetic sensibility confronted with the horror of modern warfare. Sorley was only twenty when he was killed. He died before the inevitable blight of disillusion had affected his poetry. He had written poems of the Wiltshire downs showing a promise which, but for his early death, must have brought him among the first poets of his generation.

THE VARIETY OF THE GEORGIANS

IF no great figure comparable to Browning or Tennyson towered above his contemporaries during the Georgian period, poetry of a high standard of excellence was composed in all types. Georgian lyrics, if they are not often profound, show as wide a variety as those of any previous period. Katharine Tynan and W. H. Davies wrote as artlessly, as spontaneously, as Robert Herrick ; James Joyce produced his exquisitely wrought songs in the early Elizabethan manner—*Chamber Music*, as he aptly called them ; G. K. Chesterton sang out lustily of cakes and ale ; Walter de la Mare captured a haunting, other-worldly note ; Ralph Hodgson produced one or two delicate, sustained pieces, among them *The Bull* and *The Song of Honour* ; and a great many more poets wrote equally fine lyrics.

Narrative poetry is best represented by Masefield. He reverted from the psychological kind introduced by Browning to the simple tale ; his *Reynard the Fox* (which should be compared to the episode of Wat the Hare in Shakespeare's *Venus and Adonis*) is as good narrative as is to be found anywhere in English poetry. Robert Bridges' *Testament of Beauty* is a representative Georgian philosophical poem. The best satirical poetry of the era was written by Chesterton and by Lord Alfred Douglas.

W. B. Yeats is the most notable poet of the Georgian period. Yet he is not properly a Georgian at all—any more than he is an Englishman. His sources are remote from the English stream, he is a Celtic poet reaching for his subjects into the realms of mysticism, among the systems of Plotinus and the neo-platonists, into ancient Celtic myth and legend. The World War passed him by, rapt in remote contemplation. Some of his best poetry was written after the War. He takes little or nothing from contemporary events. He stands alone, an indubitably great poet—and one, incidentally, who

"Reynard the Fox," hero of Masefield's fine narrative poem.

has suffered more than any other from anthologists ; two or three early poems of his, quite unrepresentative of his later development, recurring in verse collections time after time.

POETRY STILLED BY THE HORROR OF WAR

MANY young poets went singing into the World War ; none came singing out of it. In the days of the romantic revival Byron had seen a little service in the cause of Greek liberty ; he has described scenes of slaughter with gay cynicism in *Don Juan*. Many of the Elizabethan and Caroline lyricists had fought at home or abroad. Henry Howard, Earl of Surrey, was a soldier ; so was Sir John Suckling. All poets who were courtiers were, *ipso facto*, fighting men, obliged to draw in defence of their sovereign when called on. So it would not be altogether true to say that the poetic sensibility was first brought face to face with the reality of war in 1914. It would be true to say, though, that it was brought face to face with something it had not encountered before—a white heat of horror that laid it waste and shrivelled it up completely. Rupert Brooke and others sang out bravely during the first days ; then, abruptly, the heroic note was stilled—at least, among the front-line fighters. The next phase of War poetry registered disillusion and horror and rage against generals at the base (Siegfried Sassoon's poetry notably), and then silence. When the monster of modern war had ravaged far enough, when it had destroyed not only beliefs concerning the causes and aims of the War, but had withered away all a man's belief in himself, had shattered his own values as well as those he had once supposed he was fighting for—then poetry itself died. Many of the Georgian poets went on writing during and after the War. But to those who had been in the fighting, such verses seemed to be intoned in a mausoleum. In the spiritual desolation effected by the War there could be no living response to the old notes.

A POEM THAT WAS MISUNDERSTOOD

FROM the poets composing during the first post-war years one name stands out, that of T. S. Eliot, American by birth and English by adoption. The appearance of *The Waste Land* in 1922 marks as important a point in English poetry as did the publication of Wordsworth's *Lyrical Ballads* in 1798. Both volumes profoundly influenced the course of poetry. For a long while critics and readers failed to find anything in *The Waste Land* but a mass of erudite allusion, including a quantity of parodies, it seemed, of well-known and obscure passages in the literatures of various countries.

Parlour games were invented among the literary-minded where the fun consisted in spotting the reference. Lost among the learned details of the poem, people never thought to read it as a whole. Nobody can reasonably be expected to understand all the points in *The Waste Land*; few have the leisure to read extensively enough to comprehend even the majority of them, though any one who is interested should undertake the preliminary course in " key " books suggested by the author in a note at the end of the poem. But, as Hazlitt wrote of the maze of allegory and allusion in Spenser's *Faërie Queene*, if one lets these things be, they will not bite one. If, without worrying with all the obscurities, one reads the poem through, preferably aloud, there should emerge a response something akin to gratitude.

The time through which the War generation passed is there expressed. It has been looked upon boldly; it has found complete poetic expression : the waste land in that generation's spirit, the mockery, the irony, the desolation. To be able to apprehend all this—the triviality, the sordidness, and frustration set against such a vast background of mankind's spiritual aspirations—myths, religions, literatures —is to be in a measure soothed. Much post-War unrest came from not daring to acknowledge it all. Eliot did dare, and though after achieving this analysis of ruin he entered a period of religious synthesis and the satirical vein left his poetry, his chief importance is as a poet of transition, of a period of bewilderment perhaps unparalleled in any age.

THE AFTERMATH OF WAR

WHEN the spiritual vortex caused by the World War had quieted down, when *The Waste Land* had appeared, two tendencies began to emerge in English poetry : one, represented by T. S. Eliot himself, towards a new classicism, the other towards a new romanticism. D. H. Lawrence, more through his prose than his poetry, is the chief influence of the latter movement. The new romantics are in revolt both against the " tawdry cheapness " of an industrialised, standardised west and against arid intellectualism in poetry. They are for feeling and for the body as against a mind that is in danger of losing its body, propelled continuously about the metropolis on wheels. As the romantics at the beginning of the nineteenth century looked towards the French Revolution, the post-war romantics look towards Soviet Russia. Yet their difficulty consists in this, that they cannot reconcile their revolt against an industrialised, mechanised west with their faith in a new régime which is nothing if not completely mechanised, whose success rests upon this. One cannot be both a pagan and a robot.

Poetical campaigns carry many supernumeraries along with them. The best poets frequently belong to no school. There are one or two individual poets writing to-day who may be remembered long after the representatives of the -ists and -isms, who war with each other in the monthly and quarterly periodicals.

PATHS THROUGH THE GARDENS OF POETRY : SOME GOOD ANTHOLOGIES

"POETRY," wrote Coleridge, "is the blossom and the fragrancy of all human knowledge, human thoughts, human passions, emotions, language." Anthologies of poetry collect the blossoms and bring them within the reach of everybody. The beginner should procure at least two anthologies : *The Oxford Book of English Verse* or *The Albatross Book of Living Verse*, and an anthology of modern verse, then proceed according to his or her tastes. For example, if you are attracted by stirring deeds and heroic subjects, begin with Tennyson's *The Revenge*, or Macaulay's *Lays of Ancient Rome* ; then go on to an early ballad, *Sir Patrick Spence*, and compare the condensed, episodic treatment of the early poem with the more elaborate forms of the nineteenth-century ones.

Those who are interested in forms of poetry should take, for instance, the heroic couplet and see how little it deserves the stricture of being a limited form by reading successively an extract from Keats's *Endymion*, Chaucer's *Prologue to the Canterbury Tales*, and Dryden's *Absalom and Achitophel*. A good way to approach the lyric would be to begin with W. H. Davies (any poem in the Albatross collection), then read Shelley's *Ode to a Skylark* (noting how much more charged this is with philosophic thought), and then go on to compare a seventeenth-century religious lyric such as Henry

Vaughan's *The Revival* with an Elizabethan lyric such as George Peele's *Harvester's Song*. Observe how carefree the one is, what grave ecstasy informs the other.

Apart from the anthologies mentioned, other very good ones are Walter de la Mare's *Come Hither* (charmingly annotated), Palgrave's *Golden Treasury*, and Alice Meynell's *School of Poetry*. When enough poetry has been read for an interest in the characters and circumstances of the poets to have been acquired the reader may turn to Izaak Walton's *Lives of Donne and Herbert*, Samuel Johnson's *Lives of the Poets* (both in the World's Classics Series), and De Quincey's *Recollections of the Lake Poets*. A succinct account of English prosody is given in H. W. Fowler's *Modern English Usage* (Clarendon Press). Other useful books are Humbert Wolfe's *Signpost to Poetry* (Cassell), and *The Nature of English Poetry*, by L. S. Harris (Dent).

ENGLISH DRAMA : LIVING EXPRESSION OF ITS AGE

by BARBARA NIXON

THE play, unlike the novel, is the most rigid of literary forms, with the exception perhaps of the sonnet. In a novel the author has an almost free hand. He can tell his story quite objectively, he can make himself the hero, he can translate his characters' most secret thoughts. He can make his novel a hundred, or five hundred, pages in length, and his story can last twenty-four years or as many hours. But the dramatist has no such easy task. He has to present a story within certain dimensions : he cannot avail himself of the almost unlimited fields of the novel and of the film. Practical considerations play an important part. In the first place, because it is presenting rather than relating a fact, a play must be confined to a certain length, for the reason that no audience can sit still for more than a few hours. In the second place, the characters have to speak for themselves, their motives and thoughts have to be made clear by their actions. And now, since the school of naturalism has won the day, they are not even allowed the simple, though sometimes ridiculous device of the soliloquy, by which, in talking to himself, a character tells the audience facts necessary for the development of the plot. Even the place of action is limited by the inability of the stage-hands to change more than a certain number of scenes in a given time, and by the more crude considerations of cost.

WHAT IS A PLAY ?

A PLAY is fundamentally an actual representation ; it is the nearest approach to a reproduction of life, as we see the characters move, and hear them speak. But dialogue alone will not make a play, although many would-be dramatists suppose that it will. A play need not be packed with events and often fabulous happenings, as were the Horror Tragedies and Victorian Melodramas, but the dialogue must always bear a relation to action. In England, Bernard Shaw has perfected the play of conversation and ideas. The discussion in the last act of *On the Rocks* continues for over half an hour, but the dramatic force of the scene lies in the fact that as a result of the discussion the Prime Minister's Cabinet will stand or fall ; and it is this which keeps our interest more alive than if we were listening to a lecture on the state.

A play depends mainly on its action and on its characters, and more especially on the balance between the two. The " Horror " tragedians of the seventeenth century filled their plays with so much action that there was no room left for the characters. To-day there is a tendency to spend so much attention on the characters that the action disappears. In domestic drama and the old humanistic tragedies, the importance of good and " round " characterisation is very great if our sympathies are to be moved. But an excellent play may have a problem instead of an eventful plot, and types or symbolic characters instead of personalities. An essential of any play is conciseness of idea and conciseness of construction. Extraneous detail which is necessary to give the impression of real life must be strictly controlled, and subtly connected with the main issue.

HOW TO JUDGE A PLAY

JUDGMENT, whether it be of plays, novels, architecture, or murder trials, is necessarily to a very large extent a personal and subjective matter, and, therefore, cannot be a hundred per cent. reliable. That jury is fortunate which is faced with passing judgment on a man " caught in the act " ; usually it has to consider how the weight of circumstantial evidence is balanced *pro et contra*. In the same way, with art there are no absolute rules of judgment, and those rules that there are, are not infallible. Neither can judgment be based on predilection ; " I like a play, therefore it is good," is a supremely individualistic attitude to an existent material fact, ignoring the importance of historical significance. Many parts of Shakespeare's plays would be condemned to-day by some occupants of the stalls, if they did not know who the author was.

It becomes much easier to assess the value of a play after a lapse of years, partly because there is the verdict of other critics to help one, and partly owing to the perspective given by time. Just as one cannot possibly tell whether the architecture of a house is good or bad when one is ringing the door bell, so it is difficult to estimate the worth of contemporary art. The Victorians liked their pseudo-Gothic, over-decorated monstrosities, but most people to-day are convinced that they were not only a lapse of taste, but an error of judgment. Mere fashion has relatively little ultimate influence in art ; it should never be more than a means to an end, a provocation rather than a satisfaction.

It is easier to judge classical than romantic drama, for the style demands a conformity to certain rules of time, place, and action, which will be dealt with in more detail later. But even when these are subscribed to, only half the battle is gained. There is still the content to be considered : the passions raised must be of the grand order, the conflict must be vital, and above all, there must be a philosophy. The bulk of English drama, however, is in the romantic tradition, and content is predominant over form. It is Shakespeare's philosophy of human nature, not his technical construction, which makes his plays masterpieces.

Judgment of a play, therefore, is as difficult a matter as judgment of the whole field of art. Rules may help to a certain extent, but they are not invariable. The rules of unity of time and place which played a great part in traditional drama are, for instance, unnecessary with the expressionistic method. The problem of judging modern plays is the most difficult. One may enjoy a comedy for two and a half hours immensely, and in less than a day it has become a completely unimportant part of one's experience. Moreover, in England to-day the value of drama is hidden under the curse of entertainment, and what may be good entertainment has not necessarily anything to do with good art. The commercialisation of the theatre—not to be confused with its popularisation, which unfortunately does not exist in this country to-day—has almost ruined the drama as a serious art form. The other arts, being more individualist by nature, have not suffered to such an extent. Epstein can continue to express himself regardless of the disapproval of the majority. T. S. Eliot can still write for a cultural coterie, and ignore the popular market. But a play needs the co-operation of many people, and is, therefore, so expensive to produce that it has become as much a business concern as the advertising of domestic commodities.

Plays are now written for the few who have sufficient money to go to them, and, therefore, deal with subjects which amuse *them*, but which are not necessarily important to the mass of the population, or to the history of art. English plays to-day are often well constructed ; they less often, but still at times, show dramatic situations ; occasionally they are moving ; in London, at least, they are nearly always well performed ; but they show a marked deficiency when compared with accepted great works both of this country and abroad. Comparison is one of the surest foundations of informed criticism.

GUIDE-POSTS TO DRAMA SET BY TRADITION

THE Greek authorities ruled that the place of action must be consistent with reality ; that the action of the story must last the time taken by the actual presentation ; that only three hours of the hero's life, and naturally, therefore, the most important three hours, should be shown. They regarded it as inadmissible to change the scene by more than twenty or thirty yards. A scene in a temple or house could be followed by one just outside that temple or house, but the action was not allowed to go much farther afield. The Greeks maintained in their plays a strict intellectual naturalism of construction. But their solution and climax were generally contrived by the appearance of a god or goddess who, with divine autocracy, disentangled the coils of the plot. This *deus ex machina*, however, is not comparable to the abrupt devices used in the conclusions of modern farce. In early Greece it was not even illogical. Greek religion depended on the active participation of the gods in the affairs of mortals. Doctrines of freewill had not yet been evolved, nor was there any conception of the more abstract Deity of Christian faiths.

The Elizabethans ignored the tradition of unity of place. They used no scenery, and, therefore, a bare stage which was now meant to be England, could equally well be Persia in twenty minutes' time. As long as the author can handle his plot with sureness and dexterity there is no good reason why this should not be so. Marlowe's *Tamburlaine* has a large number of scenes, and hardly any of them take place in the same country. But the figure of Tamburlaine is so powerfully drawn it outweighs any impression of confusion. Many a modern play which is dutifully restricted to one set, falls to pieces because the characters are too insipid to sustain our interest for more than thirty minutes.

The Augustan Age insisted on the classical unities, just as they modelled all their literary forms on Greek lines.

The convention has persisted up to the present day more for economic than artistic reasons. With the realistically built scenery of the late nineteenth and early twentieth centuries, it was imprudent, for reasons of expense, to construct more than three sets. In the case of the colossal musical shows to-day, this argument naturally does not hold, as they depend for their effect on their two-thousand-pound scenery as much as on their artists, and more than on their plots.

It is unwise to judge literature, and especially dramatic literature, apart from the age in which it was written. It is not merely capricious fashion which makes artists of one period scorn the work of the one preceding. Because it depends on direct representation, drama must express the spirit of the age if it is to live. The pre-Raphaelites missed greatness because they reverted to a culture which was dead and foreign to them, without even attempting to adapt it to their contemporary situation. It is history which makes art, much more than art which makes history. It is, therefore, valuable to look at drama from the point of view of its historical significance.

GLORIOUS PLAYS FROM EUROPE'S GOLDEN PAST

In early Greece drama had its beginnings in religious festivals, in the dances and songs for the feast of the god, Dionysus. In the course of years these dances became regularised, until by the time Æschylus wrote his great tragedies the tradition was strongly founded—so strongly founded, that it has become the basis of all dramatic art throughout Europe. The importance of the Greek influence has been two-fold. In the first place, it was responsible for the technical side already mentioned. It was the Greeks who invented the " rules of the game " which have been followed in varying degrees ever since. In the eighteenth century, the revival of classical tradition became so strong that plays were frequently judged good or bad, simply by their conformity to hard and fast rules, and not by their dramatic or philosophic content.

But apart from making the rules, the Greeks, and in particular Aristotle, established the moral significance of drama. All art is a representation of life. This is even more true of drama than of other literary forms. The audience is not merely shown an incident, as in a painting, or told about it, as in a poem or novel, but it actually sees it happen. The educational and propaganda value of plays is therefore enormous, though there are clearly dangers if the art falls into the hands of the irresponsible. The religious element remained in Greek plays to the last. The hero is a great man, far greater than the average mortal, but even he is helpless without the aid of the gods. The purpose of tragedy, according to Aristotle and to most great tragedy-writers, is to purge the emotions of the audience through the use of terror and awe, to show a picture of life, but life enlarged and at the same time simplified, so that its moral significance and purpose, which are lost to sight in the chaos of daily routine, become apparent. Comedy with the Greeks was entirely a matter of social and political satire—a point that should be remembered when critics attack Bernard Shaw, saying that his plays are propaganda and not art.

HOW ENGLISH CHEERFULNESS MADE ENGLISH COMEDY

IN England, drama began independently of the Greek tradition, but in the same way it has its roots in religion. In the Middle Ages the Church stood for all the culture that there was, and it was quick to see the propaganda value of dramatic presentations. It realised that actual people presenting scenes from the lives of Noah or Moses, or Joseph and Mary, had a far greater educative value than even the longest sermon from the pulpit. Plays or sketches were first presented inside the church buildings. Then as they grew longer and more complex, they were moved into the church porch or yard. In the fifteenth century they were taken over by the Trade Guilds, and became the foundation of English drama as we know it. The religious theme was still maintained for a time, but the innate cheerfulness of the English led to the interpolation of scenes of comedy— comedy of a type that still survives in our pantomime to-day. Noah's wife was made a shrew, who refused to go into the Ark unless all her gossips were included also. One of the shepherds in the Wakefield Nativity play steals a sheep and pretends that it is a baby. Suddenly, while he is being tossed in a blanket for his sins, a chorus of angels appears and sings Hosanna.

Each Guild was responsible for one play. It is often easy

to see the process of selection. The Shipwrights did *The Building of the Ark*, the Goldsmiths *The Adoration*, the Bakers *The Last Supper*, and the Bedmakers *The Dream of Pilate's Wife*. Apart from the dramatic versions of actual Bible stories, there were Miracle plays dealing with legends of the saints, and the Moralities. The best known of the latter is *Everyman*, in which the hero Everyman is accompanied on his journey through life by the various virtues and vices personified, such as Good Deeds, Gluttony, Mercy, and the rest. The Morality plays gradually became less moral and more secular, moving away from allegory towards romance and comedy. About 1553 we get the first true English comedy, *Ralph Roister Doister*, by Nicolas Udall.

The next stage in the advance towards the secular is found in the Interludes. They show a distinct break not only with the Mysteries, but even with the Moralities, since they appear to have been written for amusement, and not with any didactic purpose. Most of the best known of these plays have been attributed to John Heywood. Though Heywood lived during the reign of Henry VIII., when the Protestant-Catholic dispute was raging, he maintains a refreshingly a-moral and satirical point of view, reminiscent to a certain extent of Chaucer. *The Four P's* is the story of a Pardoner, a Pilgrim, a 'Pothecary, and a Pedlar, who arrange a contest in which the prize is to go to the biggest liar. The Pilgrim wins.

The name Interlude implies that these pieces were acted between two more serious plays, or used like a modern curtain-raiser, but there is no evidence to show whether this was the case or not. They are written as dialogues, sometimes witty, it is true, but they have no great dramatic value as there is even less action in them than in many of the earlier religious plays. Their importance is that they are an early sign of the growth of individualism which came with the Renaissance ; of the rise of the middle class which was already beginning to assert itself, claiming the right of the individual to criticise the authority of the feudal lords, and the doctrines of Divine Right and Infallibility. Satire was impossible in the Dark Ages when the Church and the lords claimed power over body and soul, and individual criticism was damned as a heresy. It is necessarily a product of intellectualism. Rabelais in France had already shown what immense possibilities it held both as a social and a literary weapon.

The sixteenth century came like a clear dawn after a stormy night. The darkness of medievalism was passing, the days of the feudal lords were finished, and the ascendancy of the urban bourgeoisie or trading class was beginning. For those who wished there was everything to be discovered, new lands, new cultures, new philosophies. In an age with such possibilities of adventure and romance, it is not surprising that there was so phenomenal an output in literature, especially in the drama. Life was exciting, and the theatre presented the most exciting form of art.

The Elizabethan Age can be said to be the age of the sonnet and of the drama. Both were derived to a great extent from the Italian Renaissance. Culture now became a secular instead of an ecclesiastical prerogative, largely owing to Lutheran influence. Young gentlemen were not considered thoroughly educated until they had travelled on the continent for two or three years. These travellers brought back with them the old classical legends, tales of fifteenth-century Italy, and the stories of Boccaccio, which were quickly pounced upon by the playwrights. There was so much to be learned and to retell, the problem of originality and the sin of plagiarism, which vex authors to-day, did not arise. Out of Shakespeare's thirty-seven plays, only one has an original plot. Even the text is sometimes " lifted " from other sources. One of the most beautiful passages in *Antony and Cleopatra* is directly inspired by North's prose translation of Plutarch's *Lives*.

TRAGEDIES OF MEN WHO WRESTLED WITH FATE

OF the early Elizabethans Marlowe is the most interesting and typical. In *Tamburlaine*, the hero sweeps, in glorious blank verse, from conquest to conquest until he is Emperor of the Eastern World. No one can oppose him, all countries fall before him, till at the last Death comes, and what is all his earthly power worth ? In *Faustus* the thirst for culture as well as for adventure is shown. Dr. Faustus has so insatiate a desire for knowledge that he sells his soul to the devil to purchase it. At this price he learns the mysteries of philosophy and magic and the wonders of early Greece, but, like Tamburlaine, he finds that his gain is worth little when he comes to die. Marlowe's conception of tragedy is simple. It is embodied in the greatness of man, the glory of his achievements, and his insignificance when faced with the laws of life and death. He was popular with his audiences partly because of this very simplicity of philosophy. He put all the adventure and recklessness and passion of the new spirit into magnificent verse. But he pitted his characters against the gods, Shakespeare against themselves. Nothing can destroy Tamburlaine except death, but *Hamlet* would still be a tragedy even if the hero were not killed in the last scene. It is in Hamlet himself, in his own nature, that the tragedy lies.

In the ten years between *Tamburlaine* and Dekker's *Shoe-maker's Holiday*, Elizabethan drama progressed a long way. Marlowe was only capable of the heroic and adventurous spirit which discovered America and was ready to fight the world. Dekker was of the world of trade which was just beginning to prosper, and he wrote of the small middle-class man who believed that honest shoemaking was better than six fine battles. This change from the glorious to the domestic can be found gradually taking shape throughout the works of Shakespeare, in the transition from *Love's Labour's Lost* to *Henry IV.* and *Twelfth Night*.

WHERE SHAKESPEARE'S GREATNESS LIES

As no other artist has ever done, Shakespeare stands for and typifies the whole of his age. True, he also towers above it more than any other giant of literature ; but his real greatness lies less in the fact that he stands out, than that he stands *on* his age, rising out of it to unsurpassed heights, but never forgetting the foundation of the society to which he belonged. In this, the most vital period in English history, drama and art were, in the fullest sense of the word, popular. The classicists of the Augustan Age wrote for the intellectuals and scholars ; the Restoration dramatists wrote for the court ; the pre-Raphaelites so loathed their age that they refused to understand its problems, and reverted to mediævalism as a cult. But Shakespeare took the subjects beloved by the mass of Elizabethan people, and made from them plays which continued to appeal to the mass and yet had deep, abiding interest for the greatest minds of his own and every succeeding age.

Marlowe was a great poet, as we see, for example, in Tamburlaine's lament over Zenocrate :

> " Black is the beautie of the brightest day ;
>   The Golden Ball of heaven's eternall fire,
>   That daunced with glory on the silver waves,
>   Now wants the fewel that enflamed his beames,
>   And all with faintnesse, and for foule disgrace,
>   He binds his temples with a frowning cloud."

But Marlowe was not so great a playwright as Shakespeare, because his plays lack the breadth of appeal and the deep human understanding of Shakespeare. The one wrote for the cause of art, the other for his audience.

The Elizabethan audience was mixed. It was more popular and more truly traditional than an audience has ever been since. There was a small body of courtiers who sat on the stage itself and hampered the plays considerably, both by their presence and by their frequent and apparently loud comments. In the gallery there were the merchants and shopkeepers ; and in the pit the " groundlings "—the smaller shopkeepers and apprentices—who came to the theatre as an alternative to the bear-baiting and cock-fighting gardens. All these sections had to be pleased. The gentry and merchants wanted to see the doings of noble personages, the groundlings wanted comedy and good horse-play. (This interest in horse-play accounts for the large number of battles and duels in Elizabethan plays. These were not the laboured efforts that we know to-day, but elaborate and skilled displays.) Every one wanted to see a picture of life, and this picture Shakespeare gave them far better than his more highbrow contemporaries, Marlowe, Webster, and Jonson.

THE COMEDIES, RINGING WITH ENGLISH LAUGHTER

SHAKESPEARE'S early romantic plays all show the Italianate influence of the Renaissance. *Love's Labour's Lost* is a charming, but not a great work. The best characters in it are the comedians Holofernes, Dull, and Costard, who do not belong to the atmosphere of Navarre, but to the local parish of a Stratford-on-Avon. In *Two Gentlemen of Verona* Shakespeare still has not found his strength ; both the characters and the situations are unreal and forced. But in *A Midsummer Night's Dream* he harnesses, for the first time, Italian romanticism with native English realism. Moreover, in this play it is the romantic side which is the weaker. We cannot take a live interest in the affairs of Theseus and Hippolyta, or of the lovers, even though they have pretty lines ; the greatness of the play lies in the fairy scenes, which are largely based on traditional English folklore, and in the rustics, Bottom, Flute, and their friends, who come straight from Shoreditch and Clerkenwell, and have really nothing to do with Athens.

In the later comedies, *As You Like It* and *Twelfth Night*, the combination of the two worlds is more cleverly adjusted. But the Forest of Arden could more easily be found in England than in France, and Sir Toby Belch and Sir Andrew Ague-cheek can be seen to this day, in London clubs and at county horse shows.

In pre-Elizabethan days there had been a few *Chronicle* plays, lengthy and tedious chronicles of the events and speeches in the reigns of earlier kings, having almost no dramatic value. After 1588, when the Armada had been beaten and scattered, Elizabeth, for the first time, sat securely on her throne, and England acquired a stability and prosperity it had never known before. The increased prestige abroad (though the English never ceased to be ridiculed for their odd and insular fashions in dress) quickly made itself felt at home in the awakening of national pride. English kings and lords began to take their place as heroes, where only ancient Greeks and Italians had been considered worthy enough to stand before. The middle class had been steadily growing in strength since the time of Edward III., and the middle class is the backbone of nationalism. On the crest of this wave of enthusiasm for things English, Shakespeare, as well as many other dramatists, wrote a series of historical plays. All of these plays show an immense improvement on the old *Chronicles*, though only Marlowe's *Edward II.* can hold a candle to any of Shakespeare's.

ENGLAND'S KINGS AND QUEENS ON SHAKESPEARE'S STAGE

SHAKESPEARE mixed his historical figures with fictional characters drawn from his observation of living people— often to the detriment of the former. Falstaff drives King Henry and all the Dukes of Westmorland off the stage. One of the greatest tributes to Shakespeare's power of creating characters is in Morgan's criticism in the eighteenth century. So impressed was he by Falstaff that in some three hundred

Sir Andrew and Sir Toby : conspirators (in " Twelfth Night ").

pages he tried to prove that Sir John must have actually existed, and gave lengthy dissertations on his hypothetical private habits, the sort of country house he must have lived in, and his even more hypothetical moral philosophy. No greater tribute, though of a foolish kind, could be paid to a dramatist's power of characterisation. It has only been rivalled by more modern though equally ingenuous critics, who fill volumes speculating how many children Lady Macbeth had, or might have had.

The most typical of the Histories is *Henry V.*, but dramatically it is one of the poorest. Henry V., as an ancestor of Elizabeth, had to be so glorified that he becomes an idealised figure-head, and Nym, Bardolph, and Pistol are not given space enough to be much more than a distraction. The two parts of *Henry IV.* are the richest of these plays. Here the historical and fictional sides are better balanced than in the others, and Henry Hotspur almost holds his own against twenty-stone Falstaff. *Richard II.* is an earlier and more serious play. Except for one gardener, there is no comedy to offset the history. Its place is taken by the " philosophy " of melancholia. Richard's poetical philosophising about worms and music is of course an anachronism—that is to say, Richard expresses ideas and thoughts which were unknown at the time when he actually lived—but the Elizabethans were too bold to be much concerned with such details. As the stability and peace in the country increased, the early glamour of adventure and war died. Men were less active and had more time for thought, so that a pensive melancholia became fashionable. Richard II. is the first of Shakespeare's characters to show this trait, but he is succeeded by Jacques in *As You Like It*, who can " suck melancholy out of a song as a weasel sucks eggs." Later it is ridiculed gently in Malvolio (*Twelfth Night*), and finally most perfectly developed in *Hamlet*.

Richard II. can almost be counted the first of the tragedies. Richard fails through the flaws in his own character, and the victory of Bolingbroke is artistically as well as historically inevitable. *Romeo and Juliet* and *Julius Cæsar* must be discussed apart from the others. Though the first is one of the most beautiful love stories ever written, and the second contains excellent work in the character of Brutus, they both have the same weakness, that the climax is not inevitable, but is brought about by accident. There is much pathos but no deep tragedy. True, Cassius says the fault lies " not

in our stars, but in ourselves," but the facts and the supernatural portents in the play belie him. For the Greeks it
was sufficient that the gods should be against a man, because
their religion and their philosophic code was formed on that
basis. But after the appearance of the doctrines of humanism and
freewill, such a view of the world could no longer be accepted.

"GORGEOUS TRAGEDY IN SCEPTRED PALL"

SHAKESPEARE was the first, in *The Merchant of Venice* and
in the great tragedies, to create the imperfect hero.
Tamburlaine in his glory stood above criticism. In Shakespeare it is Antonio, Horatio, Macduff, and Kent who are
the just and upright men of noble spirit ; but they are
insignificant puppets beside Shylock, Hamlet, Macbeth, and
Lear, men who are greedy, indecisive, or insanely selfish.
They are magnificent, but they are inevitably betrayed by
their own flaws of character.

Macbeth sweeps with terrific dramatic force to its bloody
climax. The action is developed with almost savage speed,
but despite this it is the least great of the four tragedies.
Among other things, there are too many topical details which
side-track the issue. The witches, though they lend atmosphere, do not give power to the play. They were probably
inserted out of deference to James I. who was a firm believer
in witchcraft, and whose book on dæmonology had just been
published. The long speech about the King's Evil was also
put in for political rather than dramatic reasons, and is far
more irrelevant than, for instance, Cranmer's eloquence
about the future of the baby Princess Elizabeth in *Henry VIII*.
The interest in *Macbeth* lies in the contrasted natures of
Macbeth and Lady Macbeth, and in their reactions to each
other, and to their guilt. With the disappearance of Lady
Macbeth, the vitality of the play wanes.

In the early days of James I. there were signs of an intellectual disillusion beginning to creep into drama. With the
increased stability, the old values of life were changing.
There was a tendency for emotions to be exaggerated, rant
took the place of rhetoric, and horror the place of tragedy.
Among the greater writers there was a bitter resentment,
such as we see in Donne's morbid preoccupation with Death
and worms, and in the savage fury of *King Lear*, and in
Measure for Measure.

King Lear contains some of the finest verse in the language.

There is no fictional character grander than old Lear. But, in a sense, the play is a retrogression to the old *Chronicle*. Shakespeare has used a crude, early British story as a basis for his plot, and he has not taken sufficient pains to relate the story to the characters whom he wished to create. Nevertheless, the magnificence of the old king and the poignant meanderings of the Fool make us forget the imbecilities of the first scene and the crudities of the " wicked sisters." This play was in the vogue of the " Horror " drama, which was then beginning, and well shows Shakespeare's genius and the power of his mind. When lesser dramatists—Fletcher, Massinger, and later, Middleton and Shirley—attempted to write this kind of play, they failed abysmally. They paid less and less attention to character-drawing, and scenes like the blinding of Gloucester became of primary, instead of incidental, importance.

HAMLET AS THE HERO OF A VENDETTA

IN *Hamlet*, Shakespeare's skill as a dramatist again makes him triumph over unpromising material. The plot is founded on that used in Kyd's revenge play, *The Spanish Tragedy*. It moves through crime and horror to a melodramatic ending where corpse is rapidly piled on corpse. But the characters, and, in particular, Hamlet himself, are so surely observed and so convincingly drawn, that we forget all the improbabilities and absurdities of the story. Hamlet holds our imaginations enthralled and gives us food for meditation long after the play is over. It is true that the melancholia, the questioning of the value of life, was fashionable then in intellectual circles ; but Hamlet is far more than a philosophising dilettante. The indecision which forms a part of all of us is in him acute. His is a case of such a refinement of sensitivity that almost any action becomes abhorrent. He is the most complex of all Shakespeare's characters, and more volumes have been written about him, as to why he does or does not do anything, than about any other figure in literature. Critics have expended thousands of words discussing whether or not he is really mad, and explaining away his callousness about Polonius and his brutality to Rosencranz and Guildenstern.

Several of these questions are very much simplified when the tendencies of the age are considered. In the first place, madness was already becoming a popular stage device, a device that was later used by many *ad nauseam*, surviving even Sheridan's satire in *The Critic*, until it passed away with the death of the Victorian melodrama. It is possible that Shakespeare never decided whether Hamlet was to be mad in reality or not ; in either case it is not of very great importance, although it makes a better play, if a more unkind character, if he is feigning. In the second place, the drama of " horror " had taken a firm hold on the public. The audience came to the playhouse wanting to have its blood curdled. A parallel can be found in modern times in the popularity of *Grand Guignol*. Italy, with its Machiavellian methods of disposing of enemies and its Borgian refinements of the art of poisoning, supplied ample material for plots of the most gruesome kind. From Italy also came the code of revenge. Inherited possibly from the classical legend of Orestes and Agamemnon, and only eradicated in Corsica within living memory, revenge and the family vendetta was growing rapidly to a peak in seventeenth-century Italy. In England, fortunately for individual safety, the idea never took a wide practical form, but for dramatists it was an extremely opportune device. It allowed the hero to be the centre of all the excited interest of a well-staged murder, and yet to remain a hero because his action was justified by his motive.

Shakespeare, more often than we realise to-day, allowed himself to incorporate the current fashions in his works. In *Hamlet* he provided the motifs of philosophy and madness to suit the tastes of the ruling class, and a duel, a crime to be avenged, and several murders by poison and other means, for the " groundlings." But even though we do not relish these particular details so much nowadays, the play has lost hardly any of its appeal, and none of its greatness. Shakespeare in the last period of his life had gained such a universality of outlook that he could make fiction more real than reality. *Hamlet* is the great tragedy that it is because Hamlet is precisely what he is. Had Horatio been faced with the same problem we should have had an exciting revenge play, but no more. Fate sets Hamlet the problem, and the tragedy lies in the fact that he is the one person who must, and the one person who cannot, unravel it.

HOW SHAKESPEARE BUILT HIS PLAYS

" OTHELLO " is structurally Shakespeare's most perfect play. Except for the first scenes in Venice, it even satisfies the demands of the classicists for the unities of time and place. It is the most compact in form and the least distracted by irrelevancies of any of the plays. It was not an easy task to make a play out of the love affair of a jealous Moor—in those days, a negro. But *Othello* is so masterfully handled, and the Moor himself so magnificently drawn, that the play would almost conquer the colour prejudice of America. Even the fourth act does not make such a hiatus in the plot as usual.

The construction of Shakespeare's plays would have been ridiculed by the Greeks, just as it was deplored by the neo-classicists a century later ; and indeed, his juxtaposition of tragedy and comedy, romance and broad farce, is a dangerous weapon in the hands of a less sensitive artist. But the multiplicity of characters and scenes did not matter in Elizabethan conditions, when actors wore their own clothes, even for Roman plays, and when no scenery was used. The absence of scenery accounts for much of the descriptive poetry in which Shakespeare, especially, excelled. As each scene began, the audience had to be told what part of the country it was, whether it was night or day, wet weather or fine. This description was often beautiful, but it was also necessary. It only shows the irrationality of convention that the habit was kept up long after the introduction of scenery. In Victorian days, actors still referred to the " cærulean blue," or " the pearly dark," when an unsteady cloth painted with palms or castles, was in plain view of the audience.

Both in the plays of Shakespeare and of the other Elizabethan dramatists, the fourth act is always the weakest spot, and appears to have been written mainly to fill up space. To-day, the public expects to be entertained for two and a half to three hours, and a three-act play serves that purpose. But, according to most authorities, the Elizabethans insisted on at least four and a half or five hours, and that meant a five-act play. One of the most obvious faults in Elizabethan drama is the tendency to ramble and the frequency of extraneous details, and this must have been aggravated by the necessity of spinning out the story to the requisite length. Three acts are much easier for the author to manage. The first act has to plant the situation, indicate the characters, and awaken interest. The second sustains that interest by presenting the action. The third attains the climax, and resolves the initial situation. A master can build his drama through four acts, but Shakespeare himself proves that no man has successfully managed five. The construction of the perfect play might be illustrated thus :

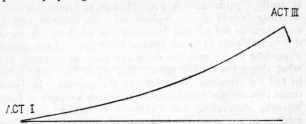

The Elizabethan play, after the drop at the end of the third act, has to collect itself together again and prepare, throughout the fourth act for a second, and final, climax in the fifth. The outline may be illustrated thus :

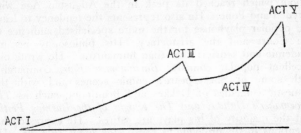

In the poorer plays the fourth act is filled, to gain time, with extra murders or extra comedy. In the better, particularly in the great tragedies of Shakespeare, it serves as a lull in a gale, before the final devastation of the hurricane. But even at its best a lull for the whole of an act causes a serious loss of attention in an audience.

THE EXUBERANCE OF ELIZABETH'S AGE

SHAKESPEARE'S tragedies are the great justification of romantic drama. The classic rules which were followed exactly in France by Corneille and Racine, insist on a rigidity of form, and a stereotyped grandeur of content. The exuberance of the Elizabethans broke these bounds ; content gained precedence over form, the first became contemporary and realistic, and consequently the second became looser. Of the two methods the second has more possibilities, but also more pitfalls. If the playwright intends to write of contemporary subjects, he must decide which aspect of contemporary life is really significant. A play of topical trivialities may be amusing but is always ephemeral; its interest and value evaporate as its subject becomes out of date. A romantic dramatist needs to be an artistic historian. If the content *is* important to the age, the form can take, to a certain extent, what shape the author wills. But when the content begins to fail the romantic form falls to the ground. In Jacobean times this content became more and more a matter of fantastic legends, depending on vicarious excitement rather than interest to slur over the looseness of construction. To stem the degradation of the drama Ben Jonson turned to classical methods.

Jonson was admired by his literary confrères far more than Shakespeare. He is the founder of the neo-classical school which reached its peak in the Augustan Age with Dryden and Pope. He also represents the tendency to leave the popular playhouse for the more specialised audience of the Court and the aristocracy. His philosophy became academic and satiric rather than humanistic. He wrote one excellent popular comedy, *Bartholomew Fair*, comparable with some of Shakespeare's comic scenes and with the domestic comedies of Dekker and Beaumont, such as *The Shoemaker's Holiday* and *The Knight of the Burning Pestle*. But the majority of his plays are satires. He expressed his intentions in the prologue to *Every Man in his Humour*. He would write of

> " Deeds and language such as men do use,
> And persons such as comedy would choose,
> When she would show an image of the times,
> And sport with human follies not with crimes."

His scorn, however, is often greater than its object; it is more worthy of the crimes at which Swift lashed than of the follies of greed and lust.

DRAMA IN DECLINE CALLS HORROR TO ITS AID

BETWEEN 1620 and 1642 drama shows a growing artificiality in subject and treatment. The Elizabethan need for individualism and the optimism of nationalism were waning; the new Tudor merchant class had become landed monopolists, and the struggles of the provincial merchants were voiced in the demands for greater Parliamentarianism. In an age of transition art is apt to fall back on its outworn precedents, unless there comes a genius to found a new school. The dramatists of this period did not understand the shift of emphasis from the individual to the social group, and in consequence much of their work is decadent. Some definitely went over to the Court, and produced masques in which all considerations of content were sacrificed to spectacular effect. Nevertheless, masques are important theatrically, because they were the first attempts at elaborate scenery. Jonson saw the dissolution of the old standards but did not recognise the cause, and wrote to reform the old rather than to lead the new. Others, such as Ford, Webster, Middleton, Shirley, and Massinger did not see the change and continued the old traditions, striving for novelty through melodrama. Ford and Webster wrote some magnificent verse, and there is a sordid grandeur in Webster's best-known plays, *The Duchess of Malfi* and *The White Devil*. These, with Ford's *Tis Pity She's a Whore* and Middleton's *The Changeling*, are the best of the time. But they show a poverty of thought covered by excesses gross enough to tickle the palates of the most jaded age. Attempts were made by Dekker and Heywood to keep the domestic drama alive. The majority of the plays, however, are filled with a blood-curdling quantity of murders, rapes, tortures, and incest, so it is small wonder that when the Puritans, with their antagonism to the Court and all its manners, came into power, the theatres were closed from 1642 until the Restoration.

PLAYS TO PLEASE A WANTON KING

THE Puritans regarded the theatres as hothouses of sin. There are still people to-day who hold the same opinion. Actors remained legally " rogues and vagabonds " until the late nineteenth century. Up to the end of the seventeenth century the civic authorities of London refused to allow theatres to be built inside the city. The law was circumvented by the growth of private theatres such as Blackfriars, just as the actors evaded the vagabonds Act by becoming nominally attached to various Lords or Ministers—as the Lord Chamberlain's men, or the Lord Admiral's men. But still the authorities continued to regard the playhouse as a nuisance, and worthy burgesses were indignant because the private rooms in the theatres became the rendezvous for courtesans.

It is true that the condition of the drama in 1630–40 gave the Puritans some justification in closing the theatres. But they made no distinction between the decadent plays of the moment and the general and ultimate value of drama. As a result of their action the theatre ceased to be popular, so that later dramatists were driven to write for coteries and for comparatively narrow circles of intellectuals. The theatre cannot really live without popular support. The coffee-house wits and Restoration dilettantes could not keep it alive, because drama is the most realistic form of art and must be concerned with reality. The Puritans considered all forms of amusement wicked, so completely ignoring the moral and propagandist value of dramatic art which the Greeks and the Early Church had both recognised. They confused for ever the minds of the majority by linking the private lives of actors and actresses with the intrinsic value of the plays. They drove drama out of the reach of the middle and working classes.

In 1660 Charles II. returned and old actors reappeared while new ones quickly sprang up. At first Charles allowed only two companies to be formed, which played at Dorset Garden and at the Theatre Royal, whereas in Elizabeth's reign there had been six public theatres. The audience was almost entirely composed of the courtiers and their belles, and of those who hoped to join this circle and aped its ways.

Apart from the altered atmosphere of the audience, there were other practical changes in the theatres themselves which exercised a great influence on the plays. The theatres were no longer built on the Elizabethan model, in which the apron stage jutted out into the middle of the auditorium, and made the intimate soliloquy an easy matter. The stage was now at one end of the hall, and cut off by a proscenium arch. There was still a certain amount of " apron," but not very much. This meant that far more could be made of spectacle than before. The early masques were remembered and elaborate scenery came to be used, with the natural consequence that the carpenter became to a large extent the master of the author. Performances were now invariably indoor amusements, so there were far greater possibilities with lighting. Charles also introduced actresses. When boy-actors played the women's parts authors were chary with their female characters. In Shakespeare there are only two women to twelve or more men. But now it was possible to keep a juster balance, and indeed, as the Ann Bracegirdles and Mrs. Mohuns leapt into fame, parts had often to be written in for them.

FANTASTIC CARICATURES OF HUMAN EMOTIONS

CHARLES brought back with him the traditions of French tragedy according to Corneille and Racine. The plays of these authors were adapted and imitated, and the result was the English " Heroic," dealing on classical lines and in grandiloquent verse with affairs of " Honour." The old free blank verse gave way to the formal, rhymed heroic couplet. Individualism disappeared before the attack of convention and dogmatic idealism. A mass of these plays was written, fantastically flamboyant in matter and manner, with no psychology of character, and no philosophy of moral conflict. Heroes rant of their Honour and their Love, heroines of their Chastity and their Duty, while the villains gnash their teeth in sub-human villainy. Villiers parodied the exaggerations of the age in his *Rehearsal*, which formed the model for Sheridan's *Critic* one hundred years later. But even his preposterous satire is hardly more ridiculous than the originals themselves. Otway, in *The Orphan* and *Venice Preserved*, deserves exception. Although there is in these two plays a quantity of intolerable bombast, there is also some strong dramatic writing. Otway had a more true, though still a wavering, conception of tragedy than the rest, and based his tragedies on fatality rather than on accident. But particularly in *The Orphan* he confuses the tragic with the pathetic, thereby bringing the ruin of true tragedy. The Elizabethan was too robust an age to bother with pathos, but it is a far easier emotion to express than grief, as it depends on circumstance rather than on character, on chance rather than on a consistent philosophy. In the less virile centuries that followed writers succumbed all too easily to Otway's example.

Dryden is the pillar and the justification of the heroic style. His heroes are as honourable and as dull as Horatio in *Hamlet*, but his plays have a far deeper intellectual content than those of any of his contemporaries. Others accepted the fashion blindly and unthinkingly, Dryden consciously endeavoured to adapt the classical style to English thought. He recognised the greatness of Shakespeare, but could not understand in what it lay, and he attempted to cover the void by an insistence on form. He is pre-eminently the apostle of Reason. In *All for Love* he deliberately set himself to copy and to alter *Antony and Cleopatra*. He realised the suitability of blank verse to the English language, and abandoned the rhymed couplet; he co-ordinated and condensed the play, reducing the multiplicity of scenes to a minimum. Much of the verse is very fine, but it lacks the freedom and beauty of the original; the sentiments are noble but they have lost their fire. There is an atmosphere of stilted grandeur throughout which commands admiration but not sympathy. The pendulum of reaction has swung to the other extreme.

WIT SPARKLES IN A DISSOLUTE AGE

AFTER the forced restraints of the Puritan régime, comedy formed a more natural means of expression than heroics, and well suited the dissolute nature of the Court. Real heroism was growing out of date and manners were taking its place. The influence of France, as in the heroic drama, is here very marked, that of Molière being particularly strong. There still exist many translations and direct adaptations of French comedies. Many of the plays are purely licentious, but the best have also a serious purpose. All of them are of a higher quality than the falsely heroic tragedies. They are extremely witty, and give a vivid picture, if not of the age, at least of the dominating class of that age. For the first time in the story of drama, social snobbery plays an important part. The snobbery of the cultured London aristocrat and dilettante towards the uncultured country squire, the snobbery of the gentleman who has wasted his legacy towards the wealthy middle-class merchant, formed good subjects for laughter and satire. The proud but impoverished aristocrats could not afford to despise the bank accounts of the merchants. They had to accept loans under humiliating conditions; they retaliated with the only weapon left them, cultural superiority, and developed that snobbishness for which England is famous throughout the world.

It cannot, however, be asserted that the greater writers of the period wrote merely to flatter the vanity of the audience. Wycherley's satire is often brutally savage, Etheredge maintains a saner and more critical balance, Congreve with brilliant rapier thrusts exposes the sham and the poseur. These three and Vanbrugh are the masters of artificial comedy in England. Their artificiality is an essential part of the society to which they belonged. It is useless to object that characters in the full sense have been replaced by types. With very few exceptions this is true, but the plays were written for such a very narrow circle that nothing else would have been apposite. Satire is at its best when it lashes at the typical, not only at the eccentric.

The titles alone of the plays of this period are enough to give a fair idea of their contents. We have Dryden's *Marriage à la Mode*, Etheredge's *The Man of Mode*, the works of Mrs. Aphra Behn and Nahum Tate, *The Town Fopp*, *Sir Timothy Tawdrey*, *Madame Fickle*, and *The Citizen Turned Gentleman*. Many of these are bawdy to a degree; many are frivolous, shallow attempts to raise laughter from a dissolute audience; their construction is certainly far from perfect; the story is lost in a maze of confusions; but almost all are of a very high standard of writing. The prose is easy and talented, the wit entertaining even to-day when the many topical allusions have lost their point. Congreve anticipates Bernard Shaw by introducing the play of conversation. All his plays, except *Love for Love*, are loosely constructed; it is a hard task to retell tersely the plot of any of them, yet *The Way of the World* can still be a stage success to-day. His wit has a brilliant finesse, and he is an unsurpassed master of light prose.

Wycherley's first plays are of the frivolous type dealing with fops and fools. Even in these there is a more bitter note than can be found in the work of any of his contemporaries. But in *The Plain Dealer*, his satire becomes almost puritanically savage. The flippancies and artificialities of the age seem to have goaded him into a fury. His plays are the best theatrically, and he is the only writer of the time whose satire has a genuine reformist intention, though it never reaches the merciless iciness of Dean Swift.

TRAGIC GRANDEUR WATERED DOWN TO SICKLY PATHOS

WITH the accession of William and Mary the Court became a more staid institution. Anti-swearing rules were made and the gallants had to learn to restrain their tongues. Farquhar and Vanburgh continued the tradition, but in a much empered form. Compared with *The Country Wife*, *The*

Beaux Stratagem could be read at a drawing-room tea-party.
It is more domestic and less artificial, but it has lost some of
the sparkle and wit. With Queen Anne, circumspection
turned to sentimentality. The delicate blush and the convenient swoon began already to replace the bold sophistication
of the ladies of Charles II.

Queen Anne was not interested in the theatre ; George I.
understood a dozen words of English, and apparently wished
to understand even less. Royal patronage, therefore, which
had meant so much before, both financially and culturally,
was withdrawn, and with it a certain amount of the old
glamour and excitement disappeared. The middle classes
were becoming stronger and richer every day. The social
climbers among them, who had married their daughters into
the penniless aristocracy, came to the theatre ; but although
they wanted to like the fashions of society, they brought with
them their own sentimental morality. The result on the
drama was disastrous. Some appallingly mawkish plays
were written, and worse, Shakespeare was altered and his
tragic grandeur watered down to sickly pathos. *Romeo
and Juliet* was given a happy ending and *King Lear* altered
to bring Cordelia miraculously to life again. A scene was
inserted in *The Merchant of Venice* showing Shylock returning to his empty house, a desolate old man robbed of his
daughter.

This was an age more pedestrian than dramatic and the
proper medium of expression was, therefore, the novel, not
the play. The middle class was the important class, and the
middle class stayed at home in the evening. The novel
could be taken home and read among the family by the
fireside, whereas at this time the play could not. Defoe,
Addison, Steele, and later Johnson, all catered for this new
emphasis on the home. Newspapers with editorial sermons
sprang into being, and Richardson began his letters from
" men of feeling " to young ladies of sentiment. Nearly all
of these writers tried their hand at plays, but with very little
success. Johnson's *Irene* is a ponderous affair, on strictly
formal lines. Addison's *Cato* is the most praiseworthy.
It conforms to all the classical rules of unities and number of
characters, and it is well constructed ; he makes a gallant
attempt to leave aside the traditional and now mawkish love
element, by making his hero a politician. But the play is
dull.

GOOD PLAYS RUINED BY CLUMSY TECHNIQUE

THOUGH there had been several attempts to establish " Little " theatres, the city authorities sternly refused them licences. The two remaining theatres, Drury Lane and Covent Garden, were vast, and effectively destroyed the few last hopes of the drama. They were unsuitable for Shakespeare ; the beautifully free blank verse had to be bawled and the soliloquies became ridiculous. They were even more unsuitable for the intimate Restoration comedies. Playwrights, however, still insisted on putting in lengthy asides, because they were not sufficiently at home with their medium to evolve a new technique. Here we see the foundation of the most stupid convention of the stage as we inherited it at the beginning of this century—that of the aside delivered in a full-throated roar sufficient to reach the gallery, and apparently insufficient to penetrate the ear of another actor only three feet away. The stage, set in its proscenium arch like a picture in a frame, became a spectacle remote from the audience. The latter went to see rather than to participate in the performance, and plays became more unreal and out of touch with the lives and interests of the spectators. Emotion, if it was to " get over," had to be stretched outside all bounds of possibility. The quick dialogue of the Restoration comedies was lost. Now, since we have returned to the conversational style of acting, only the more recently built theatres are suitable, and the old heirlooms will only serve for musical comedy and spectacle.

Ironically enough, the last stick was added to the funeral pyre of the drama by the actor himself. The perfect production is a collective and co-ordinated effort of author, producer, actor, and scene-designer. The rôle of each is important, but chiefly important in its relation to the others. The over-emphasis of one will destroy the whole balance. The scene-designer had already had his day in the masque and spectacle play, and has it now in the opera and pantomime ; in the late nineteenth century it was the turn of the author, and now it is that of the producer. But in the eighteenth and nineteenth centuries it was the turn of the actor, and he seized his opportunity. It is unfortunate that the period richest in actors should have been the poorest in plays.

Garrick and Mrs. Siddons, we learn from contemporary writers, were histrionic marvels, but the trash in which they frequently appeared was deplorable. Plays began to be written especially for them, plays with two grand and glorious parts running through the whole gamut of tawdry emotions, but with no other point about them. Any discrimination between a good performance by an actor and a good dramatic entertainment was lost, and has remained buried up to the present day, with very few exceptions. Good drama is of historic importance, and is for all time ; good acting, however magnificent, is ephemeral, and should never be allowed to dominate the former. The current phrase became not " went to the play," but " went to see Siddons or Garrick."

TWO MERRY WRITERS RELIEVE THE GENERAL GLOOM

A MINOR result of the decay of drama was the rise of the burlesque. But the contemporary plays were so uniformly bad, that relatively little burlesque was possible. One cannot burlesque the same thing many times. Three, however, are important : *The Tragedy of Chrononhotonthologos* by Carey, Fielding's *Tom Thumb*, and later Sheridan's *Critic*. The last two give a better idea of the current state of affairs than volumes of critical analysis. Puff in the *Critic* shows the imbecilities of the plots when he says : " It is a received point among poets, that where history gives you a good outline for a play, you may fill up with a little love at your discretion . . . a play is not to show occurrences that happen every day, but things just so strange, that though they never did, yet they *might* happen." Nor does he spare the inanities of convention :

> PUFF : Now enter Tilburina !
> SNEER : Egad, the business comes on quick here.
> PUFF : Yes, sir . . . now she comes on stark mad in white satin.
> SNEER : Why in white satin ?
> PUFF : O Lord, sir . . . when a heroine goes mad, she always goes into white satin . . . don't she, Dangle ?

The only bright gleams in the English drama of this period, Goldsmith and Sheridan, were both Irish. Goldsmith makes a gallant attempt to stem the surge of sentiment by reviving a healthier, robuster form of comedy, reminiscent of Shakespeare and Dekker. In *The Good Natured Man* he is still sentimental, but in *She Stoops to Conquer* he turns his back both on that and on the comedy of manners. Mr. and Mrs. Hardcastle are genuine, living characters, and Tony Lumpkin is a refreshing boor. Even the heroine Kate has nothing of the insipidity of Richardson's young ladies. So far had the pendulum swung towards conventional and drawing-room sentiment, the audience found even Goldsmith coarse in parts, but though our censor would not dream of allowing any of the Restoration comedies if they were written to-day, he would have no hesitations about *She Stoops to Conquer*. Sheridan is more brilliant in his dialogue, his satire is hard and biting, but he lacks the understanding and humanity of Goldsmith. Mrs. Malaprop in Sheridan's *School for Scandal* is a caricature, whereas Mrs. Hardcastle is a portrait. Sheridan carries on the tradition of the comedy of manners, purged of its licence and bawdry. His plays show up the scandal of the drawing-rooms, and the tawdriness of the poseur. For a brief period Goldsmith and Sheridan raised the standard of the drama, but there was no one to take their place. They are the last flicker of the fire that was to smoulder in banality and melodrama for a hundred years.

The French Revolution brought a fresh impetus to poetry, the Industrial Revolution to the essay and the novel. Neither affected the play. Poets in their lyrics were fired by the new ideals of freedom and liberty from the individualistic point of view ; Burke and Smith and J. S. Mill were inspired in their prose by the forces of social reformation. Here was one of the most vital situations in English history, and there was no one who could harness it with the artistic realism of the stage. It needed more courage than the poets were capable of, especially in an age when poetry was only too frequently a means of escape ; and it needed more imagination than the prosodists could command. Nevertheless, several of the romantic poets attempted drama : Keats, Wordsworth, Coleridge, Shelley, Byron, have all left plays, some of which have been produced. Keats's *Otho the Great* is of very little worth ; even the poetry is ponderous and characterisation is nonexistent. The same can be said of many of the others. Exception, however, must be made for Shelley's *Cenci*, and Byron's *Sardanapalus* and *Cain*.

The ideas of freedom and liberty characteristic of the romantic movement were reflected in poetry, and led, among

other things, to the use of new verse forms, which broke away
from the formalities of the classicists. But, in drama, Byron
still insisted on the old rules. In a preface he says that he
has attempted to approach the unities, because " with any
very distant departure from them, there may be poetry, but
can be no drama. He (Byron) is aware of the unpopularity of
this notion in present English literature ; but it is not a system
of his own, being merely an opinion, which, not very long
ago was a law of literature throughout the world, and is still
so in the more civilised parts of it." Byron's temperament was
the most suited to dramatic technique of all the romantic
poets : his very virility has something theatrical about it.
But even so, his plays are more to be read than to be seen,
and should be classed with Milton's *Samson Agonistes*, Hardy's
Dynasts, and Browning's *Pippa Passes*.

PLAYS WHICH COULD NOT BE PERFORMED

IT is worth a brief digression to consider these works, although
they are, in reality, quite apart from dramatic tradition.
Byron writes in the preface to *Sardanapalus* that the play was
not " composed with the most remote view of the stage."
But if so, it has no more than a formal right to be called a
play. A play not intended for production is like a battle
fought between two ex-colonels with tin soldiers on a green
baize-covered table. Milton's *Samson Agonistes* and Shelley's
Prometheus Unbound are really poems ; the authors might
just as well have inserted " then So-and-so spoke," instead
of writing the name of the speaker in the margin. They
chose the latter method for its virtues of conciseness and
avoidance of unnecessary detail. Shelley's *Cenci* is the most
actable of all these plays ; it has dramatic force, some characterisation, and it is written in superb verse ; but it is weakened by presentation ; the atmosphere of the macabre and
the sombre disappear under even the dimmest footlights.

Actual representation is an essential of drama. These plays
make excellent reading, but they must always be regarded as
poems not plays. Hardy's magnificent work *The Dynasts*
might create a better effect if recited by actors and a full
chorus *in the dark*, but put the lights up, and the whole conception would be made tawdry. But as a poem the dramatic
form in which it is cast adds vividness to the imagination of
the reader. It gives a greater illusion of experience and reality
than the mere telling of a tale.

ENGLISH DRAMA SWOONS INTO THE ARMS OF MRS. GRUNDY

THE period from 1740–1860 is most enlightening when we look at drama from a critical point of view, because, though a great deal was written, it was nearly all bad. It is often easier to adduce positive qualities from their negatives. The Industrial Revolution and all the vast fields that it opened were not touched by any playwright until Hauptmann wrote *The Weavers* and Toller *The Machine Wreckers*, in recent years. The more dramatists shirked the vital problems of their age, the more they fell into the vapid, the ridiculous, and the banal. Cumberland's comedies have one or two noteworthy scenes and characters, but they have no lasting value. Joanna Baillie's *Plays on the Passions* (1798 and later), written for an audience which had forgotten what passion was, are both ridiculous and dull. Each play deals with one passion and only one, whether it be Hate, or Pride, or Jealousy. She shows little ability and less understanding. Mrs. Inchbald's comedies have a flicker of the old verve, but invariably it peters out long before the last act. Had it not been for the " star " actors the theatre might have died. Indeed it is questionable whether it would not have been better had it done so, in order to be born again unshackled by worn conventions. Plays became progressively worse until they finally sank into the abyss of melodrama, with its false incident, false characterisation, and, worst of all, false sentiment.

Little Lord Fauntleroy is the triumph of sentimentality. It is outrageous that any audience could have been reduced to tears over such rubbish. The full-blooded hardness of the Elizabethans had gone ; the shallow but brilliant glitter of the Restoration had gone. There is not a little truth in Virginia Woolf's description of the era in *Orlando* ; the Victorians were left with massive ivy on their pseudo-Gothic houses, fringed antimacassars on their upholstered furniture, and heavy plush curtains on their doors to keep out any breath of air from the disturbed and dirty world outside. Tragedy was too brutal, comedy apt to be too coarse, and all that was left was pathos. The damp had certainly set in. The upper classes still went to the theatre, but they had not the taste or culture of their predecessors. The working class had no leisure and little money. The middle class sat by its family hearth, in an impregnable plush-covered fortress, and listened to the teachings of Wesley, many of whose followers preached more bitterly than the Roundheads that the theatre was the House of Sin, the Rendezvous of the Ungodly, and drama the inspiration of the Devil.

DRAMA IN OUR OWN TIMES

ROBERTSON'S play *Society*, produced in 1865, shows the earliest signs of a revival in dramatic art. He is the first of the new school of dramatists who sought to draw drama away from Gothic castles and pure, sobbing heroines, back to life as it really was. He and his more famous successors, Henry Arthur Jones and Sir Arthur Pinero, wrote for the middle class, and about the middle class, and initiated the bourgeois drama with its naturalistic production, as we know it to-day. Jones wrote of the greed of the petty shopkeeper, the superficial vices of the middle class, Pinero of the conflict between actual life and emotion, and the idealistic convention of the day. Neither of them, however, would probably have written so well, nor the movement spread so widely in England, had it not been for the appearance of Ibsen on the continent.

HENRIK IBSEN : FOUNDER OF ALL MODERN DRAMA

IBSEN laid the foundations of all modern drama. Even in translation, his plays have become such classics that one is apt to forget that he was a Norwegian and not one of our own English writers. He is responsible not only for the growth of realism, but of symbolism also, a second very important factor in the present-day theatre. Neither is this as contradictory as it sounds. Symbolism is a natural outcome of true realism. Realism, it must be remembered, should never be confused with naturalism. The drawing-room comedies of to-day are intensely naturalistic, but they are not real, because although the sets look exactly like our own rooms and just as solid, and though the actors make their jokes, smoke their cigarettes, get up and sit down as though they were at home, there is no realism in the plot or in the idea. Realism concerns life, not manners and fashions.

Ibsen began with historical plays, but quickly turned from them to choose subjects which were important to his own day. In *The Enemy of the People* and *Pillars of Society*, he shows up the graft of politicians, and the moral ruin caused by commercialism. These sound like subjects for a treatise, but he maintains a dramatic balance by the vividness of his characterisation and his picture of the human being pitted against society. In the early twentieth century " society " takes the part played by " Fate " in the seventeenth. It is the stumbling-block of idealism and good intentions, it is an iron wall far more impregnable than the gods of the Odyssey. Ulysses could hope to split the gods and range some of them on his side ; but the ranks of society are solid, and the individual who revolts batters his head in vain. Ibsen saw the dramatic possibilities of this conflict, and seized them. It is Dr. Stockmann, the kind-hearted idealist, who is forced to become the enemy of the people, and it is the irony of this fact that creates the dramatic situation. In *The Doll's House* Ibsen shows the unreality of the popular belief in, and worship of, pretty little women. A lesser man would have been content to shatter the old myth, or at most rage bitterly against it. Ibsen understands that it is not the fault of the Noras that they are dolls, but that it is a rôle forced on them by the whole of society, although they succumb to such humiliating treatment only too easily.

Ibsen's characters are all of them living people, but there is a sense of forces stronger than man in his plays, and it is this that makes them great, that makes them tragedies rather than serious satires. Frequently he heightens his effect by the use of symbolism. In *Rosmersholm*, the conflict between the characters of Rebecca West, Rosmer and his wife, is sufficiently strong to move inevitably to the climax, but the symbolism of the white horses of the mill-race adds a great intensity. It is the same in *The Wild Duck* and in *The Lady from the Sea*. It is equally symbolic that it is the building of a tower, the peak not only of his architectural skill, but of his ideals and aspirations, which causes the death of the master-builder. Ibsen wrote his plays with part of the room divided off to make a stage. Even the construction of his stage directions is always consistent with reality, he never even puts his doors in impossible places. He broke as much with the style of the old theatre, with its fantastic extravagances, as he did with the content of the plays.

POIGNANT SATIRES FROM THE PEN OF A RUSSIAN MASTER

AN influence almost equal to that of Ibsen has been exercised on English drama by the Russian, Anton Tchehov. He shows with more beauty of expression than Ibsen, though with perhaps less understanding, the quagmire into which society had sunk, the stupidity of the old ideals, and the absence of anything new to take their place, the absence even of a real wish to find anything new. No writer has equalled Tchehov in the complete naturalism combined with poetry of his dialogue. His plays are poignant satires. It is unfortunate that in this country they have generally been treated as tragedies, when they were conceived as satiric comedies. The line between a deep and therefore cruel satire and tragedy is very fine indeed, and consequently easily missed by temperaments not used to such subtleties.

Tchehov employs symbolism with great effect. In *The Cherry Orchard*, the orchard itself is symbolic of the futile but charming romance of the old régime. Madame Ranevsky cries bitterly for her cherry blossom when her very existence is threatened by the relentless advance of the new bourgeoisie. The appearance of the tramp, typical of the spirit of unrest springing up all over Russia, startles the family rudely out of their dreams and fancies in the twilit garden. Except the parvenu bourgeois Lopahin, they all cling to a world that has gone ; the student talks of the " New Life," but it is only so many words, and even old Firs, the servant, would rather be back in the old days when he was a serf. The last scene of the play, when Firs, who has been treated with sentimental affection, is forgotten and left to die in the empty shuttered house, is Tchehov's nearest approach to tragedy. In the *Three Sisters*, the same futility, the same refusal to face facts, is apparent. It is a vivid picture of the stagnation of life in provincial backwaters, with Moscow as the Mecca, always hoped for with futile optimism, and never reached.

THE PLAY OF MODERN PROBLEMS

A HOST of dramatists followed in the footsteps of Pinero— Miss Baker, Miss Sowerby, St. John Hankin, Stanley Houghton, and many others less famous. Their works are all concerned with real problems, many are sordid, most are depressing. Their construction is fairly good, their character-isation often convincing, but they invariably miss their climax. The matter is tragic, the manner only pathetic. Granville Barker in *The Madras House* and *The Voysey Inheritance* shows clearly the influence of Ibsen. His plays deal with the revolt against standardisation, the corruption of com-mercialism, and the futility of convention. He has a deeper understanding than his predecessors, as well as a greater mastery of dramatic technique and characterisation. There is always a wider generality in his treatment of a subject : in *Waste* it is the social, not merely the personal, aspect of the sex problem ; in *The Voysey Inheritance* it is the penalty exacted from the individualist in a class issue, irrespective of which side he takes. In *Madras House*, Constantine finds a personal solution in escape to the Moslem religion, but that does not help the conscientious Philips who, for all their good intentions, are beaten by the social prejudice around them.

HOW TWO GREAT DRAMATISTS HAVE SEEN SOCIETY

WHAT Barker saw vaguely, the increasing importance of class antagonism in modern history, Galsworthy saw with a lawyer's dispassionate clearness. His plays are never tragedies, they are the perfection of the problem drama. With intellectual coldness he holds the balance between opposing forces. Without any emotional comment he observes, in *The Silver Box*, that there is one law for the rich and quite another for the poor, and in *Loyalties*, that the old virtues of Honour and Truth have been superseded by the creeds of a clan and the need to keep up a bold façade. In *Strife*, his hard business men are not villains nor his workers' leaders heroes ; both are driven by the weight of the class behind them. *The Skin Game* is an English parallel of *The Cherry Orchard*, but in comparison it is pedestrian and sordid. The squire and his wife detest the advance of industrialism, but, unlike Madame Ranevsky, they fight against it. To save the view from their manorial windows they stoop to dirtier methods than their enemy, the hard-fisted *nouveau riche*, would ever use. For future historians Galsworthy will be important, as he gives a true though unflattering picture of his times. He maintains the chronicler's attitude of impartiality. He is the type of Liberal who sees both sides of the question so well that there is no solution possible.

Bernard Shaw, who burst on the complacency of the late Victorian days like a tornado, exposes ruthlessly the shams of modern life. He attacks by ridicule the idealist whose income depends on the exploitation of the slum-dwellers, the respectable gentlemen who finance organised prostitution ; even the sanctity of the medical profession is not secure against him. He explodes the popular idea of the young hero. His young men are not noble, but rather stupid adolescents, ignorant and bumptious ; his young ladies do not faint, nor do they swoon, they do not even flirt ; they are masterful young women filled with either an urge towards a philoprogenitive Life-force or with a crude intellectualism ; his burglars perversely *want* to get arrested ; his emperors become conceited little captains ; his Cleopatra and his Cæsar, a minx and a prosaic politician.

He has far less sense of personal drama of character than Ibsen or Galsworthy. We do not care very deeply what happens to any of his heroes or heroines. With Galsworthy we see the struggles of human beings, powerless against a social cause ; with Shaw we see the social cause with various fairly human beings concerned in it. For this reason he has never written, and will presumably never write, a tragedy in the Shakespearian sense ; nevertheless, his indifference to human beings certainly does not hinder his plays from being very great. He has followed Congreve in his choice of the conversation play—his prose is less polished but his wit is more biting. He is the master of the social problem drama in England. No other writer has his powers of brilliant dialogue, which can sustain interest for a whole act in which nothing happens, but ten men sit round a table and talk.

The Shavian play is the play of ideas rather than of action. Even in *St. Joan*, in the most romantic story that it is possible to find in European history, Shaw carefully avoids any attempt at romantic treatment. Joan is not an individual heroine, she is the tool of history. The emphasis throughout is on the historical situation. The most entertaining scene, between the Earl of Warwick and the Bishop of Beauvais, is a Shavian discussion on the decay of feudalism and the rise of bourgeois nationalism. Both Joan and the Grand Inquisitor are, contrary to the history books, rational rather than fanatical.

THE INTELLECTUAL ACROBATICS OF GEORGE BERNARD SHAW

IN his earlier plays, culminating in *Heartbreak House*, Shaw deals with one problem in each. Latterly in *The Apple Cart* and *On the Rocks* he has chosen the whole social system. This makes the plays no less interesting intellectually, but certainly weaker dramatically, because it is difficult to find a solution which will suit both the characters and the author. Latterly, also, Shaw's old venom against the sham shows signs of degenerating into a little demon of perversity. He sets up his characters and then proceeds to knock them down one by one, leaving not one, nor a hope of one, standing. He is so intent on revealing the hidden side of every branch of the tree, he saws off the very one on which he is sitting. The apostle of rationalism, he has even shown the inadequacy of rationalism. His is not the rancour of tragedy, nor the venom of satire, but the pessimism of despair.

Shaw's plays are at their weakest in their climax. The penalty of choosing as a subject a real situation is that the need for a resolving solution becomes greater. Shaw cannot or will not face the problem of solution. In his excellent picture of the decadence of pre-War society in *Heartbreak House*, he finds it in the bombs of a German air raid. In this play he explodes each of his characters in turn, the young girl, the whole family with its wives and husbands, the burglar, and finally, old Captain Shotover himself ; his philosophy turns out to be derived from rum and he, too, is exposed. The knowledge that all the characters are poseurs, however, does not stop their conversation ; they might go on until Doomsday, but with the suddenness of the Greek *deus ex machina*, bombs drop in the sandpit. In this case the solution has the merit of historical truth ; the War did end that style of life, and probably nothing else could have done. But in *On the Rocks*, after building up to a dramatic climax, Shaw evades the issue on the flimsy argument that the hero, who sees the urgent need for, and has even conceived of a remedy, is not the man for the job because it does not suit his personality. The solution of the problem, also of the play, is postponed to another occasion.

Another exponent of the problem drama in England is St. John Ervine. His plays have great dramatic quality. *Mixed Marriage* deals with the struggles in Ulster after the Belfast riots, while *Jane Clegg* is a play of lower middle-class English life. One of the disadvantages of the social problem play is that it is apt to be treated as history, and the theatre public has little interest in the history of yesterday, until it has become at least two generations old. In spite of this, however, *Jane Clegg* has been revived about three times since it was first produced in 1911.

CHARMING PLAYS OF DELICATE FANTASY

IN opposition to Shaw and the realists, there were before the War two other schools of drama in England, the whimsical fantasy of Barrie and Milne, and the mystical symbolism of

Synge and Yeats, which influenced our poetic playwrights Masefield and Drinkwater. Both schools are interested in "the other world." But whereas with Barrie this interest is the outcome of a fanciful sentimentality, with the Irish authors their Celtic mysticism is not only innate in them, but it is closely bound up with the political struggles of Ireland for her freedom. Their "little people" are symbols of the Irish soul, Barrie's are fairies out of picture books. Synge in *The Riders to the Sea* and *The Playboy of the Western World* showed himself a master of both tragedy and comedy. His combination of realism and symbolism, and his subtly satiric humour, are reminiscent of Tchehov. Masefield in *The Tragedy of Nan* has caught some of Synge's tragic spirit ; the flood-tides of the river Severn add an inevitability to Nan's death, as well as a mystery and a beauty. It is one of the very few modern English tragedies. In *Melloney Holtspur* and *Philip the King* he tries to get the same effect by the use of ghosts. The incursion of the supernatural here becomes an irrelevant trick and certainly weakens the plays.

Barrie lives in fancies of the "might have been." His is a philosophy of escape, an attempt to look at a sordid world through rose-coloured glasses, a charming but rather a futile occupation. He ignores reality and creates a Lob or a Peter Pan, who refuses to grow up. Barrie shares the delusion of the older generation, which sentimentally believes that childhood is the happiest time of life, that freedom from responsibility and financial cares is compensation for the lack of any rights, even the right to own the smallest thing beyond a toy. In *Dear Brutus*, Lob provides the characters with another chance ; in a fantastic wood they are allowed to see what they "might have been," an incautious procedure, reminding us of the words of Hamlet, that it is better to face "the ills we have than fly to others that we know not of." Barrie steals the prerogative of the novelist, in that he tells us more about his characters in his amusing and lengthy stage directions than they show of themselves in their actions.

THE DRAMA AS WHIPPING-POST FOR MAYFAIR'S PLAYBOYS

POST-WAR comedy, at its best in the hands of Noel Coward and Somerset Maugham, has its roots in the works of Gilbert and of Oscar Wilde in the 'nineties, and further back in the Restoration. Maugham, however, has left light comedy for bitter and mordant satire. His plays come as near tragedy as satire can, but they consciously reject it ; for him, the state of man's soul is so rotten that it is not worthy of tragic treatment. In *Our Betters*, Maugham exposes the shams of society, showing the rot underneath the fine façade. In *Rain*, he attacks the hypocrisy of religion, in the clergyman who deceives himself that he is saving the soul of a prostitute, when he really wishes to become her lover.

Wilde inaugurated the paradox as the medium of modern wit, and he and Noel Coward have revived the comedy of manners. Wilde's *The Importance of Being Earnest* and Coward's *Hay Fever* are extremely witty commentaries, the first on the decadence of the 'nineties, and the second on the social decomposition of the post-War period. But brilliant as they are, they have side-tracked modern English dramatic effort away from the fundamental to the superficial. Coward himself now seems, in *Bitter Sweet* and *Cavalcade*, to have turned more towards a complacency of sentimentalism.

But where Coward can tread with dexterity and financial success, his would-be followers flounder in a quagmire of cheap wit and impossible manners. In *The Youngest Drama*, Ashley Dukes has admirably summed up the present position of the English theatre. He says : " Drama may be either a mirror or an expression of the times. But for the most part the stage . . . is sunk in the torpor of yesterday's gentility, like a half-pay colonel in a Bloomsbury lodging. The dramas of our distracted world are played elsewhere. . . . The theatre of the hundred thousand has no more to say to us, the theatre of the million does not yet exist. The old audience is enfeebled and exhausted, the new audience of the people's theatre is still a dream of the future."

THE FUTURE OF ENGLISH DRAMA

DRAMATISTS in England are prolific as they have never been before. Plays come on and come off in illogical profusion. A good drama may last ten days, the stupidest farce ten months. The thriller has taken the place of the melodrama of the 'eighties, and the drawing-room fancy of the comedies of manners of the 'thirties. The theatre is non-popular. For the most part it is superficial, and has not a wide enough appeal to regain much strength. Most dramatists have shut their eyes to the fact that the competition of the cinema has made a new technique essential. The theatre to-day is better equipped in lighting and scenery than ever before, but the cinema is better equipped still. The thrilling and the supernatural are far more convincing on the screen, and the spectacular is more impressive. Even the monopoly of colour will soon be usurped by the films. The most frenzied and expensive elaborations of the musical-comedy stage, such as real water and solid scenery, cannot compete with Hollywood, where, for example, the whole of the royal palace at Vienna can be shown from a six-foot model.

With a straight dramatic story the camera again has the advantage ; it can follow the hero down the stairs, along the street, and through the traffic, building up the final situation all the time. The cinema has invaded the dramatic field, and drama, at least in its present condition, seems to have lost hope of competition. To compete it would seem necessary for it to seek other fields, to aim at simplification rather than elaboration, to attempt the dramatic treatment of an idea rather than the representation of a story or simple fact. It is noticeable that Shaw's plays make the worst of films. A film must have continuity of movement, not only of idea.

HOW THE CINEMA HAS INFLUENCED THE STAGE

THE modern movement in dramatic art has been influenced in many respects by the cinema. It is an attempt to negate the very confinements and definitions of the stage hitherto. Many camera devices have been tried, but to use them requires great skill. The camera can always force emphasis by the use of a close-up or a symbol or an angle. But on the stage there is no such easy means of compelling the attention of the audience. In a cinema the audience looks at the screen whatever happens, but in a theatre it may be looking at the background, a scenic effect, another actor, or at almost anything, unless the focus point is made very clear.

Cinema tricks are apt to be a distraction on the stage, in a straight story, though they can be used to great advantage in the type of play which deals with a mass problem or a general idea. Take, for instance, two modern plays, *Late Night Final* and C. K. Munro's *The Rumour*. Both use variations of the same technique. In the first, however, the devices and the multiplicity of scenes are distracting, because the play is not meant to be a picture of American life, but the story of a conscientious journalist and his personal struggles. But *The Rumour* is a play about war and its causes—not one particular war, but war generalised. In this case it does not hinder but helps that the action takes place alternately in Downing Street, Paris, the Stock Exchange, the docks. There is no hero ; his place is taken by the rumour of war, and rumour is not confined by rules of time and place.

WHAT IS MEANT BY "EXPRESSIONISM" IN DRAMA

REINHARDT and Piscator in Berlin, and Meyerhold in Moscow, have contributed substantially to a revival of drama, precisely by experimenting in new methods of expression— Meierhold by the use of different stage levels, Piscator by the use of films. The latter used the film in stage plays for the purpose of generalisation, to bridge the gulf between time and place. After, or at the same time as, showing, for instance, a strike on the stage, he showed films of strikes in other cities and other countries. But we are an insular people, and these movements have had only occasional influence in this country. Even Gordon Craig, who contributed so much in the early part of this century to the revival of the theatre by his imaginative productions, has to-day left the field.

In the German play *Masses and Men*, by Ernst Toller, the hero is not an individual, he is not even a type ; he is a symbol of the mass. One man speaks the words of many, and one man represents a crowd. The symbol in this expressionistic play is a symbol of reality, and differs from the symbols used by Ibsen and Tchehov and the Irish poets. Symbolism with those dramatists is a mystical and extraneous force introduced to heighten the artistic effect ; it is secondary, whereas in expressionism the symbol is the element out of which the structure of the play is built.

A GREAT IRISH PLAYWRIGHT WEAVES TRAGEDY WITH LAUGHTER

TO-DAY once again, as with Sheridan and Goldsmith, Synge and Shaw, Ireland has provided us, in Sean O'Casey, with our chief hope of a revival in our theatre. Sean O'Casey began his career by writing in the realistic style. In *Juno and the Paycock, The Plough and the Stars*, and *The Shadow of a Gunman* he has caught the atmosphere of the Dublin tenement and of the tenement dwellers, as Synge caught the spirit of the Irish peasant. With Shakespearean judgment and modern technique, he weaves together tragedy and comedy that is almost farce, with brilliant results. In *The Silver Tassie* he has gone even further, by combining realism and expressionism in the same play. The play begins as before in Dublin, but O'Casey realised that the War was too vast a subject to be treated realistically with noises and bombs " off." He sets a symbolic howitzer in a ruined church, and the soldiers chant their prayers to the gun as their only god. It is a great play, but the mixture of technique is not altogether successful. What is surprising, however, is that the alternation of moods and techniques comes so very much nearer to success than one could have imagined. The war scene is completely expressionistic, and gives the impression of the ghastly nightmare quite out of human control that the War was. In the last scenes the author returns to realism, but a realism that is still permeated by the fantastic horror of the scene before. He shows the mingled neglect and patronising of the maimed War victims. Susie, who, before the War, doted on Harry, the football hero, with a spinster's fever, brushes him carelessly aside now that she is a nurse and he is paralysed. She says : " If you'd passed so many through your hands as I, you'd hardly notice *one*." The play reaches a climax of bitterness, and Harry the paralysed and Teddy the blind half-chant together of their despair :

> HARRY : The rising sap in trees I'll never feel.
> TEDDY : The hues of branch and leaf I'll never see.
> HARRY : There's something wrong with life when men can walk.
> TEDDY : There's something wrong with life when men can see.
> HARRY : I never felt the hand that made me helpless.
> TEDDY : I never saw the hand that made me blind.
> HARRY : Life came and took away the half of life.
> TEDDY : Life took from me the half he left with you.
> HARRY : The Lord has given, and the Lord has taken away.
> TEDDY : Blessed be the name of the Lord.
> HARRY : The Lord has given, and man has taken away.
> TEDDY : Blessed be the name of the Lord. . . .
> TEDDY : Come, Harry, home to where the air is soft. No longer can you stand upon a hill-top ; these empty eyes of mine can never see from one. Our best is all behind us.

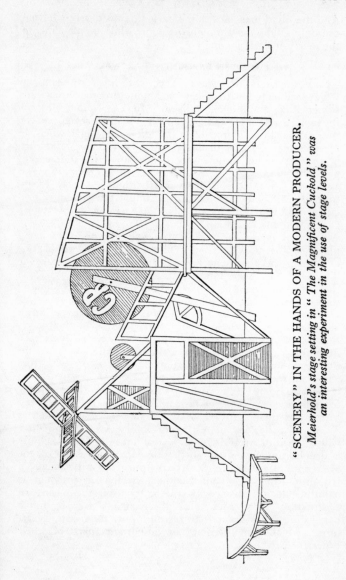

"SCENERY" IN THE HANDS OF A MODERN PRODUCER.

Meierhold's stage setting in "The Magnificent Cuckold" was an interesting experiment in the use of stage levels.

And the blind man pushes the chair that his paralysed friend can only guide, out through the door, while the dancing and the merry-making go on.

WHY MODERN EXPERIMENTS ARE VALUABLE

AMONG writers who have flirted with expressionism and experimented with a new technique are the Americans, Elmer Rice, and Eugene O'Neill. In *The Adding Machine* the whole action of the play, after the first scene, centres round the brain-storm of a middle-aged clerk when he receives his notice of dismissal. O'Neill's *Strange Interlude* is an exercise in rudimentary psycho-analysis, and is only partially successful. The characters speak their thoughts as loudly as their speeches ; this affords an easy escape from the difficulties of motivation, but it often comes perilously near the ridiculous. His *Hairy Ape* is far better in conception and execution.

Evreinov marks the peak of this type of experiment in his play *The Theatre of the Soul.* The scenery is a large diagram of a man, the characters are the three egos which make up his personality—the rational ego, the emotional ego, and the sub-conscious ego. The action lies in the conflict of these three. It is to some extent a Freudian version of *Hamlet.* The play is important mainly as an experiment, and the virtue of these experiments lies less in themselves than in the hope that through their fusion we shall succeed in finding a new realism—a realism as different from the photographic naturalism of Granville Barker as he is from Victorian melodrama. O'Casey has shown a new path, but it remains to be seen whether there will be others capable of following his lead. The problem plays of Barker and Shaw, and their more recent and slighter successors such as *Young Woodley*, are interesting and often excellent, but they will not lead to a real dramatic revival until dramatists acquire a deeper understanding of the fundamental issues of the age, until the theatre is freed from the atmosphere of trivialities and light entertainment which is proving as stunting to its advance as the coterie of the Court in Restoration days, and until theatre-goers regard drama not as an after-dinner distraction, but as a serious art form, which can become an important part of their experience.

PLAYS TO SEE AND PLAYS TO READ

" To the play " is one of Pepys's most frequent jottings in his *Diary*, and it is to the play we must go if we wish to cultivate an interest in the drama. For plays are generally written primarily to be produced. There are dramatists to-day whose plays represent every type of drama. One should not miss an opportunity of seeing Noel Coward's or Somerset Maugham's cynical social satires, Sean O'Casey's tender, passionate pieces, or of admiring Shaw's intellectual gymnastics. Former plays by such living dramatists as these, besides the best plays of Ibsen, Strindberg, Tchehov, and Wilde, are constantly revived, and should not be missed. Shakespeare's popular plays may always be seen.

But the theatre cannot do all the work for us. There are great plays which are seldom or never produced nowadays ; and there are great plays—notably those of Shakespeare—which cannot be fully appreciated unless they have been read before they are seen. Those interested in drama should read first Marlowe's *Doctor Faustus* and Webster's *Duchess of Malfi* ; then for the Restoration period, Congreve's *Way of the World*, or Wycherley's *Country Wife* ; Goldsmith's *She Stoops to Conquer* is the finest example of an eighteenth-century play. Shakespeare reading should begin without notes with comedies which make amusing reading, though they are not often produced, such as *The Merry Wives of Windsor*, *Measure for Measure*, or *Troilus and Cressida*. *Othello* is a good tragedy to begin with. When acquaintance has been made with the Elizabethan period, the reader should turn to that other great period of drama, that of the classical Greek drama. Professor Gilbert Murray has made a good translation of the finest Greek plays.

The best book on English Plays is Allardyce Nicoll's *British Drama* (Harrap). For particular periods reference should be made to Rupert Brooke's *John Webster and the Elizabethan Drama* (Sidgwick and Jackson), and two excellent works by Bonamy Dobrée, *Restoration Comedy* and *Restoration Drama* (Clarendon Press). Hazlitt's *View of the English Stage* and Charles Lamb's dramatic essays make fascinating as well as informative reading.

HISTORY : "RICH WITH THE SPOILS OF TIME"

by M. J. MOULTON, M.A.(Edin.)

HISTORY to many people is often a memory more or less unpleasant of their schooldays. Tables of dates, accounts of battles, and scenes of bloodshed, deaths of kings, quarrels of nobles, and fierce disputes over religion seem to fill the panorama of history to those who have not extended their knowledge of the past beyond that amount of it acquired at school. History is a difficult subject to teach, and methods of history teaching practised in the schools have often been responsible for killing that enjoyment of the past which comes naturally to people endowed with a lively intellectual curiosity. The best way of recovering our zest for the past is to leave aside the ordinary text-books of history and return to the study of the subject by way of the works of those men of letters who have employed their genius in describing the life of past generations. For history is not a matter of politics or of warfare only ; it is the story of the manner in which people have lived in the past, what they have thought, and what they have done. Since history deals with affairs of such vital human interest, it is obvious that it must be included in our study of literature, for literature may be called the written record of the story of mankind.

Not all histories, however, can be termed "literature." Some histories are so deficient in human interest, so badly written that they fall beneath the level of literature, but this complaint cannot be brought against histories like Gibbon's *Decline and Fall of the Roman Empire* and J. R. Green's *Short History of the English People*. History only differs from other kinds of literature in its adherence to facts and in the width of its scope. A novel such as Tolstoy's *War and Peace* may give a picture of society, but the novelist is not obliged to keep strictly to facts. A biography, such as Boswell's *Life of Johnson*, must be true to facts, but its scope is not so wide as that of history. The biography narrates the story of the life of an individual ; history is the record of the life of society, or of the nation.

ARRAYING FACTS IN ATTRACTIVE COSTUME

THE primary task of the historian may be to ascertain and narrate the incidents of the past, but he will not succeed in writing great history if he limits himself to a matter-of-fact statement. In that case his work would be deficient in the imaginative grasp of life and in the luminous quality of style that are characteristic of a literary masterpiece. For instance, if a historian informed us that a Parliamentary debate on an Irish Home Rule Bill was held in 1886, that certain members spoke in support of the motion, certain others against the motion, and that the Bill was thrown out by a certain majority, he would be recording facts, not writing a history. The genuine historian would describe the state of popular feeling in Ireland and England, show the sequence of events leading up to the debate, indicate how the various speakers had arrived at their conclusions, picture the crowded House of Commons, the eloquence and effect of the speakers, the emotions aroused by the result, and its consequences.

For the historian, it is equally important to endeavour to trace the causes and results of events as to record the events themselves, although it is not always easy to say what causes produced a certain event, what motives induced a man to perform actions which have had an important effect on the men of his own and of later generations. In this matter the historian must use his judgment, and to do so effectively he will need a considerable degree of imagination, as he has to put himself into the place of the character whose motives he is trying to discover, and in addition he has to try to realise the conditions of society at that time. Hence it follows that imagination and sympathy must form part of the historian's equipment, if he is to live through past epochs of history, feel as men felt at that time, think as they thought, and be animated by the same ideas and hopes.

THE HISTORIAN'S PATIENT SEARCH FOR TRUTH

PERHAPS more than in any other branch of literature it is important that we should try to establish some standards for testing the value of a history. If we are not aware what qualities are necessary in a history we are liable to be misled and to form a false conception of the past. How, then, can we be satisfied that the historian is presenting a true picture ? In the first place, the historian must be accurate in his facts.

Brilliant literary gifts may enable a writer to produce a readable history, but, if it lacks accuracy, its value as history is diminished. The historian has to undertake an immense amount of labour to ascertain the true facts of the social and political life of past epochs. Suppose a historian is going to write the history of the reign of Queen Anne. What methods will he employ to ensure the highest possible measure of accuracy ? He will consult all the official records available, such as Acts of Parliament, records of the Privy Council, the archives of public offices, the dispatches of generals, and the reports of committees. By this means he will collect the facts of political events from the official sources. But all men are not of the government's way of thinking. The historian must ascertain the state of popular feeling on political events. For this purpose he will consult the pamphlets produced by party writers of the time. The pamphlets of Defoe, Swift, Arbuthnot, and other writers indicate the state of political feeling in Queen Anne's time.

Then, what were the people thinking about religion at that period ? The official documents of the Church will have their value. The pamphlets poured forth at the time of Dr. Sacheverell's trial will reflect the differences between the High Church and Low Church parties. The historian will further want to inquire into the social life of the Queen Anne period. The essays of Addison and Steele will give him some insight into the fashions of the time. Memoirs, diaries, and letters will supplement his knowledge of the manners of the English of the early eighteenth century. Patient research, therefore, must be done by the historian if he is to accumulate facts concerning the past, and if he is to gain a full knowledge of all the aspects of a particular period of society.

PREJUDICES THE READER MUST DISCOUNT

However much evidence the historian accumulates by consulting various sources, many occasions arise when he has to use his own judgment. If there is conflicting evidence on some point, if one pamphlet says one thing and another pamphlet asserts the opposite, how is the historian to decide between them ? He will have to use his judgment and decide the matter in the light of his knowledge of the period. But the historian's judgment may be affected by his point of view. For a long time history was written by Liberal historians, and consciously or unconsciously their interpretation of past political events differed from that which a Conservative historian would have given. The religion of the historian will also influence his view of the past. To a Protestant historian the Reformation may appear as a glorious episode, the triumph of freedom in religion, and the beginning of democracy. To a Roman Catholic historian the Reformation may appear as a tragedy which disintegrated the religious and cultural unity of Europe.

The nationality of the historian may distort his judgment. An English and French historian would form different estimates of the character and achievements of Napoleon. To illustrate this point let us consider the different conclusions formed in regard to Cromwell by Carlyle, a Protestant historian, and by Hilaire Belloc, a Roman Catholic historian. Carlyle saw Cromwell as a type of the hero, or the strong man. Belloc in a monograph on Cromwell attacked Carlyle's estimate, urging that Cromwell was really a man of mediocre ability whose family had risen to power and influence through wealth acquired from the plunder of abbeys. Both historians support their theses by citing evidence.

In these cases when historians disagree among themselves over the interpretation of facts how can the reader form his opinion ? We may allow for the bias produced by adherence to a certain creed or party, but the extent to which this bias operates calls for a nice judgment. We can read historians writing from opposite points of view and try to decide what measure of truth is in each, but in all circumstances the reading of history calls for the exercise of the reader's judgment. The main temptation we must guard against is allowing ourselves to be convinced too rapidly by historians with whose political and religious faiths we are in agreement. The ideal historian ought to approach history with an open mind and allow himself to be guided by facts, but in actual practice such impartial historians have been rare or uninteresting. The most popular historians have approached their subject with a decided point of view.

Accuracy and impartiality are commendable qualities in a historian, but by themselves they produce very colourless history. History is a subject that should not be treated in a dry-as-dust, colourless manner. The drama of political events, the tumult of popular passions, the colour of social life should inspire the historian to inform his work with the highest literary art, to present it as vividly as it deserves. The historian must have a lively appreciation of the sparkle and variety of life, and endeavour to give a graphic reconstruction of past scenes and historical figures. To perform this task well the historian must have a sense of the dramatic and the dramatist's gift of showing the clash of personalities and its consequences. Historical episodes do frequently occur that lend themselves to vivid, dramatic treatment, but yet history is not entirely a sequence of episodes dramatic in their appeal. It is a tale of steady development, more rapid at some points than others, but always moving onwards. Hence the historian must also have a faculty for narrative writing. He must not allow his history to be so clogged by details that it seems to remain stationary. Further, the writing of history demands the ability to design a work, to plan its perspective in the same manner as the architect designs a building. The best history, we may say, is one narrative in form with moments of drama and executed with all the skill of a literary architect.

SEEDS OF HISTORY SOWN IN THE MONASTERIES

IN the early centuries of English history the monasteries were centres of instruction and learning. In their libraries the monks copied out the Scriptures, works of poetry and of philosophy, and embellished their copies with beautiful artistic designs. Among other things the monks were accustomed to keep a record of important events, a kind of monastic log-book in which they entered the affairs of the monastery and such information about outside events as reached their ears. At first the records were kept in Latin, and it was probably from such records that, in the eighth century, Bede compiled his *Ecclesiastical History of the English People*. Bede's *History*, which was written in Latin, is invaluable for the historian of the Anglo-Saxon Conquest and the coming of Christianity.

The keeping of monastic records in English was due to the encouragement of King Alfred. In his efforts to restore learning, which had suffered during the Danish invasions, Alfred had the famous *Anglo-Saxon Chronicle* begun about 892. *The Chronicle* appears to have been kept first by the monks at Winchester, but later copies were sent to various monasteries, such as Canterbury, Peterborough, and Abingdon where the monks continued the record and added entries concerning local happenings. Accordingly several versions of *The Anglo-Saxon Chronicle* have survived. Sometimes the entries consist of a date and the bare record of an event; sometimes they consist of passages of vivid and stimulating narrative. Alfred's struggles with the Danes from 893-97 are described in some detail. The renewed warfare with the Danes during the years 911-24 is recorded in a fluent, glowing style. *The Chronicle* was carried on for almost two hundred and fifty years after the death of Alfred, the Peterborough version extending to 1154. *The Anglo-Saxon Chronicle* is the earliest national history possessed by a modern European nation written in its own tongue. Apart from its historical value, it reaches in some of its descriptive passages the highest level of old English prose.

A FRENCHMAN'S GLOWING TRIBUTE TO THE SPLENDOUR OF THE ENGLISH COURT

AFTER the Norman Conquest, chronicles were usually kept in Latin, then the common language of European scholars. By the fourteenth century, however, writers were beginning to use their mother tongue instead of the sonorous, ecclesiastical Latin. It was in this century that the French writer, Froissart, produced his famous *Chronicles* which are doubly interesting to English readers because they were translated into English in 1523 by Lord Berners, and because parts of the *Chronicles* deal with contemporary English history. Froissart, who was born about 1337 and died in 1410, spent most of his life at the courts of princes where he picked up as much information about current affairs as possible. In 1361 he arrived at London, won the favour of his fellow-countrywoman, Queen Philippa, and remained for five years at the English court, then the most brilliant in Europe. In his *Chronicles* he included all that he could learn about English history and described the manners of the English court as he saw it. A note of the longing that rises in the mind at the thought of past happiness is perceptible in passages like the following when he refers to the English court : " I could not tell nor recount, no, not in a whole day's talk, those noble dinners and suppers and feasts, those joyous meetings, those gifts and guerdons and jewels that were freely given."

The affairs of Flanders, France, Scotland, Spain, and Portugal are narrated in the *Chronicles* as well as those relating to England. For the most part Froissart was dependent on oral testimony, which is generally far from trustworthy, but many events he described were the result of personal observation. Thanks to his lively interest in things great and small, and to his restless activity (at one point in his *Chronicles* he remarks : " It greatly annoyed me to be idle "), he acquired a prodigious amount of information which he conveyed in a vivid, easily flowing, and readable style. According to his lights, Froissart was an honest chronicler, for he tells us that he spent his time travelling, " to the intent to know the truth of deeds done in far countries."

THE HISTORY THAT SHAKESPEARE READ

NOT until we come to the Elizabethan Age do we find an historical work in English of interest to the student of literature, and even this work derives its chief interest from the influence it had on the greatest figure in English literature. *The Chronicles of England, Scotland, and Ireland . . . faithfully gathered together and set forth by Raphael Holinshed*, published in 1578, have some intrinsic merit, but it is safe to say that most readers make their acquaintance in the course of their study of Shakespeare. Shakespeare went to Holinshed for the material of his historical plays, *Richard II.*, *Richard III.*, *I. Henry IV.*, *II. Henry IV.*, *Henry V.*, and also for part of the plots of *Macbeth, Lear, and Cymbeline*. Holinshed's *Chronicles* were largely a compilation made by several writers. A William Harrison contributed an introductory description of Britain, which is followed by a history of England to the Norman Conquest by Holinshed himself.

Next we find a history and description of Ireland written by Richard Stanyhurst, a native of Dublin. Holinshed derives the history of Scotland from the Latin chronicles of the Scottish historians, Boece and Major, and follows a translation of their work by a continuation of English history up to the time of writing. The author claimed that he " had an especial eye into the truth of things," but this did not prevent him from accepting legends as sober historical facts. Yet Holinshed's *Chronicles* have gained an outstanding place in Elizabethan literature, and his plain, clear style is an added attraction to the inquiring reader.

A DIGNIFIED RECORD OF A LOSING FIGHT

HOLINSHED'S *Chronicles* are perhaps more valuable as literature than history. With *The History of the Rebellion in England* by Lord Clarendon we come to an historical work important to the historian and to the student of literature. Clarendon's work is half memoirs and half history in form. It is the narrative of the Civil War between Charles I. and Parliament, and it is also the memoirs of one who was actively engaged in the struggle. Clarendon was at first on the side of Parliament, but his devotion to the Church, which the Parliamentarians were bent on attacking, threw him into the party of the King. After the King's defeat Clarendon went into exile and returned, in 1660, with the restoration of Charles II. For seven years Clarendon was High Chancellor, but in 1667 the intrigues of his enemies drove him into exile in France, where he died. Clarendon's experience of public affairs and his wide knowledge of men give a peculiar dignity and breadth of outlook to his history. Most of his life he had fought a losing battle, and in consequence an atmosphere of tragedy seems to hang over the narrative. The most striking feature of Clarendon's *History* is the wonderful gallery it contains of historical portraits. Charles I., Cromwell, Strafford, Hampden, and many others are described in a masterly fashion. Every trait of their characters is included, and no detail, however trivial, is omitted which would increase the graphic quality of these sketches. Clarendon was Royalist in his political sympathies, but he was not unfair to his opponents. He may have had his prejudices, but he does endeavour to be judicial and fair-minded.

Though very different in style from the stately record of Clarendon, Bishop Burnet's *History of My Own Time* belongs to the same kind of historical writing. It is the history of a man who has taken an active part in the events he describes. Gilbert Burnet was born in Edinburgh in 1643. He became a priest in the Scottish Episcopal Church, and later gained eminence as a theologian, politician, and writer. Burnet went to London and made himself popular by his eloquent preaching. He attached himself to the party of William of Orange, being one of the people who conducted that prince to England. As a reward he received the bishopric of Salisbury. In the course of his busy life he met in person the most conspicuous characters in politics and in the Church.

These characters, such as Charles II. and William of Orange, are described very convincingly by Burnet. " It seems as if he had just come from the King's closet, or from the apartments of the men whom he describes, and was telling his readers in plain, honest terms what he had seen and heard," wrote Horace Walpole.

The *History of My Own Time* begins with an outline of the Civil War and the Commonwealth, and proceeds to give a detailed narrative of the succeeding period down to 1713. The book was published in 1723, eight years after the author's death. Burnet was no impartial historian. He wrote in the conviction that Whig politics were what England needed. Consequently his history has been assailed by writers of a different political point of view. In spite of his partisanship Burnet was an honest, well-meaning historian, less dignified than Clarendon, but a writer who must be read by those wishing to become acquainted with the great figures of English history in the late seventeenth century.

THE GOLDEN AGE OF HISTORY

IN Clarendon and Burnet history has not yet evolved into a distinct branch of literature, but is still allied with memoirs. In the eighteenth century the practice of history as we know it arose. At the beginning of the century there was no history in the modern sense of the term, yet not long after the middle of the century Hume could say : " This is the historical age," and before the end of the century Gibbon had produced the masterpiece of English history. What accounts for this sudden blossoming in historical writing and its rapid rise to a foremost place in literature ? In the first place more material was put at the disposal of the historian. Thanks to the labours of antiquaries, collections of state papers were printed and made accessible to students. Then an impetus to English historical composition was given by the example of French historians like Voltaire, the author of a history of the reign of Louis XIV. Finally, the cool critical temper of writers of the eighteenth century was exceptionally favourable for the production of histories.

In 1752 David Hume, the philosopher, became Keeper of the Advocates' Library in Edinburgh, a position which gave him access to much historical material. He used this privilege to engage in historical work, and two years later he issued Volume I. of *The History of Great Britain, Containing the Reigns of James I. and Charles I.* The second volume, which appeared in 1756, brought down the history to the Glorious Revolution of 1688. In the third volume, Hume returned to 1485 and narrated the course of English history up to the death of Queen Elizabeth. He completed the work in a fourth volume which covered the period of English history from its beginning up to 1485. Hume's book remained the standard work on English history for a century but it has now been superseded, mainly because Hume was not a scientific historian. He did not practise the painstaking researches of modern historians, but made the best of what material he could find. Consequently inaccuracies have been discovered in his history. From the literary point of view, however, Hume is still interesting. " The first quality of an historian is to be true and impartial ; the next to be interesting," he once declared. Hume may not always be exact, but he is always interesting. He brought to history a clear mind and a lucid style which made his narrative eminently readable.

ERUDITION LEAVENED BY TRENCHANT WIT : GIBBON'S COLOSSAL MASTERPIECE

HISTORY only emerged in the eighteenth century as a literary art, but to that period belongs what is universally acknowledged to be the masterpiece of historical composition in English, Gibbon's *Decline and Fall of the Roman Empire.* Gibbon had prepared himself for the task of the historian by a course of long and extensive reading. The idea of writing the history of a phase of the Roman Empire came to him during a visit to Rome, in 1764. " As I sat musing amidst the ruins of the Capitol," he tells us, " while the barefooted friars were singing vespers in the temple of Jupiter, the idea of writing the decline and fall of the city first started into my mind." The task was forbiddingly difficult. Gibbon was to explore a vast tract of history, only parts of which had been charted. He had to reduce masses of material into order and present the narrative of the decline of Rome and the birth of modern Europe. " At the outset all was dark and doubtful ; even the title of the work, the limits of the introduction, the division of the chapters, and the order of the narrative ; and I was often tempted to cast away the labour of seven years." But he pursued his intention and, in 1776, the first volume of his history appeared.

Its popularity was immediate and lasting. "The first impression was exhausted in a few days ; a second and third edition were scarcely adequate to the demand . . . the book was on every table, and almost on every toilette." Hume wrote to the author : "Whether I consider the dignity of your style, the depth of your matter, and the extensiveness of your learning, I must regard the work as equally the object of esteem."

In spite of its popularity not every reader of *The Decline and Fall* admired it as much as Hume. It was received with a chorus of protest on the part of the clergy and other devout people who were offended by Gibbon's treatment of Christianity. He described the origin and growth of Christianity as if it were not supernatural in any way. In effect, his ironic attitude to Christianity amounted to a covert attack on revealed religion.

THE ARTIST'S VISION AND THE SCHOLAR'S CARE

THE most striking quality of Gibbon's history is its wide range. Other historians have confined themselves to one epoch or one country. Gibbon covers fifteen centuries in his account of the decline of Rome and includes all Western civilisation in his survey. Had he not possessed the artist's gift of treating every period in its right proportion he could never have presented the events of these centuries within the compass of a single narrative. What is a still greater tribute to his mastery of the art of history is that Gibbon's account is substantially accurate in spite of the immense ground it covers. Modern research has discovered facts of which Gibbon was unaware, but no serious flaws have been detected in his work. Width of range and accuracy of statement are not the only merits of *The Decline and Fall*. It has an epic grandeur. History in the hands of Gibbon becomes a momentous account of great events and great figures. He lavishes all the wealth of his literary resources on the description of memorable occasions, such as the Death of the Emperor Julian, the Taking of Jerusalem, and the Capture of Constantinople. Figures such as Mohammed, who dominated the stage of history during a thousand years, are portrayed with remarkable insight and skill. The greatness of the subject is reflected in the splendour of the style. The balanced phrases, the stately rhythm, and the sonorous roll of the sentences build up a style entirely in keeping with the dignity of the subject.

THE ROMANTIC REVIVAL CHANGES THE SPIRIT OF HISTORY

THE art of history has never reached a higher level than that attained in the works of Gibbon. Other historians of that age were too ready to judge the people of past epochs by their own standards. They came to history with their minds made up concerning questions of religion, morality, and politics. They took it for granted that mankind was the same in all ages and in all countries, and though this may be true enough as far as it relates to the fundamental qualities of men, at the same time there are differences in beliefs, thoughts, and manner of living between one age and another. This failure of the eighteenth-century historians to take account of the changes of society from one generation to another was not repeated by their successors in the next century. Indeed the latter were remarkable for their endeavours to understand the life of past ages, to realise how people did live in former times ; they did not assume that they were similar in outlook to themselves. The great change that is evident in the works of historians like Carlyle, was due to that movement which is known as the Romantic Revival.

A HISTORIAN WHO WROTE FROM THE HEART

THE spirit of the Romantic Revival is clearly manifested in such a work as Thomas Carlyle's *History of the French Revolution*, which is informed with sympathy and vivid understanding. When he laid down his pen after completing the work, Carlyle remarked to his wife : " . . . this I could tell the world ; you have not had for a hundred years any book that comes more direct and flamingly from the heart of a living man." History to Carlyle was not something to be studied and recorded dispassionately. The facts of history were not dead, but a living lesson. His belief that the events of history exhibited the workings of moral laws made the past intensely alive to him. Carlyle had a vivid imagination and he employed it fully in an effort to bring to life again the drama of the French Revolution and its principal actors.

As a result, his history pierces deeper than any mere narrative of cause and effect could do ; with his matchless sympathy he unfolds the motives and passions of the people. He

8

shows us men living and acting among perilous circumstances, sometimes failing and sometimes triumphing. No history has so much of the stuff of poetry in it. Carlyle saw all history as an illustration of the text that what a man sows that also shall he reap, and the French Revolution which brought a terrible retribution to the aristocracy for centuries of oppression was to him a striking instance of this truth. For one who wishes to know the unvarnished, prosaic truth about the French Revolution, Carlyle's work may not be ideal, but nowhere else will such graphic pictures of men like Mirabeau, Danton, and Robespierre be found, and nowhere else are events, such as the taking of the Bastille and the carnage of the Swiss Guard, presented in such vividly phrased descriptions.

A RIPE JUDGMENT AND A PRODIGIOUS MEMORY

THE work of Macaulay, the next great historian, has not quite the same depth of imagination. It has indeed, both in style and outlook, more resemblance to the work of eighteenth-century writers. Macaulay read incessantly, and was endowed with a prodigious memory. All his interests lay in the direction of history. " I am nothing if not historical," he declared once. On leaving Oxford, Macaulay read for the Bar. He entered Parliament in 1840, and from 1834–38 he served in India on the Supreme Council of India, performing much useful administrative and legal work. This experience gave him inside knowledge of the working of government, knowledge which enabled him to write with a ripe judgment on history.

Macaulay gained a considerable reputation as a writer by his historical essays, but his great work is *The History of England*. In the breadth of its information and in its minute description of events this history shows the fruits of his vast reading and the tenacity of his memory. By the brilliance of his style he makes history read like a novel. His style is oratorical and striking, like that of an advocate presenting his case, and, like the speeches of an eloquent speaker, it never fails to hold the reader's interest. In his desire to make his descriptions effective, Macaulay is sometimes given to exaggeration. Thus, describing the Massacre of Glencoe, he makes the frowning mountains higher and the gloomy pass darker than they actually were in order to create a fitting background for that tragedy. This tendency to exaggerate,

Thomas Babington Macaulay, master of descriptive history.

however, does not seriously impair the value of his history.

The history has been chiefly criticised, particularly since Macaulay's death, for its political bias. Macaulay did write history from the Whig point of view, but he was far from being a blind partisan. In any case the accuracy of Macaulay's history matters singularly little to the average reader who prefers literary skill to absolute scientific accuracy. Even if he were completely misleading, which he is not, Macaulay could be read with pleasure. The brilliance of his descriptions, his vivid, revealing character sketches, his fertility of illustration, are merits that give him a place in literature, whatever his value as an historian.

EXULTATION OF A PATRIOTIC ENGLISHMAN

JAMES ANTHONY FROUDE read Carlyle's *Reflections on the French Revolution* and was greatly struck by its imaginative qualities. He came to know Carlyle personally in 1849, when the latter inspired him to write history. Froude inherited Carlyle's sense of the drama of history and his faith in the importance of great men, but he was wise enough not to imitate the prose style of the master. His principal work is *The History of England from the Fall of Wolsey to the Defeat of the Spanish Armada.* These events are chosen as the beginning and the triumph of the Reformation in England. Froude writes from the point of view of a patriotic Englishman proud of the triumph of Protestantism and of the victory of England over Spain. His narrative of the rise of Protestantism and English national feeling never fails to be interesting, but its value as history is diminished by Froude's carelessness.

Although he did a large amount of original research, he was not an exact scholar and occasionally was guilty of inaccuracies. These inaccuracies aroused furious controversies when the history was published. Froude's historical judgments were hotly attacked by the rival historian, Freeman. It has been discovered that Froude's inaccuracies, after all, are minor ones, and his history still survives on account of its literary merit. He has a special talent for sketching graphic portraits of historical characters, such as these of Henry VIII., Mary, Queen of Scots, and Elizabeth. Froude's prose style is one of the purest and clearest to be found among historical writers. *The History of England* is his most important work, but the same literary art on a smaller canvas is revealed in the collection of essays entitled *Short Studies on Great Subjects*, and in the accounts of the English explorers, entitled *English Seamen in the Sixteenth Century*.

AN ENGLISH CHAMPION OF THE ARYAN RACE

FROUDE'S fiercest critic was a fellow-historian, Freeman. Freeman was a man of violent opinions and passions, and was easily moved by strong personal likes and dislikes. His historical work shows evidence of profound learning, but he was more of a scholar than a man of letters. He specialised in the early history of England and the result of his researches was the *History of the Norman Conquest*. Freeman approached his work with the fixed idea that the Anglo-Saxon element was of supreme importance in the evolution of English history and English institutions. He disliked the Celts and the French. His enthusiasm for the Anglo-Saxons affected his prose, and also induced him to use words of English derivation in preference to those borrowed from Latin. His style accordingly is rather diffuse and awkward. The material he accumulated has proved more valuable than his actual writing.

Macaulay, Froude, and Freeman had written on separate periods of English history, doing valuable research work in each epoch. The time was opportune for a more summary account of English history and this was presented in *A Short History of the English People*, by J. R. Green. No work covering the whole range of English history has met with greater popularity. Green possessed exactly these gifts required for making history a popular subject. In spite of his ill-health (he suffered from consumption) he was a man of amazing energy, throwing himself with great enthusiasm into any work he had to perform. He had a wonderful faculty for entering sympathetically into the lives of past generations, especially into the thoughts and feelings of the common people. Consequently a sense of the vitality and growth of the national life runs all through his history. He could reconstruct past scenes and episodes with singular vividness and his style rivals that of Macaulay in brilliancy and picturesqueness. By reason of all these qualities Green's history remains a thoroughly enjoyable account of the story of the English people.

One of the most popular of nineteenth-century historians was the American writer, W. H. Prescott. Prescott's two best-known works deal with the Spanish occupation of South America. The *History of the Conquest of Mexico* tells the story of Hernando Cortes' expedition, the Cortes whom Keats in his sonnet *On First Looking into Chapman's Homer* inaccurately represents as the discoverer of the Pacific. Prescott's history was received with a chorus of applause by the public who gave a similar reception to the parallel work, *The Conquest of Peru*. These works have enjoyed continued popularity because they read like historical romances.

MAKING THE PAST LIVE : THE MODERN IDEAL

MOST of the historians of the Victorian age were professors of history at Oxford or Cambridge as well as being men of letters. During the last century history first became a subject of study at the universities, and by the end of the century it had fallen into the hands of professors and academic students. Physical science, with its methods of accurate research, dominated intellectual activity, and attempts were made to study history by the same methods of scientific approach. In *The Times Literary Supplement* of March 16, 1922, the writer of an article entitled *History in Letters*, expressed views that had long directed the work of historians. " Absolute accuracy of fact in the trained researcher as he edits his charters and collates his records is the first and last need. It is science, the stern new governess of the Muses, which has set us to our modern way of writing history."

The supremacy of scientific investigation in history was challenged by Professor G. M. Trevelyan in a letter to the editor of the same paper, a fortnight later. " Critical sympathy with bygone passions," he wrote, " thoughts, religions, politics, ambitions, and aspirations, and above all, the power to understand how men act and are acted upon in large masses or small groups, these qualities are necessary as well as ' the absolute accuracy of fact in the trained researcher.' " Professor Trevelyan's views on the writing of history have triumphed. Accurate scientific research is given its due place by modern historians, but they also cultivate the literary qualities of an attractive style and vivid narrative.

A HISTORY THAT SPARKLES WITH UNDERSTANDING

As well as any living writer G. M. Trevelyan combines the qualities of the trained, scientific historian and the man of letters. In view of Trevelyan's ancestry his success as an historian is not surprising, for his father, Sir George Otto Trevelyan, the nephew of Lord Macaulay, was also an historian of considerable merit. In the *Life and Letters of Lord Macaulay*, Sir George Trevelyan produced one of the classics of biography, but its success has rather eclipsed his other works. Like his uncle Lord Macaulay, Sir George had a good deal of experience in public affairs before he began the composition of history. His favourite period was the last half of the eighteenth century, with which his best historical works, *The American Revolution* and *George III. and Charles Fox*, are concerned.

G. M. Trevelyan's principal works are *British History in the Nineteenth Century*, *England under the Stuarts*, *The History of England*, and *England under Queen Anne*. These histories reveal in an eminent degree sympathy with the passions, thoughts, hopes, and fears of past generations. Trevelyan possesses the breadth of imagination that enables him to identify himself with the way in which men used to live and feel. The facts of history are irradiated by a full understanding of their significance. History in the hands of Trevelyan is no mere recital of facts, of battles, sieges, and deaths, but a full account of the politics, religion, economics, and social life of a period. He incorporates the fruits of much research in his histories, but he knows how to present his knowledge in an attractive fashion. The style of his great ancestor Macaulay is hardly more vigorous, sparkling, and lucid, and his works are scarcely more readable.

H. G. WELLS SURVEYS THE PARADE OF THE CENTURIES

NONE of H. G. Wells's numerous novels and treatises has caused more sensation in the literary world or been more successful than his *Outline of History*. Other historians had written the history of a nation, of an epoch, or a movement that affected several nations. Wells boldly essayed to write the history of mankind. Wells does not believe in nations, for to him they seem petty and provocative of strife. He writes in the firm conviction that mankind is one family, and his history is meant to provide some justification for this international or rather supra-national attitude. It aims at supplying the world with those historical ideas without which there can be no common peace or prosperity. Even admitting that Wells has no historical qualification for his task beyond a wide general knowledge, one has to recognise that the *Outline of History* is an extraordinarily stimulating book. The novelty and freshness of the point of view that transcends a national outlook lends the book a peculiar interest. The emergence of life on the earth, the story of pre-human beings groping their way to civilisation, the account of the rise and decay of one civilisation after another, Greek succeeding Egyptian, Roman succeeding Greek, and passing away in its turn, the influence of Christianity, the appearance of science and its effect on society, all these form the subject-matter of a fascinating record.

CRITIC AND CATHOLIC: HILAIRE BELLOC

"THE OUTLINE OF HISTORY" provoked much criticism as well as enthusiasm. One of its severest critics was Hilaire Belloc who found it necessary to publish *A Companion to Mr. Wells's Outline*, containing a refutation of statements which seemed to Mr. Belloc erroneous. Belloc has shown himself a voluminous writer on many subjects, but his connection with history has always been closer than that of Wells. His purely historical works are *The French Revolution* and *A History of England*, but his biographies of Marie Antoinette, Richelieu, Wolsey, James II., and a monograph on Cromwell are of great historical interest also. As a staunch Roman Catholic, Belloc writes in the conviction that the Catholic Church has been the greatest factor in European civilisation, a position which it requires no distortion of facts to establish. His value as an historian is slightly impaired by his tendency to assume that a Catholic is probably a good man and a non-Catholic probably not so good a man, but his bias is so frankly stated that it does no harm. Above all, he is independent in the conclusions he arrives at from a study of historical documents.

DEEP LEARNING BENEATH A LUCID STYLE

ANOTHER Catholic historian, not so obtrusively Catholic and provided with an even deeper and more solid fund of learning than Belloc, is Professor Christopher Dawson. In his trilogy, *The Age of the Gods*, *The Making of Europe*, and *Progress and Religion*, Professor Dawson has successfully accomplished a work of colossal magnitude. He has traced the development of European culture, with special reference to the part played by religion in determining its nature, from primitive to modern times. His work has not gained the same popularity as that of Wells and Belloc, but its value as history is no less. Dawson's style is admirable in its dignity and scholarly character ; it is the reflection of an exquisitely cultured taste.

Wingfield-Stratford, the author of *The History of British Civilisation*, is Catholic in outlook but strictly impartial in intention. " It is the business of the historian to tell a story and that with as little fuss and intrusion of his own opinions as may be," expresses his attitude to historical composition, and this ideal of self-suppression he never violates. He attempts to give a complete survey of the development of British civilisation and not a cross-section dealing with politics or economics or social life. Beginning with the Stone Age his history traces the changing phases of political life, forms of government, religion, social life, everything that shapes the temper of a people.

SOME FINE EXAMPLES OF MODERN HISTORY

HISTORICAL writing has become too large a department of modern literature to be fully considered in anything less than a series of volumes. In addition to the historians mentioned above there are several important writers, like Professor F. J. C. Hearnshaw, Professor Ramsay Muir, and R. B. Mowat, whose concern with history is academic but who are also endowed with the gift of literary expression. Philip Guedalla has several historical works to his credit which enhance the reputation he has won as an essayist and biographer, and which are marked by artistic concealment of a vast amount of historical knowledge.

The eventful years of the World War have naturally inspired a considerable amount of historical literature. *A Short History of the Great War*, by Professor A. F. Pollard, and *The Great War : 1914–18*, by C. R. L. Fletcher are two competent records produced by trained historians. From a military point of view, *The Real War*, by Captain Liddell Hart, is a valuable book. It has been described by experts as one of the best histories on a small scale yet written on the World War. Another interesting work on this subject is *An Outline History of the War*, by G. V. Carey and H. S. Scott. *The Origins of the World War*, by an American writer, Professor S. B. Fay, shows signs of careful investigation.

HISTORY BOOKS TO READ AND ENJOY

HISTORY, according to Emerson, is the lengthened shadow of a man. For those readers of history whose interests are primarily literary the best approach to the subject is, not to start straight away with the shadow, but to read history as a background, for the living, actual reality—man himself as he appears in great novels, plays, memoirs. The fascinating chronicler, Holinshed, should be read after Shakespeare, who took much of his material for his historical plays from this source. Then, when one has become interested in the period of the Commonwealth through reading Bunyan, Pepys, and Milton, one should proceed to read extracts from Clarendon's *History of the Rebellion*, especially his character sketches which supplement those in Pepys and Evelyn. And similarly with each period. If one is particularly interested in the eighteenth century, in the parade of the gay and learned, the corrupted and holy characters, who jostle through the pages of Swift's *Journal to Stella* and Boswell's *Life of Johnson*, the background of historical perspective should be supplied by reading G. M. Trevelyan's *England Under Queen Anne*, and W. M. Thackeray's *The Four Georges*.

The study of more comprehensive histories should begin with such works as Wells's *Outline of History* or Hilaire Belloc's *History of England*, both written in a clear, easy style. Then one should proceed to Macaulay. His *History of England*, despite its length, makes as interesting reading as a novel. The same may be said of a work that might next be tackled : Gibbon's *Decline and Fall of the Roman Empire*, written in an elaborate, yet always witty style. Read after this Carlyle's *French Revolution*, and compare his vivid rush of words with Gibbon's eighteenth-century sobriety and restraint.

There is no standard book on history considered primarily as literature, but useful books on particular historians are : Froude's *Carlyle*, and Sir George Otto Trevelyan's *Macaulay* (Nelson).

BIOGRAPHY AND MEMOIR : NOBLE LIVES OF GREAT MEN

by M. J. MOULTON, M.A.(Edin.)

"**B**IOGRAPHY is, of the various kinds of narrative writing, that which is most eagerly read and most easily applied to the purpose of life." This remark of Dr. Johnson's applies equally well to modern biography. With the exception of the novel, no form of literature is more popular or more eagerly read. Johnson's remark indicates also the reason for the popularity of biography during the past two centuries. It is more easily applied than other kinds of literature to the reader's personal life. Its popularity, like that of the novel, is explained by the fact that it gives readers an opportunity of entering into the private lives and experiences of other people.

Treatises on mathematics or physics seldom become popular because they deal with matters remote from everyday life. The novel, in most cases, deals with the experiences of one or more characters whom the novelist by his art can make as real, as actual, as living people. The biography, also, tells the experiences of a single character, but in this case the human interest is stronger because we know that it is the narrative of a real, flesh-and-blood person. We believe that men like Soames in Galsworthy's *Forsyte Saga* existed, and do exist, but, at the same time, we feel that Soames moves in a different world from ours, that his experiences have not much bearing on our lives. With the character in a biography the case is entirely different. We know that he existed ; therefore, all his experiences can be compared with our own, whether to realise their differences or their similarity. Also, nothing is more interesting than to penetrate into the lives of men whom we knew only as Parliamentary figures, authors of books, or great religious leaders, and see them in the intimacy of their private affairs.

HOW BIOGRAPHY DIFFERS FROM THE NOVEL

THE biography resembles the novel in its appeal to human interest, but, since the biographer is relating the life-story of a real person, he has to stick to the facts of that life. The novelist can create any character he pleases, endow that character with any qualities and experiences he pleases, so long as he preserves the illusion of reality. In other words, the novelist depends on his creative imagination. The biographer cannot give rein to his imagination. His character was born in a certain year, married a certain person in another, and so on. But, though the facts are there, the motives are not always evident. The biographer must, therefore, use his imagination to enter into the mind of his character, to sympathise with him, and to understand what motives impelled him to certain actions. Nevertheless, biography demands observation and understanding more than creative imagination. In this respect, then, the biography differs from the novel.

THE BIOGRAPHER'S SEARCH FOR TRUTH

LET us now consider what qualities are essential in a bio-graphy and how we can tell whether a biography is good or bad. If the biography contains the record of the life of an individual it is obvious that that record is worthless and mis-leading unless it is truthful. The first essential quality of a good biography is truthfulness. No falsification or suppression is permissible. Sometimes out of consideration for the feeling of relatives, biographers have suppressed disagreeable episodes in the life of their subject. But if the truth cannot be recorded without injury to the feelings of relatives, the biographer should wait until time makes his disclosures less painful.

There can be no question about the necessity of truthful-ness in a biography, but the further question arises how far is it possible to attain the truth ? The life of an individual is so complex, he is actuated by so many motives which another can never fully understand that the task of the biographer seems impossible, especially if he is writing the life of a man long dead whom he never knew personally. Perhaps the biographer can never attain truth with scientific accuracy, but by making good use of his material he can make an honest endeavour to get at the truth as far as is humanly possible. The good biographer goes to the letters, diaries, journals, or any other writings his subject has left and uses them as evidence in the revelation of his personality. Truth-fulness is a quality that must be insisted on in a biography, because a biography deals with facts.

HISTORY SEEN IN BIOGRAPHICAL PERSPECTIVE

IN this respect the biographer resembles the historian who seeks to record past events accurately. History, like biography, is concerned with the lives of prominent men who have profoundly influenced the society of their time. The distinction between history and biography is that biography describes the life of an individual, whereas history describes the evolution of society and all the forces that influence it. The single person in the eyes of a biographer has value for his own sake ; in the eyes of the historian he is only important if his writings or actions affected the rest of society. Milton to the historians appears as a man who wrote pamphlets in defence of Cromwell's government and was typical of the puritan spirit. To the biographer Milton is a human being whose development as a poet was disturbed by his domestic troubles and the turmoil of civil war.

A biography may be exact and truthful in its story of an individual, but it may still be unreadable if it is not a work of art. It is not enough for the biographer to collect all the facts he can about his subject, and verify these facts ; he must present the account of his subject's life in a readable and interesting way. For this purpose a clear, lucid style and a talent for narrative writing is necessary because the author has a story to tell. Selection of details is also necessary and the biographer must show a fine tact in their selection. In addition, he requires a sense of perspective. His aim should be to present the study of his subject's life as an artistic unity with all the details placed in their proper order and relation.

BIOGRAPHY IN EARLY TIMES

ALTHOUGH biography appears as an independent form of literature comparatively late, its origins lie far back in the history of our literature. When a man possessed any striking quality that impressed his fellows, such as leadership, saintliness, or poetical genius, they naturally preserved his memory after his death by recalling his deeds or his sayings. In order to preserve his memory better they took to writing down their recollections of him instead of handing them down orally. It is to this desire to commemorate the dead that biography owes its origin.

The earliest biographies were written in Latin by monks to preserve the memory of the saints and, at the same time, to teach the people by giving them examples of saintly lives to follow. Adamnan's *Life of St. Columba*, written about 690, and Bede's *Life of St. Cuthbert*, are the best-known examples of these lives of the saints. The weakness of these biographies is that the writers accept stories of miracles and legends about the saints as long as they point a moral. The biographers are not interested in their subjects simply as human beings, but as models to hold up for the instruction of the people. Consequently they do not make any serious attempt to get at the truth about the lives of their subjects. The first life of a layman, the *Life of Alfred the Great*, by Bishop Asser, written in the ninth century, shows little advance on the lives of the saints. It is in part a chronicle and a collection of notes on events, and gives no great insight into the personality of Alfred. For some centuries after Asser's *Life of Alfred* biography disappears, and what details we have of the lives of great men are included in chronicles or annals.

Biography was revived in the sixteenth century when a fresh impulse of patriotic feeling aroused interest in the lives of prominent men. Two important biographical narratives were written in the middle of this century, Roper's *Life of More* and Cavendish's *Life of Wolsey*. Roper was married to a daughter of Sir Thomas More, lived in his household, and composed his biography shortly after his father-in-law's execution. It is a readable account of More's life, embodying interesting scenes and conversations, but its tone is perhaps too biased to make it an accurate record. Cavendish wrote about twenty-four years after the death of Wolsey, and was able to write with greater detachment than Roper. Cavendish's biography is written with lucidity of style, with tenderness and charm. Its theme of the changing nature of human fortune raises the *Life of Wolsey* to the level of a tragedy.

In 1579, North's translation of *Plutarch's Lives* was published, and its effect on later English biography was profound. Plutarch, in the first century A.D., had written the lives of prominent Greeks and Romans in pairs, each pair consisting of one of each nationality. Plutarch wrote in the conviction that the conspicuous events in a man's life are not so illuminating as the circumstances of his private life. Yet, in spite of the example of Plutarch, English biography did not flourish in the early part of the seventeenth century. Authors were diverted from the writing of full-length biography to the compilation of character sketches. Numerous imitations of Theophrastus, a Greek writer of character sketches, were produced, and individuals were regarded as types of one quality or another and not simply as human beings. Several writers, such as Aubrey, Wood, and Fuller, collected biographical notes, but these are too fragmentary and disconnected to be regarded as biographies.

THE CHARM OF WALTON'S "LIVES"

THE first outstanding biographer in English literature was Izaak Walton, the author of that ever-popular book, *The Compleat Angler*. Walton was born, in 1593, at Stafford, but most of his life was spent in London where he carried on business, probably as an ironmonger. He enjoyed the friendship of men of letters and divines whom he attracted by the charm of his character. Walton's biographical writings consist of a collection of five miniature studies : three of personal friends, Donne, Sir Henry Walton, and Dr. Sanderson, and two of contemporaries, George Herbert and Richard Hooker, with whom he was not personally acquainted. He wrote from memory with the assistance of the accounts of some friends, and without making much careful research. The principal merit of Walton's *Lives* is the charm of the style which reflects his studious and devout temperament.

Walton's *Life of Dr. Donne* is perhaps the best of the collection, and an analysis of it will indicate the method employed by the writer. He traces the events of Donne's life in a rather summary fashion, informing us about his birth, his education at Oxford and Cambridge, his travels in preparation for public office, his romantic marriage which antagonised his wife's relatives, his subsequent hardships which were relieved by his entrance into the Church where he concluded a pious ministry by becoming Dean of St. Paul's. After tracing the incidents of Donne's life, Walton discusses the traits of his character. " Now the English Church had gained a second St. Austine, for, I think, none was so like him before his Conversion ; none so like St. Ambrose after it ; and if his youth had the infirmities of the one, his age had the excellencies of the other ; the learning and holiness of both." From a consideration of Donne's character Walton returns to describe his last sermon which was delivered in spite of severe illness and was followed soon after by his death.

The dignity and rhythmical beauty of Walton's style may be appreciated by reading his final observations on the character of Donne. " He was earnest and unwearied in the search of knowledge ; with which, his vigorous soul is now satisfied, and employed in a continual praise of the God that first breathed it into his active body ; that body, which once was a Temple of the Holy Ghost, and is now become a small quantity of Christian dust ; but I shall see it re-inanimated."

"LITTLE LIVES" BY A GREAT MAN

AFTER Walton we find biographical sketches, but no outstanding biographies until we come to the next century, when Johnson wrote his *Lives of the Poets*. In a way, these Lives are rather biographical sketches than biographies. Johnson was commissioned by a bookseller to write " little Lives and little Prefaces to a little edition of the English Poets." The length of these introductions which form the *Lives of the Poets* vary according to the poet's importance. Johnson's method was similar to that of Walton—that is, he wrote out of a full mind without making exhaustive researches. He wrote these *Lives* towards the end of his own long life, most of which had been spent in the study and practice of literature. He had come in contact with many men of letters and acquired a vast amount of information about literary affairs which was stored up in his retentive memory. It was fortunate that he should have received this commission ; otherwise his rich knowledge of the details of the lives of men of letters might have died with him.

THE PRINCIPLES THAT GUIDED JOHNSON

JOHNSON had no great faith in painstaking research ; he stated on one occasion that the business of adjusting the minute details of literary history was tedious and unnecessary. His greatest contribution to the practice of biography was his resolute endeavour to get away from panegyric and record the truth. " We have had too many honeysuckle lives of Milton," he said to Malone, " mine shall be in another strain." With his passion for truth he combined a keen interest in the peculiarities of individuals, in those points where they differ from others. The best of the *Lives* are those of Milton, Dryden, Pope, Addison, Swift, Collins, and Gray, although the last is not very sympathetic. Equally important with Johnson's practice are his theories on the writing of biography.

In some of his essays, among other things, he points out the interest intimate and homely details give to a biographical work. The biographer should "lead the thoughts into domestic privacies, and display the minute details of early life!" When we find the literary leader of his day discussing the art of biography it is evident that we are on the threshold of important developments.

THE MASTERPIECE OF ENGLISH BIOGRAPHY

THIS important development was the triumph of biography in Boswell's *Life of Johnson*. But before we consider this masterpiece it is necessary to glance at a work which considerably influenced Boswell. William Mason's *Life of Gray*, issued in 1775, was something of an innovation in the writing of biography. Previous biographers had inserted occasional letters for the purpose of illustrating the life of their subject, but Mason determined to make the fullest use of Gray's available letters by arranging them so that they would tell the story of his life. He explains his method when he says : " In a word, Mr. Gray will become his own biographer. . . . I might have written his life in the common form perhaps with more reputation to myself ; but surely not with equal information to the reader ; for whose sake I have never related a single circumstance of Mr. Gray's life in my own words, when I could employ *his* for the purpose."

Boswell, who was a careful student of biography, saw the advantages of this method and developed it when he came to write the life of Dr. Johnson. During the years of his friendship with Johnson he had accumulated a vast amount of material in the form of letters, records of conversations, and reminiscences of Johnson related by his friends. He was able to use his material to the best advantage because he had definite ideas on the right method for the biographer to adopt. This is shown when he says : " Mason's *Life of Gray* is excellent, because it is interspersed with letters which show us the man. His *Life of Whitehead* is not a Life at all ; for there is neither a letter nor a saying from first to last. I am absolutely certain that my mode of biography, which gives not only a history of Johnson's visible progress through the world and of his publications, but a view of his mind in his letters and conversations, is the most perfect that can be conceived and will be more of a Life than any work that has ever yet appeared." Accordingly, Boswell narrates the particulars of Johnson's life from year to year. "I do it chronologically," he says, "giving year by year his publications, if there were any; his letters, his conversations, and everything else that I can collect. It appears to me that mine is the best plan of biography that can be conceived; for my readers will, as near as may be, accompany Johnson in his progress, and, as it were, see each scene as it happens."

THE QUALITIES THAT MADE BOSWELL SUPREME

THE enduring value of Boswell's biography, its position as the greatest of English biographies, is due to Boswell's industry, his accuracy, and his grasp of the function of the biographer. His painstaking research is beyond all praise. The enduring charm of the Life, however, does not depend entirely on these qualities. It remains the most widely read and best loved biography owing to its vivid pictures of an arresting personality. Johnson appears before us with his huge frame, short-sighted eyes blinking from a face pitted by small-pox, his body rolling, his hands gesticulating, and his voice thundering as he pronounces the final word on some disputed point. Johnson's appearance, his odd manners and his habits draw to him the affectionate regard we reserve for peculiar but likeable people. The picture of Johnson is no superficial one, however. Boswell reveals also Johnson's massive, intellectual strength, his sincere piety, his courage, and unfailing charity.

Boswell's *Johnson* deserves to stand as the supreme example of English biography because it embodies the three qualities we have noted as necessary for a good biography. Its accuracy has been established by the researches of later scholars. A hundred and fifty years of careful research has added little but unimportant scraps to our knowledge of Johnson. Boswell never leaves his subject to digress into contemporary affairs. The other men of letters who appear in the biography do so only in so far as they are connected with Johnson. Boswell's powers of artistic construction are evident from the use he made of his material. His skill in joining together isolated conversations, in maintaining the narrative interest, is such that the reader will hardly observe that that period of Johnson's life before he met Boswell is treated in proportionately much less space than the period of their acquaintance. Yet Boswell knew Johnson only for the last twenty years of his life. In addition to his qualities of accuracy and artistic sense, Boswell has the further merit of sympathising with his subject. His attitude to Johnson is admirable. He suppresses himself, records without judging, stands aside and lets Johnson reveal himself. This rare tact is supplemented by an easy narrative style which makes the biography in Boswell's own words " one of the most entertaining books ever written."

A SON-IN-LAW'S FAITHFUL PORTRAYAL

LOCKHART'S *Life of Scott* carried on the Boswell tradition so successfully that his biography rivals Boswell's masterpiece. By general agreement it is considered as the second of English biographies, while some critics have even assigned it first place. Before he undertook to write the *Life of Scott* Lockhart had already gained practice in biography by writing a *Life of Burns*, one of the few works on that poet which is neither an attack on his character nor an apologia for his life. As Scott's son-in-law, Lockhart had ample opportunities of enjoying his company, of understanding his character, and gaining knowledge of his life. For his biography he could draw on personal reminiscences, Scott's journals, and an enormous collection of letters. In his portrait of Scott, Lockhart attempts to remain scrupulously honest and to remain unbiased by his family connection with him. He says : " I have endeavoured to lay before the reader those parts of Sir Walter's character to which we have access as they were indicated in his sayings and doings through the long series of his years—making use, whenever it was possible, of his own letters and diaries rather than of any other materials, but refraining from obtruding almost anything of comment. It was my wish to let the character develop itself." Lockhart followed Boswell in employing the material his subject left, but he wisely refrained from reproducing actual conversations. Johnson was a brilliant conversationalist ; Scott did not shine in company.

Lockhart's biography is much more extensive than that of Boswell. Carlyle, while admiring its frankness, criticised its construction, maintaining that it was a compilation rather than a work of art. Carlyle's criticism is partly justified. Lockhart is rather fond of massing details, but he is at the same time a skilful narrator. The reader is presented with the fullest information on the events of Scott's life, but the narrative does not flag in spite of its leisurely manner. Because his information is so complete, because he treated his subject with absolute frankness, because he approached him with understanding and sympathy, Lockhart has painted as vivid a picture of Scott as Boswell has done of Johnson. In the pages of Lockhart, Scott appears in his true light, as one of the most admirable, most generous figures in literature.

METHODS DICTATED BY VICTORIAN DELICACY

WITH the Victorian age a change came over the spirit of biography. Boswell and his followers had not suppressed the little weaknesses of their characters, but the Victorians felt that it was undesirable to record disagreeable details. The conception of the great man as the hero arose and the revelation of his weaknesses was thought to detract from his merit. " What business," said Tennyson, " has the public to know about Byron's wildnesses ? He has given them fine work and they ought to be satisfied." The notion that the biographer should present the great man's life as a model to his contemporaries comes back into biography. By this time biography had become firmly established as a literary form, and it was taken for granted that the life of every prominent man of letters or affairs should be written. Usually a relative was nominated for this task ; indeed a biographer was appointed with almost as great regularity as an executor.

This type of commemorative biography generally took the form of a Life and Letters The *Life of Arnold* by Dean Stanley set the Victorian fashion of respectability in biography. Mrs. Grote wrote a charming study of her husband, the historian. Mrs. Kingsley performed a similar office for her husband, Charles Kingsley, the novelist. Sir George Trevelyan's *Life and Letters of Macaulay* which belongs to this category is a work of real literary value. It is particularly interesting in the account it gives of the precocious child Macaulay was and of his almost incredible feats of memorising.

THE FEMININE TOUCH IN BIOGRAPHY

A NOTICEABLE feature of Victorian biography is the appearance of women as biographers—a rôle for which feminine sympathy and intuition make them eminently suitable. Margaret, Duchess of Newcastle, had written a life of her husband in the seventeenth century, but no ladies followed her example till the nineteenth century. We have mentioned the biographies of Mrs. Grote and Mrs. Kingsley. The outstanding work of the period produced by a woman biographer is Mrs. Gaskell's *Life of Charlotte Brontë*. When Mrs. Gaskell's work appeared it was criticised on the grounds of inaccuracy. Minor inaccuracies there may be, but Mrs. Gaskell's biography is likely to remain a classic owing to her sympathetic interpretation of the character of Charlotte Brontë. Mrs. Gaskell had not known Charlotte long or intimately, but she made the best use of her acquaintance and of the letters Charlotte left. The strange life of the Brontë household in their remote Yorkshire parsonage is related at the beginning with the descriptive art of the novelist. Mrs. Gaskell succeeds in exhibiting admirably the contrast between the dull, practical round of Charlotte's daily existence and her brilliant intellectual and deep emotional life.

A BIOGRAPHER WHO TOLD THE WHOLE TRUTH

THE conventions of Victorian biography were challenged by Froude's *Life of Carlyle*. On his death in 1881, Carlyle left his letters, memoirs, and journals in the hands of his friend Froude, the historian. Froude determined to write a truthful biography and disregard the current notions about revealing only the praiseworthy features of great men. " By recasting the entire material, by selecting chosen passages out of his own and his wife's letters, by exhibiting the fair and beautiful side of the story only, it would have been easy without suppressing a single material point, to draw a picture of a faultless character ! " But Froude preferred to show Carlyle as he was and not as the public expected him to be. The irritability and obstinacy of Carlyle are revealed along with his courage and independence, and Froude was hotly criticised on the grounds that he had been disloyal to the memory of his friend. Now that standards of biography have changed we can take a calmer view and give Froude the credit his veracity deserved. His frankness does not diminish the greatness of Carlyle and his vivid style is admirably suitable for biography.

Father and Son by Edmund Gosse is noteworthy both for its revelation of two conflicting personalities and as a reflection of social conditions at the end of the Victorian era. It is partly a biography and partly an autobiography. It is the biography of the father, Philip Henry Gosse, and the autobiography of the son, Edmund, up to the age of twenty-one. Gosse's father was attached to the Plymouth Brethren persuasion, a form of extreme evangelical Protestantism which proved uncongenial to the son. The theme of the book is the conflict in temperament and outlook between the father and the son and the effect of this painful conflict on the son's character. Its social value consists in the fact that it is " a record of educational conditions which, having passed away, will never return." Gosse further terms it " the diagnosis of a dying Puritanism." One is impressed by the writer's courage in revealing painful episodes in his life, the recounting of which must have been attended with considerable emotional pain, and also by his powers of selecting and arranging the most revealing incidents.

Froude's departure from the orthodox Victorian practice did not seriously affect the form of biography. It still followed the Boswellian method of incorporating as much first-hand material as possible. Even in 1905, E. V. Lucas wrote a highly successful *Life of Lamb* on the same plan. He fused into narrative form all the information he could gather about Lamb from his own contemporary writings. " I have tried as far as possible," he says, " to keep the story of Lamb's life in his own and his sister's words and in those of their contemporaries." E. V. Lucas fills in the gaps between the various letters and extracts and succeeds in reconstructing the figure of Lamb as he appeared to his contemporaries.

BIOGRAPHY COMES UNDER A NEW INFLUENCE

IN 1918 a book appeared which has become a landmark in the history of biography. *Eminent Victorians*, by Lytton Strachey, contained biographical studies of four representative Victorians—Cardinal Manning, Florence Nightingale, Dr. Arnold, and General Gordon. Strachey's treatment of his characters was something new in biography. Hitherto the biographer had sympathised with and interpreted his subject. Strachey remains detached, neither indulging in hero-worship nor depreciating his subject. He does not hesitate to reveal the ridiculous sides of his characters, even drawing attention to them by his delicate irony. Strachey, who was above all an artist, saw that it was necessary to reform biographical practice in England. Biography, which he regarded as " the most delicate and humane of all the branches of the art of writing " had grown formless and inartistic.

He was appalled by Victorian commemorative biography. " These two fat volumes, with which it is our custom to commemorate the dead—who does not know them, with their ill-digested masses of material, their slip-shod style, their tone of tedious panegyric, their lamentable lack of selection, of detachment, of design ! " Strachey's own biographies are models of selection and of design. He follows his own dictum that " a brevity which excludes everything that is redundant and nothing that is significant—that surely, is the first duty of the biographer."

But Strachey's practice was not limited to making the biography a work of art. He abandoned the tone of panegyric and made a courageous effort to record the truth ; " to lay bare the facts of some cases, as I understand them, dispassionately, impartially, and without ulterior interest " seemed to him another principle the biographer should observe. If we study Strachey's sketch of Dr. Arnold's life, these innovations in biography become evident.

TWO QUEENS AS STRACHEY SAW THEM

STRACHEY followed up his biographical studies of eminent Victorians by a full-length biography of Queen Victoria. The same qualities of honesty, impartiality, and artistic construction are apparent in this book. A biographer with less power of selection might have been overwhelmed by the crowded events of Queen Victoria's life, but Strachey keeps the biography a personal record and touches but lightly on current affairs. A later work, *Elizabeth and Essex*, deals with an episode in the life of Queen Elizabeth. Strachey considered the Elizabethan period was not so much of a whitened sepulchre as the Victorian age, so in this book his destructive irony is not so frequently in play. The tortuous, capricious ways of Elizabeth are traced with fine understanding. The handsome, romantic figure of Essex, the subtle and learned Bacon, and other Elizabethan personages are described in more colourful prose than Strachey usually employed.

BIOGRAPHY BECOMES DRAMATIC

A BIOGRAPHER who has influenced English practice in biography and who has gained a European reputation is

Emil Ludwig, the German writer. His biographies of Bismarck, Napoleon, Goethe, Kaiser Wilhelm II., and Christ (entitled *The Son of Man*) have been translated into English. Ludwig brings into biography the qualities of other literary forms. His biographies read like a curious combination of a novel and a drama. The thoughts passing through the mind of the character are recreated with the imagination of the novelist. The dramatic nature of Ludwig's work, however, must chiefly impress the reader. The graphic presentation of scenes, the transition from one episode to another, is exactly in the manner of drama. In his introduction to *Goethe*, Ludwig writes : " This book will display in a slowly moving panorama the landscapes of his soul." It is significant also that Ludwig wrote a drama on Bismarck as well as a biography of him.

André Maurois, the French novelist and biographer, has more affinities with English writers in temperament and style than Ludwig. His contact with English troops during the War, when he acted as a kind of liaison officer, excited an interest in English literature and history which induced Maurois to choose Englishmen for the subjects of his biographies. His most important work is the *Life of Disraeli*, but *Ariel, or The Life of Shelley, Byron*, and *King Edward and his Times*, are biographies of outstanding merit also.

HONESTY AND ART IN MODERN BIOGRAPHY

OF the making of biographies in modern times there seems to be no end. They are produced with facility and read with avidity. Readers turn to them so eagerly because the biographer takes as much pains to win their interest as the novelist does ; he uses all his literary skill to make his narrative at once informative and enjoyable. To comment on all the modern biographies that deserve attention would be a prodigious task and require infinite space, but it may be said that both in numbers and general level of execution the biography now enjoys a prestige that it has never done previously in any period of literary history. Winston Churchill and J. L. Garvin in their exhaustive studies of Marlborough and Chamberlain respectively have added two notable examples to the list of Life and Times biographies. Edith Sitwell in her *English Eccentrics* finds material for biography in the lives of obscure but peculiar people. Hilaire Belloc has supplemented his work as an historian by writing biographies of historical figures, such as Marie Antoinette, Wolsey, James II., and Cranmer. Biographers have been especially active in reconstructing the lives of literary personages of the past. *The Stricken Deer* (a life of Cowper), by David Cecil, *Thackeray*, by Malcolm Elwin, *Byron, The Last Journey*, and *Tennyson*, by Harold Nicholson, *Charlotte Brontë*, by E. F. Benson, and *Johnson*, by Hugh Kingsmill, are some specimens of modern biography having to do with the lives of men of letters. The pattern of modern biography is naturally not standard, but its general characteristics, one may say, are accuracy based on research, honesty in interpreting the facts of the subject's life, independence of judgment, and a strict attention to the artistic features of the biography.

THE ART OF SELF-PORTRAYAL

AUTOBIOGRAPHY, a writer's story of his own life, has increased in popularity along with biography, but examples of great autobiographies are rather rarer. At first sight, it seems strange that a man should leave his life to be written by another person when he himself must best know the facts of it. Johnson declared that " every man's life should be best written by himself." Yet several factors have prevented great men and women from narrating the story of their own lives. In the first place there is the natural feeling of modesty. How can a man be certain that the story of his life will prove interesting and significant to other people ? " It is a hard and nice subject for a man to write of himself, it grates his own heart to say anything of disparagement, and the reader's ears to hear anything of praise from him," wrote Cowley.

Modesty prevents some men from writing the story of their lives. Others find it unnecessary because they express themselves in other ways. A novelist may relate his own experiences under the name of a fictitious character. The experiences of David Copperfield, for instance, follow those of Dickens's own life to some extent. When a writer expresses his personality in creative work an autobiography becomes superfluous. Various motives, however, have impelled writers to set modesty aside, and tell the story of their own lives. Sometimes an autobiography becomes necessary to clear away misunderstanding. An accusation of intellectual dishonesty levelled against him by Kingsley provoked Newman to write his spiritual autobiography. Other writers have composed autobiographies to amuse their leisure hours. Such was the origin of Gibbon's *Memoirs*.

OBSTACLES TO TRUTH IN AUTOBIOGRAPHY

COMMENTING on the comparative scarcity of good autobiographies, we made the obvious remark that a man should be better acquainted with his own experiences than any other person, however sympathetic that person may be. A man should be certain of the facts of his life, should recall his motives, his feelings, his inner strivings in a manner that an outsider can never do. It would seem, then, that an autobiography is bound to be more truthful than a biography, and that it will represent the nearest approach to an accurate record of an individual life. Several obstacles, however, stand in the way of complete accuracy in an autobiography. First of all, there is the natural tendency to forget past events and feelings in our lives. Few people can remember very clearly their childhood experiences; only several outstanding incidents of this time of life remain distinct in the memory. A man looking back over a crowded life will inevitably find blanks at certain points, and the task of tracing his entire development becomes difficult when these gaps intervene.

In the second place, there are episodes in his life which the writer will hesitate to reveal owing to their disagreeable nature. A sense of shame will prevent some disclosures, while some unpleasant episodes will be unconsciously omitted for, as psychologists assure us, we tend to forget incidents that arouse painful memories. Yet the episodes the writer omits may be important for the understanding of his emotional make-up. A biographer, provided he has access to information about disagreeable episodes in the life of his subject, would be less hesitant in recording them than the man himself.

Thirdly, the autobiographer will omit details which do not appear essential in order to preserve the unity of his narrative. A man's experiences are so manifold, so complex that he has to exercise selection in narrating them. The autobiographer will tend to trace his development in some particular direction, say his spiritual or emotional development. Therefore, he may not present a picture of his character in its full complexity. For these reasons an autobiography may give us more insight into the life of a man, but it may not contain a fuller record than the work of a biographer on the same subject. Finally, knowledge of oneself is exceedingly difficult to achieve and, in any case, a study of a man is not complete unless we learn how he appears to other people. For this reason autobiographies and biographies may be regarded as complementary, one revealing how a man appears in his own eyes, the other how he appears in the eyes of contemporaries or of posterity.

THE NEED TO CONQUER RETICENCE

IF we ask what are the qualities we should expect to find in a good autobiography, our question must be answered in the same terms as that relating to biography. Truthfulness, we may say, is a quality essential in a good autobiography. The reader must be convinced that the writer is giving a faithful account of his own life, that he is sincere in his desire to record the truth, that he is frank even to the extent of relating his weaknesses and mistakes. Any feeling that the writer is posing, that he is anxious to show himself in the best light, that he is suppressing anything that would make an unfavourable impression, obviously diminishes the value of an autobiography. The autobiographer should relate his experiences, his motives, and purposes without any self-approbation or apology, and leave the rest to the reader's judgment. The autobiographer is telling the story of himself as an individual. He should include everything of significance that illustrates the development of his personality, but he should not aim at portraying people he has met or at tracing contemporary events unless these people or events have had a profound influence on his life.

The third essential feature of an autobiography is that the writer should select his details and construct his narrative so that the whole appears as a work of art. An old man reviewing his life would recall his experiences haphazardly and incoherently, mingling the important and the accidental. The purpose of the autobiographer is not so much to inform us of all that he has done or has had done to him, but to show us what he *is* and how his outlook has been formed. He must present us with the narrative of his life so ordered that we can follow the formation of his character, realise what influences shaped it, what ideals the writer set in front of him, what were his intentions, and how far he has succeeded in achieving the work he wished to perform. For this delicate analysis of one's own character the intuition and literary skill of an artist are necessary.

AUTOBIOGRAPHIES PROMPTED BY RELIGIOUS ZEAL

THE type of autobiography that occurs perhaps most frequently in English is that written by authors or religious thinkers to trace their intellectual and spiritual experiences, leaving out of account the more trivial details of their lives. The religious autobiography has usually been written after a spiritual crisis, such as conversion. *The Confessions of St. Augustine*, the classic example of the religious autobiography, describes his conversion from paganism to Christianity. Bunyan's *Grace Abounding to the Chief of Sinners*, though not professedly an autobiography, is an account of his awakening to the saving grace of Christ. It reveals the deep religious experiences of the writer and the intense struggles of his soul in the fight against sin.

With this record of the spiritual life of a Puritan written in the seventeenth century, we can compare Cardinal Newman's *Apologia pro Vita sua* written in the nineteenth century, and describing his conversion from Anglicanism to Roman Catholicism. An unprovoked slander from Charles Kingsley who accused him of intellectual dishonesty aroused Newman to vindicate himself. He took his pen, wrote day and night, often weeping under the emotional strain, setting down his religious experiences just as he felt and remembered, and finally achieving a work moving in its sincerity and conviction. Although he wrote without any premeditation, the style of Newman's *Apologia* is a model of English prose. He triumphantly answered his accusers and gained himself a place in the affections of all readers who value honest, sincere, and courageous thought.

LITERARY MEN COMMENT ON THEIR WORK

SEVERAL literary men have written their autobiographies as commentaries on their work, to show their intellectual development, what opinions they have cherished or abandoned, and what purpose they have set before themselves. Autobiography of this kind appears in the eighteenth century, when we find three interesting personal documents produced by Hume, Gibbon, and the American politician and author, Benjamin Franklin. Hume prefixed an autobiographical sketch to his *History of England* (1777). This short autobiography, written just before his death, contains little more than the history of his writings and of their reception by the public, but even from this short sketch the reader gains an impression of the modest, equable, friendly nature of the writer. Benjamin Franklin's *Autobiography* was written for the benefit of his son. It is a straightforward, direct narrative of the varied experiences of the writer and his rise to fame as an American statesman. The reader is left with the impression that Franklin was a man of prudence, sagacity, and eminent good sense. His autobiography is enlivened by the attention he pays to the trivial but illuminating episodes of his life. Thus he describes himself entering Philadelphia eating one roll while he carried the others under his arm. Touches like these introduced in a natural, unstudied fashion make the reader acquainted with Franklin the man, as well as with Franklin the statesman.

The autobiography with the greatest literary value of these three is Gibbon's *Memoirs*. Although the title Memoirs is used, the work is autobiographical in intention and form. The word autobiography was first used in 1809. Gibbon did not write an intimate account of his life. He outlined the main facts : his parentage, his education, his soldiering in the Militia, his residence in Lausanne, his activities in Parliament, and so on, but he was no believer in exposing his sentiments and inner strivings. The book contains the story of Gibbon, the historian of the Roman Empire, rather than of Gibbon the man. He records with some care his preparation for his great book, *The Decline and Fall of the Roman Empire*. He tells of his historical studies, his choice of a subject, his first attempts at writing, his revisions of the earlier chapters, and finally he describes the completion of the work in a memorable passage where for once the calm dignity of his style is tinged with emotion.

THE FASCINATION OF UNSHRINKING CANDOUR

ONE type of autobiography which has not been greatly practised in English, and the best examples of which belong to foreign literatures, is the confessional autobiography. The writers of Confessions endeavour to give a full and unashamed account of their lives, of their emotional as well as of their intellectual and spiritual experiences. The unshrinking candour of these writers lends a fascinating quality to their autobiographies. They reveal the ridiculous, mean, and sordid aspects of their lives, concealing nothing they have done or thought, however unworthy. Benvenuto Cellini, an Italian writer, in his confessional autobiography relates the story of his adventurous life, and confesses to theft and murder. His life story reads like a picaresque novel in its variety of incident and its pictures of low life.

Rousseau, the French philosopher, gives us an equally frank account of his life in his *Confessions*. " I wish to show to my fellows a man in all the truth of nature, and this man will be myself," he declares. Without any suppression he relates what he did, what he thought, what he was. He says : " I have shown myself such as I was ; despicable and vile when I was so, good, generous, sublime when I was so ; I have unveiled my inner being such as you have seen your-self." The character of Rousseau, a strange blend of generosity and selfishness, of strength and weakness, is fully displayed in the pages of his *Confessions*. The philosopher who extols parental love leaves his own children to subsist on charity. The autobiographies of Cellini and Rousseau are extremely interesting as the records of the complex natures of two men of genius, their vices, their inconsistencies, their endeavours, their hopes, and their failures.

AN OPIUM ADDICT REVEALS HIS DREAMS

No autobiography so frankly confessional as those of Cellini and Rousseau exists in English. The first English autobiography of this kind was written in the seventeenth century, by Lord Herbert of Cherbury. At the age of sixty he " thought fit to relate to my posterity those passages of my life which I conceive may best declare me." Herbert had some standing as a poet and a philosopher, but those passages of his life he judged more important related to his travels on the Continent, his early marriage, his visit to the Court of Queen Elizabeth who tapped him on the cheek and declared it was a pity he had married so young, his expedition to the Low Countries, and his residence as ambassador in Paris. The restless, impetuous spirit of the man, which induced him to lead an adventurous life, and his vanity, which was flattered by the attentions his handsome figure gained him, emerge in his autobiography. Swinburne declared this autobiography was one of the hundred best stories in the world.

From its title De Quincey's *Confessions of an Opium Eater*

might seem to fall into the same category as Rousseau's *Confessions*. In reality the candour of Rousseau was abhorrent to De Quincey. " Nothing indeed is more revolting to English feeling," he wrote, " than the spectacle of a human being obtruding on our notice his moral ulcers and scars." This remark of De Quincey's explains the comparative scarcity of this type of autobiography in English. The English are too reticent to write confessions. Yet De Quincey does penetrate deeper than most English autobiographers. He does not confine himself to the story of his external life, but reveals his more hidden emotions. Although De Quincey traces the effect of his fatal addiction to drugs, one has not the feeling that he is delighting in exposing his vices to a scandalised world. The gorgeous quality of De Quincey's prose almost becomes a disadvantage because, by its splendour, it tends to distract the reader's attention from the story of his actions and emotions. What really prevents the *Confessions of an Opium Eater* from achieving the first rank of autobiography is the verbosity of De Quincey. In spite of this defect De Quincey's confessions remain unique as a record of abnormal experiences.

THE ENGAGING CONFIDENCE OF MOORE

THE popularity of the autobiography has increased in modern times and distinguished examples of this literary type have been produced by men of letters. George Moore, the novelist, carried on the traditions of Rousseau in his *Confessions of a Young Man*, supplemented by *Hail and Farewell*, an account of his later life in a similar confessional vein. Moore tells all about himself, about his life in Paris and his meetings with fellow-artists with an engaging frankness and simplicity. He takes an artist's interest in himself and his doings ; he excels in the art of confiding and of taking all the world into his confidence. His autobiographies, moreover, are marked by the delicate skill in handling words, the apparent simplicity that conceals consummate art, which have gained Moore a high reputation as a literary craftsman.

Very different in spirit and style from the *Confessions of a Young Man* is the *Autobiography of a Super-Tramp*, the life-story of the poet, W. H. Davies. In his straightforward direct manner Davies narrates the story of his adventurous life, of his truancies from school, his organisation of his companions into a robber gang, his voyage to the United

States, and his experiences as a tramp in that country. *The Autobiography* resembles nothing so much as a picaresque novel in the variety of the adventures it relates, in its humour and high spirits, in its pictures of low life, and especially in the descriptions of the odd characters the author encounters.

ENCHANTING STUDIES OF CHILDHOOD DAYS

" EARLHAM," by Percy Lubbock, and *The Innocent Eye*, by Herbert Read are both autobiographical fragments, the first containing reminiscences of childhood vacations, the second embodying the author's recollections of his life up to the age of ten. Both books are written in exquisitely beautiful prose, and the childish memories of the authors are concerned with places and persons more than with themselves. Lubbock's grandfather was rector of Earlham, near Norwich, and Lubbock spent his vacations in the old rectory. " The slightest turn of memory," he says, " takes me back at any time to Earlham, to the big sunny hall where we used to assemble for morning prayers." The house itself, the garden, the river flowing past the garden, the old church a little way from the house, where grandfather, a scholarly old gentleman, used to preach and where grandmother, her voice still clear and sweet in spite of age, used to sing are indelibly printed in the writer's memory and rendered doubly charming by the passage of time. In *The Innocent Eye* Herbert Read describes the surroundings amidst which his boyhood was spent. The farmhouse, the stables, the green, the orchard, and finally the vale in which the farm was situated, are seen again in the writer's imagination. Seldom have the boyhood days of any writer been described with more delicacy and beauty of style.

MEMOIRS OF A SOCIETY LADY

WHEN any modern personage of importance publishes his or her autobiography or memoirs, there is almost invariably some excitement in the literary world, which varies in intensity in proportion to the frankness with which the writer comments on contemporary personalities and events. Few memoirs have aroused more excitement than the autobiography of Margot Asquith, later Countess of Oxford. The book is entitled *An Autobiography*, but it is more a series of impressions of people and places than an attempt at self-study. In the preface the authoress states : " When I began this book, I feared that its merit would depend upon how faithfully I could record my own impressions of people and events." Her life has given her abundant opportunities for forming vivid impressions of the leading figures of the day. The daughter of a well-known Scottish Border family, the Tennants of Glen, she became acquainted with Gladstone, Morley, Lord Balfour, Lord Rosebery, and other famous statesmen, on all of whom she makes candid comments, and whose conversation she sometimes reports in detail. The book is, indeed, remarkable in its sheer vitality and frankness. It is the mirror of a mind restlessly energetic and keenly interested in the spectacle of life.

One of the best modern autobiographies is Lord Haldane's account of his life, which deals almost entirely with his public career. His boyhood is passed over in a few sentences, and he proceeds to trace his legal and political career, his occupancy of the War Office, his part in the war, and finally his attainment to the position of Lord Chancellor. Lord Haldane was a distinguished philosopher as well as politician, and this book, written towards the close of his long life, is marked by a mellow philosophic wisdom.

A POET IMMERSED IN THE HORRORS OF WAR

THE *Memoirs of a Fox-Hunting Man*, and the *Memoirs of an Infantry Officer*, both by Siegfried Sassoon, the poet, provide a contrast to the memoirs of the politicians. The first deals with the author's life up to the outbreak of the World War. Brought up in the country at the house of an aunt, he passed a lonely childhood, its most memorable incident being the instruction in riding he received from the groom. The writer became a keen huntsman, and most of the book is occupied by accounts of the various meets he attended. The atmosphere of the English countryside and the spirit of fox-hunting pervades the pages of the first volume of his memoirs. The background of the second volume is very different. From the quiet English countryside we are transported to the roughness and horrors of trench warfare. The descriptions of attacks, of a brigade going into action, of patrols going out at night, stumbling through shell-holes, and finding themselves baffled by the barbed wire of the enemy, excite a lively impression of the actualities of warfare. The life of a soldier is depicted with great

9

fidelity ; moments of suspense during action are followed by periods of relaxation.

> " Out there it's just one thing after another, and one soon forgets the bad times ; it's probably something to do with being in the open air so much and getting such a lot of exercise.   It's only when one gets away from it that one begins to realise how stupid and wasteful it is.   What I feel now is that if it's got to go on there ought to be a jolly sound reason for it, and I can't help thinking that the troops are being done in the eye by the people in control."

Such is the author's opinion of the War expressed during a conversation with a friend.   In many places during a lull in the warfare, one encounters passages evidently the work of a poet whose senses were keenly alive to the sights and sounds around him.   " Next evening just before stand-to," he says, " I was watching a smouldering sunset and thinking that the sky was one of the redeeming features of the war. Behind the front line where I stood, the shell-pitted ground sloped sombrely into the dusk ; the distances were blue and solemn, with a few trees grouped on a ridge, dark against the deep-glowing embers of another day endured ! "

MEMOIRS OF THE WAR'S MOST MYSTERIOUS FIGURE

No one in modern times has written a more absorbing account of his experiences than Colonel T. E. Lawrence, the famous Lawrence of Arabia, and no one has had a more adventurous career.   The *Revolt in the Desert* is a graphic narrative of the part Lawrence played in inciting the Arabs to rebel against the authority of the Turks during the World War.   It is a story of thrilling adventures unequalled since the days of the Elizabethan explorers.   In *Revolt in the Desert*, which is an abridged version of *The Seven Pillars of Wisdom*, Lawrence did not devote much space to his own personality, but was more concerned with the campaign which he carried to a successful conclusion.   Yet the reader cannot help being struck by the daring, originality, and resolution of the man.   Lawrence wrote with a natural clearness and vividness.   His descriptions of Arabia, its towns and deserts, are impressive in their clear-cut strength.

Lawrence was as shrewd in estimating the characters of the Arabians as he was quick in catching the spirit of the

Lawrence of Arabia.

Arabian land. The acuteness of his judgment appears in this estimate of the Sheriff Abdulla, second son of the Grand Sheriff of Mecca.

> " His eyes had a confirmed twinkle ; and though only thirty-five, he was putting on flesh. It might be due to too much laughter. He jested with all comers in most easy fashion ; yet, when we fell into serious talk, the veil of humour seemed to fade away, as he chose his words, and argued shrewdly. . . . I was playing for effect, watching, criticising him. The Sheriff's rebellion had been unsatisfactory for the last few months (standing still, which, with an irregular war, was the prelude to disaster) ; and my suspicion was that its lack was leadership : not intellect, nor judgment, nor political wisdom, but the flame of enthusiasm, that would set the desert on fire. My visit was mainly to find the yet unknown master-spirit of the affair, and measure his capacity to carry the revolt to the goal I had conceived for it. As our conversation continued, I became more and more sure that Abdulla was too balanced, too cool, too humorous to be a prophet ; especially the armed prophet who, if history be true, succeeded in revolutions."

The number of autobiographies and memoirs that have been produced in modern times makes it impossible to enumerate any but the outstanding, but mention must be made of the remarkable autobiography of H. G. Wells in which the development of an unusual personality is finely described.

SECRETS INGENUOUSLY TOLD BY THE DIARY

THE writers of autobiographies and memoirs have some purpose in narrating the story of their lives and experiences. They may be writing in response to a desire for self-expression, but they are writing for publication also. They feel that their personalities and experiences are interesting enough to deserve the attention of the public. But what motive can a person have in sitting down every night to record what he or she has done during the day ? The urge to express oneself must explain the production of diaries and the unremitting industry of the people who have kept them, for the majority of those personal documents were never intended for publication, and the writers were usually so undistinguished that they could never have hoped that their daily experiences would have much general interest.

It is precisely because they were not intended for the satisfaction of public curiosity that diaries prove such fascinating reading. The writer confides in his diary, never dreaming that thousands of eyes will pry into his secrets. No kind of literature reveals the feelings and thoughts of the writer more intimately than the diary because there is no disguise. In other forms of literary expression the writer is deliberate, and conscious of the effect he wants to produce.

We have assumed that the diary is a form of literature, although it might be legitimately argued that scrappy, disjointed entries in a diary cannot be called literature. Diaries are indeed defective in artistic construction, but some diaries are literature because of their inexhaustible human interest. Literature depends not only on the skilful manipulation of words, but it is also the expression of human personality in words.

THE INIMITABLE PEPYS

BY one of the coincidences of literature the two best-known diaries in English were written by two men living at the same time and acquainted with one another. Samuel Pepys and John Evelyn both lived in the second half of the seventeenth century, both have left us valuable commentaries on the society of that period. Pepys was born in 1632 or 1633, and was educated at St. Paul's School and Cambridge. He entered the Government service and attained the responsible position in the Admiralty of Clerk of the Acts, an office which carried with it the Secretaryship to the Navy Board. Pepys's busy life as a Government official, which brought him into contact with people prominent in the Court and politics and put him in the way of the latest information concerning public figures and events, afforded plenty of material for his diary.

Pepys began to keep his diary in January 1660. He describes the Restoration of Charles II., the Dutch War, the Plague of 1665, the Fire of 1666 that burnt down a large part of London, and many other incidents of great historical interest. Pepys was a regular theatre-goer and his entries relating to the theatre indicate the dramatic taste of the time. His lively interest in current affairs makes the diary valuable from an historical point of view. But it is as the reflection of Pepys's personality that the Diary will chiefly interest the reader. Pepys enters his domestic affairs, grumbles about his wife, makes some observations on pretty " misses " he has noticed, criticises sermons he has been listening to, and makes shrewd remarks about the people he has been meeting. He is not a great man nor even a good man, but the Diary has a peculiar charm which can only be explained by Pepys's naïve ways, his complete frankness, his engaging curiosity. This charm is heightened by the style, which is not literary English but something Pepys has fashioned for his own use. It has the qualities of quaintness and originality. It belongs to Pepys and expresses him admirably. Many writers have tried to parody his style but it remains inimitable.

Evelyn's Diary covers a longer period than that of Pepys. He began to keep a diary in 1652 and continued it almost to the end of his life in 1706. Thus we have a record of the same period from two men very different in temper and outlook. Evelyn's Diary has not won the affections of readers to the same extent as that of Pepys, probably because he is more reticent in his entries. He does not reveal the secrets of his heart in the same way as Pepys. Evelyn was a gentleman by birth and nature, a man of scholarly habits and unusually wide interests. He was educated at Oxford and travelled for ten years on the Continent. He was interested in the arts and sciences, becoming a fellow of the newly-formed Royal Society. He wrote poems and plays, became an authority on gardens and trees, prepared a plan for rebuilding London, and was interested in the question of smoke abatement. His home was at Deptford and in the course of his public duties he saw much of the life of the Court. Although strongly royalist in his political sympathies, he deplored the vices of the court of Charles II. All his varied interests are reflected in his diary. He was especially fond of recording his opinions of the trees and gardens of other people.

Evelyn's Diary has not the intimate, personal appeal of that of Pepys, but the external events he describes belong to an interesting period of English history. Yet in its very reticence the diary reflects the personality of Evelyn who was

Samuel Pepys dines at home in the attic.

too grave and serious to enter the trifling but illuminating incidents Pepys was accustomed to do. The impression of Evelyn the reader gains from the diary will probably coincide with that of Pepys who, after meeting Evelyn one day, wrote in his diary : " In fine a most excellent person he is and must be allowed a little for a little conceitedness ; but he may well be so, being a man so much above others."

GLIMPSES OF A CLERGYMAN'S DINNER TABLE

DIARIES have usually been published after the death of the writer, sometimes lying for many years in manuscript before they found an editor. After remaining among family papers for more than a hundred years, the diary of an eighteenth-century clergyman, James Woodforde, has been made available to readers. The diary of the Reverend James Woodforde is a fascinating book. The writer was remarkable for nothing. Born in 1740 and dying in 1803, he lived an uneventful life in a Norfolk rectory. For forty-three years he sat down daily to record the details of his life, such as where he dined, what he ate, how his servants were behaving. He shows little traces of emotion and his spiritual life was quite tranquil. But even his entries of the dinner menus have a fascinating quality, derived from his obvious relish of eatables.

Sometimes he grows a little sarcastic : " My sister can't bear to hear any one praised more than herself in anything, but that she does the best of all." The following passage is a fair sample of the delightful flavour of the diary :

> " We breakfasted, dined, supped, and slept again at home. My Nephew and self walked to Church this morning at 11 o'clock and there I read Prayers only, being a day appointed for a general Fast, on account of the War with the Americans. I had a large congregation. My Servant Ben went after dinner to his Father's unknown to me, and did not return home till near 11 at night and when he came home he went to bed without my seeing him and I believe not very sober. It is very bad of him."

For a complete view of English village life in the second half of the eighteenth century one cannot do better than turn over the pages of Woodforde's Diary.

PERSONAL JOTTINGS IN FULL DRESS :
THE JOURNAL

THE difference between a diary and a journal is not easy
to establish. A diary is a daily record of the writer's
life, a journal may sometimes be kept on the same chronological plan, but in general the entries are fuller. A journal
is not so much of a private document as the diary. The
writer of the diary writes for his own benefit ; he keeps the
diary as a private confessional. The writer of the journal,
although he may not intend to publish it immediately, does
not regard it as a private possession. Wesley, for instance,
used to publish extracts from his *Journal* for the instruction
and comfort of his followers. A journal, again, may
be written for a specific purpose, to describe some
journey.

One of the earliest and best of English journals was that
kept by Dean Swift. The reader who knows Swift only as
the narrator of Gulliver's adventures and the aloof satirist
of human follies will find his *Journal to Stella* a particularly
attractive work. Swift's ecclesiastical duties kept him in
Ireland for most of his life, but every year he spent a few
months in London. During his absence, Swift wrote
regularly to his dear friends, Esther Johnson and her
companion, Rebecca Dingley, who shared his home in
Ireland.

When he was secretary to Sir William Temple, Swift had
met Esther Johnson, who was a member of Temple's household. Esther was educated by Swift. Every night during
his visits to London, when he had come home to his lodgings
and was lying comfortably in bed, Swift wrote a minute
account of what he had done that day for the information
of his female friends. He tells what people he met during
the day, and Swift, who was a very influential writer at this
time, courted or feared by the leading politicians who knew
the power of his pen, met everybody of importance. Swift
learned all the London gossip, and this he recounts, knowing
the female curiosity of Stella and her companion. The
journal is written in a pleasant conversational style full of
affectionate terms and lively remarks on various people. It
reveals a charming side of Swift's nature one would scarcely
suspect from his other writings.

A POET DESCRIBED BY HIS SISTER

DOROTHY WORDSWORTH, the sister of the poet, wrote several journals at different periods of her life. Sometimes they take the form of a diary and record trivial details, such as, " To-day I mended William's shirts." Dorothy kept her first journal from January to May, 1798, while William and she were staying at Alfoxden in Dorsetshire. This journal is especially valuable for the account it gives of Coleridge's visits and of his relations with Wordsworth. When they removed to Grasmere in Cumberland, Dorothy resumed her journal, still in the form of a diary. Her Grasmere journal contains exquisite descriptions of the scenery of the Lake District as it appeared amidst the changes of the seasons. Later, Dorothy toured Scotland and the Continent, keeping careful records of her journeys. Apart from its value in throwing light on the political activities of Wordsworth, Dorothy's journals have intrinsic interest because they reveal in her an understanding of Nature and a gift for describing scenery scarcely inferior to that of her brother.

YOUTH WRITES IN THE SHADOW OF DEATH

JOURNALS have shared the popularity of other kinds of autobiographical writing in modern times. One of the most remarkable personal documents ever written is *The Journal of a Disappointed Man*, by W. N. P. Barbellion, the pseudonym of Bruce Cummings. Cummings was a young scientist, who might have become a distinguished biologist if death had not intervened. His journal begins in 1903 and ends in 1917, about a month before his death, at the age of twenty-eight. Much of it was written under the shadow of approaching death, which was due to creeping paralysis. The journal records the progress of the disease and the writer's thoughts on the life he is soon to leave. Sometimes he is depressed : " It is too inconceivably horrible to be buried in the earth in such splendid spring weather. Who can tell me what is in store for me ? Life opens to me, I catch a glimpse of the vision and the doors clang to again noiselessly ! "

But the last entry in the journal reads : " I am only twenty-eight, but I have telescoped into those few years a tolerably long life ; I have loved and married, and have a family ; I have wept and enjoyed ; struggled and overcome, and when the hour comes I shall be content to die. . . ." The journal provides Cummings with an outlet for his emotions : " I fall back on this Journal just as some other poor devil takes to drink." Because it is the record of a brave spirit, because it is written in a style fresh and frank, not aiming at literary excellence, but at sincere expression of feeling, *The Journal of a Disappointed Man* is impressive and inexpressibly poignant.

The Journal of Katherine Mansfield has some points of resemblance to *The Journal of a Disappointed Man*. Katherine Mansfield died prematurely in 1922 after several years of suffering from a lingering disease. " Those huge complaining diaries," which she mentions in one entry of her journal, provided her also with an emotional outlet. Her journal was compiled after her death by her husband, Middleton Murry, from diaries and scraps of personal documents. Few people have loved life more than Katherine Mansfield, and this eager enjoyment of living, working, seeing places and meeting people, colours the journal and enhances the tragedy of her early death.

TALKING WITH THE GREAT : SOME INTRODUCTIONS

" THE proper study of mankind is man " ; in beginning a course in biographical literature the only difficulty is to choose which man—or woman—to study first. It is best to begin with some modern character in whom the reader is already interested, and this should be easy since contemporaries have been prodigal of their memoirs. Margot Asquith reveals as fascinating a personality as any one in her *Autobiography*. Many famous politicians are referred to, among them Winston Churchill, whose own writings would lead one on to his life of his ancestor, Marlborough. This fine biography deals with the reigns of James the Second, William of Orange, and Anne. The fascinating Pepys and the informative Evelyn wrote diaries during this eventful period and to these one should turn next, following them with Swift's *Journal to Stella*, written during the reign of Queen Anne.

Another line would be to start with the collection of biographies entitled *Great Victorians*. This contains an article on Carlyle which would take one back to Carlyle's own biographical writings. When his *Frederick the Great* has been read, his essays on James Boswell will afford an excellent introduction to the study of Boswell's own master-piece, the *Life of Samuel Johnson*.

Those interested in autobiographies which are largely self-analytical should begin with *The Journal of Katherine Mansfield* and go on to Barbellion's *Journal of a Disappointed Man*, or Marie Bashkirtseff's *Journal*, and then try Newman's *Apologia pro Vita Sua*, or Wesley's *Journal*. For auto-biographical reading in which adventure predominates a good start would be made with T. E. Lawrence's *Seven Pillars of Wisdom*, followed by Benvenuto Cellini's *Auto-biography* or Casanova's *Memoirs*.

The best writing on biography is contained in Carlyle's essay on Boswell. Boswell himself has valuable words to say on his art in the opening pages of his *Life of Samuel Johnson* (Everyman). Lytton Strachey has a few illuminating remarks on biography in the preface to his *Eminent Victorians* (Phœnix Library), and Harold Nicholson's *Development of English Biography* (Hogarth Press) provides an interesting history of the subject.

CRITICISM : THE WHY AND HOW
OF A WORK OF ART

by WRIGHT WATTS MILLER, B.A.(Lond.) ;
M.Ed.(Manchester)

IT is difficult for a reader, whether professional or amateur, not to regard literary criticism from one or the other of two standpoints ; either to accept it as paramount authority, or to reject it as unwarrantable interference. One type of reader will do his best to digest any work of literature so long as it is " recommended," " accepted," a " standard," or " classic " by the bench of critics ; another type, observing the chaos which has at many times existed in criticism, and mistrusting the claims of any dictatorship of taste or intellect, will fling guidance overboard and vow to be his own critic. Of these two men the second has possibly more of the root of the matter in him, though if he passes by books simply because they are " classics " the limitations of his field of enjoyment will soon become obvious. One might compare the first man to the tourist plodding round a foreign city, *Baedeker* in hand, and the second to the tourist, more typically English perhaps, who takes a general look at the city, has a drink in a café, and then walks out into the country to look for a golf course.

There must be some fundamental reason, it may be surmised, why the authority of the expert in literature should be so warmly debated, often by the uninitiated most of all, while that of the expert in other spheres, such as sport, mathematics, or navigation, is accepted with little dissent. Is not the difference that such subjects as literature, politics, economics, or education (subjects on which every one feels qualified to express an opinion) are human studies, whereas the other subjects quoted are mainly a matter of more impersonal technique and skill ? The very significance of literature, in particular, depends on the intimate and complex psychological chords it can touch : it would be strange if the valuation of literature should escape the infinite reactions of the personal element. The establishment of psychology as something like a science is at the basis of all the schools of criticism which have arisen during the present century.

But there were psychologists before psychology. The judgment of such men as Dryden, Dr. Johnson, or Coleridge was delicate, intimate, and trenchant enough to need little aid from modern scientific psychology, and the history of such judgments is one of the most important aspects of the history of English literature.

THE CRITIC MUST HAVE SYMPATHY

How are we to recognise a good critic ? We remember first that literature is a communication of one person's experience to another person. The reader, partly through his own deficiencies, partly through those of the author, is never, or very rarely, able to grasp the complete and perfect experience exactly as the author wished to communicate it. A good critic is surely, therefore, able before anything else to approach as nearly as possible to this complete understanding. For this he must have sympathy, sincerity, honesty. He must not be prejudiced. Yet which of us can avoid prejudice ?

Let us examine more concretely the sympathy which the critic must have, and the prejudices he must avoid. When we speak of his appreciating the author's full " meaning," we are using a very inexact word, as I. A. Richards has brilliantly pointed out. Borrowing Richards's analysis, we cannot deny that " meaning " is commonly used to cover four different ideas : (1) the Sense or " matter," the nucleus, such as the skylark's song in Shelley's *Ode to a Skylark*, or the bare story of a novel. (2) The Feeling with which the author conveys his sense—Shelley's joy and longing in the *Ode*, or Dickens's indignation in *Oliver Twist*. (3) The Tone, or the attitude which the author deliberately takes up in order to adjust himself to his particular audience. The tone of a political speaker may obviously be very different from the feeling he really has about his theme ; there are always inconvenient members of his audience who are capable of recognising both aspects and asking uncomfortable questions. (4) The Intention of the author—the effect he is endeavouring to produce. He cannot write without producing some sort of effect, whether the one he intends to produce or its opposite. When we say of an insincere writer " he does everything for effect," we mean that his intention is to display his own cleverness. The sincere writer usually intends to affect either our hearts or our minds.

WHAT THE GOOD CRITIC TRIES TO DO

A GOOD critic is one who is able to appreciate these four aspects of his author's work. He may be said to have four aims. (1) He tries to have sympathy with the author's Sense or Matter. He will not condemn Shakespeare's fairies and ghosts, for example, merely because they are fairies and ghosts. (2) He tries to have sympathy with the author's feeling. He does not object to the yearning quality of much of Shelley's poetry simply because he does not feel like yearning himself. (3) He has sympathy with the tone of the writing. A formal speech at a funeral, for instance, will not be criticised for its banality and stiff phraseology, which have probably been chosen to avoid stirring the most painful and intimate aspects of grief in public. (4) He tries to have sympathy with the author's intention ; he will not complain of light comedy that it " does not promote any political or religious truth."

A critic may legitimately complain if an author's tone, or feeling, assorts badly with some other aspect of his work, as when Thomas Moore writes verse intended to be wistful and melancholy in the galloping metre of " The Assyrian came down like a wolf on the fold." But the critic must always regard the work as a whole ; he must consider one aspect only in relation to the total aspect, one portion only in relation to the whole.

The qualities we look for to-day in a critic are not so much heavy-handed authority and the separation of good from bad books, as a true appreciation—an entering into what the author meant to say and a perception of how far he succeeded in saying it, or of how he has said more than was within his intention or control. The critic may be himself a creative writer in some other field, like Coleridge, Arnold, or T. S. Eliot, or he may work almost exclusively in criticism, like Hazlitt or I. A. Richards. But the true critic is in any case himself a creator. He may reveal more about the author than the author knew ; he can relate an author to his background, and show his significance to his whole period or country. Each generation is likely to lay stress upon different aspects of a dead author's work, though without necessarily affecting his immortality. Each generation may also have different ideas, arising from political, economic, or other than literary causes, about the function of literature, or the elements in it which should be stressed. Thus the critical literature of a past age, though it might seem at first sight academic, professional, technical, and generally unremuner-ative, is actually one of the most direct keys to the feeling and conscience of that age. It reveals in a special way, however objective it may try to be, the humanity of its period, the humanity which is the fundamental reason for past literature still meaning anything to us.

CLEARING PATHWAYS THROUGH ENGLISH POETRY

THERE were many battles to be fought before English criticism was clear-sighted enough to attain sympathetic judgment. Criticism has had to cast aside many notions as irrelevant to its purpose as the philosopher's stone or the elixir of life were to the beginnings of natural science. English itself had many battles before there was any criticism worth the name. The history of criticism is largely the history of these battles, finding out in the first place what was or was not good English, then what should be the rules for English poetry, what should be the difference between poetry and prose, or how far one's judgment of a book should depend upon its subject-matter. The chief problems of English criticism have been these :

(1) The quarrel of the Ancients and the Moderns. Ought English literature to follow the example of Latin and Greek, or seek its own standards ? This quarrel lasted until approxi-mately the end of the eighteenth century, when it was merged in the perennial discussion of :

(2) Classicism versus Romanticism—a problem in which " classic " has ceased to mean " following the Ancients," and now stands for authority as opposed to individual liberty in literature, or in extreme forms, tyranny as opposed to libertinage. It is now generally agreed that there is natural ebb and flow between these two poles ; in contemporary literature we may even detect both tides pulling at once.

(3) Disentangling poetry from prose. This was achieved at the end of the seventeenth century. The early confusion of the two forms of expression can be seen by comparing any of Dryden's prose with the strange poetical prose of the preface to the Authorised Version of the Bible.

(4) The problem of how far art should conform to the accepted standards of morality. Should art be practised only

" for art's sake," or should it try to teach and improve ? The vast reading public of to-day gives new point to this old question.

When English literature was firmly established, there arose the great school of historical, or scientific, criticism (most active in Germany), which applied the methods of science, and particularly the evolutionary principle, to amassing vast quantities of facts in attempts to explain a work of literature. The material collected was often very valuable, though the conclusions drawn often needed correction by the newest and most human of the sciences—psychology. To-day we have the very important psychological schools of criticism, which apply psychological methods to discovering what the author really meant, and give less attention to the merely museum-like discovery and collection of " sources " and " influences " upon his work.

HOW ENGLISH BECAME A LANGUAGE

THE greatness of English literature is largely due to the fact that English is, and has been for some three or four hundred years, one of the most expressive and flexible languages in the world. It has not, however, always been so. The language of the Angles and Saxons was primitive, like the language of the Norsemen, which it resembled. Its literature was like the Norse sagas in tone, though it was inferior to them in quality. The language that Chaucer wrote, at the end of the fourteenth century, was a fine medium for poetry, but it was not strictly a language ; it was a dialect only, the dialect of the London district. Dialects differed so much in Chaucer's time that during the next century it became urgently necessary, for mere intelligibility, to stand-ardise one of them, especially as England was then unified after the Wars of the Roses, foreign trade was increasing, and printing had been introduced. Caxton, himself a Kentish-man, complained much of the confusion of dialects. The London dialect, partly through the prestige given it by Chaucer, established itself naturally as Standard English ; no authority imposed it on the rest of England. The English which every Englishman reads and writes to-day is the de-scendant of the London dialect of the fifteenth century, though the English which he speaks may show traces of what is left of the other dialects. Interesting dates showing the standardisation of English are 1535, when the first complete version of the Bible in English was published, and 1549, the date of the Church of England Prayer Book.

It was hardly to be expected that criticism should flourish in a language so unstable as mediæval English ; there is none until the Elizabethan period, except for scattered comments such as Chaucer's ballad-parody of *Sir Thopas*, or his gibe at Western men and their old-fashioned alliterative poetry, or *gestes* :

> " . . . I am a Southren man,
> I can not geste—rum, ram, ruf, by lettre,"

says the parson when asked to tell his tale.

But though the dialect difficulty had been settled by 1500, another great problem had arisen during the Middle Ages— the huge absorption of French and Latin words. It is these which give modern English half its value as a language, but it is these also which make it peculiarly difficult even for a native. The most uneducated Englishman rarely mishandles or misunderstands the Saxon part of our language, but the profusion of necessary but foreign words (what he calls " long words "), and the frequency of some foreign constructions, make it hard for him, even after these six or seven hundred years, to read much of the best in English or to write English well in more than a simple way. For a Frenchman, German, or Spaniard, the equivalent barrier of education in his own language is less difficult to surmount. The foreign element mingled itself with the Saxon element in our language, not only because of the Norman Conquest, but because Latin was the language of the Church and the second language of every educated person throughout Europe, and further because most English literature during the Middle Ages was based on French (or sometimes Latin or Italian) models. French literature is at the base of most of Chaucer's work, of the old ballads and carols, of " Sumer is icumen in."

The immense revival of interest in Greek and Latin civilisation at the Renaissance, beginning in Italy, came to England late. Again the English vocabulary was flooded with foreign words, some of them to die out again rapidly, many of them, such as " insular " and " concise," to become essential and common words. The real work of the Renaissance was to spread ideas of a broad and humane culture. It was the time of the founding of many of the most famous English

schools, and there was a great attempt to lift education out
of the routine and logic-chopping, the limited aims and
curriculum of the Middle Ages.

EARLY QUARRELS OVER POETRY

SUCH was the soil which produced the first English literary
critics. They had a new-found pride in a national
language, but a language which was spoken by comparatively
few persons in Europe, which had produced little literature,
and in both these respects held something of the place that
Dutch or Swedish does among languages to-day. The
problems were to give the English language and literature
their own standards, and to weld in the influences of the
great Ancients and perhaps of the Italians. Three great
educationists were among the first to call for pure English,
to object to French-English, Italian-English, or pedant's
English; they were Thomas Wilson, in his *Art of Rhetoric*
(1553), Sir John Cheke (first regius professor of Greek at
Cambridge), and Roger Ascham, in *The Schoolmaster* (1568),
and in *Toxophilus* (1545).

But mixed with this worthy concern for pure English
was a concern for pure morals which, unfortunately, caused
many distractions and misconceptions. Poets in this period
were frequently treated as liars because they composed
works of imagination. Rhyme also fell into bad odour
because it was found in low ballads and the literature of the
modern languages only, whereas the literature of the supposedly virtuous ancients never descended to such jingling.
Poets were abused as " a rakehell rout of wooden rhymers,
not attaining to the parings of the Latin or Greek tongue."

HOW RHYME WAS WON FOR ENGLISH POETRY

HERE was the great barrier to true literary criticism for
over a century. The poets put up defences, one of
them—Sidney's *Defense of Poesie* (1580)—an important work,
but they also could not get away from the moral attitude.
They sought to defend poetry by examples of its moral,
irrespective of its literary, value. Both parties seemed to
overlook the fact that the most moral literature cannot convince unless it has the power of convincing as well as the
matter to convince ; it must, in short, be good literature.
Rhyme was rather feebly defended for some time, and charming poets like Campion tried unsuccessfully to write unrhymed

lyrics in imitation of Horace or Anacreon. But there was too much good poetry being written by men who, like Shakespeare, had " small Latin and less Greek," for rhyme to lose the day. It became recognised that rhyme was a natural embellishment of a strongly accented language like English, even though it might not have suited a measured language like Latin.

Although the prejudice against rhyme lingered in scholars such as Milton, its triumph was established as early as 1603 in the poet Daniel's *Defence of Rhyme*, written in reply to Campion's *Observations in the Art of English Poesy*. Both are interesting essays, and much less abusive than most Elizabethan criticism.

BEN JONSON : A CLASSIC IN A ROMANTIC AGE

THE most intellectual and learned of Elizabethan critics was Ben Jonson, who failed in criticism, as he did in drama, to preserve the essential vital contact with popular and natural taste. It was natural that Jonson should regard Bacon as having " performed that in our tongue which may be compared or preferred either to insolent Greece or haughty Rome." He mistrusted functions of prose other than the philosophical, for which Bacon employed it, and frankly preferred rhetoric to the clear and simple prose needed in the best sort of personal essay. He granted rhyme in English verse, but anticipated Dryden and Pope in preferring a severely formal type of verse, such as the stopped couplet used by Pope, to the freer forms of poetry we find in the Elizabethan lyrics. He was the Classic of a Romantic Age.

JOHN DRYDEN : THE FATHER OF ENGLISH CRITICISM

SO much of the seventeenth century was occupied in other than literary quarrels that a big gap is left before we reach the next critic whose work is of permanent interest and value. This was John Dryden who is puzzling at first in his versatility, but it was this very quality which made him our first great critic. He was the first to ignore those irrelevant preoccupations with the imagined rules of the Ancients, with the moral wickedness of " fiction " in poetry and drama, with the gentle birth or otherwise of an author, and to take actual literature—the whole of it—as his starting-point.

John Dryden.

When he attempts to make rules he does sometimes fall
into the old formalism, but when he examines an individual
work he cannot keep his broad sympathy from judging
it on its own merits. He says : " Delight is the chief,
if not the only, end of poesy : instruction can be admitted
but in the second place, for poetry only instructs as it
delights." It may indeed appear remarkable that this
simple fact of psychology had not before been noticed
by the Puritan wranglers, or by the defenders of poetry.
Dryden's task was to ask in every case why a book gave
pleasure.

His first critical work is the *Essay of Dramatic Poesy* (1668).
At the time of its composition, he said later, he was " sailing
in a vast ocean, without other help than the polestar of the
Ancients, and the rules of the French stage, which are extremely different from ours, by reason of their opposite taste."
He sailed so well that he produced one of the classics of
English criticism. The Essay is in the form of a dialogue.
Dryden himself, under the pseudonym of Neander, deals
one by one with the artificial objections the others make
to Shakespeare and the English stage in general. If a play
must be " an imitation of nature," the English plays must
be the better because the more natural, however many rules
they break. Why should one object to the mixing of tragedy
and comedy in a single play, or to the presence of an under-
plot as well as a main plot ? Is not life like that ? Then
comes his famous description of the dramatic character of
Shakespeare.

Most of the rest of Dryden's critical work consists of
prefaces to his poems, plays, or translations, a form of
pamphleteering, common at the time, which enabled him to
answer his adversaries publicly, but without special publication for the purpose. The most important are the *Dedication
to the Aeneid* (1697), and the *Preface to the Fables* (written
in 1700, the year of his death). The latter contains his
famous praise of Chaucer. This ability to admire a mediæval
author, though at the same time rendering him into modern-
ised " Fables," was only one more aspect of the wide and
penetrating sympathy of Dryden. There was no critic like
him in Europe, during his own time ; there have been few
so well equipped since. Dryden wrote little about English
prose, which by his own example he made so sound and
clean an instrument.

After Dryden's time there is little difficulty about distinguishing poetry from prose. What is found later on is not so much poetical luxuriance in prose, as prosaic regularity in poetry. The liberties won for poetry by the Elizabethans had been sadly abused by such poets as Cowley and Crashaw in the middle of the seventeenth century. Noble imagination had given place to wild fancy, and freedom in rhyme and metre had become disorder, or else something with which to play tricks. It was, for example, possible to write a poem which should take the form, on the printed page, of a cross or a gravestone. The steadying movement in English prose had its natural counterpart in a severe regularising of English verse at the beginning of the eighteenth century. This desire for order came partly from France, and though the Ancients were appealed to again and again, it is the element of order rather than the element of Latinity which justly earns this age the names of the Classic Period, the Age of Reason, the Augustan Period (after the great age of Latin literature under Augustus), or even the Age of Prose. Poetry sought relief in the standardisation of the couplet of five feet, a form of verse in which the rhyme is necessarily so insistent that the only thing to be done is to take advantage of the insistence, and make the rhyme half the point of the verse, as in :

> " The hungry judges soon the sentence sign,
> And wretches hang, that jurymen may dine."
> *(Rape of the Lock).*

Thus wit became the principal criterion of most verse for a time. The age was dominated by ideas of Good Taste. There was in England at last a society that considered itself " polite," able to compete with the salons of Louis XIV.'s Paris on their own ground, and so it was very important that there should be no disturbing authors, no impolitely exciting metres, to mar the elegant picture. Pope, as Lytton Strachey has pointed out, earned a colossal sum of money, not by his original verse, but by translating Homer into the fashionable couplets, giving the age " a Homer after its own heart," far removed from the barbaric Greek. This was to some extent realised by Pope's contemporary critics. Richard Bentley, the greatest scholar of the age, said of the translation : " A pretty poem, Mr. Pope, but you must not call it Homer."

THREE CRITICS WHO REVERED AUTHORITY

IN criticism the conflicts of this period are now mainly of antiquarian interest. There was a dispute over the Ancients and the Moderns, which led Swift to write the immortal *Battle of the Books*, where he imagines the books in the library getting down from their shelves to join the fray. But the substance of the essay is no longer of importance ; it is a classic of our prose, but not of our criticism. Actually the Moderns' view of the Ancients was so coloured by Modern prejudice that the quarrel was more apparent than real. The finest expression of the rules of the age is Pope's *Essay on Criticism*, which is written in heroic couplets. But it is the consummate neatness of the expression we admire to-day, rather than the matter.

The greatest representative of the " politeness " of the age is Addison, who really did a great deal to refine society and its attitude to women in the pages of *The Spectator* and *The Tatler*. He simpers, however, and the limitations of his attitude are obvious to a generation in which education is more widely accessible to all classes. He devoted several numbers of *The Spectator* to an examination of *Paradise Lost* which consist almost entirely of a comparison of Milton's poem with the great epics of the Ancients. Milton was exalted to a position of almost tyrannical authority for the whole of the eighteenth century, because he is the one scholarly English poet who followed the classics and remained great. Misguided though many of the critical ideas of the period were, however, they form the first general attempt to examine literary problems objectively. Eighteenth-century critics were badly hampered, but the notions that hampered them were at least literary notions for the most part. And finally, as has often been observed, nearly all the rules they formulated, though irrelevant for poetry, are admirable for prose. It was not an accident that the greatest writers of the century, such as Swift, Fielding, Addison, Steele, Berkeley, Johnson, Gibbon, and Burke, expressed themselves in prose.

A GIANT OF COMMON SENSE : DOCTOR JOHNSON

THE list of Dr. Johnson's works is apt to seem strangely out of accord with the magnitude of his reputation : some not very good poems in the fashionable manner, a rather dull novel, some not very good papers in *The Rambler*, an undeniably great achievement in the *Dictionary*—what else is there but Boswell's *Life* ? The answer lies in Johnson's last work, the *Lives of the Poets* (1779–81), begun when he was seventy, and also in his scattered critical work, his introductions to Shakespeare and other writers. Here is the only record written by himself of that vast insight and common sense which otherwise spent themselves in argument and conversation, to be recorded by the inimitable Boswell.

Johnson could not avoid some of the prejudices of his age, but his mistakes in over-emphasising the classical side of criticism have been too strongly insisted on by later and less gifted critics, such as Macaulay. Johnson took a leading part in exposing the literary frauds of James Macpherson, the author of *Ossian*, he made many valuable suggestions for readings of corrupt lines in Shakespeare, and he defended Shakespeare against the foolish taste which would condemn him because he did not observe the rigid rules formulated for the Greek and later for the French drama.

Though Johnson applies the measuring-rod of the rather limited criteria of his time to all the poetry he examines, from Cowley to his own day, there is always profit to be had from observing his application of it, even if the conclusions he comes to are sometimes biased. *The Lives* are full of such general reflections as : " The true Genius is a mind of large general powers, accidentally determined to some particular direction " ; " Books without the knowledge of life are useless ; for what should books teach but the art of living ? " Johnson objects to the continual recourse to classical mythology for ornament, even in poems such as *Lycidas*. In this he is preparing the way unconsciously for a new and more imaginative treatment of ancient fable such as we find later in Shelley and Keats.

The second half of the eighteenth century saw a considerable revival of interest in literature other than " classical." Gray read Anglo-Saxon, Norse, and old Welsh ballads ; Spenser and Spenserian verse came into favour again ; Bishop Percy published his famous *Reliques* (a collection mainly of forgotten old English ballads, many of them very familiar to-day ; Joseph Warton questioned whether Pope was a great poet, or even a poet at all, and his brother Thomas Warton produced a really notable work—the first *History of English Poetry*. The ground was being cleared for the casting off of all Latin or French or " polite " shackles—for the great liberation called Romanticism.

THE TRIUMPH OF NATURAL ENGLISH

ONE of the most noteworthy dates in the history of English poetry is 1798, when Wordsworth and Coleridge published *The Lyrical Ballads*. An equally important date in the history of English criticism is 1800, when the second edition of the *Lyrical Ballads* appeared with the famous *Preface* by Wordsworth. It is largely due to these two poets that poetry to-day is still generally regarded, not as composed by rule, but in a vague way, as " mystic " or " inspired," and that wild natural scenery is appreciated as the source of some of our noblest emotions, instead of inspiring horror or repulsion, as it seems normally to have done during the Age of Reason. Wordsworth was so impressed with the degenerate taste of his age, so fired with the new doctrines of the " noble savage " and other ideas which inspired the French revolutionaries, that he set about a further radical reform in poetry—the reform of diction. Since the virtues were reputed to be found most commonly among rustic and humble peasants, such as he knew in Cumberland, he would choose the language of these men, rather than the language of the university or the court, for poetry. He would reject all personification ; he would reject all " poetic diction " such as tempted his older contemporaries to write " nymph, tube, azure " every time they meant " girl, gun, blue." He goes so far as to declare that the language of poetry is identical with the language of prose, but is forced to admit that " metrical language " may add charm. He then explains poetry, in the well-known phrase, as " emotion recollected in tranquillity." Wordsworth was so great a poet that even the simplest of diction could not always spoil his quality. The poem, *I wandered lonely as a cloud*, is written in very plain language, but is still one of his finest productions. Nevertheless, much of his best work, such as the *Ode on Intimations of Immortality*, and the sonnets, is undeniably a triumph in language quite other than that " normally used by men." Many of his failures were due to his deliberate choice of simple language, and he probably succeeded more often in spite of his theory of diction than because of it.

His friend and associate Coleridge, one of the very greatest critics in English, pointed out with extreme clearness
both the fallacies and the virtues in Wordsworth's theory.
Coleridge's criticism suffered, like the rest of his work, from
his lazy and desultory habits, and except for *Biographia
Literaria* and the essays on Wordsworth, it is generally fragmentary. But he was nevertheless the great formative spirit
of the Romantic Period, as revered in his later years as
Johnson had been in his time. He was able to look at
poetical problems in an objective way impossible to Wordsworth and Shelley, if not to most Romantic poets, while
his authorship of *The Ancient Mariner* and *Kubla Khan*
left no doubt, on the other hand, that he understood in
the highest and most intimate degree the nature of poetic
experience.

Shelley's *Defence of Poetry*, the source of some familiar
quotations such as " Poets are the trumpets that sing to
battle," was not so much a critical essay as a " defence " on
the highest moral grounds, in the old Elizabethan manner.
It represents some of the spirit which really animated Wordsworth, but which seldom appears in his attempts to state
poetical doctrine. It is one of the most romantic documents
of all the Romantic Period. Keats, had he lived, might
have been a better critic than them all, for his *Letters* contain
flashes of insight which unmistakably indicate genius, and
rare genius at that.

But the most striking example of the enthusiasm and
individuality of the age is Hazlitt, who, though imperfectly
acquainted with any literature but English, and always
pushing himself well into the foreground, had the gift of
entering into another's personality so vividly that he has
been to many the means of introduction to a favourite author.
In his power of penetration he may be called one of the first
psychological critics, but he fails at times because, when he
could not adjust himself completely to an author, he had no
more fundamental standards to fall back upon. He defended
Keats against the general taste of his time, but was notoriously
unjust to Shelley. If one is to like Hazlitt one must swallow
him whole and not expect much logical presentation. In
criticism the Romantic Period saw at last the triumph of
appreciation. Perhaps in direct consequence of this it
produced a great deal of critical literature which is in itself
a pleasure to read.

CRITICISM THAT WAS BLUNTED BY PROSPERITY AND CANT

No great critic in English has tried, since the eighteenth century, to make precise rules for literature, though many have tried to lay down general principles. But the purpose of literature has been as much a theme of discussion as ever. That is to say, literature has remained healthily in touch with its roots—the life of its time. Arguments over literature are often simply arguments over the way life should be lived. The Victorian period took morals very seriously; consequently its judgments on literature tended to be moral judgments. Not only were the works of Byron banished, and Browning banned on account of his " immoral " Italian subjects : even Tennyson was censured for descending to such subjects as the guilty love of Lancelot and Guinevere in the *Idylls of the King*. (There were not wanting, however, critics who also condemned Tennyson for the sentimental weaknesses in his poetry for which he is often despised—too much despised—to-day.) It is significant that one of the most famous dictums of the period is Matthew Arnold's definition of poetry as a " criticism of life." Alongside its too well-known complacency, the Victorian period was troubled by many and serious doubts : we may take Macaulay as typical of the complacency, and Arnold and Ruskin as typical of the doubt.

Macaulay began with literary criticism, but later grew more interested in social and historical problems. In neither field can he be said to have pursued knowledge for its own sake. In history he seems to be asserting the glories of his own age rather than patiently depicting the past. His vivid powers of description confined themselves to material and external things—the signs of prosperity rather than the signs of culture. He disliked all abstract speculation, and dismissed the ancient philosophers, in a notorious phrase, as having " filled the world with long words and long beards." His judgment of writers was affected by his opinion (often a snobbish one) of their character and rank.

SCOURGE OF THE PHILISTINES : MATTHEW ARNOLD

In material things the Victorians were not badly off ; in the world of ideas they were sadly troubled. It is small wonder that the greatest critics of the age are those, such as Carlyle, who chastised it. Passing over Carlyle's literary criticism as small in bulk, we must name Matthew Arnold one of the five or six masters among English critics. His writings have had the rare effect of adding a word to the language, the word *philistine*, which is now used even by many who are ignorant of its origin. " The people," said Arnold in *Culture and Anarchy*, " who believe most that our greatness and welfare are proved by our being very rich . . . are just the people whom we call the Philistines." An inspector of schools by profession, Arnold laid much of the foundations of our national system of education. *Culture and Anarchy* (1869) is still as much a classic of our education as of our criticism. Arnold attacked the material standards of the age, and the one feature which might have been considered spiritual he attacked as the most anti-civilising influence of all ; he attacked the provincialism of English Protestantism and Nonconformity. Its noble and austere virtues he praised as Hebraic virtues, but what was needed in the Church, and in English life in general, he said, was more of the Hellenic element—more sweetness and light—more of the Greek element in Christianity, the element of which Dean Inge, for instance, is the chief champion to-day.

In literature Arnold profoundly mistrusted the historical method of criticism, which was becoming widely practised, because he thought it tended to give too high an opinion of one's own age, to lead the critic into the vulgar error of a Macaulay. He demanded that the subject should receive attention in literature, and that we should refresh ourselves at the fountain of Greek civilisation because of its " high seriousness." " Criticism," he said, " is the attempt to know the best that is known and thought in the world." Arnold was an invaluable antidote to the materialism of his time, and to the slovenliness into which the freedom of Romanticism had sometimes allowed poetry to fall. But Arnold's admiration of French logic and clearness of thought and expression blinded him to some extent to much of the excellence of the incurable anarchism of the English character ; he blundered badly in at least two famous passages in *Essays in Criticism*, once when he called Shelley " a beautiful and ineffectual angel," and again in describing Keats's love-letters as " the love-letters of a surgeon's apprentice."

THE REDISCOVERY OF ART : RUSKIN AND PATER

THE ugliness which had been created haphazard by Victorian prosperity (there is not a town in England which does not still suffer from it) cried out urgently for cure, or at least palliation. Arnold attacked it through literature and religion. Ruskin and William Morris attacked it through the visual arts : Morris painting, weaving, building, printing, designing, writing poetry, and preaching Socialism, and Ruskin lecturing, sermonising, and expressing his indignation at it all for nearly sixty years. Ruskin's master, Carlyle, said " the soul of society is diseased." Ruskin and Morris realised the extent to which the diseases of the social body affected its soul. Ruskin sometimes indulges in wild contradictions and enthusiams which detract from his value as a critic of literature, but he was of first importance in spreading ideas of sweetness and light among a wider circle than was reached by the austere Arnold. *Sesame and Lilies* (1865) is perhaps his most characteristic and possibly his best work.

Ruskin had an uphill task. A notable group of writers at the end of the nineteenth century shrank from it, not only in the material world, but in the world of literature. Led by Pater, they turned their backs in hopelessness and disgust upon the ugliness of most men and most of the works of men, and cultivated their æstheticism in their own little circle. They proclaimed the doctrine of Art (in which they included literary art) for Art's sake. They affected queer tastes, as in Max Beerbohm's *Defence of Cosmetics*, merely to annoy the public. Yet the Decadents—Wilde in literature or Whistler in painting—left a very important mark in both fields, though their own movement dwindled into nothing. Its surviving representatives are the critic and poet Arthur Symons, the unique Max Beerbohm, and one who has long since rejected the outward trappings of the movement, James Joyce.

Pater was a good writer and a sensitive interpreter ; his *Studies in the History of the Renaissance* (1873), and *Appreciations* (1889) show his intuition at its best. The doctrine associated with his name is hedonism, the belief that pleasure is the chief good. To this there is a corollary, that the highest, most sublime pleasure is the chief good since lower pleasures destroy the capacity for enjoyment of more sublime ones. Only once in his Oxford retreat did Pater frankly reveal his doctrine, in the conclusion of the *Renaissance*, where he says : " Not the fruit of experience, but experience itself, is the end." Pater, who was a great stylist, borrowed from such French stylists as Flaubert the doctrine of the *mot juste*, which has since been of the highest importance to English literature. According to this theory, there is only one phrase which will say exactly what the author means to say, and the secret of good writing is to search for and find this phrase. Pater himself took infinite pains to discover the right words to express his meaning.

THE SCHOLARLY CRITICS OF THE NEW CENTURY

AFTER the collapse of the æsthetic movement, though not of its influence, by the early death or suicide of most of its members, there is a lull in critical controversy until after the Great War. The interval was admirable for the scientific amassing and presentation of material for the study of literary history. The spread of education produced a large and still increasing number of scholars who turned out, particularly in America and Germany, monographs and theses upon every conceivable aspect of older literature, from " The Influence of Dutch Literature on English " to " The Derivation of Ancient Building-Terms," or " The Laundry-Bills of the Great Poets." The work entailed in such research is always long, dull for the most part, and dusty in both the literal and the figurative sense. Sneers at this kind of work are common, not only from the general public, but from many of the brighter and more impatient students in universities. It is true that much research has been done in the false scientific spirit of the early collectors for museums, who did not know how to interpret the importance of facts, and were not much interested in interpreting them. But these collectors nevertheless provided information of the highest value for those truer scientists who knew how to interpret. Every scientist who discovers a new law to-day, though he may perform thousands of verifying experiments himself, must still depend for about 90 per cent. of his information upon facts gathered by other and perhaps more humble scientific workers.

The good and the bad points of literary research may both be illustrated by the Bacon-Shakespeare controversy. On the one hand a great deal of unnecessary and often ridiculous labour was wasted in endeavouring to prove an impossibility which would have been obvious to any sane Baconian if he had read the few very uncultured and scornful words that

Bacon ever had to say, in the writings commonly recognised as his, about poetry, or love. On the other hand, a vast number of facts were brought to light about the handwriting of both Shakespeare and Bacon, their styles were analysed more observantly than ever before, and the net result is at least that, if a lost Shakespearean play should one day be recovered, we shall have a number of tests for its authenticity which might not otherwise have been discovered.

GOLDEN QUALITIES OF A TRUE SCHOLAR

FOR the ordinary reader the human aspect and the social background of literature are all-important, since he is apt to dismiss a classic as dull because he has insufficient knowledge of its milieu to find it interesting. But the human aspect of his knowledge of an author depends very much upon research done by others. The man who can consider all the available facts, discover some more for himself, and then, without losing sight of the wood for the trees, weave the whole into a coherent picture of an author, truer than had existed before, he is the true scholar. His qualities of patience, selective intelligence, and wide grasp are rare. The greatest critics of the early twentieth century—Professors Sir Walter Raleigh, Sir Arthur Quiller-Couch, W. P. Ker, and George Saintsbury—were such men. Their successors to-day are Livingston Lowes in America and Louis Cazamian, a Frenchman writing in English, who is one of the very greatest living authorities on English literature.

THE MODERN SCHOOL OF PSYCHOLOGICAL CRITICISM

THE discovery of scientific psychology is the ultimate cause of the apparently chaotic state of criticism to-day. But in spite of apparent dissension, the present is a very notable period in English criticism, and critical literature was never more the mirror of the mind, or minds, of the nation than now. The exaggerated interpretations of the early psychoanalysts, who would assign all our actions, for example, to the working of the sex instinct, are already being corrected, and it is realised that psychological laws, like the supposed rigid laws of the early stages of the theory of evolution, cannot be arbitrarily applied. The psychologist must take into account all the facts relating to the individual whom he is examining ; he must not interpret a recurrent dream of falling, for instance, in exactly the same way for each of his neurotic patients. Similarly the critic who uses psychological methods must take into account all the facts. Working along these new lines, a number of important revaluations of great figures of the past, and of the whole field of literature, have been made, notably by Aldous Huxley, J. Middleton Murry, Havelock Ellis, Herbert Read, Harold Nicolson, and the late Lytton Strachey.

The picture of the literary world to-day presents a wide and dangerous divergence : a flood of popular and for the most part ephemeral works selling in their tens and hundreds of thousands, and on the other hand a narrow vein of experiment reaching into stranger and stranger fields, and intelligible to fewer and fewer readers. (We must except the rare genius, such as D. H. Lawrence, who has something to say to every type of reader.) Criticism necessarily reflects this divergence. On the one hand there is a large body of professional critics, some of the calibre of Desmond McCarthy or Sir John Squire, some much less gifted, who report on current literature to a public which demands of book reviews entertainment and information, but rarely critical doctrine. The opposite pole of literature is reflected in the critical work of Ezra Pound, and of the associates and followers of James Joyce. Here indeed we have the *mot juste* pushed to the utmost limit of sense, half-reflections of words, dreamwords, puns of the unconscious mind, invented " portmanteau " words, used in a desperate attempt to make expression yet more personal, yet more individual.

It is perhaps significant that most of these super-analytic writers exile themselves to Paris, the home of literary cliques and cults. Meanwhile, the majority of readers who are seriously interested in literature, seek rather desperately for guidance ; they are ready to accept authority, to meet a new Classicism half-way. Fortunately there are two contemporary critics of rare sensibility who are capable of bridging this confusing divergence in literature : the scientific psychologist I. A. Richards, and the poet T. S. Eliot.

T. S. Eliot might be called the high priest of Order and Discipline in literature to-day. He brings to their service a mind of rare analytic powers, and a lucidity of style which makes *The Use of Poetry and the Use of Criticism* (1933) a classic among histories of English criticism. In this work he seems to have conquered the vagueness and double meanings which were sometimes annoying in his early work.

10

His account of the acquirement of taste is a masterpiece of restraint and clarity.

MODERN CRITICS WHO PIERCE TO THE ROOT OF LIFE

IT is quite safe to say there has never been a critic like I. A. Richards. For a start, one may read, in *Practical Criticism*, of his experiment in giving his students thirteen poems, not likely to be previously known and with no author's name attached, and asking the students to read them more carefully than they would normally do, and then write their criticisms of them. They wrote long and interesting reports upon these poems, and their incredible misreadings and false judgments show the amazing and usually quite unrealised difficulty of fully appreciating a poet's meaning. Richards's analysis of the four kinds of meaning has already been given. It will be found applied with great subtlety and clarity in *The Meaning of Meaning*, *Principles of Literary Criticism*, and in the short and provocative essay entitled *Science and Poetry*.

For T. S. Eliot tradition is fundamental both in religion and literature. I. A. Richards is a psychologist who suggests, particularly in *Practical Criticism* and *Science and Poetry*, some standards of value and rules of life for those who hold no religious belief as the term is commonly understood. But in the field of literary criticism Eliot and Richards meet : indeed, though they often disagree, their books are full of acknowledgments of each other's work. Eliot seeks less to impose authority than to educate sensibility. Richards talks of classical authors rather than of the modern school of disintegrated writers. His exercises are all exercises in sensibility. To the person who has lost faith in the old views of the universe, he is able to point out that poetry still exists.

Poetry may create an illusion, but the illusion is a psychological fact—it is real because the poem is a communication of the real experience of another man. Poetry is a real language of real men. It is the most sublime form of language which men possess. To those who, as a result of the terrible and destructive analyses of the latest physical science and of psychology, have lost faith in any kind of supernatural communication, poetry offers a meaning which is still, for men, a real meaning. If you accept the destruction of the old beliefs, poetry, says Richards, may save you, if you will make the effort to understand it, from the blank despair of the apparent modern dilemma. If you can still accept something fundamental from the old beliefs, says Eliot, poetry can help you to interpret them, and the minds of others who accept them, too—if you will make the effort. Thus, in these latter days, literary criticism has become indeed a criticism of life, the stuff and source of literature.

HOW BEST TO APPROACH LITERARY CRITICISM

LITERARY criticism, when it is general, nearly approaches æsthetics and philosophy ; when detailed, it is meaningless until the reader is well acquainted with the work of the author criticised. Caution should therefore be exercised in the approach to criticism for fear of incurring mental indigestion on the one hand, and disappointment on the other. To read more than two critical works of any kind straight after one another is to court disaster.

A good introduction to the principles and practice of literary criticism is provided by Professor George Saintsbury's *Loci Critici*, an anthology of famous or significant passages taken from the works of authors ranging from Aristotle to Matthew Arnold. The reader is advised to begin with the general passages such as Arnold's *Preface to Poems* (1853–1854), Hazlitt's essay *On Poetry in General*, or Sir Philip Sidney's *Apology for Poetry*, and is urged not to read a passage such as Dryden on Shakespeare until he has first read some Shakespeare.

Loci Critici may with advantage be followed by Matthew Arnold's *Essays in Criticism* (two series) or *Culture and Anarchy*, either of which provides a very interesting contrast to the work of the earlier and of the later critics. Among the most stimulating modern literary criticism is I. A. Richards's *Practical Criticism* and *Principles of Literary Criticism*, Herbert Read's *Form in Modern Poetry*, and T. S. Eliot's *The Use of Poetry and the Use of Criticism*.

A helpful and reliable account of English literary criticism from the earliest times to the end of the nineteenth century may be found in Professor Saintsbury's *History of English Criticism* (Blackwood).

TIME CHART OF

Showing the major movements, and their leaders, in

PERIOD	POETRY
1400–1599 From the death of Chaucer to the death of Spenser.	*Tottell's Miscellany*, 1557 (Wyatt and Surrey), Marlowe, EDMUND SPENSER, SHAKESPEARE, the Elizabethan Sonnet Writers.
1599–1660 Late Elizabethan and Jacobean Literature, up to the Restoration of Charles II.	JOHN DONNE and the " metaphysical " poets, especially Herbert, Vaughan, and Crashaw, Herrick, Lovelace, Suckling, JOHN MILTON, Andrew Marvell, Cowley, Waller, Denham.
1660–1765 The Augustan Age and the Age of Reason.	JOHN DRYDEN (1631–1700), Lady Winchelsea ALEXANDER POPE, Thomson, Collins, Gray ; Percy's *Reliques of Ancient English Poetry*.
1765–1824 The Romantic Movement.	Cowper, Crabbe, BURNS, BLAKE, WORDSWORTH and COLERIDGE (*Lyrical Ballads*, 1798), Southey, Scott, BYRON, SHELLEY, KEATS.
1824–1870 The " Victorian " Age.	TENNYSON, BROWNING, E. B. Browning, Matthew Arnold, THE " PRE-RAPHAELITES " (ROSSETTI, MORRIS, Christina Rossetti, SWINBURNE.)
1870–1914 From the death of Dickens to the outbreak of the World War.	Meredith, Bridges, KIPLING, HARDY, Housman, G. M. HOPKINS, FRANCIS THOMPSON, Alice Meynell, Masefield, Yeats.
1914–1922 From the beginning of the World War to the publication of *The Waste Land*.	J. E. Flecker, Rupert Brooke, Wilfred Owen, C. H. Sorley, Edward Thomas, Siegfried Sassoon.
1922—to the Present Day.	T. S. ELIOT (*The Waste Land*, 1922), Edith Sitwell, Sacheverell Sitwell, C. Day Lewis, Wisten Auden, Stephen Spender.

While giving the outstanding dates and movements in English Literature, the Chart also shows the periods at which the various genres have been at their best or worst. Note especially the blank periods in the Drama division, covering 1642–1660 and 1765–1865.

ENGLISH LITERATURE

Poetry, Drama, and the Novel, from 1400 to the Present Day.

DRAMA	NOVEL
Mystery Plays. Morality Plays. Interludes. *Ralph Roister Doister*, John Heywood, MARLOWE, Lyly, Peele, SHAKESPEARE (1564–1616), Beaumont and Fletcher, BEN JONSON, Ford, Dekker, Webster. ⊙ *In 1642, the Theatres were closed until 1660.* JOHN DRYDEN, Vanbrugh, Congreve, Wycherley.	⊙ *No novels were published before 1660, but the earlier works helped the development of this literary form.* *Euphues* (John Lyly), *Arcadia* (Sir Philip Sidney), Deloney. John Earle, Thomas Overbury.
	Bunyan, Defoe (*Robinson Crusoe*), Richardson, HENRY FIELDING (*Tom Jones*, 1749), Smollett, Sterne, Oliver Goldsmith.
Sheridan, Goldsmith.	
No outstanding Work or Writer.	Horace Walpole, Mrs. Radcliffe, SIR WALTER SCOTT, JANE AUSTEN.
	CHARLES DICKENS, W. M. THACKERAY, EMILY BRONTË (*Wuthering Heights*), Charlotte Brontë, George Eliot, Trollope, Charles and Henry Kingsley.
Robertson (*Society*, 1865), Henry Arthur Jones, Sir Arthur Pinero, OSCAR WILDE, Granville Barker, Sir James Barrie, St. John Ervine, J. M. Synge, John Galsworthy (1867–1933), GEORGE BERNARD SHAW (1856-) (*Widowers' Houses*, 1892, *St. Joan*, 1924), John Drinkwater, SEAN O'CASEY, Noel Coward, Somerset Maugham.	MEREDITH, HARDY, Gissing, Arnold Bennett, Henry James, R. L. Stevenson, Conrad, JOHN GALSWORTHY, H. G. WELLS, Hugh Walpole, E. M. Forster.
	JAMES JOYCE (*Ulysses*, 1922), D. H. LAWRENCE, Aldous Huxley, Virginia Woolf.

The Chart mentions only the most outstanding authors. For the modern period the distinctions drawn are necessarily rather arbitrary. Living authors are not included in the present-day division where their names were made and their styles already formed before 1914.

THE STORY OF ENGLISH LITERATURE

by WRIGHT WATTS MILLER, B.A.(Lond.),
M.Ed.(Manchester)

THE history of English literature is the history of the ways in which Englishmen have thought and written about the eternal affecting themes—love, the mystery of life and death, and man's relation to God and to Nature. It has taken a long time to learn how to express such thoughts in the difficult medium of words, and some such thoughts will always be better expressed through music or painting or some other medium. Each fresh discovery in the way of expression in words may be said to have added something that did not exist before, something permanent, to the inheritance of all Englishmen. Each generation has been interested in different aspects of these eternal themes, or has been stimulated to contemplate them by circumstances rather different from those which have stimulated other generations. The history of English literature is largely the history of these differences, and of the discoveries that have been made for their expression ; it is the history of the English nation as well as the history of a succession of individual great men.

WHERE OUR POETRY WAS BORN

ENGLISH literature before 1100 is a closed book to those who have not given a little time to the study of the language. Nevertheless, and limited though the range of Anglo-Saxon literature was, it is not cut off from the main stream of English literary history. The Angles and Saxons brought over with them from the Continent a kind of heroic epic poetry, common to all the Germanic tribes. There is no rhyme in this poetry, and no metre of the regular kind used in modern English, but each line is divided into two halves, bound together by alliterating syllables, and each half containing two strongly-accented syllables, with from two to seven unaccented ones. That is, the unknown authors of these poems had grasped two fundamental facts about the language.

The principle of accentuation (instead of proceeding by regular numbers of syllables, as in French or Latin) is still the foundation of English verse ; it enables us to use three hurried syllables as equivalent to the regular two of a poetical foot, or to vary the position of the accent, as when Shakespeare writes :

> " . . . my way of life
> Is fall'n into the sear, the yellow leaf."

Here *into* should strictly be accented on the second syllable, to conform with the scheme of the line, but only advantage results from accenting it, in the natural way, on the first syllable. Alliteration is also a great power in English poetry, not only in obviously imaginative passages such as *The furrow followed free*, but in other passages where it makes its effect less noisily but none the less surely—*The rarer action is in virtue than in vengeance.*

The old Germanic poetry exalted the deeds of traditional heroes, and regarded courage, self-control, and endurance as the noblest virtues. Only one complete heroic epic remains in Anglo-Saxon, the not very good one of *Beowulf*, which in the form we have it is a tenth-century version of deeds which happened on the Continent in the sixth century, before the Angles came to England. The old heroic spirit, fatalistic and often pessimistic, is also preserved in short personal poems, generally laments, such as *The Wanderer*, and *The Seafarer*, and *Deor*, which are the finest things in old English poetry. But all Anglo-Saxon literature is preserved through the Church ; it is not surprising, therefore, that the bulk of it is religious in subject. The versions of parts of the Old and New Testaments, generally assigned to Cynewulf and to Caedmon, have much of the old epic grandeur, and often present characters as pagan rather than Biblical heroes. But the Christian influence, conversely, had already weakened what was left of the native pagan poetry ; there are obvious clerical insertions and weaknesses in the form of *Beowulf* which we have to-day.

Apart from the laments, lyric poetry probably only existed in Anglo-Saxon in the form of popular charms and riddles. The amazing combination of pagan and Christian elements in some of these leads us to speculate much on the possibility of popular and pagan ballads having existed in Anglo-Saxon and being lost. But beyond speculation we cannot go. We do know that as late as 991 the Danish wars produced the vigorous poem of *The Battle of Maldon*, and other late examples of the old type of verse are not wanting.

THE OLD AND THE NEW STYLES IN CONFLICT

IN the history of both English language and English
literature the biggest break comes from 1100 to 1200. It
is not a complete break, but it marks the influx of a foreign
element so powerful that it was not properly assimilated for
three or four hundred years. It is difficult to say much
about English literature during the twelfth century because
there is so little of it. Yet from its later flowering we can
only conclude that it continued, probably in a spoken rather
than a written form. Even during the Anglo-Saxon period,
of course, most literary work thought important was composed
in Latin. Such was Bede's *Ecclesiastical History* (finished in
731), and a great deal of what remains to us in that halting
medium, Anglo-Saxon prose, consists of translations of such
works as this. Latin reached the common people through
the Church services, and from the metre of the early Christian
Latin hymns they began to learn to write poetry of the kind
which we know to-day. For these hymns, instead of being
based on alliteration and crude accent, had rhyme and regular
metre, with an arithmetical scheme of syllables. (A familiar
Latin song of this type, though secular and much later, is
Gaudeamus Igitur.) So the rather crude poetry of the
twelfth and thirteenth centuries exhibits as a rule a great
conflict going on between the old system of free accentuation
and the new regularity.

Layamon's *Brut* (a verse history of England), the *Ormulum*,
the many verse romances of King Arthur's knights, all
illustrate the growing pains through which poetry was passing.
Not only did it learn from the Latin hymns, but also from
the French, who had themselves learned the patterns of their
poetry from the troubadours of Provence, that fountain-head
of examples for the whole of mediæval and modern poetry.
And so in the fourteenth century appear the first genuine
lyric poems in something like modern English. Of these
Sumer Is Icumen In is one of the earliest.

Lyric poetry in French had of course already been written
in England for some time, and many English poems were
now composed with a French or Latin refrain to each verse.
Mediæval English lyric poetry is often much more natural
and unsophisticated than French and Provençal poetry,
though it is far from being naïve. Lyrics of divine worship
are often so passionately composed that they might be taken

*Beowulf, traditional hero of the one complete heroic epic
which remains in Anglo-Saxon.*

for love-lyrics, and *vice versa*. Many of our finest carols were composed in this period, and the bulk of the lyric poetry is either religious or amorous in subject, though there are also ballads of personal satire, songs to good ale, and to hunting. Nature poetry as understood to-day does not yet appear, though its element is clear enough in some of the best-preferred images, as in the love-lorn poem beginning " Lenten is come with love to towne."

THE DAWN OF ENGLISH LITERATURE

CHAUCER (1340 ?–1400) is the first real man of letters to write in English. He not only drew full advantage from foreign literary models (having travelled often in France and Italy on diplomatic business) but also enjoyed to the full the richness of native English life and character. He turned the long-windedness of the conventional romance into more human and affecting stories, in such poems as *Troilus and Cressida*, and in *The Canterbury Tales* we find at last a vivid consciousness of the daily life around its author—a state never reached in any literature until it begins to show signs of maturity. Chaucer is the first English writer to show great powers over the precise and incisive phrase or epithet ; he is also the first to show a wide and varied command over the true accentuation of natural English poetry. In him the Anglo-Saxon, French, Latin, and Italian elements begin for the first time to be harmoniously assimilated.

Contemporary with Chaucer, however, there was a remarkable renaissance of the old alliterative verse (though a little weakened in metre) in the West Country, which spoke a different dialect from Chaucer's more sophisticated London English, and in its comparative isolation also had rather rigorous ideas about morals. So the poems of this little renaissance are mainly religious—*Pearl*, *Patience* (the story of Jonah), and *Cleanness*, and best of all Langland's wonderfully real and vivid picture of the England (mainly the corrupt England) of his time—*The Vision of Piers Plowman*.

A LOCAL DIALECT THAT BECAME OUR NATIONAL TONGUE

THE fifteenth century contains no great authors except Malory, but it was a period of important adjustments. The English dialects had become so divergent from each other that the London dialect, the language of the court and of Chaucer, as well of many merchants, established itself as the king over the others for the mere sake of convenience and comprehensibility, being thus the ancestor of modern Standard English. One of the last flourishings of literature in any of the other dialects was in the Border Ballads, such as *Chevy Chase*, most of which can be assigned, though vague in date and nearly all anonymous, to the fifteenth century. There is little other than folk-poetry, indeed, during the century.

Prose literature naturally shows the effects of the standardisation of the language—mainly in the translations of the Bible, and in the popular sermons and religious treatises of such men as Pecock, who now found it necessary to forsake Latin in their exhortations. Caxton also had to choose the standard dialect for his translations (which were the first books printed in English), though it was an effort for him to adjust his own broad Kentish for the purpose. He printed also in prose the *Morte d'Arthur* of Sir Thomas Malory, which had been written in 1470, gathering together the old legends into one of the most successful romantic narratives in English.

RELIGION AS THE CRADLE OF ENGLISH DRAMA

THE greatest number of English Mystery and Morality plays belong to the fifteenth and early sixteenth centuries. The mystery plays (presented by the guilds) arose out of earnest and sincere desires to present sacred stories to the people, and gathered about them a whole mass of extraneous interests, such as wrestling-matches, music, personal satire, political satire, and carol-singing. They naturally preserved the dialects of their districts to a very late date, some of the most important groups of mystery plays coming from York, Wakefield, Chester, and Coventry. The morality plays personified vices and virtues, and often extended to a deadly dullness of preaching, but they served to develop the idea of regular acts and scenes and properly balanced personages. They developed early in the sixteenth century into the Interludes, in which genuinely created characters, as understood by the modern stage, first appear.

SEEDS OF A MIGHTY POETIC FLOWERING

THE great flowering of the Italian Renaissance reached England late, mainly by way of France, and much diluted in vigour. It is reflected in the great number of sixteenth-century translations from the classics, including such still famous versions as North's *Plutarch* (1579) and Chapman's *Homer* (1598–1616) ; in the strivings towards humane education by Ascham, Sir Thomas More, and others ; and in the very direct influence of Italian poetry upon two important minor men : Wyatt (1503–42) and Surrey (1517?–47).

It was these two who brought the sonnet to England : Surrey is also the first known Englishman to write in blank verse. The accentual principle of English verse here gave birth to a new form, which was to become the vehicle of the greatest triumphs of the Elizabethan period in poetry. The work of Wyatt and Surrey was not published, however, until 1557, in the famous Tottel's *Miscellany*, along with the work of many other new poets still struggling with the language. After 1557 the publication of poetical miscellanies was frequent.

Ascham, Sir Thomas More and his fellows, had a vital problem to deal with—the acknowledging of the status of English as a language. Ascham's first book, though called *Toxophilus* (1545), was a treatise in English on archery—" English matter in English speech, for Englishmen." The battle for English English, against Latin or Greek English, was fought bitterly all through the sixteenth century, and its echoes continue, indeed, through almost all English literature. English English, however, was becoming steadily fixed among plain Englishmen, if not among the more scholarly, by such triumphs as *The Prayer Book* (1540) and the first complete version of the Bible in English, by Miles Coverdale, in 1535.

THE ENGLISH LANGUAGE COMES INTO ITS OWN

THE name " Elizabethan " is only a rough one ; in literature the period is said to begin with Spenser's *Shepherd's Calendar*, in 1579, when Elizabeth had been on the throne twenty-one years, and it cannot be said to show any signs of changing or ending until James I. was near the end of his reign. Actually the period is the genuine and late-flowering English literary Renaissance, tallying in a way with the Italian fourteenth-century Renaissance, but much more homely, and displaying the genius of the language to all the greater perfection on account of its later development

Edmund Spenser (1552?–99) is generally called " the poet's poet " to-day and perhaps unfairly neglected on that account. He is the first English poet of genius to realise and to develop the possibilities of his native language as a language fit for poetry and worthy to produce a literature ultimately as fine as that of Greece, Rome, or Italy. *The Shepherd's Calendar*, a collection of twelve experimental pastoral poems, none of them Spenser's best, sets out frankly with this aim, and is therefore often regarded as a landmark.

Spenser looked back to the only great predecessor he could find in English—Chaucer, who, it must be remembered, wrote in dialect, since there was no standard literary English in his day. From him Spenser borrowed hundreds of antique words and phrases which he resurrected, often in comically inaccurate forms, with the idea of adding dignity to the language. Some of his most inaccurate borrowings, such as " derring-do," have become standardised through Spenser's success in using them. *Prothalamion, Epithalamion*, and some of the sonnets, are probably easiest to appreciate to-day, but *The Faërie Queene* remains Spenser's greatest monument. The achievement of the " Spenserian stanza ", so admirable for narrative in its variation, was itself no small thing. The purpose of the poem—" to fashion a gentleman or noble person in vertuous and gentle discipline "—is often forgotten. The allegory of the whole—the twelve virtues to be presented in twelve books, if the whole poem had been finished—is lost again and again in allegories within allegories as the stories unfold one upon another. *The Faërie Queene* has been and still is a treasure-house for all English poets to plunder.

The problems of Spenser were the problems of all Elizabethan poets—how to reconcile classical models and the genius of native English, and how to avoid the stigma of " idleness " attached to poetry. It was this stigma that gave rise to Sidney's great essay, whose title must seem so strange to-day, *The Apology for Poetry* (1580). Sidney himself (1554–86) wrote some excellent sonnets, though they appeared in a long sequence addressed to his lady, on the model of Petrarch's sonnets to Laura, a model which served for nearly every Elizabethan poet who attempted the sonnet. For these poets were intensely serious about their work ; when read in bulk it becomes obvious that the conventional idea of a fresh dawn of sprightly young poetry among the Elizabethans is a little exaggerated. The delightful songs of Campion, Nashe, Heywood, Jonson, and scores of others which appear in all the anthologies are indeed a creaming of Elizabethan poetry. Not till Daniel's *Defence of Rhyme* (about 1602) was it even settled that English poetry ought to rhyme ; classical poetry never rhymed—was not rhyme therefore a barbarous invention not to be tolerated ?

POETRY'S ADVENTURES IN THE THEATRE

POETRY, of course, soon got out of the hands of the pedants, and nowhere more than in the theatre. Blank verse, discovered by Surrey, was brilliantly handled for the first time by Marlowe (1564-93) in *Tamburlaine*, *Dr. Faustus*, *Edward II.*, and other plays, and Shakespeare, in one of the few personal references in his plays, acknowledges him as his teacher in verse. Greene, Peele, Kyd, Lodge, Nashe, and others practised the same medium, and the sudden growth of Elizabethan drama after Marlowe's début in 1587 is remarkable. Marlowe and his associates are often referred to as the " University Wits," because their work was heavily influenced by the classics. But the stage had been developing slowly since the morality plays and interludes, as the stage must always develop independent, to a large degree, of the printed word.

It is no accident that Shakespeare (1564-1616), with his " small Latin and less Greek," is the greatest man of the Elizabethan theatre. The amazing stagecraft of his best plays excites wonder still, and makes the clumsiness of Marlowe's plays primitive indeed. Shakespeare was born a poet, and to live by poetry one had in those days to write for the stage. We need not suppose that the Elizabethan audiences were more eager to hear poetry than prose, but we are sure, from their racy talk recorded in a hundred places, that they had a quicker and more varied gift of phrase, both in appreciation and creation, than most of us have in these days of wide reading. Simple poetry they could not help knowing, since they all sang part-songs as one of their commonest amusements. Naturally enough they never quite took to the more academically planned plays of Ben Jonson (1573-1637), but preferred the free, romantic comedies of such as Beaumont (1584-1616) and his associate Fletcher (1575-1625), whose *Knight of the Burning Pestle* is often revived to-day with success.

There was also in the Elizabethans, however, a very vivid preoccupation with the imminence and mystery of death. The tragedies of Shakespeare or of Webster (*The Duchess of Malfi* and *The White Devil*) were concerned with a reality perhaps easier for them than ourselves to appreciate. Even Kyd's early *Spanish Tragedy*, a crude story of revenge, remained one of the most popular plays in the London repertoire for about thirty years.

PROSE THAT KEPT "THE COMMON TOUCH"

THOUGH few Elizabethans had yet learned to write ordered prose as we understand it to-day, they could write prose racily in touch with the speech of common people, prose which appealed to all the senses and not merely to the intellect, as a modern critic has said. A minor classic in this kind is Nashe's story *The Unfortunate Traveller*. There was also much pamphleteering, much writing of voyages, as Drake's *The World Encompassed* (set down by his chaplain) and Hakluyt's (1553-1616) great anthology of voyages, and there was above all *The Authorised Version of the Bible* in 1611.

This version does not all date from 1611 ; much of it is drawn from older versions such as that of Miles Coverdale, and the English of *The Authorised Version* is consequently often old-fashioned even for 1611. But it is as true to-day as ever it was to say that " there is no better English anywhere than the English of the Bible." In no country has the language of the native version of Scripture had more influence than in England. Not only are Milton, Bunyan, Wordsworth, Ruskin, D. H. Lawrence, to pick a few at random, saturated in it, but hundreds of its phrases have become so current in everyday speech that their origin is usually overlooked. *The Authorised Version* has been one of the most powerful elements in English national culture.

The one great figure in Elizabethan prose is Bacon (1561-1626), whose greatest work, the erection of a new scheme of inductive and empirical knowledge, was set down in Latin, so that it might be more universally read, in the *Novum Organum*. Bacon's *Essays* are the slightest of his work ; their condensation is that of an accomplished lawyer, and their simple, pointed prose is of a kind no other Elizabethan could touch. *The Advancement of Learning* is his best exposition in English of his revolutionary point of view.

LYRICS WOUND ROUND DELICATE IMAGERY

IT is unreasonable to cut off the Elizabethan period sharply from its successor, but in poetry we detect the growth, in the early seventeenth century, of two strains much less artificial than that hankering after the classics and the Italians which still troubled the Elizabethans. The first strain is called the Metaphysical, and its father is Donne (1573 ?-1631). There was never before a poet (and few since) who could more poignantly express emotion by way of a strange image as Donne. The blending of intellect and emotion in his best work is unsurpassed. Others, such as George Herbert (1593-1633) and Vaughan (1622-95), applied the same intensity of poetic imagination to religious themes, as in *Sweet day, so cool, so calm, so bright*, and *I saw Eternity the other night*. All these poets, and others, such as Crashaw, Carew, and Cowley, often overreached themselves and made ridiculous instead of sublime images, but no group of poets has surpassed their best work in subtlety.

The second new strain shows a greater cheerfulness, and a kind of semi-pagan acceptance of fate rather than the gloomy fore-realisation of the Elizabethans. It is best illustrated by Herrick (1591-1674), whose *Fair Daffodils, we weep to see*, is typical of the best of the Caroline poets (so-called merely after the reign of Charles I.). Herrick wrote scurrilous personal verses and simple divine ones, as well as the type just quoted. It should be noticed that he is not a " Nature poet " ; he writes about daffodils, roses, violets, and a few other flowers as symbols, but he is not interested in the essential spirit of Nature, as, for instance, Wordsworth was. There are really no " Nature poets " yet.

A POET WHO SCORNED THE "BARBARITY" OF RHYME

MILTON (1608-74) is perhaps the most difficult of great English poets to appreciate or even to place properly in literary history. He is best regarded as a man a little behind his time rather than in front of it. He scorned the ways of the Metaphysicals and the Carolines. He was brought up in the true Renaissance tradition, and was one of the few to see the real meaning of " humane " or classical studies. He wrote always with Latin and Greek in his head, and his English, in *Paradise Lost*, for instance, in consequence compares unfavourably with Shakespeare's for variety and richness of flavour. He rejected the " barbarity " of rhyme scornfully in all his major works. In short, he was still a man of the Renaissance and had not quite realised the possibilities of the independent life of the English language.

We read Milton now for his sublimity, his grand grasp of grand situations, and are often surprised to find how simple his language really is, and to recognise familiar phrases such as the light that " made darkness visible." He spent the middle part of his life in active work for the Puritans, with whose narrowness he was nevertheless constantly in conflict, and wrote his three greatest works when blind, disillusioned, and afflicted, after the Restoration. But the most brilliant of his younger contemporaries, Dryden, could say of him : " This man cuts us all out and the Ancients too."

THE SOBERING INFLUENCE OF THE PURITANS

PURITANISM not only produced one of England's greatest folk-classics, *The Pilgrim's Progress* (1676), and one of the greatest English tracts, Milton's *Areopagitica*, which was directed against the press censorship of the Puritans themselves ; it also closed the theatres and helped to break the tradition of Elizabethan blank verse entirely. It provoked some of the finest pulpit oratory in English, though more often from the side of the Established Church than from among its own followers. Its steadying and limiting effect was parallel with a change in English prose. The old ornamental, almost voluptuous, prose makes about its last appearance in the work of Sir Thomas Browne (1605–82) —*Urn-Burial*, and *Religio Medici*.

The new age realised that prose had to be capable of expressing sober exactitude as well as soaring invention. Under the influence, not indeed of the Puritans, but of the new spirit of scientific inquiry first inspired by Bacon, the Royal Society was founded in 1662, and one of its first aims was to achieve " a close, natural way of speaking . . . to return back to the primitive purity, and shortness, when men delivered so many *things* in almost an equal number of words." In short, it was becoming clear that the English language could now express such a variety of ideas that its intellectual and its imaginative functions ought to be, to some extent at least, differentiated, the one being kept for prose and the other for poetry. No more would a Walton write a treatise on scientific angling (1653) in which poetry of words and sentiment mingles inextricably with the information so whimsically imparted. The rise of the Puritans was but one symptom of a general ordering and regimentation of ideas.

THE "CLASSIC" PERIOD BEGINS

THUS the Restoration of Charles II. in 1660 marks a real break. Though England became " merrie " once more, it was a much more conscious and e'egant merriment than the Elizabethans had enjoyed. In 1660 begins the great " Classic " period of our literature. It is probably best to understand this as signifying an ordering, rather than a following of the Greeks and Romans, for though that strain was prominent enough its nature was more influenced by contemporary ideas than such a movement had been before.

It needed a great man to lead such an ordering. He was Dryden (1631–1700) " the father of English prose," " the father of English criticism," and a great example to English verse as well. Blank verse was already falling into incoherent semi-prose when the closing of the theatres put an end to its use in drama for a while ; lyric poetry, in the hands of men less gifted than Donne and Herbert, was becoming an exaggerated straining after fresh " conceits " on the lines of the Metaphysicals. Metre and even rhyme were becoming lost sight of under the exaggeration of more intellectual pre-occupations. The quasi-standardisation of the heroic, or five-foot, couplet for English poetry for about a hundred years seems to us at first sight perhaps trivial and unnecessary. Actually it was very much needed.

Heroic couplets had been written before—some as early as 1623 by Waller, and a little later by Denham, who both came to be regarded as the forerunners of the Classic School. Dryden, a man of great wit, more interested in the controversies of his time than in the life of the individual man's passions, made of the couplet a biting weapon for satire, in which he excelled. The proper use of the couplet demanded a technical care which had been missing from English poetry. It demanded that the rhyme, instead of dinning monotonously in the ear, should carry so much of the point of the satire (as rhyme does in the last line of a limerick) that it became one of the chief merits of the poem. From this it followed that the sense was usually complete within a couple of lines, or a multiple of two, and that variation was secured by a clever change in the sense, usually by way of antithesis, in the very middle of each of a great number of the lines. There is thus as much genuine intellectual pleasure (without excluding the possibility of emotional pleasure) in a good poem of Dryden or of one of his successors, as there is in a good fugue by Bach.

Dryden was always conscious that he wrote at an age of transition, both in poetry and prose. The alterations he made in later editions of his prose works illustrate very well the kind of elegance and exactitude which was coming to be demanded. It is certain, at any rate, that Dryden was the first to write consistently in a prose which can still be called lucid modern English. His *Essay of Dramatic Poesy* and *Preface to the Fables* are classics of our critical literature.

The drama reflected more closely than other forms of literature the abandonment which followed on the Restoration, but even the bawdy wit of Wycherley (1640–1716) and Congreve (1670–1729) is of a mannered and intellectual form, so that on the modern stage some of the wittiest, even the bawdiest, passages, are too quick and subtle for a good third of the audience. The " classicism " of the age was not a cold academic classicism, but rather the precise code of a consciously elegant society. Of that society we can read, of course, in the pages of Pepys (1633–1705).

THE "POLITE" AGE OF THE AUGUSTANS

No fashions in English literature have lasted so long at a time, without modification, as some of the fashions of the classic period. Correct couplets, very little different from Dryden's, were still being written in the eighteen-twenties. The eighteenth century was quite conscious of its correctness, and suggested for itself the name Augustan, as a parallel to the glorious age of Augustus, the first emperor of Rome. It was not only the form of verse that was so near fixation ; it was also the diction and the spirit. The age is characterised by a preference for words of classic origin in its poetry, and an avoidance of the homely Saxon, unless a word itself of literary associations, such as " swain." General-isations are preferred to individualisations, as being more " sublime." It was an age when kings were depicted in togas rather than in the dress of their own age, when an " Ode to the Passions " trooping vaguely along one by one was thought of more merit than any poet's account in blood and tears of his own passions.

Not unnaturally, the greatest poetical triumphs of the age are in satire, mainly the work of the greatest modern satirist and writer of couplets—Pope (1688–1744). No one has ever got such a sting into a bare half-line of verse as Pope. With a couplet he could ruin a reputation irretrievably and unforgettably. His own ideas were derived and shallow, but his wit must always excite the greatest praise, especially in the *Satires* and *Epistles* rather than in the better-known *Rape of the Lock* or *Essay on Criticism*.

Many tried in vain to compete with Pope in personal satire. Outside this field, however, other uses were found for the couplet ; Gay (1685–1732), author of *The Beggar's Opera*, wrote *Trivia*, a book of rules for walking the streets of London, and others wrote mock-epics on frivolous subjects such as cider and hunting. No one, however, dared to compete with the Ancients in the realm of genuine epic ; some attempted in tragedy and failed inanely ; the age for the most part had the good taste and sense to stick to its own standards. It could even laugh at its own diction, beautifully parodied by Gray, for instance, in his *Ode on a Favourite Cat Drowned in a Tub of Goldfishes*.

PROSE : THE GLORY AND JUSTIFICATION OF THE AUGUSTANS

THE Augustan period was not quite at ease with the passions nor with seriousness. Its greatest triumphs after Pope's verse are in the sober medium of prose. And in prose, at least that of the greatest masters, the shackles of would-be classic diction seem to fall away. Pope had as contemporaries one of the greatest of all English prose-writers—Swift (1667–1745) ; two great masters, almost the creators, of the " middle " style in Addison (1672–1719), and Steele (1672–1729) ; and a great master of the simple style in Defoe (1659–1731).

Swift's irony is of a peculiar kind. Often it turns upon itself and laughs at itself, so that one does not know which way to laugh with this morbidly sensitive satirist. His greatest satires are probably the short sketches such as *A Modest Proposal* rather than *Gulliver's Travels*, but the perennial appeal of the latter, as a pure narrative, to children of every generation, is a testimony to the lucidity of his style. It has been held that *The Tale of a Tub* is " one of the very greatest books of the world." There is no more consistently lucid writer in English.

Addison and Steele were the natural growth of the " polite " age in which they lived, when culture was becoming fashionable, so long as it did not demand too serious an application, and women were allowed to take a greater part than hitherto in men's conversation. Looking at the original copies of *The Tatler* and *The Spectator* to-day, it is difficult to realise how avidly they were read for their literary worth, and how uncritical their readers must have been of the very small amount of news which heads each issue. While Steele, the more human and even boisterous of the two, was actually the creator of *The Tatler* and of the character of Sir Roger, Addison was the more restrained, fine, even finicky spirit. Indeed, to Swift he appeared little more than a poseur. But even his posing, and the very delicate and harmless satire which accompanied it, helped to bring smoothness of manners into a society which had still more of the barbarian North than the elegant French in its composition.

THE DISCOVERY OF THE NOVEL

OF all writers Defoe has the greatest gift for presenting fiction as if it were fact. No one believes that his *Journal of the Plague Year* is not an eye-witness's account until it is pointed out that when the Plague was raging Defoe was but six years old. Similarly not only *Robinson Crusoe*, but his accounts of the lives of doubtful characters such as *Moll Flanders* and *Captain Singleton*, are all told with an innocence and absolute sincerity which is irresistible. Yet these books are not quite novels. They follow the fortunes of a single character in a manner which had been in vogue ever since prose literature began. They have the length, but neither the depth nor the breadth of a novel. Addison, in *Sir Roger*, was near to contributing one of the elements for a successful novel.

But the first novel in English is always held to be Richardson's *Pamela*, no earlier than 1740. Often morbid or sententious, it is nevertheless a remarkably moving account of the emotions of a young girl in service, persecuted by a master to whom she was too attractive. It was read in its thousands and translated all over Europe. To follow, in prose, the experience of so living a character, was a new event in literature. In 1742 Fielding, a much broader man, and a great prose-writer, began a parody of the, to him, sickly *Pamela*, but soon discovered that he was writing a novel of his own— *Joseph Andrews*—a book more varied in appeal than any that had yet appeared. He called it aptly " a comic epic in prose." His greatest work, *Tom Jones*, followed in 1749, and Richardson's *Clarissa Harlowe* in 1748. Smollett (1721–71) was now also writing his rollicking stories, and Sterne (1713–68) his unique *Tristram Shandy* and *Sentimental Journey*.

THE NEGLECTED MASTERPIECE OF A GREAT GENIUS

THE novel obviously could not have appeared until prose had been made a flexible enough medium for writing novels. Prose in the eighteenth century could achieve anything. We must hurry over Gibbon (1737–94), and Goldsmith (1728–74), to sum up the Augustan period in its greatest and most typical figure—Dr. Johnson (1709–84). Apart from his *Dictionary*, the reader is sometimes puzzled to know what literary work earned Johnson his undoubted place, and to wonder whether he would now hold that place without Boswell's *Life*. The answer is to be found in a work too little read—the *Lives of the Poets*, finished when Johnson was over seventy.

Here are indeed the Augustan obtuseness about flights of imagination, and the stickling for rigid diction, but here also are some of the finest and most profound critical reflections in English, as applicable to-day as ever. Johnson was a born critic, but he preferred talking, at which he excelled, to writing. He has confessed that writing was laborious to him and he would not have practised it had he not been obliged to earn his living. He wrote the *Lives* almost as he talked, consulting few references. They make one of the finest introductions to all that was of solid worth in the Augustan age.

HUMAN EMOTIONS PLAY A BIGGER PART

QUITE early in the eighteenth century there are many signs that the prevailing formality was ill-suited to many minds. Many of the century's most interesting poets seem to have led secluded and strange lives, and some died insane. It was not a good time for men of romantic sensibility. But quite early, many poets secured a great vogue without writing in the fashionable couplet. (The history of metrical forms is always a sure guide to taste.) Thomson's *Seasons* (1726–30) in blank verse, and *Castle of Indolence* (1748), in Spenserian stanza, and even in semi-Spenserian language, and Young's *Night Thoughts* (1741) in blank verse, all had a large public. As the century went on, men grew conscious that abandonment to natural feeling was not necessarily something to be ashamed of, and in the second half of the period there was a flood of tearful novels. More fundamental changes in feeling, such as the rise of the Methodist Movement, were also going on. Men of fashion met the new tendencies half-way by giving up some of their fashionable worship of the classics and turning to the Middle Ages. Imitation Gothic ruins, and dead trees to accompany them, were erected in gardens ; but there was also a genuine interest in the neglected Middle Ages. Gray (1716–71), for instance, was a scholar not only in Latin and Greek, but also in Anglo-Saxon, Old Norse, and Welsh. Though much of his poetry had all the characteristics, and even the faults, of the Augustans, in subject he was different. Collins (1721–59) and Cowper (1731–1800), both shy and retiring, were writing poetry about fairies and winter walks. Gray, Collins, and Cowper scarcely wrote any heroic couplets at all. Chatterton (1752–70) made capital out of his imitative ability and the popular taste for the mediæval. Burns (1759–96) wrote Augustan English but unsurpassedly natural Scots. The last strain of folk-poetry in Britain probably died in Burns.

HOW THE GROWTH OF CITIES FOSTERED A LOVE OF NATURE

BUT the strongest new force gathering through the eighteenth century was that romantic interest in wild nature and scenery which is now regarded as so typical of English poetry and the English race. It could not have arisen before, since Englishmen still lived in small towns and vil-lages, in close contact with the life of the soil. They did not need to refresh themselves with " Nature," though their poetry showed often enough that they were not blind to her. But as the Industrial Revolution advanced, and men were herded more together, the contrast between town and country life became more obvious. Thousands of men now lived and died without natural contact with the life of the soil and of the seasons. To-day, of course, the greater portion of our population come under this category. A conscious seeking after what we have lost is therefore inevitable. The feeling for Nature showed itself fitfully in Thomson, Gray, Collins, Cowper, and many minor men, and with amazing intensity in the isolated poet Blake (1757–1827), whose mysticism was so powerful that he lived almost unrecognised by his generation, and was happy so. His models in poetry were quite obviously Shakespeare, Chaucer, and the Elizabethan lyrists.

But real understanding of Nature is perhaps not shown until Wordsworth (1770–1850) and Coleridge (1772–1834). Their joint publication of *Lyrical Ballads* in 1798 marks that year as one of the most significant dates in the history of our literature. They were both profoundly inspired by a reaction against the artificiality of life in towns and of poetry as they knew it. They had immense poetic gifts, and they set out quite consciously to rescue their generation by a deliberate return to simplicity of language, of character, and of subject. The supernatural they welcomed in all seriousness ; Coleridge's principal contribution to *Lyrical Ballads* was *The Ancient Mariner*, and of his other poems *Christabel* and *Kubla Khan* are certainly the finest. They desired to recapture the sense of mystery, without burying themselves in any false mystifications ; Wordsworth writes of trees on a lonely pass talking " the ghostly language of the ancient earth."

Wordsworth's preface to the second edition of *Lyrical Ballads* in 1800 (not that it had a very large sale) is still one of the finest documents on the function of poetry. It contains also his own theories that the language of poetry should be " a selection of the language actually used by men," and that only among the simplest peasants are true virtue and fit subjects for poetry to be found. But Coleridge himself pointed out the fallacies of this attitude. Many of Wordsworth's greatest successes were achieved in very literary language indeed, as in, for instance, the *Ode on the Intimations of Immortality*. Apart from the three poems mentioned, Coleridge's greatest work was done in the field of criticism. He had possibly a keener sense of what is true poetry than any other critic.

THE ROMANTIC SENSIBILITY REVOLTS AGAINST REASON

THE dazzling poetical period 1798 to 1824 is generally called the Romantic Revival. The often didactic Wordsworth and Coleridge deserve the epithet romantic less than their younger contemporaries Shelley (1792–1822), Keats (1795–1821), and Byron (1788–1824). With these men the floodgates of emotion, of sentiment, and of sensation were opened. A comparison of Keats's *Ode to a Nightingale* with any work of Pope's will show the change that had taken place. No English poet has justified so well, in so short a space of time, the choice of purely personal experience as his main theme. Had he lived, he might have shown as broad a humanity as Shakespeare. Shelley, with his head full of dreams of liberation, gathered from the French Revolution, is the finest poet in English for certain imaginative powers which may roughly be termed " of the intellect." The *Hymn to Intellectual Beauty* and *Epipsychidion* illustrate this. He almost never came down to earth. His skylark and his west wind are mere convenient symbols to carry his own longings.

But the popular poet of the time was Byron, who writes much more like Pope, except in a few lyrics such as *The Isles of Greece*, than like a true romantic. He was " romantic " only in his choice of yearning themes. All the dangerous side of the romantic movement was by now in full swing— " albums " of verse, uncritical surrender to emotions, and an easy tripping or galloping metre spoiling the sense of a poem. These faults are shown in Thomas Moore, often in Hood when he is serious, in Southey and Campbell, and in a host of poetasters.

It was not only poetry, of course, that underwent the change to " romance." Scott (1771–1832), after writing nothing but stirring ballads at first, turned to the novel, and produced the first historical novels in English. His style was often unpruned and hurried, but he is still one of our greatest story-tellers. After Scott followed Ainsworth, Lytton, and others in the historical field, Lever, Lover, and Marryat in a more boisterous and realistic vein, and Peacock (1785–1866) rather apart, as a brilliant satirical novelist, from whom none of the shams of the romantic movement were hidden.

Rather late in the eighteenth century, Fanny Burney and some other women had begun to write novels. Literature was now accepted as a possible calling for women. In Jane Austen (1775–1817) we have perhaps our most distinguished woman writer. Quiet and limited though her subjects are, she has an irresistible delicate irony which is essentially feminine in quality. She has done something that no man could have done.

The *Spectator* type of essay lasted all through the eighteenth century, and along with it the rather more natural literature of letters and diaries. The letters of Lady Mary Wortley Montagu and of Horace Walpole have interest for even the most modern readers. With the nineteenth century the limitations of " elegant writing " were perceived, and we get a period of great distinction in solid periodical criticism, in the newly founded *Edinburgh* and *Quarterly* and *Fortnightly Reviews*. Lamb (1775–1834) made something new of the personal essay; Hazlitt (1778–1830) wrote some of the most enthusiastic criticism we have; De Quincey put the mistiest of romanticism into prose; solid historians such as Grote continued to write an echo of Augustan prose; and downright William Cobbett (1762–1835) produced some of our most memorable simple prose, even if its hectoring tone was not all that polished literature could desire.

DOUBTS THAT TROUBLED THE VICTORIANS

THERE is a curious break of ten years between the principal romantics (except for Wordsworth, and even his best work was certainly done before 1820) and the first work of the Victorians such as Tennyson (1809–92) and Browning (1812–89). The ardour of the Romantics had spent itself when these two began to write. That ardour derived in good measure from the French Revolution, whereas the younger men found themselves in a time of great maladjustment. Reform Bills and Factory Acts failed to check the growing abuses of industrialism, and every socially sensitive person was bound to feel, all through the century, that all was not well with the State. In 1859 Darwin's *Origin of Species* gave, for a time, a shock to religious belief—at least to some kinds of belief. So that although our own generation tends to scoff at the Victorians for their unbounded assurance, the greatest of them, it will be seen, were actually all troubled by doubts and very critical of their age. The one possible exception is a man of very severe limitations—Macaulay (1800–59), whose confident pride in the achievements of his age, and scorn for philosophy and the more profound adventures of the human mind, make it impossible not to find him vulgar.

TENNYSON : A MASTER OF METRE AND MUSIC

TENNYSON, Poet-Laureate in 1850 after Wordsworth, was certainly most fortunately adjusted to his age. He is perhaps our only Laureate who has been able to compose good poetry upon set occasions, such as the death of the Duke of Wellington. His real gift lay in his command of metre and music and in his keen eye for significant detail in description

His poems on contemporary themes, such as *The Princess*, dealing with the emancipation of women, were rarely successful. He felt the contemporary zeal for reform keenly, but had not the literary courage to exclude this and perfect his own sweeter gifts, which were in the direct line of descent from Keats. Tennyson's career as a poet is thus largely a record of hesitation and dissatisfaction.

Browning (1812–89), on the other hand, is distinguished by an almost blatant assurance and vigour, and it has been thought that his philosophy might be summed up in the optimistic lines of Pippa's *Song :*

> God's in His heaven—
> All's right with the world.

It should be remembered that the lines are sung by Pippa, not by the poet. A close study of his work shows he was aware of many of the distressing problems of his age and it has been suggested that his approach to them was strangely in tune with twentieth-century ideas.

Browning tried, if not always successfully, to see and understand all sides of a question and to take into consideration motive as well as fact. He is less concerned with the murder than with the murderer, as may be seen in his poem *Porphyria's Lover*. Browning is perhaps best represented by his love lyrics. Many of his finest poems are included in the collection entitled *Men and Women*. *Bishop Blougram's Apology* well reveals his love of argument and his dramatic ability.

The Victorians, generally speaking, wanted a sweet refuge from the ugliness of the world created by the Industrial Revolution, and welcomed in consequence the romantic mediævalism of William Morris (1834–96) or Dante Gabriel Rossetti (1828–82), the *Rubaiyat* of Edward Fitzgerald (1859), the devotional poetry of Christina Rossetti (1830–94), or the swirling choruses of Swinburne. It should be noticed that the Middle Ages as " re-created " by Morris, for instance, or Greece as " re-created " by Swinburne, were no true Middle Ages or Ancient Greece. It is the fantasy that is the point in these poets.

THE CITY YIELDS ITS ROMANCE TO A GREAT NOVELIST

THE most typical of Victorian writers is to-day generally thought to be Dickens (1812–70), though it should be remembered that many of his contemporaries, particularly among the upper classes, never ceased to regard him as vulgar. But we can pass over his sometimes excessive sentimentality and his failure at depicting characters above him in social station, and can see him as the first great novelist of industrial England. The romance of the Romantic Revival comes down to earth in his novels as the romance of life in great modern cities. The romantic appreciation of Nature is notoriously absent in Dickens. Instead we get romanticised characters (albeit the atmosphere that surrounds them is generally humorous) and a romanticised background—crooked houses setting off crooked morals, quaint gardens setting off quaint old ladies, and so forth. It is this quality which has caused Dickens to be so often accused of caricature.

Thackeray (1811–63) has been accused of sentimentality as often as Dickens. But Dickens was in passionate revolt against the injustices of his age ; his tearfulness was usually the tearfulness of exasperation and of his great sympathy. Thackeray, on the other hand, was too much the perfect clubman to rebel violently against his age. He had, however, a very keen eye for hypocrisy and insincerity, and in drawing aside the veils of these qualities which enshroud almost everyone's true nature, he took up a gentle, bantering, half-serious attitude which has been alternately called cynicism and sentimentality. In a freer age he might have been a more powerful and passionate writer. His works remain as perfect pictures of upper and upper-middle-class society. It should be noted how, not infrequently, as in *Pendennis*, he castigates contemporary manners for their blind and hypocritical attitude to the relations between men and women.

The reformist novel and the historical novel were popular all through the century, in the hands of such men as Charles Reade (1814–84) and Charles Kingsley (1819–75), and the novel of contemporary society, in the hands of such as Trollope (1815–82) and George Eliot (1819–80). The accent of sincerity, however, is lacking in too many Victorian novels ; against them stand out the remarkable work of the Brontë sisters, particularly Emily Brontë's *Wuthering Heights*. The faults of the Brontë's novels are the faults of inexperience, not of bad taste or hypocrisy.

EXTRAVAGANT PROSE OF THE NINETEENTH CENTURY

THE exuberance of the Romantic Revival left behind it a rather long-winded and often extravagant prose style, so that there is very little nineteenth-century prose which can be read to-day with the same ease and pleasure as the simple prose of Swift, Defoe, or Fielding. Carlyle (1795–1881) created for himself a rhetorical, half-biblical, half-German style which has found no successful imitators. Ruskin (1819–1900) wrote some of the most massive sentences in English. Both Carlyle and Ruskin were fired against social injustice and cant, but their protests were individual exasperations rather than considered and constructive criticisms. Carlyle found refuge in a deification of the great man or hero, Ruskin in the mission of art against ugliness, and in an æsthetically conceived and imperfectly realised socialism.

The most constructive critic of the Victorian age was Matthew Arnold (1822–88). His poetry in the main sought refuge from his age in a rather thin-blooded resurrection of the classics, but in criticism he was probably the greatest apostle of true culture in the history of English literature. He realised the materialism of his age, and pointed out, in such works as *Culture and Anarchy*, the insufficiency of science as a guide to conduct. He foretold the growth of a vast popular literature of very low quality, and pointed to poetry— the record of " the best that has been thought and said in the world "—as the guide which was needed and would be needed more and more. His own prose was less ornate than usual in his age, but often rather hectoring in tone.

Much of the best prose in the Victorian period was written by lesser men who followed a limited theme without caring much for the great stream of literature. Kinglake in his *Eothen* (1844), a brilliant, unromantic book of travel, Surtees in his hunting novels, and Richard Jefferies (1848–87), a more or less self-taught writer of Nature sketches, were examples of these.

THE " LILIES AND LANGUORS " OF THE DECADENTS

AFTER the pseudo-mediæval and pseudo-Hellenic fantasies of the middle century, the desire for romance decayed into the " æsthetic " movement of the 'nineties—the absorption of Oscar Wilde (1854–1900), Walter Pater (1839–94), Ernest Dowson (1867–1900), and others in " art for art s sake." Fragments of individual passion, fading lilies, cameos in the Japanese style—such were the themes of their work. Almost the only writer of any importance surviving from the period is Max Beerbohm (*b.* 1872), who, in such works as *Zuleika*

Dobson, has transfigured romance into a fascinating satire on itself. At heart still a romantic, Max Beerbohm is too conscious of his world to do other than poke perfect fun at romance.

The Decadents, though so soon forgotten for their own sake, had pointed out something very important—that English literature must become more precise in subject and in its choice of the right mood if it was to preserve a vigorous life. At the end of the century three big changes began to show themselves by degrees. One or two men began to write with deliberate simplicity : A. E. Housman's *Shropshire Lad*, for instance, appeared in 1896. (The old fantastic style of men like Meredith did not lose its power, however, until after the War.) Secondly, Kipling, Shaw, Wells, and others began to take the changing world around them as proper subject-matter for literature. The poets did not follow suit until a little later, with Masefield and others. The idea carried over from nineteenth-century romance that poetry should be " sweet " and " musical " and pretty in subject is still, of course, very powerful among the general public to-day. It prevents, among other things, the proper appreciation of satire as a form of poetry. Thirdly, every kind of writer began soon to make a genuine attempt to see his subject realistically, to set down the truth so far as he could imperfectly see it, even if the result was a piece of work without the shape and finish to which the nineteenth-century public had been accustomed.

AN EARLY EXPONENT OF THE SHAVIAN IDEA

ONE of the most powerful influences in the modern period came from Samuel Butler, who, though he lived from 1835 to 1902, was as untypical of his age as possible, and naturally but little appreciated by it. He satirised both orthodox religion and the pretensions of science, turning accepted ideas upside down, in such books as *Erewhon* and *The Way of All Flesh*, in the now familiar manner of Shaw. His *Notebooks* (not published until 1912) are the best illustration of his revolutionary ideas. " The deepest quality of a work of art," he said, " will always be the quality of the mind of the producer." With this remark he threw overboard all the pretentious formality and romanticism of the nineteenth century.

The characteristics of the work of Bernard Shaw, whose first novel was published in 1885, are too well known to need description. The decay of the evils which he attacked may cause some of his work to lose its interest, but time cannot spoil the lucidity of his prose, which displays one of the finest simple styles since Swift. His early associate in the Fabian Society was for a time H. G. Wells, whose first work, *The Time Machine*, appeared in 1895. It is certain that no two writers have had more influence during the last thirty years than Shaw and Wells, Wells possibly more of the two, on account of his being less provocative and more reasonable. It is true that in his later works Wells has inclined to repeat both his Utopian themes and his type characters, but he remains perhaps the most influential teacher of his age.

Rudyard Kipling, whose *Plain Tales from the Hills* appeared in 1888, will surely retain a place in English literature by his brilliant short stories. The conciseness and vigour of their style is best illustrated in the early Indian themes ; little of Kipling's most appreciated work has been done since 1900. The short story flourished brilliantly in the eighteen nineties in the hands of Kipling, Wells, and others ; there had been few earlier short stories which had concentrated so powerfully upon small themes exactly suited to their length. Some of the most notable post-war literature also consists of short stories, such as those of Katherine Mansfield and T. F. Powys.

SOCIAL REFORM REVIVES LITERATURE

THE themes of Wells, Shaw, and (to some extent) Kipling, were an indication of the reorientation of society which was going on. Social reform was no longer a matter for the philanthropy of a Ruskin or 'the sympathetic passion of a Dickens ; it was becoming the inescapable occupation of every thinking person as it has continued to be increasingly ever since. This fundamental change showed itself also in the powerful revival in the theatre in the eighteen nineties. Since the comedies of Sheridan and Goldsmith, in the middle of the eighteenth century, there had scarcely been a new play with genuine life in it. The theatre had fallen to a level of degraded romanticism which appears ridiculous to-day ; it was more out of touch with reality than any other form of Victorian literature.

The new impulse in the theatre came principally from Ibsen, whose attacks on false ideals and shams of all kinds had been growing familiar to English audiences as early as 1880. Shaw's *Widowers' Houses* (1892) was the first English play to follow Ibsen in dealing with normal people in normal situations, instead of stereotyped characters in stereotyped situations, generally ones of romantic love. Shaw was followed rapidly by Granville Barker (*b.* 1877), Galsworthy (1867–1933), and others less distinguished. Meanwhile there was a renaissance of poetic drama in Ireland, with the work of Synge (1871–1909), Lady Gregory (*b.* 1859), and Yeats (*b.* 1865). The English Provinces also showed a renewed interest in the theatre, and good plays were both written and produced in Manchester, Liverpool, and elsewhere.

Though Thomas Hardy (1840–1928) published his last novel in 1896, he cannot quite be called a Victorian—nor yet a modern. His style is indeed Victorian in its heavy and often clumsy qualities, but his outlook is too independent, too ironical, to be that of his own age. He struggled against conventions but was born perhaps too soon to realise a new outlook entirely, falling into a kind of fatalism which has had no disciples.

The apparent fatalism of Joseph Conrad (1857–1924) is different from Hardy's. Conrad wrote only of what he knew —all his stories can be traced to their originals—and what he knew was the implacable sea. He does not romanticise the life of the sea ; his novels are popular among seafaring men for that reason. But neither does he invent a blind " fate " when no fate is there. What he does not and cannot know he leaves unsaid or barely hinted at, instead of imagining an ironically playful deity, as Hardy did. " My task," said Conrad, " is, before all, to make you see. That—and no more, and it is everything."

LITERATURE AT THE CROSS-ROADS : THE TWENTIETH-CENTURY DILEMMA

IT is to be wished that the pitiless honesty of Conrad had inspired more novelists since. Twentieth-century literature is faced with a problem which has never existed before in the history of literature. Universal education has made reading a very general amusement, and the cheap press and the cheap novelette date their appearance from about the same time as the first work of Shaw and Wells. The danger of permanently lowered cultural standards, foretold by Matthew Arnold, is more imminent than ever. A mass of writers earn their living to-day by writing frankly to please.

They give a supposedly weary public various dreamlands—
of South Sea Islands, marriage to millionaires, adventures in
the wild spaces of the world. Above this level of amusement
there is an intermediate type of literature, very difficult to
classify and to separate at its upper end from the genuine
literature now being produced—which is probably no more
and no less than at any other period. Many novelists have
begun with honest intentions and been betrayed, not only
by the need to make a living but by the desire to please, to
conform to the standards of society in which they would otherwise find themselves isolated. The author of genuine merit
need not, though he may, be difficult to understand at his
first appearance. Cults have grown up around certain authors
implying that their difficulty alone must be proof of their
merit.

For these reasons, therefore, the remainder of this article
will deal with few names—those of men who have undeniably
had a new outlook and a new influence. There may prove
in fifty years' time to have been others whose permanent
qualities have slipped quietly by, unappreciated by our own
age, though it is one of the virtues of the present scale on
which reading is done that it is very difficult for genuine work
to be without appreciation, if only the appreciation of a few.
It is so easy, however, to be temporarily attracted by the
subject-matter of a book that it would be unsafe here to pass
judgment on the crop of new novels, for instance, which appeared between 1921 and 1931. We shall do no more than
mention the work even of Arnold Bennett (1867–1931), or of
John Galsworthy (1867–1933).

TWO MASTERS OF SOPHISTICATION

THE disillusion caused by the War only hastened a process
of disintegration which has been going on steadily in
English thought since 1880 or so. Some writers, shrinking
from the problems of their age, have restricted themselves
to critical work, or to the intellectual experiments of a new
kind of writing. Of the first kind Aldous Huxley (b. 1894) is
probably the most brilliant representative, and of the second
undoubtedly James Joyce (b. 1882).

It is probable that Joyce would never have been heard of
by the man in the street if his subjects had not included
those which are generally considered pornographic. Joyce's
aim, of course, is not pornography, but the elaboration of a

II

kind of writing which can express every shadow of fancy and half-meaning that flits through the conscious or semi-conscious mind. Thus the huge *Ulysses* is occupied with the experiments of one man during a single day.

Joyce has had many imitators, mostly feeble, and his methods of inventing " portmanteau " words and sometimes ignoring grammar and punctuation have opened up new possibilities to language. But the obvious objection to such work is that if it is as purely personal an expression as the author desires, it can have only one truly appreciative reader —the author himself.

THE TREND TOWARDS A SIMPLER ENGLISH

IT seems probable, indeed, that a simpler and simpler English is likely to be the aim of the next generation of writers, who will realise that unless they are in touch with their age they cannot live ; that it is useless to hide away from their contemporaries. It is certainly noticeable that simple English, though sometimes an English of a peculiarly personal meaning, has been the medium of D. H. Lawrence (1885–1930), and E. M. Forster (*b.* 1879)—perhaps the only two recent authors (other than the very young) whose work has seemed to look forward rather than stand still.

The story in Forster's and Lawrence's novels is little. It is the passionate way of experiencing and looking at life which counts. It is curious to see Forster, as early as 1905, expressing dimly, in Edwardian English, something of what Lawrence was to express much more violently afterwards in English which owed much to the language of the Bible. Both authors are concerned fundamentally with the delicate relationships between men and men, and between men and women, the subtlety and self-control necessary to behave naturally, and the absolute necessity of natural behaviour, whatever else may suffer, in the face of the artificiality, the fear, and self-suppression induced by living together in herds under modern conditions.

Of the few other writers who have tried to extend and break through the boundaries of the human spirit in recent years, some of the most important and delicate attempts have been those made by women, particularly Katherine Mansfield (1889–1923) and Virginia Woolf, at least in the latter's earlier work, such as *To the Lighthouse* (1927). Among outstanding names in fields other than fiction, Sean O'Casey (*b.* 1890) and

Somerset Maugham (b. 1874) may be mentioned in the theatre, and Havelock Ellis (b. 1859) and Lowes Dickinson (d. 1934) as humane philosophical writers. None of these men write difficult or learned English—not even the mannered English of a Tomlinson, a Belloc, or a Chesterton.

The last Victorian poet, and a good one, was probably Francis Thompson (1859–1907). A. E. Housman has already been mentioned. After his rather affected simplicity there was little new in poetry until the extraordinary, deliberately blunt and even profane *Everlasting Mercy* of John Masefield in 1911. Though Masefield has often failed through consciousness of his own manner, he gave the lead to a group known as " Georgian " poets, including Wilfred Gibson, Lascelles Abercrombie, Rupert Brooke, and the most promising and real of all, Wilfred Owen, who was killed in the War. W. H. Davies's early work, before his simplicity became too deliberate, also belongs to this period. Deliberateness, however, either of revolt or of convention, has been the mark of too many recent poets, and one of the greatest living poets is still W. B. Yeats (b. 1865), who was the greatest poet of the Irish renaissance group as early as 1889. His work shows a care and sense of responsibility, combined with a rare naturalness and delicacy of feeling, which distinguishes no other living poet except perhaps the limited T. S. Eliot (b. 1888).

A REACTION AGAINST DISILLUSION

THE disillusion of the post-War period reaches its nadir in *The Waste Land*, *The Hollow Men*, and other poems by T. S. Eliot. His methods are precise and his material very often the tenuous associations of ideas and images in his own brain ; this latter quality fills his work with meaning, but many find it very difficult to understand. His influence on younger poets, however, has been surpassed by none, though it has been rivalled by that of Lawrence's poetry. But disillusion cannot be for ever a theme, and the very youngest poets are already reacting against T. S. Eliot's outlook. His critical prose includes some of the most important essays of the post-War period, but it is interesting to see how both Eliot and Huxley, successful in criticism though they are, must turn outside their own impulses to seek constructive support. Such constructive thought as Huxley shows is mainly (and gratefully) derived from his friend D. H. Lawrence ; T. S. Eliot takes his support from the Church.

The youngest writers are now all conscious that some revolution in social outlook is necessary ; they are getting over their disillusion. At present they cling mostly to an often crude Communism. Some more spontaneous outlook will surely arise presently. The glimmerings appear in a very few, such as William Plomer, the novelist, and the poets C. Day Lewis and W. H. Auden. Whatever happens to English literature in the future, it will always be true that it is the key to the age in which it is produced, and that it is to some extent also in advance of that age. The story of English literature is the story of the English race.

SIGNPOSTS TO ENGLISH LITERATURE : SOME USEFUL REFERENCE BOOKS

THERE is neither interest nor pleasure to be got from reading a complete history of English literature before one has read a good deal of the literature with which it deals. (Many school syllabuses, unfortunately, still put the cart before the horse in this way.) But there are standard works of reference which may be consulted on individual points as soon as one's interest in literature has begun to develop at all. The most important of these is *The Cambridge History of English Literature*, whose fourteen volumes, the work of a large number of separate authors, contain much valuable critical work as well as reference matter. For biographical accounts the best source, as usual, is the *Dictionary of National Biography*. For a one-volume history, packed with facts and critical matter, it is still difficult to surpass Saintsbury's *Short History of English Literature* (Macmillan). But the story of literature in its true place in society is told in much more human values in the *History* (Dent) of two Frenchmen, Legouis and Cazamian. Their work, unlike the others mentioned, comes right up to the nineteen-twenties instead of stopping short before 1900. As a mere dictionary, however, their book is not so useful.

There are sound works on shorter periods of literature, but often a much keener insight into a period is to be had from some specific work on a smaller subject seen in its proper perspective. Such are Grierson's *Metaphysical Poets* (Oxford University Press) Tillyard's *Milton*, Livingston Lowes's *Chaucer*, or T. S. Eliot's literary essays (Faber and Faber.)

THE CRAFTSMAN IN WORDS:
LANGUAGE AND EVERYDAY LIFE

by GEOFFREY CRUMP, M.A.(Cantab.)

*D*OCTOR *JOHNSON* said that no one but a fool would write *without payment, for the sheer love of writing. If to the fool one adds the genius, the statement is probably correct. The vast majority of people, from highly paid novelists and critics to the occasional contributor to periodicals, write primarily for payment. They may enjoy communicating their thought to others, but practical needs are paramount ; they must live. Now all these people who write, or speak, for money, who use the craft of word-choosing and word-arrangement for practical purposes, will soon understand (as rejection slips come in apace, or tomatoes fly about their heads) that writing and correct speech is a craft that needs apprenticeship, like any other. Language-shaping is as skilled as carpentry, only the workshop is in the human brain. One must learn how to use the tools of self-expression, and find out all about the quality of the materials. The genius may scoff at laborious apprenticeship, the fool will babble or scribble on, but the ordinary man, with practical uses for his craft, will apply himself to master it ; for by a man's language shall ye know him.*

The former articles have given an introduction to the works of the great artists in words ; those which follow are guides to any one who wishes to become a proficient craftsman in language. They show, too, how stories and articles are constituted, and where to dispose of them.

THE proper use of language is an art. When it is used for the creation of beauty it may be a fine art, but in any event it is an art in the true sense of the word, for it requires skill. Spinning a plate on a poker may be called an art, but no one is born with the ability to spin a plate on a poker, though some learn to do it more easily than others. In the same way no one is born with the ability to speak or write ; the use of language is not a spontaneous activity, but has to be learnt.

This skill in speech and writing depends on three things : natural gifts, the attentive and critical reading of the work of able writers, and assiduous practice in speech and writing.

Those who are fortunate enough to possess an inborn facility in language generally find that the reading and writing that they need are prompted by their own inclinations ; it is such people who make their mark in the world of letters, in whatever form they write. But to the most of us, who have no literary aspirations beyond the ability to use language for practical purposes and in a cultured manner, no natural gifts are necessary other than intelligence and industry.

WRITERS MUST BE READERS

No one is likely to write or speak well without study as well as practice. A good writer or speaker needs two qualities : first, he must not only know his subject, but have a mind stored with all kinds of knowledge and ideas, for it is these that enrich his work and differentiate it from the commonplace ; and secondly, he must have the ability to express himself correctly and effectively. Both these qualities come chiefly from reading ; most of our knowledge is derived from books, and there is no better way of learning to write than to study the methods of the greatest writers.

Mere reading, however, is not enough. A vast amount of reading is done to-day, yet there are relatively few able writers. This is partly because the wrong things are read, but still more because so little reading is done in a really attentive or critical spirit. To read with the wireless turned on, or with half one's mind given to conversation, or with the mere object of " getting through " a book, is clearly a waste of labour. And no less futile is the habit of unquestioning respect for the printed word. If we allow our critical faculty to be dulled by the reputations of authors, if we accept the opinions of others instead of honestly and rationally forming our own, we must lose our intellectual independence ; and with it goes any hope of writing with precision or force, for all sense of the real meaning and power of words becomes blunted.

Those who read uncritically form no style of their own, but follow feebly in the wake of the literature they happen to favour ; thus those who read magazines tend to write in the style of cinema captions, and those who read psychology tend to write incomprehensibly. Careful writing must go hand in hand with careful reading. Language can be mastered only by first taking it to bits and then putting it together again— by analysis and synthesis. We cannot appreciate the architecture of a well-constructed sentence, or paragraph, or article, or book, unless we constantly study the best examples of these structures, in addition to making continual efforts to build them ourselves.

THE OLD BOOKS AND THE NEW

ONE other word needs to be said about reading. Good writing is not confined to the famous literary figures of the past. Those who have stood the test of time have all some quality that has made them immortal, but it is not to them, principally, that we should turn for help in the practical use of language. We can of course learn better how to express ourselves in English to-day by seeing how brilliantly Shakespeare and Dryden and the translators of the Bible expressed themselves in English of the past, and no one who desires to write well can afford to be ignorant of the great books, but for actual models of writing we should look to the best of our contemporaries. There are to-day more people writing extremely well, in all departments of life, than ever before ; what we have to do is to sharpen our judgment and pick these out from the still larger number who write extremely badly. This is no easy task, for there are many celebrated authors who write abominably, and many accomplished writers whose work is hardly known.

THE BRICKS AND MORTAR OF THE WRITER

WRITING may be usefully compared with architecture. The writer's words are his materials, and they have to be chosen, sorted, shaped, and put together ; that is to say, he must have an adequate supply and understanding of words, and sufficient mastery of grammar and syntax to be able to use them in a correct and effective manner. Secondly, just as the shape and character of the building will be completely different for a church, a theatre, a factory, or a country house, so the form of the literary composition must be governed by its purpose, though the materials may be the same ; and this form must be determined before the work is begun. Thirdly, in the same way as the proportions and efficiency of a building will depend upon sound planning and construction, so the logic and balance and purpose will be made clear by ordered and progressive thought and methodical arrangement of matter. Fourthly, such ornament can be used as may be relevant and suitable. And lastly, there is what we call the style—the spirit that gives the finished work distinction and individuality.

We have not all sufficient time to amass large vocabularies, but we can at all events determine to know the exact meaning of every word that we use, and to use none but the words that best express our meaning. This is the hall-mark of the greatest writers, not all of whom have been men with phenomenal vocabularies. A writer, like any other craftsman, should be judged by the use he makes of his materials rather than by their richness and abundance. A writer's object (in prose, at any rate) is to transfer his meaning to his reader as directly as possible, and the two unforgivable sins are therefore the use of clichés and the use of jargon.

Clichés — hackneyed, worn-out expressions — obscure thought, because the writer, instead of finding words and forming phrases to express his thought, is borrowing the phrases of others (and dead ones at that) because they resemble his thought. " Too funny for words," " terribly grateful," " O.K."—such expressions should be buried and forgotten, together with all the " unturned stones " and " unexplored avenues." It is true that slang enriches language, and forms its new blood, but it is also true that when it goes bad it poisons it. Yet would-be fine writing, or jargon, is an even more insidious enemy of the proper use of language. If to write well is to express oneself clearly and simply, it can never be desirable to use two words where one would do, or a long word instead of a short and easy one. " No " is better English than " Such is by no means the case " ; and " he was conveyed to his place of residence in an intoxicated condition " is no improvement on " he was carried home drunk."

LANGUAGE AND ITS DEAD WOOD

GRAMMAR, syntax, and punctuation are dealt with in detail in another place. But there is one important point to remember about all these. English is a living language. The correct usage in Latin may be ascertained from a Latin grammar, because the language is dead and the rules are fixed for ever. The correct usage in English is that which obtains amongst the majority of educated people to-day. The countryman's speech which we call incorrect is often only incorrect in that it is four centuries or so out of date.

In the eighteenth century, when English prose was modelled closely upon the Latin idiom, it was customary to use long and complicated constructions. Doctor Johnson, for instance, writes :

> " If by a noble and more adequate conception that be considered as Wit, which is at once natural and new, that which, though not obvious, is, upon its first production, acknowledged to be just ; if it be that, which he that never found it, wonders how he missed ; to wit of this kind the metaphysical poets have seldom risen."

This sentence is perfectly constructed, but no one would write like that now. Such involved and intricate writing has given way to shorter sentences and more frequent finite verbs ; the importance of the semicolon has increased, and the use of conjunctions has diminished. We write : " I am tired ; I am going to bed," where our grandfathers would have written : " I am tired, so I am going to bed," or even : " Being tired, I am going to bed." We must understand the principles of English grammar and construction so as not to obscure our meaning, or do offence to the accepted traditions of ordered and comely English speech. But we must also remember that to be old-fashioned in language is as much of a solecism as to be old-fashioned in dress, manners, or any other department of life.

THE AUTHOR SHOULD PLAN BEFORE HE WRITES

WRITING is at least three parts thinking. Most people find the selection and arrangement of ideas far more troublesome than the actual writing. A famous dramatist, when asked how his play was progressing, replied : " It is finished. I have only to write it now." If all literary work were approached in this spirit, the reading of it would be a much easier and pleasanter matter than it generally is. Most books, articles, and speeches are inadequately planned, or imperfectly co-ordinated, because most of us are in too much of a hurry to do more than write down the first ideas that come to us. These are the ideas that come first to every one else too, and are therefore of little importance.

The writer, having decided on his subject and the way in which he will treat it (such as novel, essay, play, or sermon), should then *collect* all the ideas he can until a promising line of thought begins to form itself. Then it becomes a task of *selecting* the material that is relevant to his purpose, and ruthlessly rejecting the rest. To keep distinct the processes of collection and selection is of the utmost importance. It then remains to arrange the subject-matter in the proper order, remembering that not only must it be grouped into paragraphs, but the logical connection between the paragraphs must be made clear by co-ordinating phrases and sentences. Ordered and progressive movement towards a clearly visualised objective is the secret of well-constructed composition. The surest way to be interesting is to be interested, and if the writer concentrates exclusively on that aspect of his subject that engages his own interest, he is likely, given the necessary technique, to carry his readers with him.

THE FINAL TEST OF STYLE

IT is sometimes said that style is personality. But style has been better defined as the impact of personality upon the spirit of the age, for a book or a building gets some of its character from the world of its day as well as from the man who made it. And even that is not all, for the subject counts for something. It is the way in which a certain subject is treated by a certain mind at a certain time that determines what we call the style of a piece of writing. But the writer need not bother overmuch about his own share in this trio. One thing is certain, and that is that style, real distinction in writing, is not the result of efforts at self-expression. The ultimate test of style is sincerity. It is a paradox that the greatest writers, those whose personalities shine most clearly through their work, are those who have forgotten themselves in enthusiasm for their subject and determination to write with the voice of their generation.

The difference between written English and spoken English should be less than is commonly supposed,. Most writing is too pretentious and " would-be literary," whereas most speech is too slipshod and clumsy. Speech, like writing, should be concise, easily understood, and agreeable ; but too often it is needlessly verbose, difficult to follow, and irritating. In ordinary conversation this is chiefly a matter of habit and temperament. Those who value their own opinions and like the sound of their own voices care little how they express themselves provided they can go on talking. Those who dislike harsh sounds and inexact or ugly expressions are likely to be at pains to express themselves pleasantly, but their speech may lack just that picturesqueness and vitality that makes the speech of less cultured people so attractive. No two people, in fact, speak exactly alike, and let us be thankful that they do not. The more we preserve our individual peculiarities the better, so long as they are not so far removed from the normal as to make our speech difficult to understand or ridiculous. The question remains : What is the normal ?

SETTING A STANDARD FOR PURE ENGLISH

EVEN among carefully educated people, dialect varieties in certain districts, particularly in the North, persist firmly. The cockney and various rural dialects are giving way very slowly, in some places not at all ; and in London and other great towns the " refained " speech of suburbia is spreading rapidly. Moreover, the pronunciation of many who regard themselves as most correct is startlingly inexact ; the Belgravian *How-d'yor-dor* and the so-called " Oxford " *Gudbah* are quite as inaccurate as the American *carnference*, the Cockney *Piper*, *lidy*, or the Glasgow *Hae ye go' a bo'le ?*

It is worth remembering that English in its purest form is customarily referred to as " The King's English." English is a language that is spoken all over the world, and foreigners are constantly surprised that we take so little pride or interest in its correct use. This is no place to enter into the vexed question of dialects ; they have great beauty, and considerable historical and sentimental importance. But it is surely desirable that all English people should at least be able to speak an English that sounds and means the same to all, and that is identical with the language of their literature.

STYLE COMES TO THE SPEAKER'S AID

THE two chief qualities required of a public speaker are intelligibility and audibility, and neither is any use without the other. Intelligibility depends upon careful choice of words and methodical arrangement ; in fact, everything that has been said about writing applies equally to speeches and lectures, which should, if possible, always be written out in full at some stage in their composition, even if they are reduced to notes or committed to memory later. Completely extempore speaking is a very difficult achievement, and most of the speaking that one hears is needlessly clumsy and involved. Even if only a few minutes are available for preparation, a clearly planned scheme should be outlined in the mind.

Audibility depends upon clear articulation of consonants, correct enunciation of vowels, and proper control of the breath. To a few people all these come naturally, but most of us need considerable practice, if not training. Microphones have simplified the task of addressing large audiences, but no microphone can turn a bad speaker into a good one.

THE THIRD ESSENTIAL QUALITY

THERE is a third quality which is as essential to a speaker as the two already indicated. He may be both audible and intelligible, but neither quality is of any use unless he is also interesting. By his manner, his language, the inflections of his voice, his use of emphasis, pause, variations of speed, gesture, illustration, and all the arts of the speaker, he must continue to hold the attention of his hearers. Audiences can easily be made to believe, by the manner of the speaker, that what is really dull is interesting ; at any rate, it is some time before they find out that it is not as interesting as it sounds. But they will never believe that anything is interesting if it sounds dull.

This point cannot be too strongly stressed, especially as it is in the interests of those who read and listen as well as of those who write and talk. Any who read these sections will be doing so in the hopes of improving their powers of expression. Let us, who may have to read what they write or hear what they say, remind them that most of us have to read and hear far more than we want to, and all we ask is that their intention should be clear, their language pleasant and economical, and their manner interesting.

HOW OUR LANGUAGE HAS GROWN

by H. K. GARVIN, M.A.(Oxon)

" EVERYBODY knows that most of the words we use to-day to express intellectual, emotional, spiritual concepts, had originally physical significance. 'Wrong,' for example, primarily implied something twisted ; 'implied' itself involves the idea of something folded within another thing—as 'involved' (to use what chance supplies !) rests on the concept of something rolled or wrapped about. 'Concept' itself, so considered, goes back to the notion of seizing or grasping ; to 'consider,' in turn, was at first to gaze attentively upon the stars ; 'attentively,' again, rests ultimately upon the idea of physical stretching. . . . But with us these vivid physical implications of the words we use have all become attentuated, they have faded out. We are no longer conscious of their primitive, more concrete meaning."

This remarkable passage occurs in John Livingston Lowes's Essay on the English Bible of 1611, which in his *Of Reading Books* he calls the noblest monument of English Prose. His assertion is perhaps all too true ; the physical implications of our vocabulary have perhaps died out ; perhaps we are no longer conscious of primitive and almost sensuous meanings of words. When we use dead metaphors such as " his fate hung in the balance " or " the empire was tottering " we fall back upon triteness only because we have forgotten the original vividness of the image. Equally, when we use a traditional expression such as " his face fell," we have forgotten that we are speaking figuratively. It is our loss. Such analysis as this of J. L. Lowes shows the enchantment and enrichment that may come to our minds from learning about language. We shall consider things more carefully when we have connected star-gazing with consideration.

THE BOND BETWEEN LANGUAGE AND THOUGHT

THE fascination of language study is twofold. Words, and the two methods of word arrangement called grammar and syntax—that is, the way in which we alter the forms of words to express fine shades of meaning, and the order in which we place them so as to convey meaning with the right emphasis and proportion—contain a volume of history and of sociology. Words are a form of thought; if we use them without care or love, we also think more or less carelessly. Those whose thought and language are the closest united are the greatest poets.

Secondly, the study of language has peculiar charm because every man carries his laboratory about with him, in his ears and mouth. The dogmatic habit of mind that seeks to dictate correctness of language is useless; it is wise to study not what people ought to say, but what they do say, what forms of speech occur everywhere, in bus and tube and shop. The personal characteristics that lead different men to select different words for the same thing, the motives of certain national and individual habits of speech and pronunciation, offer endless scope for speculation. Why do the Scots ask: " Shall we take the bus?" on a rising tune? Why do the English sink their voices step by step in asking the same question? Why do Americans usually stress the personal pronoun in such a phrase as: "Have you read the book?" and why do we stress the verb?

The questions are unanswerable, but we may learn a great deal through seeking to answer them. To study the reasons for people's locutions is often an aid to clear and more sympathetic understanding. A man who referred to Catholics as *R.C.s* was once reproached by a Catholic who thought of the expression as a term of disrespect. The user of the expression explained that he used it because he stammered and could not say initial *r*. Similarly, he explained, he was unable to pronounce initial *w*, and was forced to refer to every woman as a girl.

TRUTHS THAT LIE AT THE ROOTS OF WORDS

WHAT has been in language is not less interesting than what is. *Wrong, implied, involve, concept,* are only a few of the words that have historical significance, and often the etymology of a word will throw light on a philosophical truth. That the word *sin* in English and German is a development of the present participle of a primitive verb *to be,* changes one's conception of human fault. That the same present participle developed into another form as *sooth,* meaning truth, is equally suggestive. Our modern words *true* and *truth* replaced *sooth* when to the idea of existing fact was added the conception of faithfulness to fact. *Truth* is ultimately a feudal word denoting troth or loyalty; and in modern English, truth does imply a certain loyalty to an inner ideal. The " verily verily " of the Bible is another way of saying *truly, truly, very* being derived from the French *verai* (Modern French, *vrai*) which in its turn descended from Latin *verax*. A sad fall from dignity happened in the change from the sixteenth-century meaning of *very* to its weak modern sense as a mild intensive. Another interesting word is *good;* that it has a secondary meaning, not moral but physical, in the expression " worldly goods," shows how closely related are moral and material values.

These instances touch on profound philosophical questions, but there are lighter and more commonplace examples of the interest of words. The word *breeches*, for example, was borrowed from Celtic into both French and English. These people wore kilts; the Celts wore breeches, and when this mode of clothing was adopted, its native name came with it. Another diverting Celtic word is *whisky*, which in Old Irish means water. The poor benighted Irish learned the charms of brandy, called *Aqua vitæ* (water of life), but unfortunately they had no grapes with which to make it. They did their best with corn, and produced whisky whose name they translated from *aqua*.

Another interesting word association is the connection between *cream* and *chrism*, because the two words are the popular and the learned forms of the same word, Greek *chrisma* (oil). *Chrisma* was taken into French through Latin and became *chresme*; this latter spelling is still retained in French for the holy oil; the spelling *crême* was the final development of the word which became in English *cream*. The study of language is full of history, folklore, and poetry, and English, being a hospitable language, is even richer than most.

THE ENGLISH LANGUAGE IS REALLY GERMANIC

A CERTAIN professor of German nationality taught the history of English throughout the war in a section of the United States that was rabidly anti-Teutonic. He horrified his students by saying that English was a German dialect. Asked to recant, he asserted that not only was it a German dialect, but that it was a Low German dialect. He was correct.

All the languages of Europe, as well as Sanskrit or Old Indian, derive ultimately from a parent language called, for lack of a better name, Indo-European or Indo-Germanic.

The most important branches of this language are Sanskrit, Greek, and the Italic (Latin), Celtic, and Germanic groups, These, for various reasons, split up into a multitude of dialects which eventually became our modern languages. Only those concern us here that had an influence on English, which was a branch of the great Germanic family.   East Germanic was represented by Gothic which, before it died out, left us a translation of the Bible interesting for comparing forms of words in related languages.   North Germanic produced old Norse and the modern Scandinavian languages. Under the head of West Germanic come High and Low German, Dutch, and English.   English is thus closer in most ways to German than to any other language, but it is in some ways also very akin to the Scandinavian languages.

English was brought to the island of Britain in the fourth and fifth centuries A.D. by the tribes called Angles, Saxons, and Jutes.   The invaders needed more land than they could find at home, and they came from the part of Germany lying almost at right angles to the west coast of Denmark.   They spoke a Germanic dialect, and they were by all accounts a tall, blue-eyed, light-haired people.   When they came, the island was peopled by two sorts of Celtic-speaking peoples. One was tall and fair, the Gaels or Ghoidels, who eventually departed to Ireland and the highlands and islands of Scotland.   They were of the type seen in the film, *Man of Aran.* They spoke that Old Irish whose descendants are modern Irish and the Gaelic spoken in the highlands.   These two dialects are virtually the same, and the two branches share a common stock of folklore.

The other branch of Celts was small in build ; they were eventually pushed by the Saxon invaders into the corners of England, in Wales and Cornwall, and across the sea to Brittany.   They spoke British or Brythonic, whose descendants are Welsh, Cornish, and Breton.   So alike are Welsh and Breton still that a Breton onion-seller can make his way through Wales and be understood even nowadays.   There was some Cornish literature, and a great deal of Welsh, which had some influence on English during the Middle Ages.   The two Celtic languages, Irish and British, developed from a common Celtic stock, but were not more nearly alike than Latin and Greek. The roots were similar, but certain sound changes had operated to make specific sounds consistently different. *Mawr*, for instance, is Welsh for big, and should be pronounced to rhyme with English *sour*. The Irish equivalent was *mor*, pronounced as spelt.

THE INTERMINGLING OF IRISH AND BRITISH

THE two languages, because of the nearness of the peoples to one another, had a constantly active influence upon each other. Their influence upon the language of the Germanic invaders was, however, much smaller than would be expected. Celtic did have a considerable influence all over Europe earlier than this period, and certain of the Latin poets had names betraying Celtic origins, notably Catullus and Vergil, the first element of whose name may be compared with that of the great Gaulish hero, Vercingetorix. But the earliest period of English does not show much Celtic influence ; although, here also, certain names, such as that of the poet Cædmon, appear in a Celtic form.

Most of the Celtic words in our language either derive indirectly from a period before the Saxon invasion, or were adopted long afterwards, in the Middle Ages or later. From the early period, only a few words can be said certainly to be of Celtic origin. Old English *assa* (ass) was borrowed by the Celts from Latin *asinus*, and then transmitted to English in a Celtic form. The word *dunn* (dun) is from an early Celtic influence. The later or Middle English loan-words from Celtic include *dry* (druid), from Irish *drui*, perhaps *cursian* (to curse) ; and the word *cross* was taken from Celtic which had taken it from Latin *crux*, *crucis*. Much later loan-words are the more familiar ones such as *bog*, *brogue*, *shamrock*, and *glen*.

It is possible also that Irish syntax affected English ; possibly the progressive tenses such as " I am going," " he was reading," expressions that give such flexibility and variety to the English use of tenses, came from Celtic. But this is a highly difficult problem upon which scholars are at present working.

The Angles and the Saxons settled down in different parts of England, and it was the Saxons who provided the basis for what we now call Standard Southern English, which is our accepted literary vehicle ; but it was the Angles who gave our island her name as well as our language. Only occasionally in Latin texts was English called *Lingua Saxonica*. One of the great manuscripts containing old English poetry, *The Exeter Book*, is described as " an micel Englisc boc " (a great English book), and the island was called *Englaland*. It is somewhat paradoxical because the literary development of English owes a great deal to the carefulness of Saxon kings. The Angles settled from Northumbria down as far as the Midlands. Their name has remained in the beautiful words for Norfolk and Suffolk, *East Anglia*. The Saxons settled in the south, covering Essex, Surrey, Hampshire, Dorset, and Devonshire. Essex is of course the county of the East Saxons, Sussex of the South Saxons, and Wessex was the great kingdom of the West Saxons that won, under able kings, supremacy over the rest of England.

MODERN ENGLISH AND ITS ANTECEDENTS

THE language spoken by the men who lived in England from the sixth century onwards is difficult to read without special training because it has changed ; but the development of the language is constant, and any Englishman who learns to read Old English will feel at once that he is reading his own language. It is naturally difficult to divide the language, which is constantly changing, into cut-and-dried periods ; but scholars have roughly divided it into three periods, Old English, Middle English, and Modern English. Old English lasted until the Norman Conquest, when French was introduced as the language of the upper classes. Middle English lasted until the fifteenth century. Modern English is the period between the end of the fifteenth century and to-day. Anything written after Malory is easily intelligible to a reader who has no special training.

Old English was a beautiful language, although not in the conventional sense in which Italian and French are said to be beautiful. It was not so musical to the ear, but it had great expressiveness, strength, and solidarity of sound. Modern people too often think that only vowel sounds and liquid consonants have beauty. English, in its primitive form, had no easy liquidity but a certain harsh gravity. Consonants predominated, and consonant combinations made a splashing or crashing sound. It was more like the sounds of Nature than like artificial music. It had the heaviness of thunder, the rustling of leaves, the whistling of the wind in it. The words were largely one-syllabled, and the accent in the case of a many-syllabled word fell on the first syllable. The music of the language was in the rhythm caused by stress rather than in the vowel quality. It was a grave and serious language, suitable for treating of the necessities of life, as well as of heroic and magnanimous deeds. For all its development in subtlety and refinement, modern English has lost some of its early strength; but it still has a dignity of profoundly imaginative expression that is not found in the more melodic Romance Languages.

LANGUAGE THAT GREW OUT OF EVERYDAY NEEDS

THE syntax was straightforward, simple, and unwieldy. It was not adapted to complicated or theoretical argument. The vocabulary also was governed by the things that had to be said. In prose, such things were comparatively simple and related to the common things of everyday life. The king was *cyning*; a shepherd was a *hyrd*; the labourer was a *swan*, which was cognate with our modern *swain*. The lord was the *hlaford*, originally *hlafweard*, the warden of loaves; his lady was *hlæfdige*, or dispenser of loaves. Words for bread and meat and the sea and ships, for the land and what it grew, for life and for death, were much the same as they are now. The word *sawol*, which gave modern English *soul*, had the meaning of life or mind rather than a spiritual one. There were two words for army, *here* for a hostile and invading army, *fyrd* for the home army.

For certain things, the early English or their Germanic ancestors had to borrow from Latin or through Latin from Greek. They retained their own word for a new conception of deity; but for the details of Christianity they had to borrow. A bishop was the Greek *episcopos*. The church was from *kyriakon*, the lord's house. An angel was from *angelos*, a messenger. The devil was a new conception, for the early Germanic religions had only gods or heroes which might work to man's disadvantage, such as the evil speaker, Loki. The devil as God's adversary appeared with Judaism and Christianity, and his name in every language of Europe is a Greek one, *diabolos, diabolus, diable, Teufel, devil*.

In poetry, the Anglo-Saxons rang the changes in the word-stock of their own language, employing compounds and metaphorical and symbolical uses. Certain ideas were of great importance; the king and the lord had endless epithets such as *ring-giver, protector*, and so on. There were many names for a hero, for a monster, for the tribe, for wars and battles, for ships and the sea. For mental ideas they used compound words in a poetical way. When a man spoke, he was often said to " open his word-hoard " or his " breast-hoard." The language was rich in kennings, that is, conventional circumlocutions, such as the *whale's path* or the *swan's bath* for the sea, and the *water-horse* for a ship. Often series of such words were strung together, the method of expression being not accurate expression but amplification of a central idea. In translating the book of Exodus, the Cædmonian poet speaks of a beneficent cloud as a covering sail, for his mind was concentrated on the sea and all that it meant to the island-dwellers.

The language was still complicated in grammar, and was correspondingly awkward and stiff in syntax. The relative could be expressed in four ways, all of them clumsy. Nearly all the finer shades of meaning were expressed by endings and suffixes, different endings in the verb for number, tense, and mood ; and there were at least nine ways of declining nouns. The definite article was declined and adjectives had strong and weak declensions. The whole tendency of English has been towards simplification of grammar and clearer and more analytical expression. This has been accomplished largely by the unusual degree of influence from foreign languages.

HOW KING ALFRED INFLUENCED ENGLISH

ENGLISH owes a great deal to the wisdom of King Alfred, who was not only able politically but a cultured scholar. He was anxious to increase the dignity of his language by having classical texts translated into the vernacular, either by himself or by his friends and servants. He had, indirectly, another great effect on the language. The Danes or Norse-men had begun their swoopings down on the coast of Europe. France had had to sacrifice Normandy, which is still in appearance a Viking land with its blonde, blue-eyed inhabitants. England was saved from wholesale Danish spoliation by Alfred's wise arrangement granting the Danes for settlement the part of England north of Watling Street. This district was called the Danelagh, signifying land under Danish law. The invaders were converted to Christianity and lived comparatively peacefully. Their language, Old Norse, was like English, and many of the roots of the words were the same.

The consequence was that the foreigners, in an effort to make themselves easily understood, would use the root only and let the ending be. They hastened in this way the simplification of inflections.

Danish sounds were much the same as English, but some had different developments. Words which originally began with *ga* or *gi* in English developed to *ya* and *yi*. In Danish the hard initial *g* was preserved, and many words with this sound were borrowed and supplanted or remained beside their English equivalents with slightly different meanings. Thus *yard* is English, whereas *garden* and *garth* are Scandinavian. *Gate* also is Danish, and has replaced except in dialectal speech the native English *yate*, which is still heard in the south. The Middle-English verb *to yeve* or *to yive* was replaced by the Danish form *give*. Modern German has also kept the hard pronunciation of the *g* which sufficiently explains why our word *yellow* appears in German as *gelb*. Another set of words of Scandinavian origin is that which has initial *sk*, such as *skill*. The English development of this sound gave *sh* as in *shall* and *ship*, formerly *scal* and *scip*. Some Scandinavian influence affected vowels also. The Old English for *swain* was *swan*, which would in the natural course of development have given *swone* just as Old English *stan* produced *stone*, the long *a* having been kept only in Scots. The modern word *swain* comes from the Scandinavian form of the same word, *sveinn*.

Even after the Danish treaty in the ninth century, England had a long period of Danish influence culminating in the rule of the Danish king, Cnut. The effect of this continuous although spasmodic influence was to add many Danish words to the vocabulary. The preposition *till* is Scandinavian ; so are the forms of the personal pronoun *they* and *their*. Certain classes of words show foreign influence. The Danes were our rulers for a time, and they were also very well developed as regards internal politics and law. Consequently many legal and political words were introduced. The word *law* itself is of Scandinavian origin, and others are *outlaw*, *grith* (legal security), *wapentake*. Other miscellaneous loan-words include *awe*, *saw* (Danish *saga*), *crave*, *get*, *fellow*, *husband*, *hit*, *leg*, *low*, *root*, *skin*, *thrall*, *want*, *wrong*. Some words, such as *sister*, represent a Scandinavian form of a cognate English word ; in this case the English equivalent was *sweostor*, which is much nearer to the German *Schwester*.

The farther north and east one goes in England the more Scandinavian words one finds in the dialect of the country people.

THE GROWTH OF OUR LANGUAGE UNDER THE NORMANS

THE most important event in the development of English was the Norman Conquest in 1066. Celtic, Latin, ecclesiastical, and Scandinavian influences had not altered the structure and character of the language. The coming of the Normans changed its whole nature, and in changing the form of the language inevitably modified English methods of thought. There were several reasons for this. In the first place, there had been no previous conquests of the same order. The Celts had been a fragmentary and defeated people. The Latin influence of the Church was not political but pervasively spiritual ; its influence on the language was analogous. The small degree to which Latin terminology influenced religious language is some measure of the comparatively small change brought about in manners and thought by Christianity in its early stages.

The Norman Conquest was an entirely new phenomenon, the invasion of a people unified, well organised, and superior in culture to the inhabitants. In more ways than one, the invaders inaugurated a new era. They were of Norse origin, it is true, and thus they were akin in some degree to the English and the anglicised Danes. But they were French speaking and brought an entirely new culture, civilisation, and mode of thought. Their basis was solid Germanic with its loyalty, fierce enthusiasm, and solidity. Their development was Gallic, with wit and humour and a certain amount of refinement and breadth of thought. It is largely owing to this mixed spirit in the Normans that the English language of to-day has the strength and solemnity of German, something that French, Spanish, and Italian cannot attain, but also a flexibility and euphony that comes from Latin. The very strangeness of the invading influence was what made it so powerful, for contrast and novelty are often more attractive than similarity and relationship. Finally, the conquerors had the instinctive wisdom to make use of the conquered, and they did not drive them out.

The English, before the coming of the Normans, were by

no means barbarians. We have seen how Alfred cared for their education ; and their kings kept up relations with the centre of European culture that was, at that time, France. It was reproached against Edward the Confessor that he was too much of a Frenchman because he had been brought up in France. There had, therefore, been French influence before 1066, and it was useful in preparing the ground for the newcomers.

THE TWO KINDS OF FRENCH BROUGHT TO ENGLAND

THE French brought by the Normans was a French as different from French of the Ile de France as North-umbrian was from West Saxon. Norman French was a comparatively harsh Northern dialect. It is important to remember this, because later, when Central France sent its influence, it left its forms beside twin forms, as had been the case with English and Scandinavian. Norman French also represented French at an earlier stage of development. The Normans preserved longer the pronunciation *ei* for words deriving from Latin *eg*, for example, *rey* from *regem*, which developed into modern French *roi*. It also kept hard consonants, just as the Scandinavians had done ; thus our word *car* is Norman French. The later French influence produced *chariot*. *Catch* is Norman and *chase* is Central French. *Chariot* corresponds to modern French *char*, which we have borrowed much later into English in *char-a-banc* ; *chase* is represented by modern French *chasser*. In words of Germanic etymology, Normans retained the original *w* where French pronounced the difficult sound as *gu*. This explains why French has *guerre* and *Galles* where we have *war* and *Wales*.

People often wrongly think, for lack of historical imagina-tion, that from the date of the Conqueror's setting foot in England, the people began to speak French, and that English disappeared underground and burrowed like a rabbit. What actually happened was that the conquerors came and took possession of the important positions ; and lorded it in the castles and palaces. French was spoken in high places ; but the English, especially the lower classes, went on speaking English as they had before. The learned classes spoke French, and French-speakers constituted the learned class. The scribes were French, and there is therefore very little record of the English spoken at that time. After a couple of centuries, when conqueror and conquered were more or less fused, and English again became the proper language to speak in popular places, English literature emerged once more with its own strong tradition and with its structure and vocabulary much as before.

This was true of only certain types of literature, and later the learned and the popular stream became closely inter-mingled, and the result was a mixed and exceedingly rich vocabulary. For ideas and objects for which we have only one word, Middle English speakers had two or more, the French and the English equivalents. There is, for instance, the French word *uncle* and the English *eem*, both of which Chaucer uses. The joke that Scott makes in *Ivanhoe* is still worth repetition, namely, that the French were such good cooks that the animals retained their English names when in the fields, as *sheep, bull, cow, pig, deer,* but had French names when served at table, as *mutton, beef, veal, pork, bacon, venison.* Many of the names of offices such as *servant, master, butler, buttery, pantry, dinner, supper* are French ; and, among meals, only the English *breakfast* is native. Law words, and words relating to sovereignty and property, are often French, such as *court, assize, judge, prison, gaol (jail), parliament, tax, custom, royal, prince.*

NEW MEANINGS SUPPLIED TO OLD TITLES

THE French social system was more feudalised and far more complicated than our own, and the history of our titles is interesting. *King,* of course, is of English origin ; the word *queen* is one which originally simply meant *woman.* The universal *lord* and *lady* were both, as we have seen, of English origin ; and *earl,* from the Old English *eorl,* which simply meant a man of high rank, took its present meaning from the Scandinavian equivalent *jarl,* meaning the ruler of a county. *Churl,* which has now degenerated into denoting an unpleasant person, was originally simply a social distinction ; the *ceorl* was the labourer, but the term was replaced by the French *villein.* It is odd that both these words should have acquired the meaning of moral inferiority, and have lost entirely their social significance.

New titles introduced were *duke, marquis, viscount,* and *baron.* The earl's lady was called *countess* according to its French equivalent because Saxon ladies did not receive their husband's titles. The king's son and daughter were designated by *prince* and *princess*, both French titles originally meaning *first*, and it is interesting to compare the idea of the title with the German *Fürst* (prince) which also means the same, and Old English epithets *first* applied to lords with the meaning of *prince*. The English were the only people to retain a native word for *knight*. *Knights* were originally *lads*, as the German *Knecht* is to-day; the word began to acquire the meaning of military rank before the Conquest and was afterwards assimilated to the French *chevalier*. German has preserved the French idea, but has translated it. Their knight is *Ritter*, and soon after the Conquest the Anglo-Saxon Chronicle refers to the king dubbing his son as " rider " ; but for whatever reason the term was abandoned in favour of *cniht* or *knight*.

Most of the military terms were French. *War*, as we have seen, is Norman French. War on a large scale came from the conquering nation ; nearly all the Old English war terms —splendid words they were too—were abandoned for French ones, possibly because fashions and technique of war change more than anything else except perhaps clothes. *Battle, assault, siege, standard, banner, arms* and *armour, harness, lance, arbalest, hauberk, mangonel, fortress, castle*, are all of French derivation, although some of them such as *helm* and *hauberk* were borrowed by the French from the Germanic tribes. In the Middle English period, some English words for military things were still kept, such as *sheltroun*, from Old English *scild-truma*, a battle or battle-array ; but they have mostly been abandoned.

The names of artisans were mainly French, except the oldest and most fundamental. The butcher, barber, chandler, carpenter, cutler, draper, grocer, mason, tailor are all French ; only the miller, the smith, the baker, and the skinner, and some others, kept their English craftsmen's titles. All the names for relationships except the immediate ones were adopted from the French. *Father, mother, daughter, son, brother*, and *sister* were all of Germanic origin ; but *uncle, aunt, niece, nephew* are all French. *Grandfather* and *grandmother* were hybrids, half French and half English ; and in Elizabethan times, *grandson* and *granddaughter* were also invented. The parts of the body, except *face*, kept their native names. *Leg*, as we have seen, is Scandinavian ; *finger, hand, mouth, nose, eye* are all English.

ENGLAND FORSAKES HER OWN LANGUAGE

ENGLISH was undoubtedly spoken throughout the centuries after the coming of the Normans, but it did not emerge again as a literary language until at least two centuries after the Conquest. At the end of the thirteenth century, Robert of Gloucester wrote of the linguistic phenomenon as follows :

> þus com Engelond into Normandies hond.[1]
> & þe Normans ne couþe speke þo bote hor owe speche,
> & speke French as hii dude atom, & hor children dude
>   also teche,
> So þat heiemen of þis lond þat of hor blod come,
> Holdeþ alle þulke speche þat hii of hom nome
> Vor bote a man conne Frenss, me telþ of him lute.
> Ac lowe men holdeþ to Engliss & to hor owe speche yute.
> Ich wene þer ne beþ in al þe world contreyes none,
> þat ne holdeþ to hor owe speche, bote Engelond one.

It is a sad commentary.

After the Norman Conquest, more French influence came through the Plantagenets and their French wives. The wife of Henry II., in particular, the celebrated Eleanor of Aquitaine, brought a train of learned, cultured, and poetical Frenchmen with her, which reinforced the French influence in the manner that we have seen. The spelling of English became extremely erratic because the foreign scribes could not at first properly understand what they were putting down. They used the spelling *ch* for a pronunciation of *c* that they could not follow, and because of convenience they frequently spelt *u* in words containing *v* or *m* and *n* as *o* because it was easier to read. In this way we have acquired spelling forms such as *love*, *son*, which originally were *lufu* and *sunu*. The pronunciation has preserved the *u*-sound, but has shortened it.

ENGLISH REAPPEARS IN A COMPLICATED FORM

WHEN English reappeared, its dialectal variations had become much more complicated. The Old English

---

[1] Thus England came into Normandy's hand. And the Normans could only speak their own speech, and speak French as they did at home, and also taught their children. So that noblemen in this land that came of their blood retain all the speech that they took from their home, for unless one knows French, little is made of him. But humble men keep to English and to their own speech yet. I think there is no country in all the world that does not keep to its own speech but only England.

dialects were Anglian (Northumbrian and Mercian), West Saxon, and Kentish. Differences had grown so great by the thirteenth century that many more dialectal divisions have to be made in studying the texts. Northumbrian is divided into Northern and Scottish; the latter had a long and dignified literature that survived almost until Burns revived it. Mercian was divided roughly into North-West-Midland, North-East-Midland, South-East-Midland, and South-West-Midland; and West Saxon and Kentish survived as East and West-Southern. The Standard English of to-day is descended from East-Midland, which is in its turn descended from West Saxon. The differences between the dialects were not very great. Chaucer, who wrote in the London dialect which was the language of the universities and the court, takes care to make north-country speakers say *stanis* for *stones* and *taa* for *toe*. He also gives the northern forms of the verb *takis* for *takeþ*. There was a great difference in vowel values from dialect to dialect, and in the forms of the personal pronoun—some dialects retaining the older *heo* later than the modern *she*, and *hie* for *they*. The present participle is particularly interesting. In the North its ending was *-ande*—the mystery plays speak of a star " so bright shinande." The Midland dialect had *-ende* and the Southern *-inde*. The Southern dialect was the first to adopt the modern *-ing*, which was originally a verbal-noun form.

By the time we reach Chaucer, the southern language has become almost standardised, and is essentially the same as it is to-day. Chaucer's syntax, for instance, is not difficult. The grammar is only difficult because it keeps some of the old endings, and these unaccented endings add a great deal to the beauty and music of Chaucer's verse. The standardisation was brought about in various ways. The court was established in the South, and, with the two great universities of Oxford and Cambridge, it set the fashion. Chaucer himself was so famous and so respected by his contemporaries that probably he helped to fix a standard of good usage. The discovery of printing in the middle of the fifteenth century helped to fix the language and spelling.

Middle English had gained a great deal in sweetness and melody from its French schooling, but it had lost some of its primitive strength. Middle English is almost as melodic as French or Italian; the single consonants and final, almost soundless, endings replace the explosive consonants of the

Old English. The vocabulary, because of its accretions from French, was enormous and was especially rich in synonyms. It has suffered great diminution in the transition to modern English. Many words have been lost, so that scholars have not even yet succeeded in compiling a complete Middle English dictionary. Every new text that one reads provides new words surviving from Old English or borrowed from French. But the language was now definitely standardised and set in a form which was a basis for the development of modern English.

ENGLISH WAVERING BETWEEN ART AND SIMPLICITY

ALTHOUGH structurally English was set well on its way by the time of the Renaissance, prose was still undeveloped as a medium of expression. Mediæval prose was utilitarian, that is to say, it had some useful and direct motive, just as a telephone conversation is directed to clear expression rather than to artistic speech. The fifteenth century was a poor time for the development of language. There was a hiatus between the finish of the Middle Ages with its poetical accomplishment in Chaucer, Gower, and others, and the revival of learning, with its philosophical expansion. Men were too occupied with civil wars and political matters to make much addition to the language. Malory, so modern in a way in his expression, inaugurates the beginning of English prose ; and from his time onwards, prose was as dignified a medium as poetry. It is interesting to notice that the vogue of prose as a successor to poetry began in France sooner than in England. In the fourteenth and fifteenth centuries, the Arthurian romances had been translated into French prose presumably because they were more palatable to the public. Rhyme and cadence helped in the memorising of material when it was not possible to obtain many copies of a romance, or when people could not read and had to depend wholly on their aural memory. When people learned to read, prose was as interesting as poetry.

In the sixteenth century, the language was fixed as far as syntax went, and the only development made by English in structure from that time to this is that it has become in turn more elaborate and then more simple, first as it followed the

.om , as olde stozies   I will nat letten eke
ellen vs   Let euery fellowe tel
ere was a Duke that   And let se nowe, wh:
ight Theseus   And there I lefte, I
Athenes he was lozde   This duke, of who
nd gouernour   Whon he was come,:
in his tyme suche a   In all his wele and t
onquerour   He was ware, as he

The headpiece to " The Knightes Tale " from the third folio
Chaucer, " imprinted at London, by Jhon Kyngston for Jhon
Wight, dwellyng in Poules Churchyarde. Anno. 1561."
(By courtesy of Messrs. Ellis).

dictation of Latin syntax with its many clauses, and then when it returned, in the later Victorian period and in this century, to greater simplicity. There are few writers nowadays who fully understand the art of clause-construction. Their sentences are often clumsy and unrhythmical except when they contain only one finite verb. But the return to simplicity is auspicious as marking a return to the native genius of our language instead of borrowing from classical sources.

SELF-CONSCIOUS ATTEMPTS TO ENNOBLE THE LANGUAGE

THE influence of the revival of learning on the English language was considerable, and more easy to tabulate than previous influences because it was largely self-conscious. The scholars consciously sought to bring English into line with the classical languages, as if to ennoble it. It was a critical age ; writers and poets began to write prose criticism and scientific and theological prose in English as they had not done before. The prose was at first poetical and unwieldy, being a sort of hybrid between prose and verse ; the greatest influences in the development of English prose were the Bible and the colloquial prose of Shakespeare.

Although it was translated from the Hebrew and the Greek, the English Bible in the Authorised Version, and also the Book of Common Prayer, probably had more to do with dignifying English expression than any other influence. The great Bible of 1611 was influenced by the majestic cadences of the Vulgate ; and its dignity of expression has influenced common, ordinary speech in England until the beginning of this century. The reason why many people of to-day speak and write such fragmentary, thin, unrhythmical English may easily be that having no natural ear for rhythm, they were brought up without the study of the Bible that produced the grand style of Bunyan out of an unlettered and uncultivated soil. In the past, the Nonconformists especially have been influenced by this great source. Cromwell's letters—he was not a learned nor a literary man—have the characteristic beauty of rhythm of the English Bible, and a long line of Protestant writers, including Hale White, have retained the dignified simplicity and swelling prose of the Biblical school.

The prose of Shakespeare was an innovation in dramatic literature. Other dramatists of lesser and less widespread importance had used prose, but not the prose of the common people. Lyly had introduced a mannered and poetical prose into his plays ; but Shakespeare helped to establish the value of English colloquial speech. He showed, perhaps without meaning to, that a simple prose paragraph, uttering the feelings of the heart, may be of as great poetical beauty as the most ordered poetry, and that in prose the rhythm of the heart replaces the discipline of formal versification. Listen to King Henry's incognito speech :

> " For, though I speak it to you, the king is but a man, as I am : The violet smells to him as it doth to me ; the element shows as it doth to me ; all his senses have but human conditions : his ceremonies laid by, in his nakedness he appears but a man ; and though his affections are higher mounted than ours, yet, when they stoop, they stoop with the like wing. Therefore when he sees reasons of fears, as we do, his fears, out of doubt, be of the same relish as ours are : yet, in reason, no man should possess him with any appearance of fear, lest he, by showing it, should dis-hearten his army."

Another magnificent sentence occurs in the same speech :

> " Methinks I could not die anywhere so contented as in the king's company ; his cause being just and his quarrel honourable."

With Shakespeare and the Bible, English was set on a noble path, from which it has not deviated except in the cause of brevity and clear analytical expression. The basic structure of its prose was well established by the time that Queen Elizabeth was on the throne. It suffered, however, many minor changes of detail. The learned classicists attempted to bring it into line with the classical languages, and they made many mistakes in their learnedness. They attempted to spell every word according to its classical derivation, and sometimes they were mistaken. The words *doubt* and *debt*, for instance, which had come into English naturally through the French as *doute* and *dette*, had super-fluous letters restored, and appeared as *doubt* from *dubita* and *debt* from *debita*. The anomalous modern pronunciation is in accordance with the ancient derivation, which was not directly Latin but French.

THE RULES OF LITERATURE TEMPORARILY DEFIED

IN vocabulary, the Renaissance or Tudor period added something to the language, but largely by means of individual writers. The language had become somewhat restricted to a literary standard, and words not sanctioned by literature were often lost. Spenser in writing both *The Shepherds Calendar* and *The Faërie Queene* temporarily retrieved many words that had fallen out of use ; he kept ancient words such as *wroken* for *revenged* which is remembered in our *wreaked* of to-day ; *forswonck* for *tired with labour*, *queme* for *to please*, and *clincke, a keyhole*, and many others. There are many colloquial words in Shakespeare, also, that have fallen into disuse. But the Bible, within every one's reach, added many words to the language, some of which have survived and some of which have not.

The Bible of Tyndale and Coverdale gave some words which have remained with us. Coverdale gave us the word *loving-kindness*, for which it is impossible to find a translation or equivalent. Tyndale added to the language the word *long-suffering*, which is almost a household word in daily use ; and *peacemaker*, which is translated directly from the Latin *pacificus*. The word *beautiful*, one of the most useful, euphonious, completely expressive words in English, was not known to be used before Tyndale. He also introduced the phrase *filthy lucre*, and from that expression has developed the unpleasant connotation of *lucre* ; the adjective *lucrative* is still quite pleasant in connotation. Tyndale's most famous example of word-making occurs in *scapegoat*, which has been an admirable metaphorical addition to the language. The great Bible of 1611 has given permanence to such expressions as *apparel, raiment*, and *firmament*, the last of which has been used popularly even by Negro story-tellers to express the liquid with which they imagine God surrounded the earth. *Quick* for *living*, a most beautiful and expressive synonym, was kept in the language by the Bible, as well as *damsel* for *young woman* and *travail* for *labour*.

The Renaissance derived its inspiration from Greek culture, and directly from Latin culture as opposed to the ecclesiasticised Latin influence that had been disseminated before the Revival of learning. Consequently a number of Greek words appeared in English at that epoch. Before the sixteenth century there were several Greek words in English, derived from French or anteriorly from Latin. *Bishopric* is an example of a Greek word derived through the Latin Church and completed by the English suffix *-ric*, which means *district of dominion*. Other pre-renaissance Greek words are *etymology*, *geography*, *logic*, *theology*. In the sixteenth and seventeenth centuries, these rare examples of Greek influence were enormously augmented in the theological, philosophical, and scientific provinces of language, but the words adapted from Greek were treated as if they had passed through Latin channels. Adjectives, for instance, were usually anglicised by the addition of the endings *-ous* or *-al*. Examples are *autonomous* and *diaphanous*.

The modern development of science has added to these words. Many medical terms have a Latin or a Greek origin. The *sinus* is the " channel " above the eyebrow ; the *antrum*, though sounding in English pronunciation like an Irish county, is a " cave " under the eye ; *cystoscope* and *tuberculosis* have Greek forms.

There have been many changes in English between the sixteenth and our own century ; but in the main, except for the growth of the vocabulary and changes in the pronunciation of certain words, English was formed in the Elizabethan period and continued to grow in the way of classical correctness through the beautiful prose of Walton, Thomas Browne, and Dryden in the seventeenth century, through the Latinised expression of Pope, Swift, the novelists, and Johnson in the eighteenth century, finally degenerating into the often pompous and over-claused verbosity of the writers of the nineteenth century.

HOW ENGLISH HAS FARED IN THIS AGE OF PROGRESS

IT remains to see what the twentieth century, so innovating and versatile in other ways, has produced in the English language. The development of the British Empire had a great influence on the growth of English, in the additions that it brought to the vocabulary such as *topee*, *kaffir*, *wigwam*, *maori*, *trek*. The increase of relationship and communication with other countries has contributed equally. From Italian come terms associated with art such as *aria*, *cantabile*, *gamut*, *prima donna*, *aquatinta*, *chiaroscuro*, *fresco*, *intaglio*, *mezzotint*, *studio*, and *terra cotta*. The low countries have also provided some artistic terms such as *landscape, sketch, easel.* The Dutch were our masters in naval warfare for a time and from them came terms, originally Germanic, and therefore like our own words, such as *avast, skipper, dock,* and *hull.* Other languages, at different periods and in different fashions, have contributed largely to our language. There was a time when Spain and Spanish writers, and one when Italy and Italian manners, set the desirable tone, and from these times come many expressions in common use such as *attitude, fiasco, motto, stanza, umbrella* from Italian, and *ambuscade, dispatch, grandee, negro, peccadillo, renegade* from Spanish. Germany has not had a great influence on our language directly, but we have had to borrow words in fields of knowledge where Germany was leader, such as mineralogy ; from that science we have words such as *bismuth, cobalt, quartz,* and *zinc.*

Later in the historical development of English we borrowed words from other countries for objects or conceptions that we either have not or that are chiefly connected with foreign peoples. Portuguese gave us *auto-da-fé, albatross, cocoa,* and *verandah* ; Russian gave us *knout* and *steppe* among others. Turkish gave us *caftan, coffee, and horde*; Malay contributed some words surprisingly common such as *gingham, gong,* and *ketchup.* China has given *tea,* and Japan *rickshaw.* From Polynesian dialects come the words *tattoo* and *taboo.* The latter is now used for semi-religious restrictions of other countries, as well as of Polynesia. The American Indians have also given us many words whose foreign origin is forgotten, such as *squaw, tobacco, potato,* and *toboggan.*

The store of language grows with every political development. Not a few modern words in current use have been derived from foreign political institutions, and from foreign fashions and manners. One cannot always tell what words will be adopted and what not. The modern French *chic* has been so adopted into English that it has its own English pronunciation. The French were for long the arbiters of good manners, and their words *savoir-faire* and *joie de vivre* have become almost naturalised. We do not tend to take words from German wholesale ; but of modern German inspiration is *hitlerism* ; of Italian inspiration is *fascism*; and the Oxford Group has even invented a word *Buchmanism.* Indian words, Australian, Canadian, and American words, all find their way into the language, although the proportion of them that enters current and common speech is comparatively rare.

A NEW STYLE FOLLOWS THE CHANGE IN THOUGHT

THIS twentieth century, which has in so many ways attempted to throw off the conventions of thought that are felt to be outworn, has correspondingly thrown off many linguistic and stylistic conventions. This has had some good and some bad results. It is, on the whole, healthy that we have ceased to imitate the Latinism of Johnson and Addison, the rolling periods of Gladstone and other Victorian writers. The tendency to make sentences as short and as self-contained as possible is vigorous and good. The opening of the door to slang is also healthy in some ways, because it means a perpetual growth of the language. Slang comes from one of two instincts generally : one of them is to find new metaphors and expressions for old subjects ; and this is useful because it prevents language becoming stale and trite. America is especially good at inventing expressions that present something in a new and more vital way. Such expressions as : " He was so nervous that he plucked at the counterpane," or " He was as mad as a hornet," convey the meaning vividly and humorously.

Another source of slang, on the other hand, is the common tendency to laziness of expression. People who prefer not to use their own minds or imaginations, and who also prefer to be exactly like other people for fear of being inferior, tend to use stock expressions. This is not only a fault of slang users, but is equally to be reproached against educated writers who rely on dead metaphors to illuminate dullness. Any one can think of these all but meaningless phrases which are used from habit and of which people have forgotten the original figurative significance. They are used because it is easier to say : " His religious opinions sat lightly on him " than to explain clearly what is meant. A temptation of the same sort is visible in popular speech. It is considered the thing nowadays to fumble for words in a way for which our grandparents would severely have reproved us ; untidiness of thought and uncertainty of sensation and sentiment is partly the cause of it ; and it is a cause not wholly ignoble.

The present, what may be called the reigning generation—those who were brought up either immediately before or during the war—has great cause to be dissatisfied with the easy certainties that seem to have landed Europe where she is now. The easy certainties of the Churches brought no calm to souls so violently shaken in faith and goodness as most of the present generation have been. Doubting the validity of every previously established opinion, partly in a scientific, partly in an idealistic spirit that would wish but fears to believe in the eternal verities, the modern world covers its shyness and uncertainty by the use of half-finished phrases, groping dimly for expression. The result is awkward and unbeautiful, but has a certain philosophical value as recognising the infinite uncertainty of experience.

A further source of inaccurate speech is the easy use of fashionable phrases ; partly coming from imitation, partly from the English virtue or vice, usually most observed in smart circles, of baulking at a serious feeling or truth. A beautiful view is for even the best of us *awfully nice*; and the sensitive and expressive word *lovely* has begun to lose its particular value, as *awfully* has already lost its majesty and terror, and as *nice*, except in very particular writers, has lost its peculiar and accurate meaning in favour of a vague, colourless one.

"AMERICANISMS" THAT CHAUCER USED

MANY of the forces of modern science and modern communication have aided the temporary standardisation of the language. The telephone and the telegram, while they encourage a salutary brevity and economy of thought, also encourage a standardised speech as being easier to understand and more efficient to convey a meaning. While many ancient words use their ancient force, new discoveries and new modes of thought discover new words, and the extension of English over the world has enriched the language by preserving archaic expressions and dialectal expressions that would, if left to the exclusive standard of Southern English, have been ousted.

America is particularly valuable as a perpetual source of new words and of old words reintroduced. Many so-called Americanisms are in Chaucer ; *right now* is constantly used by Chaucer and by his contemporaries, and is a perfectly correct adverbial use of *right* (*direct*). Baltimore speech extends the use equally correctly to qualify other adjectives, and one often hears the vigorous phrase : " He has a right good mind." Similarly the despised " I guess " and

" I reckon " are used with their modern senses in Chaucer and Middle English generally. Another source of variety in American speech is the influx of immigrants. The country is open to foreign ideas and foreign ways of thinking, and of expressing ideas. The word *dumb* is used in the German sense of *stupid*, for instance. The influence of the old-fashioned courtly American is also to the good. Among educated people in America, the vulgarism of *like* for *as* introducing a verbal clause, and the equally unpleasant vulgarism of *due to* instead of *owing to* when introducing an adverbial clause, is heard much less often than in educated circles in England. America also, with correct speakers and writers, retains the expression *someone's else*, which, though slightly pedantic, is more attractive in sound than the awkward English *someone else's*.

There is danger from America also, however, chiefly through the influence of the film and of smart slang. Expressions, mechanically used like " Oh, yeah ? " and " Oh, boy ! " add little to grace or efficiency of expression. On the cinema, the stars who have been chosen for their beauty have rarely an innate sense of language, so that their diction and expression is stilted, artificial, and unnatural. This explains why a foreign star, such as Garbo or Bergner, often speaks English more naturally and beautifully than a star born English-speaking. They have none of the artificial standards of those who fear to be ill-bred in expression. The greatest American contribution in the way of slang is the use of language imaginatively to bring an idea home by means of a concrete expression.

THE HOSPITALITY OF OUR LANGUAGE

ENGLISH is perhaps the most completely mixed of modern European races, and consequently its language is the most hospitable and the most flexible. There are seldom two ways of saying a thing correctly in French ; and German is hampered by the rigours of its syntax. In English there are endless ways of saying the same thing, according to the speaker's personality. It would be a great pity if we ever had an academy to decide what is correct and what is not. The only true correctness in language is the grammar that is decided by good usage at the moment. What was correct several decades ago becomes vulgar to-morrow ; and, similarly, what seems vulgar now will probably be the height of fashion in a short time. Grammatical faults are unpleasant, because they are inaccurate and because they improperly represent what is to be said. It is inaccurate to say : " He do walk so slow " because *do* expresses a plural idea ; equally it is inaccurate to use the indicative " if he was " which expresses certainty as to the subject's movements when the subjunctive uncertainty is meant. In many cases of such inaccurate uses, the meaning may be clear, but sloppy habits of using parts of speech are undesirable because they may involve the speaker in vagueness and ambiguity.

The great charm of English has been its openness to change and to foreign influence. It has seldom profited by forced standards and alterations. It is in some ways a pity that there is even so fixed a standard as that provided by the British Broadcasting Corporation and *The Times*, because they make natural speakers self-conscious and artificial. It is the great flexibility of English, both as regards vocabulary and syntax, which has produced such an admirable ability to achieve different shades of atmosphere and meaning. *Maternal* and *motherly* have slightly different connotations. The word *predilection* combines something of the ideas contained in *love* and *choice*, but indefinably eludes the meaning of either.

Latin and Greek words, as well as increasing the power of expressing shades of meaning, also help to vary the rhythm of the language. Shakespeare could write a line as moving in its context and as simple as : " Never, never, never, never, never." He could also, if he wished, pile on the ponderous beauties of Latinised expression. To see the great beauty of combined Latinised and English rhythm, take any line of Milton, for instance, " Immeasurable ocean without bound," where the stability of the two final Germanic words brings to rest the fluctuating wave of the first two classically derived words. The suppleness of English expression is so great that we can have the simplest prose, such as Bunyan's ; the most artistic and refined poetry, such as Milton's ; the sweet simplicity of some of Byron's and Burns's lyrics ; the attenuated and learned prose of Pater or Sir Thomas Browne. The variety of human character is never restricted, and in English more than in any language the style really reveals the character. It is important to express ourselves as we should wish, and a knowledge of and care for our language's history should help us to do so.

WHERE THE ROMANCE OF ENGLISH IS REVEALED

THE best introductory book for those interested in the development of English is Henry Bradley's *Making of English* (Macmillan, 1925), which gives a clear and simple account for the beginner. More advanced and detailed are Otto Jespersen's *Growth of the English Language* (Oxford, 1926) and H. C. Wyld's *Growth of English* (Murray, 1907) and his *Historical Study of the Mother Tongue* (Murray, 1906) which is useful from the point of view of method. Other works, perhaps more amusing for the casual reader, are those dealing with particular aspects of English, such as Wyld's *History of Modern Colloquial English* (London, 1921), Logan Pearsall Smith's *English Idioms* (Oxford University Press), and *Words and Idioms* (Constable) by the same author. Then there are Professor Ernest Weekley's many studies of individual words and of names: *The Romance of Words* (1913), *The Romance of Names* (1914), *Surnames* (1916), *Words Ancient and Modern* (1926), *More Words Ancient and Modern* (1927), and *Words and Names* (1932). All these will be found entertaining. For place-names, the various books on the several English counties by Professor Allan Mawer are indispensable.

The clearest Old English grammar for the beginner is E. E. Wardale's, which is provided with convenient charts of conjugations and declensions, and which is accurate without being overburdened with detail. For Middle English, Joseph Wright's grammar is the best available to those who can read English only. The Oxford English Dictionary is, of course, the standard work for the study of historical English ; but it is accessible to few, and the short Oxford Dictionary will supply its place for many. Besides these there are Wyld's *Universal Dictionary*, and Skeat's *Etymological Dictionary*, which, though old-fashioned and inaccurate, is a mine of suggestive information. The standard dictionary for Old English is Bosworth and Toller's. There is no satisfactory dictionary of Middle English, but the best that we have at present, though sadly incomplete, is Stratmann-Bradley's.

THE CORRECT USE OF ENGLISH

by WRIGHT WATTS MILLER, B.A.(Lond.),
M.Ed.(Manchester)

THE correct use of a language is decided by custom and common sense. Sometimes custom is more powerful than common sense, as in the English spelling system. English grammar, on the other hand, is one of the greatest monuments to the accumulated common sense of sixty generations of Englishmen. It is a pity that, through bad teaching and association with Latin and Greek in the past, the word " grammar " should indicate such needless terrors to the average Englishman to-day.

THE MEANING AND IMPORTANCE OF GRAMMAR

A LANGUAGE is a method, more or less imperfect, by which men communicate with each other. It takes, so far as we can tell, at least several hundred years to make a language. The grammar of a language is the record of its ways and customs as they have grown up, and as they must be observed by those who wish to make themselves intelligible in the language. When we communicate with each other it is thoughts which we wish to communicate—not words, since these are but the invented tokens of our thoughts. Grammar, therefore, is *a means to clear thinking*. It is definitely not, as is sometimes implied, a set of rules established by arbitrary authority, and thrust upon the unwilling natural speaker or writer. Grammar changes from generation to generation, even in these days when the printed word tends to fix a language more permanently than the spoken word ever could. The only authority grammar can have (in English, at least) is the authority of the mass of clear thinkers, speakers, and writers at any given time.

The grammar of a language consists of two parts. The first deals with the forms of individual words ; it records, for instance, that while *seen* is the agreed word in *We have never seen it yet*, it is not the agreed word in *I seen him yesterday*. This branch of grammar is called Accidence, and has been reduced in English to a minimum. A foreigner has only a few forms to learn in English, such as that adding an *s* makes a plural, or adding an 's shows possession. The fearsomeness of the term " grammar " to the Englishman is due to the vast amount of accidence there is to learn in almost all languages but English ; whereas in English we say *I speak, we speak, you speak, they speak*, in French there is a different form of the word " speak " for each of the four. Foolish teaching has often attempted to make English grammar coincide with foreign grammar by setting the schoolboy to learn forms when no forms are there. This ignores the excellence of English, which has, by simplifying its accidence from the very large number of forms it had in Anglo-Saxon, reduced the strain on the memory to almost nothing. When an Englishman groans about the burden of a foreign grammar, he is groaning, quite reasonably, about the strain his memory must undergo before he can begin to understand the language at all.

The second branch of grammar concerns the relations of words to each other, and their proper placing in sentences. This branch is called Syntax, and it is this which English common sense has perfected to a very high degree. The strain in writing correct English is not thrown so much on the memory as on the judgment of the writer, which he must exercise anew in each individual sentence. Most of the rules for exercising this judgment depend on very simple principles, but the application of them may be a matter of the greatest delicacy. It is partly for this reason that English has become one of the most flexible and expressive of all languages, whether ancient or modern.

The practice of English syntax may be illustrated by the solution of an everyday dilemma : should we say *the public is* or *the public are* ? In some languages there might be an inviolable rule to answer that question ; " public " might be always singular or always plural. Not so in English, however, which examines the word and says : " What does it imply—a large crowd of people acting as one, or a large crowd acting severally ? " And so the answer to the question depends upon the sense of the sentence : we say *The public is one of the principal owners of iron mines in Sweden*, but *The public are slow in adding their names to the subscription list*. (Tangles would obviously arise from saying *The public are one*, or *The public is slow in adding its name*.)

Grammar, then, is essential to the expression of clear and exact meanings. To explain the distinctions between one kind of meaning and another a few technical terms are necessary, but only a few. The best way to learn such terms is to see them in actual use for elucidating problems—common errors and difficulties in English.

WHAT MAKES A SENTENCE ?

IN studying the grammar of one's mother tongue it is more practical to begin with the sentence, the unit to which we have been accustomed since the age of four, than with the word, as is necessary in studying a foreign language. The essence of a sentence is often said to be that it must contain a complete thought. We may accept this with two qualifications. " Thought " must be understood to include emotion as well as logical thinking ; it must include any mental process which we wish to communicate to some one else. Secondly, the completeness of the thought must be in the mind of its originator, and must be clear also to its recipient, but it need not be insisted on in actual words ; the completeness may be implicit but not expressed. Thus *Hurry !* is as complete a sentence as *I must hurry*, or *You had better hurry*, or *They are hurrying*, or *What a hurry he is in !*

A better way of defining the completeness of a sentence is to say that it must consist of two parts—something we wish to talk about, which is called the Subject, and something which is said about the subject, and is called the Predicate. Either of these parts may be absent in actual words, but it must be implicit in sense. The sentence *Hurry !*, for instance, is addressed to some person or persons forming the implied subject of the sentence, and whose presence is also suggested by the exclamation mark. *Hurry.* is not a complete sentence.

SENTENCES COMPOUND AND COMPLEX

WHEN we come to the end of our subject and predicate, we put a full stop or semicolon, or join the sentence to another sentence by a conjunction or joining word. This simple principle is all that lies behind the difficulties to be discussed later under the heading of Punctuation. A single subject and predicate closed by a full stop or semicolon forms a Simple Sentence. A series of such sentences joined by *and, or, but,* forms a Compound Sentence. Replace the joining words by full stops or semicolons, and the result is a series of complete simple sentences of parallel importance. Thus we may write :

> Johnson snorted, Goldsmith was peevish, Garrick ranted, and Reynolds took snuff.

or

> Johnson snorted and Goldsmith was peevish, but Garrick ranted and Reynolds took snuff.

These are compound sentences. If we remove the conjunctions we have a string of simple sentences, which must be separated by full stops or semicolons, thus :

> Johnson snorted. Goldsmith was peevish. Garrick ranted. Reynolds took snuff.

But our sentences are rarely of this constant simplicity. We more often make a main statement and qualify it by one or more subordinate sentences. We may add one of these subordinate sentences, or clauses, to explain the subject, another to explain something in the clause explaining the subject, another to tell when the action done in the predicate took place, another to tell where it took place, and yet another to explain why the actual place was chosen. It will be a useful exercise to pick out all the above parts from the following sentence :

> Sir Walter Scott, who at that time was scarcely beginning to feel the effects of the fatigue which eventually undermined his health, was to be seen any evening during the period we have mentioned, high up in the room which he had chosen for its quietness and which was to see the composition of so many of the Waverley Novels.

This is an involved example of a Complex Sentence. *Sir Walter Scott was to be seen any evening during the period we have mentioned* is also a Complex Sentence, since (*which*) *we have mentioned* makes no sense by itself. The only simple sentence present is the fundamental statement—*Sir Walter Scott was to be seen any evening*.

The test of a subordinate clause in a complex sentence is that it cannot make sense unless joined to the sentence or word which it qualifies. Each subordinate clause, however, is still composed of a complete subject and predicate, expressed or implied. The fearsome exercise called, in schools,

Analysis, deals with the parts of complex sentences. An adult person may manage without most of the technical terms employed, so long as he can pick out the true relationships of the parts of the sentence to one another—that is, the true meaning of the sentence—and can discover the subject and predicate when necessary, in each clause or sentence. Once again the rule is easy ; its application is a matter of personal skill. If one can discover the grammatical parts of the sentence *The cat scratched the dog*, one can probably discover those of a more difficult sentence. No text-book can do the work of one's own judgment in finding the parts of any sentence. Correct punctuation, as will be seen later, cannot be explained without an understanding of such processes of grammatical analysis.

THE LAWS THAT GOVERN WORDS

IT is clearly an advantage to be able to distinguish conveniently between *licence* and *license*, for example, by calling one the Noun and the other the Verb. Otherwise the distinction can be explained only by roundabout and inexact phrases, such as : " The licence is the thing you take out, and the Government licenses you when you take out the licence ! " For convenience, too, nouns are classified into Common and Proper, Concrete and Abstract. The first classification may be illustrated by the difference between *the city* and *the City* ; Proper Nouns always need a capital letter. The second classification may be illustrated by the difference between words such as *apple, hat, ball*, and *time, heat, space*. The former must always be used with an article, *an apple, the hat*, but the latter can be used alone, as in the example : *heat is tiring*. The second classification has many borderline cases such as Nouns of Multitude, like *Council*, or Material-Nouns like *iron*—not the name of any concrete piece of iron, but of the substance, anywhere, any size, undefined, with the properties which earn it the name of iron. Few common grammatical errors, however, are due to a mishandling of nouns.

Pronouns, on the other hand, cause a great deal of difficulty. A Pronoun is defined readily enough as a word which replaces a noun—*I, he, she, it, they, which, who, each, anyone*, etc. ; there are not many pronouns, and they are easy to recognise. But because their meanings depend upon some noun which has been named or implied before, it is easy to use pronouns vaguely. Much trouble may be caused in tracing the elusive *he* or *which* back to its Antecedent—the noun which it replaces —and examples of this will be discussed later. Further, since there are so few pronouns, they change their form to indicate grades of meaning. They are some of the few words which still have many variations of form in English. Chief among their variations are those showing Person and Case. (Nouns may also have Person and Case, but in English they no longer have differences of form to show them.)

There are three Persons. The First Person, indicated by the pronouns *I, me, we, us,* distinguishes the speaker. The Second Person—*you* (and formerly also *thou* and *ye*) distinguishes the person spoken to. All the rest of the world, all the possible subjects or people under discussion by the First and Second Person, are classed as Third Person—*he, she, it, they, them, him, her.* A writer often uses the First Person Plural to extend a spirit of friendliness by including his readers and himself under the one word *we,* as when he says *We are all familiar with——* The Second Person is also used, in speech more permissibly than in writing, with an effect of greater intimacy where a vague, unindividualised Third Person is really meant : *Now when you have got your Safeguarding of Industries Act, what do you find ?* Person, like most other usages in English grammar, has thus many variations and exceptions which are the result of experience and not of rigidly logical definition.

HOW NOUNS AND PRONOUNS SHOULD BE RELATED

THE nouns in a sentence stand in a relation to one another decided mainly by the part each is made to play by the verb. The same is true of pronouns. Thus in the sentence *The man hit the dog, man* is the subject of the sentence and is related to *dog* by doing something to it—by hitting it. *Dog* is the object of the sentence and is related to *man,* because something is done to him by the man. The relation of one noun or pronoun to another is shown by the case of the nouns or pronouns. In Anglo-Saxon and in languages such as German and Latin the case of a word can be recognised by its ending. Thus when man is the doer (subject) in a Latin sentence, he appears as *homo,* but when he is the one to whom something is done (object) he appears as *hominem.*

In modern English the case of a pronoun, though not of a

noun, may usually be recognised by its form. Thus *I* is always the subject of a sentence, *me* is always the object, or is in the predicate ; *he* is the subject, *him* the object, or in the predicate. The case of a noun, however, can usually only be told from the position of the noun in the sentence or from the relationship word (preposition) used with it. Compare the headline sentences, *Dog Bites Man* with *Man Bites Dog* ; or *Murder Of Officer* with *Murder By Officer*, the prepositions being *of* and *by*.

There are four Cases in English. The subject of a sentence (the man or dog who does the biting) is in the Nominative Case. The object of a sentence (the man or the dog who is bitten, for instance) is in the Accusative or Objective Case. The Indirect Object of a sentence is the person or thing affected by an action, but not most directly affected ; thus in the sentence *He passed the ball to me*, or *He bought the car for his wife*, *me* and *wife* are the Indirect Objects, while *ball* and *car*, which are actually subjected to the passing or buying, are in the Accusative Case. The Indirect Object of a sentence is said to be in the Dative Case, and in English is generally indicated by *to* or *for*, either expressed or implicit, e.g. *me* is still the Indirect Object in *he passed me the ball*. The fourth case is the Genitive Case, which includes the Possessive Case, as well as some other kinds of belonging which are not exactly possession, e.g. *a cup of coffee*. The Genitive Case is expressed by adding an *'s* or by using the preposition *of*.

The Genitive Case is the only case in English which may be shown, in nouns, by a change in the form—*the boy's hat ; in a year's time*. English pronouns, on the other hand, show most of their changes of case by changes of form. *I, we, thou, you, he, she, they, who*, for instance, may all indicate the subject of a sentence and are all in the Nominative Case. When the persons indicated by these pronouns have something done to them and become the objects of sentences, the pronouns change to *me, us, thee, you, him, her, them, whom*, and are then in the Accusative Case. We should say, for instance, *whom did you pass on the road ?* not *who did you pass ?* because *whom* is the object, just as *him* would be in the answer—*I passed him* (not *I passed he*). The Genitive Case of the above pronouns is *my, our, thy, your, his, her, their, whose*. The Dative Case is shown by adding *to* or *for* to the Accusative Case—*to me, to us, to thee, to you, to him, to her, to them, to whom*.

SOME PITFALLS IN THE EXPRESSION OF CASES

ALTHOUGH pronouns have these changes of form to show case, they are still dependent, just as much as nouns, on word-order and prepositions to show their case fully. When *Dog Bites Man* is expressed as *It bites him*, the subject still precedes the verb, and the object follows it—*Him bites it* is not permitted. Further, when prepositions are used before pronouns, the form of the Accusative Case is necessary, e.g. *by him, for me, with her, from them, about whom, after us*. And in such examples as *by it, for you, with John, from the stable*, etc., although there are no special accusative case-forms present, the pronouns or nouns are still in the accusative case. We must therefore extend our idea of the object to include not only the object of a verb but the object of a preposition. The object of a verb (which is also the object of the sentence containing the verb) is said to suffer or undergo the action indicated by the verb—*we visited John, we visited him*. The object of a preposition forms, with the preposition, a separate phrase inside the sentence—*we visited John to ask about Mary ; we visited John to ask about her*.

Most instances of the accusative case after a proposition are familiar enough to be taken for granted. *Between you and me*, however, is often wrongly rendered *between you and I*. Yet no one would say *between——I*. " Me," of course, is the object of the preposition " between." Probably *you and me* is often avoided in this phrase because *you and me* is often incorrectly used in such instances as *you and me'll have to look out*. Here " me " should be replaced by the nominative case " I," since it is part of the subject of the sentence.

We have already said that a sentence must contain a Subject (either a noun or a pronoun) and a Predicate. The essential part of the predicate is a verb, and with these two essential words—a noun and a verb—many a sentence may be constructed—*John ran, I laughed*, etc. More often, however, the meaning expressed by the verb is not complete with the verb itself. *He bought* is no use without the object —the car or whatever else was bought. But there are other ways of completing sentences than by an object. *The bread tastes dry*—the bread is not itself " tasting " anything ; *I am tired ; he feels ill*—nothing undergoes the feeling, as in *he feels the bottom*. None of these completions, which are called Complements, are affected by the action or state expressed by the verb. Rather do they expand the meaning of the subject. Particularly is this the case with complements of the verb " to be," so that several languages, such as Latin or Russian, often omit " am," " is," etc., without any confusion of meaning, and say simply *I tired, he Russian*. In these sentences obviously " tired " is the same case as " I," or " Russian " as " he "—all four are nominative. Similarly in English with *It is he*, and all complements of any part of the verb " to be." (*It is me*, however, is so sanctioned by usage that it would be pedantic to object to it in informal conversation.)

AN ANALYSIS OF THE VERB

THE simplest way to define a verb is to say that it is the word essential to the predicate of a sentence. A verb is also often said to be a word expressing an action or state. This is less satisfactory, and " action " must be taken to include all kinds of words such as *prevaricate, consider, analyse*, etc. There are two main classes of verbs—Transitive, which require an object to complete their meaning, and Intransitive, which do not. A verb may have both uses, e.g. *taste* in *He tastes the soup* is transitive, and in *The bread tastes dry* is intransitive. A transitive verb has two main classes of use, called the Active Voice and the Passive Voice. The active voice indicates the ordinary use of such a verb as " cut," the passive voice indicates that the object has been turned round and made into the subject—*The loaf was cut by Jane*, instead of *Jane cut the loaf*. The advantage of having two voices is that emphasis can be differently placed, according to the subject of the sentence, on either the loaf or Jane.

All verbs, whether transitive or intransitive, can express both the difference between singular and plural, and the difference between the three persons. These differences, however, are not usually indicated by changing the form of the verb, as in most other languages, but simply by putting before the verb a pronoun or noun which itself expresses the difference of number or person : *I speak, you speak, we speak, they speak*. Only in the Singular of the Third Person —*he, she, it speaks*, do we use a different form of the verb. (An exception is the verb *to be—am, is, are*, etc.) Even this difference only occurs in the Present of the Verb ; in the past *spoke*, for example, serves for all persons, both singular and plural.

More important variations in the verb are differences of time, called Tenses, and differences called Mood—expressions of shades of wishing, willing, likelihood, etc. English has more of these variations than most languages, and expresses them, for the most part, by adding a few conventional words, called Auxiliaries, to the simple parts of the verb, instead of taxing the memory with a large number of different parts of the verb. The difference between Past, Present, and Future is only the beginning of the English varieties of Tense. English can express the subtle differences between *I work* and *I am working*, *he will work* and *he will be working*, *they worked* and *they have been working*, *they were working*, *they had been working*, or *they had worked*.

The variations called Moods were also originally expressed by different forms of the verb, as they still are in many languages ; the solitary relic of the forms of the Subjunctive Mood in general use to-day is *if I were*, which most people still prefer to *if I was*, though they do not say *if I be*, as they would once have done, instead of *if I am*. The Imperative Mood conveys a command by using the simple form of the verb with an exclamation mark—*Go ! Stop ! O come, all ye faithful !* All other moods, including the subjunctive mood, are expressed nowadays by combinations of the auxiliaries used for expressing tenses—*had*, *should*, etc., or of parts of other verbs, such as *might* and *must*.

THE VERB AS ADJECTIVE AND NOUN

USEFUL parts of the verb are the Infinitive (*to hurry*, *to be able*, etc.) and the two Participles. The Present Participle ends in *-ing* and may serve as a part of the verb—*He is hurrying* ; as an adjective—*Hurrying crowds were delayed* ; or as a noun—*Hurrying cannot save you now*. The same forms in *-ing* make a very useful class of words called Gerunds or Verbal Nouns. Gerunds behave like nouns while doing the work of a part of a verb. In the first of the following examples " singing " is a Gerund, in the second it is a Noun : *I am pleased at his singing to-night ; I am pleased with his singing to-night*. In the first sentence " singing " could be replaced by an ordinary form of the verb—*I am pleased that he is singing to-night ;* in the second it could only be replaced by another noun—*I am pleased with his voice to-night.* The Past Participle (*spoken, written, leapt, drowned, tasted,* etc.) may also be either part of the verb, as in *He has spoken,* or an adjective, as in *the spoken word,* or sometimes a noun, as in *for the fallen.* The Infinitive is also often used as a noun —*To temporise at this moment would be fatal.*

THE DUTIES ALLOTTED TO ADVERBS AND ADJECTIVES

ADJECTIVES and Adverbs must be distinguished. An Adjective is approximately defined as a word which qualifies a noun, *e.g.* the first word in each of the following pairs : *good fellow, ridiculous boy, original composition, orderly behaviour.* An Adverb is a word which modifies or limits or adds something to the meaning of a verb, to a phrase or sentence containing a verb, to an adjective, or to another adverb. Examples of these modifications, in order, are : *He runs fast, He will probably run, exasperatingly slow, exasperatingly slowly.* While many adverbs end in *-ly,* not every word with this ending is an adverb. Thus we must not say *The troops proceeded orderly,* and since *orderlily* is felt to be so clumsy that it has never been used, we can only express our adverbial idea by an Adverbial Phrase such as *in an orderly manner.* Many words, such as *fast, only,* may be used as either adjectives or adverbs, without change of form. Many adjectives add *-ly* to form adverbs—*originally, slowly, slyly.*

Adjectives and Adverbs are also used as comparing words : in *the faster of the two,* or *He runs faster than I,* they are said to be of the Comparative Degree. Only two things are compared together here. When one thing is compared with many, or picked out from many, the adjective or adverb used is said to be of the Superlative Degree : *the fastest of all, He runs hardest at the beginning, Brightest and best of the sons of the morning !* The rules for forming the Comparative and Superlative cause occasional difficulty. Leaving out of account the words which adopt altogether different words as their Comparative or Superlative forms, such as *good, better, best*—*ill* (adverb), *worse, worst,* the rules are roughly as follows : *more* and *most* may be used to form the Comparative and Superlative, respectively, of any adjective or adverb. However, adjectives of one syllable, and many of two, more commonly adopt *-er* and *-est* : *slower, happiest.* Adverbs use *-er, -est* only when they have the same form as the corresponding adjectives : *run harder*, *sink deepest*, though *more* and *most* are not barred, and may be found in poetry.

PUNCTUATION : THE FOUNDATION OF CLEAR EXPRESSION

PUNCTUATION is in some ways the most fundamental matter in language, though some ancient languages used no punctuation at all. Many variations from the modern usages of English punctuation are found before the nineteenth century, even in the greatest authors, where their punctuation has not been altered by a modern printer. During the nineteenth century itself a divergence of practice began ; the modern tendency is generally described as under-punctuation, while the older type of plentiful punctuation still has its adherents. It is very dangerous, however, for persons who are at all doubtful about correct punctuation to assume that they may be allowed a licence in its use. Punctuation concerns the construction of sentences, and a mistake in punctuation is thus more likely to cause misunderstanding than any other, as a rule. The custom of printing legal documents without punctuation marks, or with few, is a pedantic relic of the days when such documents were written by hand, and it might have been impossible to decide whether a particular mark was a blot or a comma. It is expecting too much of language to hope that word-order alone, without punctuation, can establish perfectly clear meanings. On the other hand, a too plentiful sprinkling of commas may divide essential parts of a sentence from each other and make them appear to be straying aimlessly.

Most of the possible variations in punctuation depend on the speed of the reading—the difference, for example, between *on or about the 28th*, and *on, or about, the 28th*. Even the variation of speed may depend upon a difference of tone, which, in the spoken sentence, implies a difference of emphasis, and in the written sentence, is indicated by a difference of punctuation : in *He must come whether he will or no* the emphasis is on *come*, whereas in *He must come, whether he will or no*, the emphasis is on *must*. In the examples about to be discussed, no variation is in any case possible without its changing the meaning. Those who have thoroughly grasped the principles of sentence structure may observe for themselves in contemporary authors a few variations in systems of punctuation ; they will perhaps be surprised to find how few variations are possible without a change of meaning taking place. Alternatives are generally of the nature of bracketing or not bracketing a short phrase between commas. Single commas are more likely to be subject to rule.

THE COMMA : A STOP THAT IS OFTEN OVERWORKED

A COMMA, like other punctuation marks, is not essentially a mark for taking breath, though it often happens that one naturally takes breath where a comma occurs. There are sentences too long for a single breath in which it would be wrong to insert any punctuation ; there are others in which the commas would be ignored by the breath except in the most solemn reading. The two commonest errors in the use of the comma are : separating complete sentences by a comma instead of a full stop, and separating Subject from Predicate, or Verb from Object, by a comma. An example of the first mistake is :

> There is nothing in the way of a reduction of the tax, we expect indeed to see part of it remitted very soon.

Each half of this alleged sentence makes complete sense by itself. If the two halves are not separated by a full stop or semicolon, they must be joined by a conjunction such as *and*, *so*, *so that*. (It should be noted that *hence* and *thus* are not conjunctions but adverbs, and therefore cannot join sentences together.) An example of the second mistake is :

> He combines with the greatest personal charm and intelligence, the most selfless devotion to duty.

Omit the comma, since one would not write : *He combines, the most selfless devotion, etc.*, any more than one would write *He has, great powers.* This fault of the separation of the grammatical parts of a sentence by a comma is easy to commit in a long sentence where it is felt that a pause is needed, but commas must not be used merely to indicate a convenient pause.

> The tremendous outcry and upheaval which were raised by the crowd clamouring for admission were only equalled by the demonstrations of the crowd inside the barriers.

It would be wrong to insert a comma after *admission*, because it would be interfering between the subject, *outcry and upheaval*, and its verb, *were equalled*.

In the last sentence it would be equally destructive of the sense to enclose the whole phrase *which were raised by the crowd clamouring for admission* between commas, brackets, or dashes. The punctuation of such descriptive and inserted clauses as these (called Relative Clauses) is really a way of distinguishing two meanings, which may be illustrated by the examples :

> The referee who gave a wrong decision was lynched.
> The referee, who gave a wrong decision, was lynched.

The first referee is defined solely by the fact of his having given a wrong decision, and the relative clause is in this case known as a Defining Clause. The second referee has clearly been mentioned or implied in some previous sentence, and the relative clause mentions as in parenthesis that he gave a wrong decision, almost as casually as it might say *the referee, who wore a yellow shirt*.

Defining Clauses, however long, must never be enclosed between commas or other punctuation marks. Difficult examples of this type may always be solved by reducing them to some such blatant form as the above. Note that the following sentence is correctly punctuated, because it is not the Defining Clause itself which is enclosed by commas, but the clause and the word *countries* which it defines, while *in countries* is not so closely bound to *the natural opinion* by a relative word like " where " or " who " that it cannot be separated by the comma :

> The natural opinion, in countries where contri-
> butory unemployment insurance is not established,
> is that it puts a premium on sloth.

But this sentence could also be written without any commas at all ; the result would be to remove any slight impression that *the natural opinion* was something already mentioned.

In making lists of single nouns, or series of parallel phrases or clauses, commas should be used after each item, including both the last item and any item which precedes the final *and*.

> No Italians were allowed to leave their country,
> except diplomats, invalids, artists, and commercial
> travellers approved by the Fascists.

If there were no comma after *travellers*, the sentence would mean that any self-declared diplomat, invalid, or artist, might go abroad, whereas the meaning intended was that all four classes of person were subject to approval before they might leave Italy. *And* must, of course, be used to link the last pair in such a list. An example of a series of clauses is : *He plays cricket, walks, rides to hounds, and swims, better than he did before his operation.* Without the comma after *swims*, the meaning would be that only his swimming had been improved by his operation.

OTHER MARKS OF PUNCTUATION

DASHES, while easily overdone when used as a lazy substitute for other punctuation marks, are a help when they replace commas in a long sentence and, contrasting with other commas which are present, make it easier to determine the relative importance of parts of the sentence, *e.g.* :

> The Prime Minister had no doubt, he said, that the setting in motion of the machinery which had been established by the Conference, not only for Europe but for every country in the world, would release the long pent-up stream of trade from its barriers— barriers which it had been the first aim of the Conference to attack and remove—and set in motion again the wheels, etc., etc.

Semicolons can nearly always be replaced, in modern usage, by full stops. They are useful, however, to separate short sentences which, though grammatically complete in themselves, are too close in sequence to be separated by full stops without appearing jerky. A pair of short sentences separated from each other by a semicolon is often a useful device, and was very frequently used by Dr. Johnson to point an antithesis :

> Whatever enlarges hope will exalt courage ; after having seen the deaf taught arithmetic, who would be afraid to cultivate the Hebrides ?

Macaulay makes excellent use of semicolons in such sentences as the one expressing his notoriously vulgar judgment about the ancient philosophers :

> They promised what was impracticable ; they despised what was practicable ; they filled the world

with long words and long beards ; and they left it as
wicked and as ignorant as they found it.

Colons are sometimes used to separate two sentences of
exactly equal importance, but the semicolon is just as applicable. The colon is probably best reserved for prefixing a list.

Exclamation marks and question marks show the end of
a sentence just as though they were ordinary full stops.
They should not be omitted in rhetorical questions and
exclamations, in the gushing kind of writing which says :
What wonderful progress science has made in the last century !
Should we not therefore be grateful to these early pioneers ?
Proper insertion of these marks should remind a writer of
the vulgarity of studding his work with many such sentences.
The best antidote to a rhetorical question is to imagine always
the unexpected and derisive answer in the distance.

Quotation marks should not be used as an apology for such
a word as " funk." If the word is not good enough for its
context, use a more literary word. If the context is too good
for the word, make the context more colloquial. The
inverted commas remind one of the irritating person who
can hardly use a familiar phrase without interpolating—*if I*
may be allowed the expression.

WHAT THE APOSTROPHE STANDS FOR

THE Genitive Case is normally indicated in English either
by prefixing *of* to the noun or by adding *'s* after it. The
's is still added even when the noun already ends in an *s* in
the singular—*Reynolds's Newspaper*, and the pronunciation
also adds a syllable, as though the word were *Reynoldses*,
which indeed it would have been until the fifteenth century.
The apostrophe indicates the omitted *e*. The form *Reynolds'*
Newspaper or *Jones' hat*, without the *s*, is common, but not
so much in vogue as formerly, except in awkward cases such
as *Moses' beard*. When the *s* at the end of any word indicates
that it is plural, however, the apostrophe only is added to
make the Genitive Case : *the judges' decision* means the
decision of more than one judge. However, it is generally
clearer and neater to use *of* to form the genitive of plural
words, thus : *the decision of the judges*, etc.

In order to nail down the commonest difficulty in the use
of the apostrophe it is only necessary to think of the word
his, in which no one would think of inserting an apostrophe.

His is a Possessive word of special formation which can mean either " of him " or " belonging to him," as in *that hat is his*. Similarly, *its, theirs, yours, ours, hers, whose*, are all special Possessive words which never take an apostrophe.

The apostrophe, however, is used to indicate other omissions of letters than the *e* in *-es* which used to be the genitive ending. We write *didn't* for *did not*, *e'er* for *ever*, *he's* for *he is*, and in trying to represent dialect forms we use the apostrophe to indicate any omitted letter—*'elp ! I can't 'old the big 'un !* Thus when *it is* is abbreviated, as it usually is in speech, we write *it's*. But this has nothing whatever to do with the Genitive or Possessive.

In writing, a punctuation mark (unless a dash) should never be transferred from the end of one line to the beginning of the next.

RULES FOR PRESERVING THE SENSE OF WORDS

IT is a simple rule that a verb must agree in number with its subject—*What we want is 50,000 votes* is correct. But one often wonders whether the subject is to be considered singular or plural. Nouns of Multitude, such as *Government, fleet*, etc., vary in number according as they imply a single body or the persons who make up the body :

> The Government was powerless in this dilemma ; the Government have not many first - class brains amongst their number.
> The Fleet advances behind a smoke-screen ; the Fleet are expecting their Christmas leave.

It is only too easy to change one's mind half-way through a sentence about the number of the subject, and to commit, for instance, such monstrosities as :

> Those sort of people never make up their mind ; a terrible amount of misery and disease prevail ; for the last time there is presented to the Lower House measures inspired by . . .

The Indefinite Pronouns such as *each, everybody*, also cause confusion. In the following sentences, which are all correct, the subject is in every case in the singular :

> Everybody sees for himself that the trouble is over.
> Each of the shelves is six feet long.

No one outside the Emperor's personal party believes that restoration is possible.

Their failure was due to two reasons, neither of which was foreseen by the engineers.

I expect rapid progress if either of the new machines works at all well.

Singular nouns joined by *and* make a plural subject; singular nouns separated by *or*, *nor*, make alternative singular subjects and take a verb in the singular, *e.g.* :

If the facts are as your assistant and the specialist state,

but

If the facts are as either your assistant or the specialist states, *or* If the facts are neither what your assistant nor what the specialist states.

The word *between* implies a choice among alternatives (two or more) ; one cannot choose between one thing at a time, as is implied in such an incorrect sentence as : *Great rivalry is bound to develop between every nation concerned. Between each nation* would be just as wrong ; the word *between* has already sorted the nations out into individuals in advance, as it were, and to add another individualising word such as *each* makes nonsense. Besides, *every* and *each* are both singular. *Between nations*, or *between all nations*, would be correct. Where alternatives are specified, *between* must be followed by *and*, not *or*, since *or* separates the things between which the choice is to be made, instead of leaving them grouped together for *between* to choose from. Take the sentence :

We have to decide between a reduction of the tax and a decrease in trade, and an increase in the tax and no trade at all.

If we simplify this to such a form as *decide between an increase and a decrease*, it is clear that *or* for *and* would be absurd. We do say : *They have the chance of an increase or a decrease*, because this implies either the chance of an increase or the chance of a decrease. But replace *chance of* by *choice between*, and it makes no sense to separate the parts into *choice between an increase or choice between a decrease*. There must be more than one thing to choose from.

The Relative Pronouns *who*, *which*, *that*, can be either

singular or plural, according to the noun to which they refer ; no other noun can have any effect on the number of the pronoun, e.g. *One of the many débutantes who lend their names to Glogauer's Cream is Lady X* must not be altered to *lends her name*. *Who* refers to *débutantes*, which is plural ; *one* has its own Singular verb *is*.

HOW TO USE THE PRONOUN

A RELATIVE pronoun can only be used after the noun for which it stands has already been mentioned—it must, that is to say, have an antecedent noun. In the following examples there are no antecedent nouns for the pronouns *this*, *it*, and *which* :

> All the tools were missing from the rack, and this caused a search to be made.
> When promoting a girl to be monitor it sometimes makes the others jealous.
> Juggling on the Stock Exchange caused many prices to rise suddenly, which caused a good deal of misery to consumers.

It must not be assumed that the pronouns can be taken as referring to the notions vaguely included in the three sentences —the missing of the tools, the promotion of the girl, the rise in prices. The actual words must be there to give the names to these notions. In the first two examples the words in *-ing* illustrate a possible confusion ; *missing* and *promoting* can be nouns, but they are not being used as nouns, as *juggling* is, in the examples given. To recast the sentences so as to provide antecedents for the pronouns might take some very stiff phrases ; it may be better to use less precise words than pronouns to join the parts of the sentences together. Conjunctions will serve very well :

> As the tools were missing from the rack, a search was made.
> Since juggling on the Stock Exchange caused many prices to rise, a good deal of misery was caused.

Some people avoid this type of sentence, and write faulty ones like those given before, because they are still in the elementary stage of composing only simple sentences and then stringing them together into compound ones. It is important to be able to compose without difficulty complex sentences, in which one part can immediately be seen to be less important than another and dependent on it for its full meaning.

Even when there is a proper antecedent for a pronoun, it is unwise to separate the two so much that they do not appear to belong to one another, and the pronoun hesitates between two or three previous nouns for its reference, as in :

> The use of the pedals in this portion of the work is gradually introduced, to which special attention is earnestly recommended.

One should also be sure than the pronoun signifies exactly the same thing as its antecedent.

> Attempts have been made to lower the training college standard, but they have always resisted these.

These clearly enough refers to *attempts*, even though that word is away at the beginning of the sentence, but though *they* is meant to refer to the *training colleges*, these actual words have not been used.

The misplaced relative, that is, the relative put next to a noun to which it is not intended to refer, can produce some of the most ridiculous mistakes of all. Examples are :

> Snatching up a knife in desperation which lay on the table. . . .
> One of the neatest was the bay mare led in by my daughter, whose hocks won the admiration of the whole meeting.

In the first sentence *which* (the relative pronoun) is of course meant to refer to *knife*, and not to *desperation*, although grammatically it can only refer to *desperation*. Similarly, in the second example, *whose* refers to *the bay mare* and not to *my daughter*. Such sentences can generally be corrected by a little adjustment of the position of the words and by care in punctuation.

The Impersonal Pronoun causes much trouble in English. *One* is the only correct word, but it easily sounds stilted. It must not, for instance, be replaced by *he* or *his* further on in a sentence ; *one* and *one's* must be used. The following is American or older English, but is now generally considered wrong :

> One does not expect much advantage for himself from the new proposals, but he hopes they will improve the lot of others.

If we jib at repeating *one*, the only way out is to recast the sentence entirely, in some such form as : *Not much advantage is expected*, etc. The passive voice is often a useful way out of using *one*.

The unpractised writer often chooses *you* as his Impersonal Pronoun. This is acceptable if a person addressed in the second person—that is, the reader—is meant. But *you* must not be used to mean some person or other, as when a student writes : *The sun is highest in the sky at noon, as you can easily observe by measuring the angle.* The reader here is a teacher or examiner who is long past needing to measure the altitude of the sun for himself. One should alter to : *. . . as can easily be observed by measuring.* *Your*, properly handled, can express desirable shades of intimacy between a speaker and his audience, or a writer and his " dear reader." Comment is needless on such confusions as the following :

> When one takes up the instrument, hold it in the left hand and turn the adjusting screw with the right ; you will then see . . .

It is an unfortunate defect in English that we have no pronoun to express *he or she* conveniently in one word. *He or she* soon becomes clumsy when *his or her*, and *to him or to her*, have to be introduced later in a sentence. The simplest way out of the difficulty is to accept the legal fiction that *he* includes the meaning *she* : *It is the duty of every citizen to economise in water as much as he can* does not mean that any lady rate-payer may excusably waste water. *One* would of course be quite inadmissible as a substitute for *he or she*. It is also desirable to avoid the self-conscious use of *one* instead of *I*, due to the English vice of conscious self-effacement. The most famous victim of this was probably the don who invited a friend to his house with the words : *One's wife would be glad to see you.* It is surely better manner to accept the responsibility of *I* instead of trying to load it upon the elusive *one*.

"WHICH" OR "THAT" : HOW SHOULD WE CHOOSE?

THE Relative Pronouns *that* and *which* are to some extent interchangeable, but the tendency of English is always to make practical use of variations instead of allowing them to exist confusingly side by side. *Which* is no longer used, as in *Our Father which art in Heaven*, to replace words like

father which indicate actual persons, though it may replace
words like *company*, *Fiend*, which indicate persons collectively,
or personifications. *That* may be used for both persons and
things. The difference between the following sentences has
already been defined as the difference between a Defining
and a Non-Defining Clause :

> The match that I saw was indecisive.
> The match, which I saw, was indecisive.

It has been suggested by Fowler (*Modern English Usage*) that,
apart from the difference in punctuation, it is desirable to
distinguish the two kinds of clause further by using *that*
for Defining Clauses and *which* for Non-Defining Clauses.
Perhaps not many writers observe this rule constantly, though
most observe it now and then. At any rate, there is no other
rule discernible in the general uses of *that* and *which*.

And which and *but which* are, in general, not permissible,
unless a preceding and parallel clause has begun with a *which*.
But it must be a parallel clause.

> The climbers spent the night at Camp VI, which
> is eight hundred feet below the summit, according
> to their calculations, but which we were unable to
> verify owing to the loss of our instruments.

The second *which* refers to *calculations* and the first to *camp* ;
but should be omitted to allow the second *which* the proper
contact with its antecedent.

> A long course of training which the young man can
> bear and will fit him for any exertion.

Which must be inserted before *will*, to provide a subject for
fit ; otherwise the sentence reads *can bear and (can) will fit*.
There are some cases where *and which* is not only permissible
when no *which* has previously been used, but where the meaning would be confused if the *and which* were not permitted :

> A long course of training at the expense of the state
> and which will fit the young man for any exertion is
> not likely to be objected to.

Which, with the *and* omitted, would here refer to *state* ; the
and which is possible because the phrase *at the expense of the
state* is parallel in meaning to the which-clause. Both the
phrase and the clause give reasons why there would be no

objections. But it is as a rule neater to make a true relative clause of the first phrase in such instances as this :

> A long course of training which will be at the expense of the state, and which will fit . . .

It is useful to remember that the genitive case of the relative pronoun *that* is *whose*, and that this word may often conveniently replace a clumsy *of which*. *The committee seem to have drawn up the agreement in phrases of the meaning of which they are by no means aware* would be neater with . . . *phrases of whose meaning they are by no means aware*.

DECIDING THE MERITS OF "WHO" AND "WHOM"

A DECISION between *who* and *whom* in relative clauses may be made by reducing them to the " referee " form suggested earlier.

> The referee, who, we all saw, was incapable, was injured.
> The referee whom we all saw was injured. . . .

The second sentence may be checked by converting it to the form : *We all saw whom*. *Whom* is here the object of *saw*, and *referee* the subject of *injured*. In the first sentence the commas enclosing *we all saw* may be omitted, so long as it is realised that the phrase is a mere parenthesis and has no effect upon *who*, the subject of *was incapable*. The correctness of *whom* in such questions as *Whom did you see ?* may be checked by substituting *him* for *whom* in the answer. In speech and colloquial writing, of course, *Who did you see ?* or *Who do you mean ?* are as common and venial as *It is me* for *It is I*. One should not be misled by a relative pronoun into changing the case of another pronoun immediately preceding it : *We have no sympathy with him* retains *him* when it is expanded into : *We have no sympathy with him who would put national interests first in these times*. *Who* is the subject of *would put* ; *him* is accusative after *with*, and the analogy of *who* must not be allowed to convert it into *he*.

THE PRESENT PARTICIPLE : AN ATTRACTIVE WORD WHICH IS SOMETIMES MISUSED

D IFFICULTIES often arise in English from the misuse of the present participle—the form of the verb which ends in *-ing* and which always implies continuous action. The present participle affords an attractive way of getting over the ground quickly so as to get at the main verb in a sentence : *Running blindly in the dusk, he fell and broke his leg* is swifter in its effect than : *He was running blindly in the dusk when he fell and broke his leg*. It also puts more emphasis upon his accident than on the way in which it happened. If we wish to emphasise, instead, the action immediately preceding and causing his accident, we can again use participles : *He ran blindly on in the dusk, falling and breaking his leg*. But the participle-phrases must in each case relate to the subject of the finite verb in the sentence ; we cannot say : *Shaving in the morning, the sun shines in at my window*. If, however, the participle-phrase itself includes a noun or pronoun, this may be quite other than the subject of the sentence, e.g. : *Richard having shaved, they were all ready to go*.

In this sentence it would be wrong to insert a comma after *Richard*, as is sometimes done, under the impression that the sentence is of the same form as : *Richard, having shaved, packed his bag and went out*, in which *Richard* is the subject of the finite verb *packed* and therefore the subject of the sentence. One may test such sentences by removing the participle phrase. In the second example, *Richard packed his bag* remains, whereas in the first, *Richard* disappears and thus cannot be the subject of the sentence. Words like *considering* are of course no longer participles in such phrases as *Considering how our life is spent*, and do not come under the rules just given, though they do when they are used as participles.

MIXING PAST, PRESENT, AND FUTURE

I SHOULD *have liked to accept your invitation* is correct, implying that " if I had been able to accept it I should have enjoyed myself, though the chance of that is unfortunately over now." The mistaken form *should have liked to have accepted* would mean, if it meant anything, that " I should only have enjoyed myself when the accepting and the invitation and all the rest of it was over."

As he was doubtful of the way, he appears to have asked some tribesmen is correct. This is a report of a past event—*he was doubtful, etc.*—by some one else. It is to some one else, trying to piece the story together, that he appears, now, to have asked the way. If one had written *appeared*, it would mean that the man appeared to himself at the time to be asking the way ! This use of *appear* is obviously different from that in : *He was doubtful of the way, but appeared at last on the crest of the hill, where the guide discovered him with field-glasses.* Here the doubting and the appearing are more or less contemporary. Mistakes of tense such as those here illustrated are common with *appear* and *seem.*

PITFALLS IN INDIRECT SPEECH

IN reporting another person's words, in what is called Indirect Speech, all pronouns are turned into the third person—the speaker's *I* becomes *he* or *she*—and all verbs and expressions of time are made past tense. Further, the order of words in an original question must be turned back into the order normal for a statement. The original statement may have been as follows :

> I say that you are incapable, at present, of appreciating this point. I challenge you : how could you know what went on after the tenth of July ?

The reported statement must become :

> He said that he was incapable, at that time, of appreciating that point. He challenged him to say how he could have known what went on after the tenth of July.

A common mistake is to write : *He challenged him how could he know* . . . The rules governing reported speech are sometimes forgotten when a quotation, within its quotation marks, is incorporated in a sentence. It is often best to keep a quotation right outside the grammatical structure of the sentence, *e.g.* :

> Hamlet frightens Ophelia with the curse : " If thou dost marry, I'll give thee this plague for thy dowry : be thou chaste as ice, as pure as snow, thou shalt not escape calumny."

THE PUZZLE PROVIDED BY THE INFINITIVE

CONFUSION often arises between such pairs as *able to do a thing* and *capable of doing it ; refusal to proceed* and *objection to proceeding.* Only a full knowledge of the language can teach when the infinitive is possible and when the gerund. Usage is illogical about many of these examples. But the safest rule is to use the word in *-ing* when in doubt. A hundred mistakes like *the impossibility to improve* (for *of improving*) are found for one of the type : *refusal of proceeding.*

The split infinitive is one of the most easily detected of forms, e.g. : *to rapidly disappear*. It is, in consequence, often sedulously avoided by people who will break many important grammatical rules in complete ignorance. The avoidance of the split infinitive is not a grammatical rule. The split infinitive is very often ugly and best avoided, but in unskilled hands its avoidance may produce something much uglier and more doubtful of meaning : *We expect the young American to attain speedily high rank among racing drivers*. What on earth is *speedily high rank* ? The usual solution is : *We expect the young American speedily to attain* . . . , but there are cases where the adverb in the position of *speedily* may inescapably appear to belong to the word preceding it, instead of to the infinitive from which it has been extracted. In the following sentence, for instance, the most uncompromising opponent of the split infinitive could not alter the position of *deliberately* without making the meaning ridiculous : *Most men will hesitate to deliberately avoid irksome responsibilities incurred by chance*. The sentence might be recast as : . . . *hesitate at deliberately avoiding* . . . , but that is no essential condemnation of the split infinitive.

HARD-WORKED VERBS THAT LACK A TENSE

THE verbs *can*, *may*, *must*, and *ought* are unfortunately all defective : *must* and *ought* have no past tense, for instance, and none of them have any future tense. The distinction between *can* and *may* is often forgotten. *Can he come with us ?*, for instance, means *Will he be able to come ?—to leave his work ?—to walk as fast as we do ?*, etc. *May he come with us ?*, on the other hand, means *Has he permission to join us ?—Do you object to his coming ?* *Can* and *may* become *could* and *might* in the past, and this should be remembered when words are quoted in indirect speech :

He asked if he might come ; I said I could come to-morrow, but not to-day.

A sentence such as : *No books may be removed without permission* is sometimes altered to : *No books must* . . ., *etc.* This form means that no one is bound to remove any book without permission, but that there is nothing against any one doing so if he wishes ! The negative of *Books must be removed* is *Books must not be removed*. Or, comparing the correct and incorrect forms above in a parallel phrasing, they mean re-

13

spectively : *No books are allowed to be removed* and *No books are bound to be removed*.

Ought must never be used with *did* or *had*, as in : *He didn't ought, I hadn't ought to have done it*. The negative is : *He ought not, I ought not to have done it*. The simplest form for the past is *had* : *He had to do it, I hadn't to do it*.

TWO VERBS THAT BRISTLE WITH COMPLICATIONS

To express the simple future, with no implication of determination, compulsion, or promise, *shall* is used for the first person and *will* for the second and third persons : *I shall, we shall be there ; you, he, she, it, they, will be there*. But there are many more complications than these in the uses of *shall* and *will*. *Will* is used in the first person to show determination : *I will have my own way* (in speech the emphasis comes heavily on *will*). *Shall* is used in the second and third persons to imply a command or a promise : *You shall die ! They shall do as they are told ; he shall have it in the morning*.

The past tenses of *shall* and *will* are *should* and *would*, but are used mainly to form the conditional mood (more vividly described as the future-in-the-past) : *I should have hurried if I had known I was late*. In this sentence the hurrying would have been subsequent to the realisation of being late, though both events are now recounted in the past. For a simple conditional statement *should*, like *shall*, is reserved for the first person, and *would*, like *will*, for the second and third : *we should have hurried, they would have, you would have, he would have hurried*, etc. Comparably to *will*, however, *would* is used for all three persons to imply determination : *I would have my own way* (with emphasis on *would*). And again, *should* is used for all three persons to imply an obligation : *I should, he should, they should, we should not go to bed so late*.

A GOLDEN RULE FOR OMISSIONS

A FULL phrase such as : *As safe as or safer than the bicycle* is often wrongly abbreviated to : *As safe or safer than the bicycle*. This is equivalent to : *Safer than the bicycle or as safe as the bicycle*. When the comparing word is the same for both comparisons it need not, however, be repeated : *As safe and comfortable as the bicycle* implies *as safe as and as comfortable as*.

One of the if not the last specimens of his race is a horrible mixture of *one of the last specimens* and *the last specimen*.

One cannot pick on either *specimen* or *specimens* to do duty for both singular and plural at the same time. The sentence must be corrected to either of the following : *One of the last specimens, if not the last specimen, of his race ; one of the last specimens of his race, if not the last (of all, etc.).*

Other examples of wrongful omission are illustrated by the bracketed words, which some people would incorrectly omit, in the following :

The substance has now (dissolved) or should shortly dissolve. A simple experiment shows that the activity of ozone is much greater than (that of) oxygen.

Another instance is : *The judge remanded and granted Jones bail,* which must be altered to : *The judge remanded Jones and granted him bail.* Though *Jones* is the object of *remanded,* the succeeding word *bail* drags *Jones* after it, cutting off *Jones,* as it were, from its power of harking back to *remanded* which it can exercise in the simple form : *The judge remanded and released Jones.*

A golden rule in general is : never to be afraid of repeating a word as many times as are necessary for correct grammar and for making the meaning absolutely clear.

WHERE THE ALTERNATIVE SHOULD GO

EITHER must be followed by *or, neither* by *nor,* and the adjective *not* by *nor,* when alternatives are expressed, as in : *The obstructionists were determined that no progress should be made, nor business transacted, while their demands remained unsatisfied. Either, neither, not,* and similar words which may be used to express alternatives must be placed immediately before the alternatives which they present. The following, for instance, is incorrect : *The handkerchief is either worn in the sleeve or drooping from the breast-pocket.* This should read : *The handkerchief is worn either in the sleeve . . .* The handkerchief is being worn in either case ; the alternatives are *in the sleeve* and *drooping from the breast-pocket,* and the alternative words *either* and *or* should be directly attached to these phrases.

The same rule applies to *both* : *both in England and in France,* not *both in England and France,* since the phrases to be compared are in *England, in France,* and not *in England, France. Both* used as an adverb in this manner must be followed by *and.* It is not uncommon to find such phrases as : *Of interest both to the editor as well as to the members of the public involved.* If *both* is omitted its function is still performed by *as well as.* One of the two is redundant. One should put either : *Of interest both to the editor and to . . .,* or *of interest to the editor as well as to. . . .* In fact the original example was equivalent to : *. . . both to the editor both to the members of the public involved. Both* binds two things together ; thus it is spoiled by adding such a word as *equally* or *between* to separate the things again, as in such bad examples as : *Both of them were equally ready to give way.* (The two of them, taken indissolubly together, as connected by *both,* cannot be in any way " equal " to each other taken separately.) *It is possible to choose between both the old and the new styles.* (Read either *the old or the new styles,* omitting *between,* or keep *between* and omit *both.*)

Hesitation to use *and* as the proper sequel to *both* or *between* arises generally in a long sentence, from fear that the *and* will be lost, or perhaps confused with some other *and,* as in the example used earlier for another purpose :

> We have to decide between a reduction of the tax
> and a decrease in trade, and an increase in the tax
> and no trade at all.

The middle *and* of the three must be preserved ; the two halves of the comparison might be differentiated more sharply, however, by adding *on the one hand* and *on the other hand.*

Either and *neither* when used as pronouns apply to choice between two things only ; one must speak of *any of the angles of a triangle,* not *either angle,* or *neither angle. Neither* used as an adverb, however (*i.e.* where it does not replace a noun or describe a noun), may express choice between as many things as you please :

> " Neither my place, nor aught I heard of business,
> Hath raised me from my bed ; nor doth the general
>   care
> Take hold on me."

Neither is here equivalent to *not.*

COUPLING WORDS THAT ARE SOMETIMES MISUSED

*D*UE to is not a preposition-phrase like *owing to. Due* is still purely an adjective or participle, and therefore must be attached to a noun or pronoun. Thus we may say :

It is due to my early upbringing that I am fond of the sea (where *due* qualifies the indefinite *it*) ; or we may say : *Owing to my early upbringing, etc. . . .*, or, *On account of my early upbringing . . .*, but on no account should we say : *Due to my early upbringing I am fond of the sea.* A rule which will roughly cover most cases is : never use *due to* at the beginning of a sentence or phrase.

Try to do a thing, not *try and*, as though the trying were a different process from the doing, as in : *Go and do it.*

I did not think of doing it, not *think to do it.* *Think* cannot be followed by an infinitive, as *remember* and *intend* can, unless it means *expect*, e.g. : *I did not think to see you again.*

It cannot happen unless they know of it, not *without they know of it.* *Without* is not now a conjunction, though once it was.

The reason is that his deafness prevented him, not *The reason is because his deafness prevented him.* *The reason* is itself the " because " of the matter.

One should never be afraid of putting a preposition at the end of a sentence or phrase if the meaning is made clearer thereby. A final preposition is often ugly, but its rigid avoidance is as great a bugbear with some people as the split infinitive. *Too commonplace to be worth looking at* cannot possibly be altered to the form : *too commonplace at which to be worth looking.*

HOW COMPARISONS SHOULD BE EXPRESSED

LIKE is a preposition, *as* a conjunction. *Like* is used with nouns and pronouns only ; it governs them in the accusative case, like any other preposition : *like him, like me*, etc. *As* must be used for all other comparisons between clauses, phrases, or sentences. The four sentences following are correct :

> He was obstinate, like his predecessors.
> He was obstinate, as his predecessors were.
> Why don't you try to keep cool, like him ?
> Why don't you try to keep cool, as he does ?

Than is not a preposition, and consequently is not followed by the accusative case : *taller than I*, not *taller than me* ; *less young than he*, not *less young than him.* *Than whom*, however, has established itself, though it is often best avoided ; according to the Oxford Dictionary it is the only example of the use of *than* as a preposition.

The word *prefer* is not followed by *than* : prefer *A to B*, not prefer *A than B*. *Prefer* itself includes the sense of comparison for which *than* is sometimes falsely introduced, on the analogy of such phrases as *more desirable than* ; *prefer* means to like better than. Hence also, the adjective *preferable* cannot be qualified by *more*. If you prefer a thing you like it more than some other thing ; you do not need to say that you find it " more like-moreable " than the other thing.

Equally as is nonsense. *One is as wild as the other*, or *They are equally wild*, but not *One is equally as wild as the other*.

In comparisons, adjectives and adverbs sometimes become confused. The commonest instance is in such phrases as : *He dresses smarter than the rest*. *He dresses smartly* is obviously right ; the comparative is therefore *more smartly*. The mistake is as bad as : *He likes his beer regular*, or *He walks similar to you*. *Fast*, of course, can be both adjective and adverb ; *He runs faster* is therefore correct.

Every one agrees that *much different from* or *very improved* is wrong, but there are many cases harder to decide. The rule is that *very* goes with an adjective, and *much* with a participle —a real participle that is not being used as an adjective at the time. This may be illustrated by the following examples in which one word is employed in different uses. In the sentence : *The report of my death was much exaggerated* (*i.e.* by some one or other), *was exaggerated* is the complete verb of which the participle *exaggerated* forms part, but in the sentence : *The tyre expanded to a very exaggerated size before it burst*, *exaggerated* is a pure adjective ; it is the size that is exaggerated beyond the usual.

A FEW HINTS ABOUT CHOOSING WORDS

ERRORS in vocabulary, as in many other matters of custom and usage, are often more serious when committed by the person who thinks himself correct than when due to natural ignorance or simplicity. While the general standard of writing in popular literature, newspapers, and periodicals is probably rising, it is still disfigured by too many examples of what H. W. Fowler has admirably christene " elegant variation." Elegant variation may be permissibl in matters where elegance is the chief end intended : *dress, frock, robe,* and *gown*, for instance, though each word may have some special uses, are very imperfectly differentiated. But in other matters elegant variation is every day tending to ruin the meaning of useful words which have, or once had, a distinct meaning of their own. It cannot be too often repeated that in writing good English there are no upper-class and no lower-class words ; there are only words appropriate or inappropriate to one's meaning. It is the class-conscious who cause so much trouble with vocabulary—the people who say, for instance, *your psychology* when they mean *your mind*, or *Epic in the North Sea* when they mean *Brave deed in the North Sea*, or *Heroism in the North Sea*.

The objection to *psychology* and *epic* in these contexts is not a class-conscious objection ; it is a protest made necessary because *psychology* his its own specialised meaning as the study of the mind, and *epic* has its own specialised meaning as a long poem celebrating heroic achievements—the *Odyssey* or Dante's *Inferno*, for instance. The essence of the objection is not merely that these are the older meanings of *psychology* and *epic*, for many words in everyday use have changed their meanings unexceptionally in the last five hundred years ; it is that if the newer " meanings " prevail, there will no longer be single words to express the study of the mind, or a long heroic poem. In the list below of words subject to misuse, distinction of meaning is in each case the reason for the distinction of words ; the one exception, perhaps, is the word " *humans*," which is not yet recognised, in literary English, as a noun equivalent to *human beings*. It was never used as a noun, except facetiously or in children's fairy stories, until the early years of this century ; it is becoming so useful, however, that it seems likely that fifty years may see its complete establishment as a noun.

A good example of meaningless and confusing variation comes from a chemistry handbook :

> Whilst we will concede the name nitro-cellulose to the commercial world, we will reserve for the laboratory sphere the more correct appellation cellulose nitrate.

Probably most amateur writers could with advantage write more simply than they do. The effort is very necessary, though it is in fact harder to write the simple English of Swift or Bernard Shaw than the florid English of Carlyle or of an average local newspaper.

Another danger to vocabulary, as great as that of elegant

variation, is what I. A. Richards calls the projectile use of words. Words like *awfully* and *ghastly* are first associated with certain emotions and are then flung into the breach simply to signify those emotions. There is an element of this degradation in the misuse of *epic*. Other examples are *years !* and *hours !* to mean any period of time which seems long, and *minutes !* or *seconds !* for any period which seems short.

A third danger, that of genteel substitution, is fortunately less prevalent since the post-War return to the vocabulary which had been normal to English all through its history until the early nineteenth century. More and more people nowadays say *bitch* for a female dog, reserving the false *lady-dog* for a dog with ladylike manners, if they use the word at all. *Belly* is also returning to its own ; *stomach* for *belly* is of exactly the same order of inexactitude as *lungs* for *chest*. It is interesting to observe that *serviette* for *napkin* has become so widespread that to use *napkin* may often be legitimately thought an affectation to-day—a genteelism ungenteelised !

A LIST OF WORDS LIABLE TO MISUSE

AFFECT and EFFECT : When one is affected by anything one is moved, perhaps deeply ; one's affections are very likely engaged or one's affairs are involved. There is no noun *affect* except as a technical term in psychology. When anything is *effected* it is performed : *They effected an entrance.* It is all over ; the *effect* or result desired has been produced. *Effectual* and *efficient* may also help in remembering the meaning of *effect*.

AGGRAVATE means to make worse, or make more grave. It does not mean to annoy. It is thus incorrect to say : *What an aggravating child you are !*

AS TO WHETHER is a useless phrase. *Whether* covers all the possible meanings : *The question whether he will stay or not has soon settled itself.*

CASE as a vague word referring to a matter or occasion previously mentioned is subject to much abuse. It has been well riddled with ridicule by Quiller-Couch in his lecture on " Jargon " in *The Art of Writing*. In very many instances it is clearer to omit *case* or *in the case of*, e.g. : *In the case of late-comers a special fee will be charged.* Why not : *Late-comers will be charged a special fee* ? With *case* may b classified *side*, *part*, and some other words which are often vainly juggled with in an attempt to differentiate one abstract instance from another, e.g. : *On the psychological side there is nothing to object to in the conditions of labour.* This means : *From the psychological point of view,* etc. *When we come to the international part of the dispute* probably means : *When we come to the international aspect.* . . . With *side, part, aspect,* etc., the important thing is to decide whether a difference of viewpoint from the outside is indicated, as by *aspect,* a division of content, as by *part,* or a division of function, which can sometimes be expressed by *side* : *He is weak on the mathematical side,* and sometimes by *output* or other words according to the context. It is essential to make clear by the differentiating word exactly the kind of differentiation which is intended.

CERTAIN is sometimes clumsily used where an actual example had better be given :

> Suppose a man makes a certain proposal to another man, and this man refuses to do this certain thing.

If this sentence must be kept in general terms, it should be simplified to : *If a man makes a proposal to another* (*man*) *and is refused.* The indefinite article *a* should generally be indefinite enough by itself, and *certain* is acquiring a nasty flavour from its frequent use in newspapers to avoid prosecution : *He made witness a certain proposal.* *A proposal* would be quite as good. The unskilled writer often uses the indefinite *certain* when a well-chosen example would add both life and meaning to his sentence ; the definite can often well indicate the indefinite, so long as a pure abstraction or generalisation is not required, *e.g.* the first of the following three is the most vivid :

> A " Second Mrs. Tanqueray " scandal would be impossible to-day ; even the third Mrs. Tanqueray would excite little comment.
>
> There would be no scandal to-day about the plays which shocked the last century.
>
> A certain play which caused much scandal in the last century would hardly excite comment to-day.

COMPOSE and COMPRISE : *Comprise* means comprehend or include, and is often replaceable by *include* : *The house includes* (*or comprises*) *three bedrooms,* but *The house is composed of three bedrooms, two sitting-rooms, etc.*

CONTEXT means the text, printing or writing, which is with (con) something already mentioned. The context of " fair round belly with fat capon lined " is :

> " And then the justice
> (In fair round belly, etc. . . .)
> With eyes severe, and beard of formal cut,
> Full of wise saws and modern instances."

Context has no meaning unless there is something for it to act as context to.

CONTINUANCE and CONTINUATION : The continuance of something is the mere fact of its continuing to be in existence ; the continuation of something is the active causing of it to continue or to extend when it might otherwise die or disappear, or it may mean the portion which is added on, the extension : *The continuance of distress gives His Majesty much concern. The continuation of the debate on these measures is fixed for Friday*. It is incorrect to write : *the continuation of these measures next year*, if the measures remain the same and no Act is needed to continue them for another year ; *the continuation of the time of operation of these measures* is a correct use of continuation.

CREDIBLE and CREDITABLE : One sometimes finds : *It is hardly creditable that . . .* in mistake for : *It is hardly credible that. . . .* The confusion arises from the double application of *credit* : to credit or believe a story, and to credit a person with good or bad qualities.

DISINTERESTED means without any axe to grind. *A disinterested spectator would have said that both the home and the visiting teams were guilty of foul play* : this disinterested spectator was deeply interested in the game—if he had been uninterested in football he would not have been there—but it was not to his interest to favour one team or the other, since all were strangers to him. *Disinterested* is derived from *interest* as used in the sense : *It's in your interests that I advise you. Uninterested* is the negative derived from *interest* in the commoner sense. Whether one starts without any interest in the game, or loses interest as the game goes on, one is in either case uninterested. *Dis-* in *disinterested* has not the sense of undoing something, like *dis-* in *disconnect*.

EFFECT, see AFFECT.

e.g. is always written in small letters (*e.g.*), stands for *exempli gratia*, and means *for example*. *i.e.* is also written with small letters, stands for *id est*, and means *that is*. The abbreviations are obviously not interchangeable.

EGOISTIC is applied to a person who refers all his ideas and actions to the advantage or disadvantage they are likely to bring to himself. It does not imply a person who is simply much preoccupied with himself—self-absorbed, or introspective—nor a person who regards things subjectively, *i.e.*, as many poets do, through a strong colouring of his own emotions, instead of objectively, as an impartial investigator would.

ENAMOURED OF, not enamoured with.

ETC. should not be used out of laziness, when the *cetera*—the rest, the things that follow—could not be guessed with certainty by the reader. It is permissible to say : *They set off with a great load of picks, shovels, stakes, hammers, etc., to break up the road,* because the rest of the tools required can be guessed from those named ; but the following is bad : *Being an illiterate person, he knew nothing of Shakespeare, Milton, etc.* ; a general effect was here intended, and some such general phrase as *English literature* should have been used.

EXIT is singular ; *exeunt* is plural. *Exit the Die-Hards* will not do.

ILK means same, and nothing else. Englishmen never need the word. *Macintosh of that ilk* means Macintosh of the place called Macintosh.

INDIVIDUAL as a noun should not be used unless it means a person considered individually, in contrast with the group of which he is a member. *A seedy-looking individual* could probably be found in Dickens for a *seedy-looking person*, but is not correct, even facetiously. An example of the correct use is : *At first sight the Dinka seem a very fierce people, but the individual generally turns out to be quite amiable.*

INSTINCT must not be used loosely for any deep impulse, intuition, or inclination. A bad case in a newspaper was : *Perhaps, in spite of their deepest instincts, they gave way to the inclination to sleep and lay down in the snow. Instinct* might be used for *sleep,* but certainly not for the acquired knowledge that sleeping in the snow means almost certain death. An instinct is a fundamental tendency—to build nests, to burrow in the ground, to breed children—ingrained in the individual, man or animal, and derived not only from his own experience, but as a rule from the experience of countless generations of ancestors.

INFER and IMPLY mean much the same as *deduce* and *suggest*. *The master inferred from the shuffling of feet that the class wished to imply that the lesson was over.* The two words are not inter-changeable.

LAY and LIE. The difference beween these two verbs is that *lay* is transitive, that is, it is used with an object, as in the sentence *I lay the book down on the table*, and *lie* is intransi-tive. It is wrong to say *I lie the book down* or to say *I lay down to sleep but begin to read.* Confusion also arises because the present tense of *lay* is the same in form as the past tense of *lie.* Thus *I lay down and went to sleep* is correct. *I lay down and go to sleep*, on the contrary, is grammatically wrong. The past tense of *lay* is *laid : I laid it down just now.* The past participle of *lay* is *laid* and of *lie* is *lain.* The commonest pitfalls lurk in such sentences as the following : *Having lain down* (not *laid down*) *for an hour, I felt rested* and *I was lying down* (not *laying down*) *after dinner.*

LITERALLY means : in the actual letter of the sense. *Literally roasted* means : cooked like a joint of beef, at a similar tempera-ture and to the same extent. In its vulgar use as a mere in-tensifier, *literally* is used when the exact opposite—*figuratively* —is really implied : *I was literally melted that afternoon !*

OBLIVIOUS OF what goes on (not " to what goes on."). *Unconscious of* or *insensible to* are more exact in many of the modern instances of the word.

OUGHT is an inexcusable vulgarism for nought. The word does not exist except as a verb.

PART, see CASE.

QUITE means *entirely, completely*, and therefore cannot be qualified, as is sometimes attempted in *almost quite.*

REFER is a word much overworked. It often needs differ-entiating into such meanings as : quote, adduce, confirm, say. *Refer* covers a very limited number of the relationships possible between one statement and another.

SAME, SUCH, SAID. *Same* and *Such* as nouns, and *said* as an adjective, are a mark of the very unskilled writer. *Same* is generally resorted to in the fear of repeating a word, or of using a homely pronoun : *am hopeful of obtaining same*— why not *obtaining it ?*

SIDE, see CASE.

SUBSTITUTE. *To substitute* means to put in place of, and nothing else, e.g. : *During the War margarine was substituted for butter.* One should put the thing which replaces first.

and so avoid the mistake : *Butter was substituted by margarine* (instead of *replaced by margarine*).

THE is sometimes unnecessarily introduced by unskilled writers before a word unfamiliar to them, as though they were afraid to handle it without gloves : *Bacon was the first Englishman to delve deep into the philosophy* (instead of *into philosophy*).

UNIQUE means : alone of its kind, and therefore cannot be qualified by rather, almost, or other words.

HOW TO IMPROVE YOUR SPELLING

WORDS ending in *-ful*, whether nouns like *handful* or adjectives like *awful*, have a single *l*. To form adverbs from these adjectives add *-ly* : *awfully*, *peacefully*.

Words ending in a mute *e* drop the *e* before a vowel, in forming compounds, but not before a consonant : *lovable*, *loving*, *lovely*, *liking*, *likable*, *likely*, etc. There are a few exceptions for reasons of pronunciation, to distinguish between *singing* and *singeing*, for instance ; the *e* is preserved when it is needed to keep a *g* or *c* soft, as in *peaceable*. Other exceptions are words of one syllable such as *true*, which form compounds such as *truly*, *duly*, *wholly*, etc.

Capital letters belong to proper nouns only. It is illiterate to use them for any word which chances to be outstanding, or for the title of a piece of writing when repeated in the body of the writing, as when a schoolboy writes : " *We now come to the real Advantages of the Cinema.*" A word may need a capital or a small letter at different times, according as it is a proper or a common noun :

> The government of the country was in the hands of a clique ; The Government took office yesterday.
> Returning to the old School ; Running to school in the morning.

The plural forms of some classes of word cause difficulty : *a phenomenon*, *a criterion*, *a bacterium*, *a curriculum*, *an erratum*, *a stratum*, *a memorandum*, but several *phenomena*, *criteria*, *bacteria*, *curricula*, *errata*, *strata*, *memoranda*. Words ending in *-y* add *-s* for their plural if the *y* is preceded by a vowel—*key*, *keys*—but change *-y* into *-ies* if it is preceded by a consonant—*sty*, *sties*. Words ending in *-o* are not completely classifiable. Fowler suggests eight classes which still admit of a few exceptions. But the words most in use, and the oldest words, as a rule have *-oes* in the plural: *potatoes*, *tomatoes*, *banjoes*, *noes*, *negroes*, etc. Less common words, and words in which a vowel precedes the *-o*, generally have no *e* in the plural: *octavos*, *patios*. When it is necessary to write the plural of a letter of the alphabet, an apostrophe is necessary to avoid a possible misreading as a word of two letters, e.g.: *there are two a's in algebra*. This is the only case in which an apostrophe is used to indicate a plural. The plurals of proper names, however awkward, are indicated by adding *-s* or *-es* in the ordinary way: *there are few Spartas in the world to-day ; the Jameses have asked us to tea.*

A LIST OF SPELLING TRAPS

ALL RIGHT. (There is no such word as " alright.")

ANTI- means against, and *ante-* before, as in *antiseptic* and *ante-chamber*.

AY for *yes* and *aye* for *ever* seem standardised, except that the plural is *ayes*, in : *the ayes have it.* Pronounce *ay* to rhyme with *eye* and *aye* to rhyme with *eh*.

BRIT- : the only word with two t's from this root is *Brittany*. Others are : *Britannia, Briton, Britain.*

CHOOSE has past tense *chose*.

CINEMA, not *kinema*. *Kinema* meant something else in Ancient Greek, and was accented differently, and a film theatre in modern Greece is called a *sinema*, with a Greek s.

COMMODE, COMMODIOUS—hence *accommodation* (two c's, two m's).

COMPARATIVELY : Two a's, as in *comparable*, though the latter word is accented differently, *i.e.* on the first syllable.

DESICCATED : the prefix is *de-*, the root *sicc-*, therefore only one s is needed.

DISAPPOINT : the prefix is *dis-* ; so only one s is necessary.

EMBARRASS, *embarrassment*, have two r's and two s's.

HARASS has only one r.

HUMOROUS, from *humour*. Also *vigorous, vaporous, odorous*, etc. But derivatives in *-ist, -able*, keep the *u* : *humourist, colourable.*

LICENCE is the noun and *license* the verb. Similarly *practice* and *practise.*

LOSE and LOOSE : the verb *to loose* means to set free or to loosen, and is now mainly biblical in use.

NECESSITY : ne-cessity—hence ne-cessary, in spite of the accent's moving from the second to the first syllable.

PARALLEL, *paralleled, unparalleled.*

PENINSULA : Britain is an insular kingdom. The adjective *insular* gives the adjective *peninsular*, used of Monaco, for instance : *this tiny peninsular state.* But Monaco is situated on a *peninsula.*

PRECEDE and PROCEED : *Accede, cede, concede, intercede, recede, secede*, but *exceed, succeed.* No rule can help.

PRINCIPAL and PRINCIPLE : *Principle* means an article of faith or belief, or a universal law, e.g. *the principle of equality before the law.* The other word was originally an adjective—*principal actors*, etc.—and in every case where it is used as a noun it could be converted back into an adjective qualifying a suppressed noun which could be reinserted : principal (sum of money), principal (officer or teacher of a college), principal (person in a suit or negotiation)—*I must consult my principal* means : I must consult the person for whom I am acting.

SEPARATE, either adjective or verb ; *-a-* as in *reparation.*

SIMILE, plural *similes.*

WOOLLEN (two l's).

SOME USEFUL REFERENCE BOOKS

A VERY small number of books suffices for a complete guide to every technical matter of correctness in the English language. The only comprehensive dictionary of both common and uncommon errors and difficulties is the invaluable *Dictionary of Modern English Usage*, by H. W. Fowler (author, with his brother, of the *Concise Oxford Dictionary* and the *Pocket Oxford Dictionary*). This book discusses points in grammar, vocabulary, punctuation, style, and spelling, in a full, clear, and often very amusing manner, and some of the section-headings, such as Elegant Variation and Sturdy Indefensibles, are so useful that they seem likely to become recognised technical terms. This dictionary is alphabetical in arrangement ; much of its contents, often with fuller examples, is to be found under different arrangement in an equally amusing book by the brothers Fowler— *The King's English.*

For those who are seriously troubled by the anomalous English spelling system, there are various manuals, such as *The New Era Spelling Manual*, which arrange difficulties intelligently in classes, and are as practicable for adults as

for school-children. An equally suitable grammar of modern
English, however, is a much more difficult book to find. A
foreigner acquainted with the grammar of his own language
might prefer the formal grammar books which give tables of
the " cases " of English nouns, and the personal and other
forms of English verbs. He would soon discover, however,
that much simplification was necessary, while he would continue to be puzzled by subtle distinctions and modes of
thought which did not exist in his own language, or for which
there were no words, at least, in his own language. He would
then join with the questioning adult Englishman in welcoming
a book which discusses function rather than form, such as the
very stimulating *Our Living Language*, by Grattan and
Gurrey. Some parts of this book are very difficult, for the
adequate reason that it is impossible, in dealing with such a
subtle language as English, to make them any simpler. The
most complete and authoritative grammar for reference purposes is the *Modern English Grammar* of Professor Jespersen,
a Dane who writes in English.

IN SEARCH OF THE "MOT JUSTE"

A BOOK whose usefulness is sometimes misconceived is
Roget's Thesaurus of Words and Phrases. This is a dictionary of synonyms and antonyms, *i.e.* of words and phrases
of similar and of opposite meaning. Suppose one is search-
ing for a word to mean " severe, so that it cannot be avoided " ;
one has met with such a word somewhere, but cannot remember it. Under *severe* in the index to the *Thesaurus*
one finds eight classes of use for this word : *energetic, symmetry, exact, severe in style, harsh, painful, simple, critical.*
Harsh is nearest to the desired meaning, and turning up
harsh in the body of the book one runs through a number of
words indicating harshness until one reaches the wanted
word—*inexorable*. The meaning of *inexorable* may then be
checked from an ordinary dictionary, or more precisely by
turning it up again in the index, and tracing its uses under the
six headings there given. A dictionary of synonyms is useful
enough, but it should not be used simply as a museum of
strange words. Words do not live until they have been in
use in an actual context ; to pick *inexorable* at random to mean
severe, never having come across it before, would obviously
be dangerous ; one cannot speak, for instance, of inexorable
treatment, though one may of harsh treatment. *Crabb's*

English Synonyms, and some other dictionaries of synonyms, have the advantage of including examples of the use of most of the words with which they deal ; the *Thesaurus* covers so many words and cross-references that to include examples would probably make it of an impracticable size.

A dictionary of quotations is a necessary assistant, if only to keep one from writing *A thing of beauty and a joy for ever*, when what Keats wrote was *A thing of beauty is a joy for ever*, or *Music hath charms to soothe the savage beast*, when what Congreve wrote was *Music hath charms to soothe a savage breast*.   To verify all one's quotations, even (or especially) the most familiar, is a further lesson in the correct use of English.   One of the fullest and most practical dictionaries of quotations, not only in English but in all the languages commonly quoted in England, is that of W. Gurney Benham. Its index is very full, and there are special sections for proverbs and Biblical quotations.

THE AUTHOR IN THE MAKING : SHORT STORIES AND BOOKS

by WYNYARD BROWNE

SINCE a definition of a story must include the stories of James Joyce as well as of Dorothy Sayers, of D. H. Lawrence as well as of P. G. Wodehouse, a story is not easy to define. The modern interest in psychology is such that many of our best stories contain very little action in the old sense. Mental events have, for a time at least, obtained as much importance in fiction as physical events. A story can, for instance, be made from the thoughts of a woman as she sits by the window in the evening, trying to make up her mind whether or not she shall leave her husband, finally deciding not to, and continuing to sit by the window. Many people would complain of this story that nothing happens. They would be inaccurate. A great deal happens in the woman's mind. In fact, the only essential of the story is that *something must happen*. A story is a description of an event or a series of events.

Having begun thus pedantically, we can proceed to slightly less cautious statements. Not forgetting Homer, who had the distinction of being represented in *Great Short Stories of the World*, stories are usually in prose. Not forgetting Rudyard Kipling, who has written them about bees and wild beasts, or Lord Dunsany, who has written them about fairies, stories are usually about human beings.

THE ARTIST AS A CRAFTSMAN

THERE is no antagonism between art and craft. A good artist must be a craftsman ; and the better craftsman he is, the better his work will be. There are unfortunately good craftsmen who are not artists. Their work can be seen any month in almost any fiction magazine. For though craftsmanship can be learned, imagination cannot.

Imagination will look after itself, provided that it is not pampered and protected. But it can be rendered as helpless and useless by lack of technique as a factory-owner with one who knows how to work his machines. Guy de Maupassant owes his supreme position among short-story writers, not so

402

much to his imagination as to the careful craftsmanship which he learned from Flaubert. This despised craftsmanship, an acquisition and not a gift, enabled him to present those events which his imagination formed, in a way so perfect that they seemed to achieve the comparative permanence of crystal.

Craftsmanship can only be learned by imitation. But the process of imitation is dangerous unless it is conscious and controlled. The danger to the imitator is twofold. He may imitate bad models or only the tricks and idiosyncrasies of good models. He may—and this is perhaps the more insidious danger—imitate the stories themselves and not merely the methods of story-telling employed by their authors. A vicious circle is produced in which he can make no progress. For though he may learn to produce replicas of the models he has chosen, he will never learn how to apply their technique to his own material.

All that this article can do is to make the process of imitation more conscious. It will enumerate some of the chief problems of story-writing and suggest the kind of solution which may be expected, but it is not intended as a substitute either for reading or for practice in writing.

THE AUTHOR'S PROCESS OF CREATION

IT is often said that no good writer goes out of his way to search for material, because he has more than he can deal with already. But this must not be thought to mean that the good writer has only to sit down at his desk and the story springs like a stream from the point of his pencil. All that it means is that if you live in a small country town or in a dreary suburb, there is no need to go to the south of France or join the Foreign Legion before you can write a story.

No one has a number of complete plots pigeon-holed in his mind without any effort on his part. On the contrary, the hardest work must be done before a word of the story is written. The exact nature of the process which must take place before the writing of the story begins is impossible to describe adequately. It has been called a fusion of past experiences into an organic whole. At any rate it is probably a function of memory. But this kind of statement is not much help to some one, for instance, who wants to write a detective story. Faced by a sheet of blank paper and bothered by his unemployed genius, he demands to be told how to think of a plot.

HOW TO FIND A PLOT

THE only practical suggestion which can be offered him with any confidence is that he should ask himself a series of questions about a person or a group of people, not necessarily connected with one another in fact, whom he knows or has known in the past. The first question should usually be conditional. " *What would happen if* the Fink-Drabbles went bankrupt ? What would happen if, after all these years, old Swiveleye fell in love ? " When this first question has been answered as fully as possible, it is likely that the elements of a plot will already be assembled, and the rest of the formative process will be automatic. But if not, more detailed questions can be asked with the same conditions. " If papa went bankrupt, would young Fink-Drabble go to Canada ? What would he do there ? Would he be popular? Why not ? " and so on, until the story takes shape.

But if even then the method fails, and the wretched author's mind is as blank as it ever was, there is still another chance. Let him bring into contact two or more very different characters, not necessarily connected with one another in fact. Let him place them in some specific relation to each other, and then begin to ask questions. " What would happen if old Swiveleye fell in love with Mrs. Fink-Drabble ? Or if, when Mr. Fink-Drabble went bankrupt, his kitchenmaid won the Irish sweep ? " This type of question can be almost guaranteed to produce a plot. Its disadvantage is that the relations between the characters are arbitrarily specified. All plots depend on relations between people. The difficulty of finding a new plot is the difficulty of finding a new human relationship. To start by specifying the relation is therefore inadvisable, because it can do no more than produce a familiar plot in a new guise. Nevertheless, that is all that many writers can hope to do.

When this method of question and answer has been tried without success till it becomes a bore, our hypothetical author had better give up short stories for a time at least and try writing dialogues for the movies. It is to be hoped, however, that such a mechanical and laborious method of plot-finding will seldom be needed. The faculty of imagination, set in motion by some chance stimulus or by events and experiences in the writer's own life, works without a goad. But in whatever way the plot has come into being, whether it has grown naturally in the mind or been assembled by deliberate device, only half the work necessary before the story is written has yet been done.

HOW TO MARSHAL THE CHARACTERS

THE next process is perhaps the most crucial. It concerns what has been called the " architectonics " of the story. Just as an architect must decide, before the building is begun, how many rooms it shall have and what their function shall be, where he will put the entrance hall, where the dining-room and the bathroom and the staircase, so the writer must select and arrange the different parts of his story. To start writing before a plan of this kind has been made is in most cases to produce a shapeless, clumsy, and perhaps futile object like a house of two floors with neither a staircase nor a lift.

The importance of this architectural process cannot be overstressed. Of course the selection and arrangement of incidents, characters, dialogue, description, and the rest are subordinate to the main idea or plot. But the plot cannot be properly presented, cannot be turned into a story, without selection and arrangement. It must be given a definite shape, with a beginning, a middle, and an end. These three must be closely knit together so that there are no uncomfortable gaps or hitches in the sequence of events. The end must follow logically from the beginning. The several parts of the story must be arranged conveniently for the reader so that he receives each bit of information just at the moment when that particular information is most effective. No one should begin to write a story until he has decided what incidents he intends to describe and in what order, what he intends to say about each character, and at what point in the story he intends to say it. The success of the story depends almost entirely upon decisions like this.

The only test is the author's own complete satisfaction. It often happens that, when a story is finished, the author feels vaguely and unaccountably dissatisfied. The story is not as good as he expected, and he cannot discover why. Nearly always the reason is that he has chosen to describe the wrong characteristics and incidents or put them in the wrong order. This sounds platitudinous ; but it is nevertheless remarkable that many of those who attempt to write short stories completely fail to realise that any process of selection is necessary, or that the effect of their stories depends upon the arrangement of the selected elements.

ROUSING THE READER'S INTEREST

ANYONE who has been employed, even for a day, in reading short stories submitted to a magazine, realises how vastly important is the first paragraph. If there is not something in that first paragraph to catch the reader's attention, even if he shall continue conscientiously to the end, he will have adopted an attitude of bored toleration which would prejudice his judgment of any story.

The first paragraph has two functions. First, it must provide a minimum of necessary information, either about the place and time or about one of the characters of the story ; in other words, it must be a beginning. Secondly, it must produce in the reader a desire to know more. Very often these two functions clash. Seldom is the information which the writer can afford to give in the first paragraph interesting enough in itself to stimulate the reader's curiosity. The mere information, in fact, is more likely to stifle it. And so the first problem arises : how to present the necessary information in such a way as to stimulate curiosity ? Of course, each story has its own solution. The details of the problem are different in every case. But as a general rule the only way to stimulate curiosity is to withhold, or to appear to withhold, information.

> " What a strange idea it was of mine that evening when I chose Mademoiselle Perle for my Queen ! "

That is the first sentence of a story by de Maupassant called *Mademoiselle Perle*. It provides scarcely any information, but it directly stimulates curiosity. Why was it strange ? and who was Mademoiselle Perle ? the reader is bound to ask. The next two pages are taken up with a tantalising description of the placid, retiring, respectable household in which Mlle Perle seems to be a sort of superior housekeeper. These pages which supply the information would be almost dull had they not been thoroughly injected with mystery by the first sentence. This type of solution, by which the reader is first made curious and then forced to swallow the information as a means of satisfying his curiosity, is perhaps the commonest. But it can easily be abused.

Many stories do not admit of so obvious and undisguised a bait to the reader. They need more subtle treatment and they are undoubtedly harder to begin. A story, for instance, the force of which depends upon the fact that, although the events were strange or tragic, the people were ordinary and dull, will probably have to begin with a description of dull ordinary people. Unfortunately the description is likely also to be dull and ordinary unless some device is used. Somerset Maugham has written many stories of this kind, and perhaps his most successful device is to introduce the story as part of a conversation. He thus avoids the necessity of too much direct description, and the naturally dramatic qualities of dialogue encourage the reader. Incidentally, it may be said here that the works of Somerset Maugham can be studied more profitably by those in search of an unpretentious, adaptable, and efficient technique than the works of any other living writer.

Some stories plunge straight into the middle of the action:

> "Charlie Meadows was out of the window and disappearing down the garden path before I realised the significance of my own words.
> "'Now you've done it,' sobbed Mrs. Meadows. 'You'd better follow him quickly.'
> "I picked up my automatic from the desk and did as I was told."

This is a very decadent method. It is a desperate attempt to startle the jaded and surfeited reader from his lethargy. It seldom works, except in definitely comic stories, in which such shocks are the writer's stock in trade. If a story is any good, it can afford to begin quietly, and will only be damaged by this sort of distortion.

Sometimes it is even advisable to devote the first paragraph to creating atmosphere, a difficult business for which there are no tips or rules. A description of a tram, rattling and lurching outwards from the busy centre of a city, past cool parks and squares to a drab and ugly suburb on a hot summer afternoon, can often do more to stir curiosity and give more relevant information than any more direct approach.

But enough has probably been said to make it clear that, whatever else happens at the beginning of a story, by hook or by crook the reader's curiosity must be aroused.

HOW TO MAINTAIN THE READER'S INTEREST

IT is a mistake to imagine that readers are long-suffering. In these days, perhaps more than ever before, they are impatient ; and since it is the essence of a good story that it develops gradually, like a plant, and does not go up suddenly and fade suddenly, like a rocket, the impatient reader must be pacified, cajoled, and sometimes even deceived. If the opening paragraphs are of a specifically introductory or explanatory nature, they must either be very short or they must be disguised in such a way that the reader does not realise when he is reading them that they are merely explanatory. Rudyard Kipling, chiefly by a judicious humour and skilful compression, is expert at disguising explanations. An examination of the beginnings of his stories will show that he never gives the reader an opportunity to say, " Yes, yes, I know all this. Get on with it."

The reader is impatient, too, of tricks and coyness. He must be tantalised, but not too obviously. Many writers begin stories in the manner of complacent conjurors, as though they were saying, " Ah, wouldn't you like to know what I've got up my sleeve ? " which is perhaps even more to be shunned than mere dullness.

The beginning of a story is clearly a complicated business. The reader's interest must be aroused, the necessary information must be given, and he must not be given time to be bored nor opportunity to be annoyed. But it is equally important that his attention be directed towards the significant words, acts, and characteristics of the characters and towards the significant features of the place and time. There is no room in the short story for wandering attention. The reader must not be confused and, as it were, put off the scent by stress laid on a detail disproportionate to its place in the story. This is especially important at the beginning, because the reader does not yet know whither he is being led and therefore cannot perform an act of selection himself. It is the writer's business to see that he is led down the right paths and that what he remembers most clearly of the first page shall be that which he is intended to remember.

A most striking example of how this can be done is to be found in a story called *The Fountain Plays*, by Dorothy Sayers. The plot concerns Mr. Spiller, an escaped convict, who murders a man who is blackmailing him, only to find himself

Somerset Maugham : model of efficient, adaptable technique.

immediately blackmailed again by his butler for the very murder which was to free him from blackmail. The story opens with a long conversation between Mr. Spiller and some friends about a new ornamental fountain which he has just put into his garden. The conversation, which seems at first unnecessary, draws the reader's attention to two things, both of them very important; first, the apparently enviable financial and amorous position of Mr. Spiller, which is necessary for the irony of the story and of which the fountain is made the symbol; secondly, the fountain itself, which in the end, by wetting his victim's body, provides the butler's only evidence against him.

THE ART OF USING DIALOGUE

ERNEST HEMINGWAY, by a few tricks which are themselves little better than caricature, has started what may be a revolution in the use of dialogue. He has shown that it is possible to put into a few commonplace colloquial phrases all the atmosphere, character, and drama for which more traditional descriptive writers would need a couple of pages. His story " The Killers " in *Men without Women*, which is one of the most vivid and sinister stories that have ever been written, consists almost entirely of dialogue. There is no need for him to use those ineffectual adverbs and qualifying phrases—*grimly, angrily, sadly, with a sigh* or *with a puzzled frown*—which seem so important to many writers and which readers hardly notice. His dialogue is written so carefully that the reader knows, without being told, how it was spoken.

This should perhaps be the first object of the author of a short story, to write phrases and sentences which can only be spoken in one way. The anger, the fear, the sneer, the melancholy, or whatever emotion is supposed to accompany the words, must be inherent in the words themselves. But not only should it be obvious how the words were spoken; it should also be obvious, as far as possible, who spoke them. Hemingway, because he is not very interested in character, is not a good guide in this matter. His pages are sprinkled too lavishly with " saids." The reason for this is that his people are all alike, only distinguished one from another by the accidents which have happened to them in this unintelligible world.

FITTING THE DIALOGUE TO THE CHARACTERS

BUT for those who have not Hemingway's peculiar interest in " the dumb ox," as Wyndham Lewis has called his favourite type, it is a good disciplinary rule to write the word " said " as seldom as possible. For it then becomes essential, for clarity's sake, that each piece of dialogue shall be perfectly fitted to the character who speaks it, and that it be carefully arranged and woven neatly into the texture of the story. If a writer allows himself to specify the speaker every time, even when the scene is not crowded, he is likely to grow slack and to fall into the deadly error of thinking that in dialogue anything will do. Clarity, however, is more important than discipline, and nothing is more irritating to a reader than to have to go back to the beginning of a piece of dialogue and check up every sentence to see who said what. If it is found impossible to arrange the dialogue intelligibly without the word " said," then the word must of course be used.

THE VIVID QUALITY OF GOOD DIALOGUE

BUT although a little thought and practice can make it fairly clear how to write dialogue, it is not so easy to decide when to write it or for what purpose. That probably depends on the different facility of each individual writer. Some people can easily suggest in dialogue subtleties which they can express in no other way. Others, on the other hand, find that however hard they try, their dialogue retains a stilted and literary air, or is jerky, unrhythmical, and hard to read. Obviously the first type will employ dialogue more often and for more varied purposes than the second.

Its chief use is dramatic. " ' *I'm going to kill you*,' said the big man," is obviously a more vivid way of presenting the situation than : *The big man threatened to kill him*. Direct speech is in itself a kind of action, and the primary effect of the use of direct speech in stories is to make the presentation of action more lively. As a general rule, then, dialogue should be reserved for those parts of the story which are dramatic or need to be especially vivid. Of course, general rules must often be broken, and the most usual occasion for breaking this one arises when dialogue is to be used for the presentation of character.

There is no better and, for many writers, no easier way of distinguishing one from another of a group of people sitting round a tea-table, than to report their conversation. Their opinions on golf or mothers, expressed in their own words, can often fix them more certainly in the reader's mind than the most detailed description of their appearance or analysis of their characters. But when dialogue is used for this purpose it is important to choose opinions and phrases which throw light on just those sides of the character which have a bearing on the action. If the action depends, for instance, on the jealous nature of the chief character, it is a mistake to waste good dialogue on producing the information that she is fond of wild flowers. Emphasis must be laid on the significant points, and anything said in dialogue becomes emphatic.

CHARACTER : " THE LIFE-BLOOD OF FICTION "

UNDER the influence of political economy, many young writers have recently been insisting that their novels, unlike all other novels, would not deal with petty differences of individual character, but with great historical and socio- logical issues. " We have heard enough," they say, " of exactly how Michael or Peter got on with his parents, of exactly why Jennifer didn't marry George, and of exactly what Inez felt when she first got drunk. We are tired of psychology. We shall write of mass movements, class struggles, and historical forces." The impulse which makes them say this is intelligible and even admirable. But when they begin to write, they discover, perhaps to their disgust, perhaps to their secret relief, that the only way to present their great sociological issues is to depict some of the individuals involved.

Character is the life-blood of fiction. Even the most mathe- matical detective story or the most extravagant farce must at least pretend to deal with individuals. Laziness, lack of skill, or congenital incapacity may cause the writer to deal in fact with types. But except in fantasies and allegories this is a fault, not a virtue. Even the ordinary reader, who has never considered the unbreakable connection between variations of action and variations of character, only cares to read about individuals. " The characters," he demands, " must come alive. I will not read about abstractions. I want to feel that I have met the people about whom I have read, and that I should recognise them if I saw them in the street." Here then is an intricate problem for the short-story writer : how

to make characters " come alive " in the few thousand words
at his disposal.

What might be called the standard method is to begin by
a brief description of the type and species to which the character belongs, his profession, age, qualities, and physical
appearance. The details are then filled in by dialogue and
behaviour as the story develops. The danger of this method
is that the directly descriptive part is likely to bore the reader.
It has been used so often and applied to so many thousands
of characters that it is apt to seem stale almost before the
story has begun.

Then there is the subjective method, by which the person's
immediate thoughts and feelings are set down in such a way
as to reveal his character. This is only effective if it is done
in great detail, or if the character is one whose thoughts
are likely to be interesting or amusing in themselves. Nothing is more jejune and unconvincing than a few stray thoughts,
and there is seldom room for enough detail in a short story.

To avoid staleness and to preserve brevity, recent short-
story writers have devised a method of suggestion which is a
combination of these two with the addition of comments,
metaphors, and comparisons by the author. It is a haphazard
business, sometimes very effective, sometimes merely absurd.

> " Should he or should he not turn the young puppy
> out of the house ? In spite of his training, he was
> not very good at making decisions. Like a sea-lion
> at feeding-time, he sat up in his deck-chair and barked
> huskily. George, wondering vaguely whether the
> purple of his face was due to alcohol or sunburn,
> poured him out a whisky. He drank deeply and
> bellowed again.
> " ' That young fellow Fortescue's an ass.' "

This passage is a portrait of an Indian colonel by the hit-or-
miss method of suggestion, not at its best but at its most
obvious.

Each of these methods has some serious drawback—the
danger of staleness, of verbosity, of caricature, or of fiasco.
But there remains one which, though difficult, is more sound
and more trustworthy. The narrator limits his apparent
functions to that of a reporter. He allows himself neither
superhuman insight into the thoughts and feelings of his
people nor the pleasure of literary display and descriptive

virtuosity. He gives as briefly as possible the information about them necessary to the plot—that Mr. Welldon, for instance, is the vicar of a small country parish in East Anglia and that Toni is a Dutch gigolo domiciled at Juan-les-Pins. He then proceeds to tell precisely and without comment what Mr. Welldon and Toni did and what they said to each other. By careful selection of incident and manipulation of dialogue, Mr. Welldon and Toni can be made to " come alive " ; can be differentiated from all other clergymen and all other gigolos. Character, in fact, can be made to emerge in speech and action.

FICTION IS FOUNDED ON FACT

" THE characters of the stories in the —— *Magazine* are entirely imaginary and have no reference to real persons." If the stories are any good, this statement in itself is fiction. Every imaginary character which has the slightest resemblance to a human being must have some reference to real persons. The imagination cannot function in the void. Even mythical animals like the centaur or the unicorn are compiled of features taken from actually existing animals and combined so as to make a new imaginary animal. The creative imagination can do no more than form these new combinations. The red beard of the local police-woman is combined with the ill-temper of the author's aunt to make the tyrannical landlady of his imagination. This character will indeed be imaginary, but it will have direct reference to two real persons. Most imaginary characters have references, direct or indirect, to many more than two real persons.

But quite apart from the present state of the law of libel, under which it is possible for an unhappy author to be found guilty of libelling some one whom he has never seen or heard of, actual portraits of living people are seldom successful in fiction. The writer's invention is shackled by fact. So long as he is attributing to the character actions, thoughts, and experiences which he knows the living person to have had, there is little or no difficulty. He is not writing fiction. He is writing biography or gossip. But when the exigencies of the story make it necessary to exceed the limits of facts, to write not from knowledge but by invention, he is apt to find himself suddenly incapacitated. Fact and fiction will not blend easily in a faithful portrait. A muddled, unconvincing, inconsistent character results, which is unlikely to " come alive."

Fictional characters must be founded on the writer's knowledge of living people ; but, nine times out of ten, they are better when no attempt has been made at portraiture.

THE SECRETS OF DESCRIPTION

REALISM has made the writing of fiction much more difficult. It is no longer respectable to give fantastic or conventional descriptions of activities or places. If you describe a game of bridge or cricket, you are supposed to know precisely how these games are played. The smallest error of terminology will bring letters to the Sunday papers. If you set a scene in Rome or Vienna, you must be very careful about the geography of the streets. You must never betray the fact that you are an ignoramus like Shakespeare. So severe is the contemporary readers' demands for accuracy—at least in those things with which he is himself acquainted—that many young authors feel almost bound to qualify as pilots before they allow their heroes to fly, or to get themselves imprisoned before they can write about a convict.

This difficulty, though it is real, is not as great as it seems. If details are mentioned, whether of games or well-known buildings or machines or professions, they must be accurate. But details which cannot easily be checked need seldom be used. It must be remembered that the object of realism is to give the impression of reality. Details often hinder as well as help that impression. For just as in life most people get only general impressions, so in literature they expect and want only general impressions.

THE MISTAKE OF DESCRIBING TOO MUCH

ALL kinds of things can be described. A mood, a disease, a metaphysical system must be described before it can be discussed. We have already said that a story is a description of an event. But in speaking of literature, description usually means visual description. A good descriptive writer is some one who is good at describing things seen. In fiction the objects of description can be divided roughly into three classes : People, Places, Activities.

Now obviously it is necessary that the reader shall have some idea of what the characters of a story look like ; whether they are fat or thin ; red-faced, dark-skinned, or pallid ; smart or shabby ; tall or short. But it is not by any means necessary that their faces and clothes should be described in detail. It is much better in fact, that, given a few hints, the reader should form his own picture of their appearance. A beautiful blonde will not seem any more beautiful to many readers by being fitted out with a turned-up nose, a wide gash of a mouth, and a small neat chin. If the important fact about her is her beauty, its component parts had best be left to the reader's taste and choice. For many complicated reasons, human beings do not easily agree about physical beauty. Those people are notorious to whom the lovely Lady Dash appears merely nit-witted and vicious ; and it is very probable that the exquisite heroine of a story, when described, will become for many readers suddenly repulsive. The Greeks, with their infallible instinct for such things, realised and remembered this. Scarcely anywhere in the whole of Greek literature are to be found detailed descriptions of physical beauty. They were content to give such hints as that Athene was grey-eyed ; and yet Helen of Troy has been more generally accepted as beautiful than the most described of modern heroines.

Ugliness is easier to convey in words than beauty. A wart on the nose or a squint is rarely admired. Yet even ugliness is more forceful when it is unspecified. The description of appearance is, after all, subsidiary to the presentation of character ; and just as it is possible for people to know each other well without knowing the colour of each other's eyes, so it is possible to enable a reader to know a character well without telling him such details.

In life a person's appearance is used by others in two ways. At first sight it gives an impression which attracts or repels and enables them to form a rough and probably inaccurate estimate of character. After the person is gone it leaves an impression which enables them to visualise him or her when necessary and to recall their previous estimate. Both these impressions are nearly always general. Similarly in fiction, a description of a person's appearance should give the reader a general impression by which he may estimate the character as accurately as possible from the first, and later recall his estimate by a visual image.

THE AUTHOR AND HIS PURPLE PASSAGES

DESCRIPTIONS of places and activities are not so dangerous. The worst that can happen to your delicate account of the sunlight falling between the dappled leaves upon the ocean of bluebells where Laura lay, is that it may be skipped. No one will mind it very much ; for it is generally admitted that writers must be allowed to recognise explicitly the beauties of Nature. Similarly, no one will mind, though many may not read, your careful description of the shape and decorations of the bar-parlour or the dago's bedroom. Nevertheless, it is worth trying to make these passages not only relevant but interesting. The only way to do this is to avoid saying any thing about bluebells or bedrooms which the average reader may be supposed to take for granted.

The difficulty of describing activities—a fight, a race, a man mowing a lawn—is very much the same. Fights, races, and men mowing lawns are common enough sights ; and if a writer is to lift his descriptions of them out of the common-place, he must take care to stress those details which make the particular fight or race or man mowing different from all others. There are always differences to be found, and there is never need, though there is plenty of excuse, for common-place.

THE FUNNY STORY THAT MISFIRES

IT is remarkable how jokes which have been, or would be, very good jokes indeed in conversation become silly and irritating when they are written down. The man who is funny at a dinner-table will often find it very hard to be funny in writing. The reasons are too complex to discuss here, but it is safe to assume that the success of the spoken joke depends upon a direct personal contact between the speaker and his audience which the writer cannot make. The writer has to make a contact by proxy through the medium of his characters. Similarly, the characters only make an indirect contact with the reader through the author's account of them.

The humour, then, of a story, whether it occurs in dialogue or not, must not be direct in the way in which spoken humour is direct. It must be adapted to the roundabout method of its communication. How it can be so adapted is impossible to say. It can be discovered only by experiment. But two points may usefully be remembered. First, a deliberate joke in fiction is seldom successful unless the whole story is designed, like Saki's, as a vehicle for jokes. For what is funny in fiction is often something which in life would be an ordinary or even an exceptionally serious occurrence. A funny story,

14

told by a commercial traveller, would not be so funny in fiction as a story which is not funny, told by a commercial traveller. Secondly, most authors whose humour is good, have found it best to allow the humour to grow naturally from their characters ; to leave them, as it were, to be funny or not as they choose, and never to bully them.

HOW MANY WORDS IS MY STORY WORTH ?

TCHEKOV wrote a story called *The Proposal* of about four hundred words. Somerset Maugham has often written stories of nearly fifteen thousand. But these are extremes. The best lengths are between two thousand and ten thousand words. Anything shorter is usually better called a vignette or an anecdote. Anything longer is difficult to sell, unless the writer already has a reputation ; and it probably contains irrelevancies and superfluities, unless the writer has taken great trouble to obliterate them. From the purely commercial point of view, taking into consideration what editors are likely to want and how much they will have to pay, the most profitable length is four or five thousand words.

But there is only one real rule about length, and that has nothing to do with editors. The story must be as short as it possibly can be without losing any of its force. Padding is more disastrous in a short story than in any other form of writing. Every phrase must add something to the force of the story or it must come out. If after such a drastic excision, the story has dwindled to dwarfish and unrecognisable proportions, it must either be rewritten quite differently or abandoned.

It is quite a good test, though it sounds stringent, to go through a story when it is finished, examining each sentence to find out its function. Does it provide information necessary to the plot ? Does it add to the reader's knowledge of one of the characters ? Is the particular piece of knowledge it adds useful to the story as a whole ? Does it fill in the story's background or help to create atmosphere ? Does it make the story more realistic or more fantastic or more dramatic or more funny ?

Quite a simple sentence may be very important. It may have more than one function. " He liked to play bridge every evening from six till eight " gives considerable knowledge of a man's character. It also suggests that if, for several days, instead of playing bridge he spent the time from six to eight drinking double whiskies and staring out of the club window, his friends would know that something unusual must have happened. It helps, too, to produce an atmosphere of prosperous and complacent middle-class routine. On the other hand, in some stories, the sentence might be the most boring kind of superfluity.

Unlike a novel, a short story even at a casual first reading can be apprehended as a whole. By the time the last sentence is reached the reader has not forgotten what happened on the first page. What happens on the first page, therefore, must be directly relevant, even absolutely necessary, to the last sentence and indeed to every other sentence in the story. If there is not this close bond of necessity between each and every part of the story, the reader will be left dissatisfied and perhaps annoyed. A few irrelevant sentences in a short story are as noticeable and disastrous as a whole chapter of irrelevance in a book.

IN SEARCH OF A MARKET : WHAT EDITORS LIKE

IT is probably safe to say that more than half the difficulty in selling stories is due to inadequate knowledge of markets, which require much careful study where fiction is concerned. One editor will want stories about people of definitely higher financial or social status than the majority of his readers. Another will insist that his women readers must be able, without much imagination, to picture themselves in the same position as the heroine. Another will want stories with a twist at the end—some absolutely unexpected turn of events in the last few paragraphs. One will need two thousand words full of action. Another will consider six thousand, where the author has room to develop atmosphere and portrays character.

The biggest demand is, without question, to use an editor's words, for " stories about nice young people falling in love with one another." The fact that they do it every day in every way and that hundreds of thousands of short stories have already been written on the subject does not lessen the demand, nor, it must be admitted, does it make the task of the free-lance any easier. The theme has to be given fresh life by supplying it with new stage equipment and scenery, as it were, combining in some way the sophisticated trappings of modern life with the essential human simplicity of the " old, old story." It is not easy to do, but it is undoubtedly one of the very best ways of making money out of short stories. The writer who, from his own personal knowledge or experience, can give the story glamour by arranging the action in some place or in some sphere of activity which is comparatively strange and unknown to the average reader is lucky.

The next largest demand is undoubtedly for good adventure stories and " thrillers " of all kinds. Stories of family life are best left alone. The inexperienced writer needs more words than a short story allows him to make a family interesting. Stories of marriage tangles or illicit love need careful handling if they are to sell well. Studies in atmosphere or in psychological development are, generally speaking, only for the well-known writer, or for those seeking the more literary markets, where stories are more difficult to sell and cannot command fees comparable with those paid by popular magazines.

The writer who leans to stories of an unusual type written in a more or less popular way—and these will sometimes be successful—should remember that it is almost impossible to sell stories with morbid subjects or unhappy endings in a good paying market, unless one is well known. Artistically one may feel bound to face such subjects and such endings, but very few editors indeed can be induced to do so. For the fiction writer it is important to realise as soon as possible the kind of subjects with which one can successfully deal in a novel but which one must avoid in a short story written for profit.

THINGS THAT DETERMINE THE SIZE OF THE CHEQUE

PAYMENT for short stories varies from a guinea a thousand in small women's magazines, through the fairly usual two to three guineas a thousand in the more important magazines to the fabulous figures paid by one or two American publications. *Harper's Bazaar* pays at the rate of twenty guineas a thousand. Certain newspapers have a definite figure for a short story of about two thousand words, and this is often in the region of ten guineas. But few newspapers publishing short stories take them from unknown writers. If one's work is particularly good or has sufficiently impressed an agent for him to bargain for special terms, one would get from the established magazines more than the customary three guineas a thousand paid to the unknown writer. Payment is made on acceptance, on publication, or within a month afterwards, according to the custom of the paper or magazine. Guidance on the subject of the publications which prefer to come to some arrangement about fees before contribution is accepted can be obtained from the *Writers' and Artists' Year-Book*.

The author usually sells first serial rights only, unless some stipulation is made to the contrary. The right to republish the story in any other form or place is retained by the author. Second serial rights are frequently sold to syndicates who re-sell them to provincial or colonial papers and magazines.

Until the author has found his feet, he will probably find it more instructive and more economical to dispense with an agent, but as work increases such an intermediary becomes a necessity. A list of reputable agents may be found in the *Writers' and Artists' Year-Book*.

HOW TO PLAN BOOKS OF FICTION OR FACT

ONE of the most important differences between a short story and a novel is that the novel is longer, so that the architectural process, the arranging of parts in a satisfactory whole, is more difficult in the novel. The number of possible combinations being much greater, it is harder to find the best, and more likely that, if the best is not found, the reader will be confused and dissatisfied. Many successful novelists have said in symposia that they always make a synopsis before they begin to write. Many beginners have naturally been horrified at the thought. Nevertheless, it is probably true that some sort of synopsis, either written or kept in mind, is essential.

There is, however, no need to adhere to it very rigidly. The synopsis, like the Sabbath, was made for man, not man for the synopsis. Its use is that it enables the writer to keep the whole work in view while he is engaged on the parts. For instance, if by the end of the second chapter the character of the heroine has " developed " in some unexpected direction, the writer is able to turn to his synopsis and make those alterations in the other parts of the book which this unexpected development necessitates or suggests. In any imaginative work, such readjustments are to be welcomed as a sign of vigour rather than shunned as a sign of weakness. For this very reason, if an imaginative writer works without a synopsis, the growing book is apt to get out of hand. With one, he is able to keep it more or less consciously under control; and he is less likely to find, when he comes to the end, that half of it needs re-writing.

THE PROBLEM OF TIME AND SPACE

THE events with which a novelist deals are extended in time and space. And although there is a danger of becoming involved in mathematics when this is said, some such statement must be made. For the success of a long story depends largely upon the preservation of the temporal and spatial relations between the parts. Less pedantically: time must pass and things must move. The chief problem confronting a novelist is how to deal with this flux. It cannot be presented " in its entirety " as James Joyce has proved by his Herculean labours. A series of moments and points must be chosen which, when presented in succession, give the necessary illusion. The stream of consciousness cannot be presented without interruption. It flows too fast and deep for the shallow, narrow canal-banks of language. But there must be no apparent breaks or gaps. The progress of a story should be conceivable as a curve on a graph, simple or complex, but unbroken.

If it were possible to say how this might be done, the number of unsuccessful novels would be considerably diminished. Unfortunately, it is impossible to do more than suggest that a study of cinema technique—choice of shots, camera angle, cutting, arrangement, and " continuity "—might be of great assistance to the novelist.

For a first novel to sell, it should be about eighty thousand words in length. Much is being said at the moment about the increasing popularity of the long novel, and it may be true that long novels from established writers are more in fashion than they were. But the long first novel is not favourably regarded by publishers. Guidance is almost impossible in the choice of theme or plot, for good conception and writing can make almost any theme acceptable, though here, as with other branches of authorship, the popular market is usually the best to aim at if commercial results are the chief objective. It must be remembered that the majority of novel readers are women, and that the majority of people who turn to fiction demand of it that it should succeed in " taking them out of themselves."[1]

---

[1] For fees, terms, etc., see pp. 425–427.

SOME RULES FOR WRITING NON-FICTION

" A BOOK," said I. A. Richards in the preface to his illuminating *Principles of Literary Criticism*, " is a machine
to think with " ; and this aphorism should never be forgotten
by those who attempt to write any other kind of book than
fiction. Machines must be constructed to perform the task
for which they are intended as efficiently as possible. So
must books. An author should regard his book as a thing to
be used by the reader just as unsentimentally as a bicycle is
used, and for as definite a purpose. A biography, for instance,
of some one whose biography has not before been written,
will be needed primarily as a machine to remember with ;
and it should set out the known facts of the subject's life as
accurately and as clearly as possible, in chronological order.
But a biography of some one of whom there have been already
seventy biographies written will be needed, if it is needed at
all, as a machine to judge, to analyse, or to appreciate with.
If it is critical, it should set out only such facts in such order
as shall enable the reader to judge ; if analytical, such facts
in such order as shall enable the reader to follow the analysis ;
if appreciative, such facts in such order as shall give the reader
the fairest and most comprehensible picture of the subject.

It may be thought that these remarks are platitudinous
and unnecessary. But an examination of half a dozen biographies, chosen at random, more or less fresh from the Press,
will show how little the average biographer knows what he
is supposed to be doing. This is not altogether his fault.
The public and the reviewers are largely to blame. A bicycle
which would not move, though it were guaranteed to make
every one giggle, would be generally considered a bad bicycle.
But a book of criticism which does nothing to enable the reader
to judge, though it tells him a lot about the tastes and whimsies
of the author, is often considered, by apparently sane and
responsible people, a good book of criticism. No wonder,
then, that in such bewildering circumstances, many bad books
are written. Nevertheless, it is to be hoped that a few writers
will remember that a book is a machine and not a toy ; and
that what matters most about it is whether or not it works.

In the attempt to make a book which will work, the writer
must always consider the reader's convenience. The book
must be both easy to read and easy to refer to. The material
must be arranged logically. Arguments in the third chapter,

for instance, should not be founded upon facts which are only produced in the seventeenth. A description of the causes of a crisis should precede and not follow a description of the remedies. A definition of an Aryan should precede an account of his proper place in the world, and so on. The style, to use I. A. Richards's distinction, should be as strictly "symbolic," as little emotive as possible. Each word should precisely " stand for " something or an idea of something. No word should be used to provoke an emotional response in the reader. This does not, of course, apply to works of propaganda : but propagandists can be left to discover their own methods. In any case, propaganda probably ought to be classified as fiction.

Yet a logical arrangement of material and a lucid style are not enough. Chapter headings, sub-headings, and indexes, though not generally considered an important part nor even any part of the author's business, are essential if the book is to be convenient for reference. In these days, if a book is not convenient for reference, it is half damned. Indexes should be as full as possible. I personally prefer the kind which is almost a concordance. Indexes are useless when, as often happens, the one thing which you want to find is not there. Although an author would be rash to prepare his own index, he would be both wise and kind to see that it is comprehensive. That chapters either be themselves short or be divided into sections is also essential if the subject of the book is complex. But these divisions are useless unless the headings are clearly descriptive of the content. Nothing is more inconvenient for reference than several pages of unbroken or unlabelled text.

THE AUTHOR AND HIS PUBLISHER

JUST as a modern engineer would not dream of designing and constructing an elaborate machine without either a definite order from an industrialist or without at least discussing with an industrialist the possibility of its use, so the modern writer co-operates with his publisher in the design and construction of a book. The habit of writing books—other than novels, and poems—and then looking round for a publisher, is becoming obsolete.

If a man thinks it necessary or profitable or desirable to write another book about Sir Walter Raleigh, the first step he would take is to discuss with a publisher the kind of book it should be ; its uses, its length, its plan, and its prospects. If he does this he will save himself a great deal of time and energy. Of course, if you are a mathematician engaged upon an epoch-making theory, there is no need to discuss its shape with the Syndics of the University Press. But if you are just a poor writer, it is better to consult a publisher before you begin to write. The enormous number of books published every year makes the danger of overlapping considerable. A good publisher will know when a book is redundant and what kind of book on the same subject might be needed. The writer will have to co-operate with a publisher in the end, perhaps by making substantial alterations, certainly by helping to correct the proofs. It is better for every one's sake and for the book's that this co-operation should begin early. When the subject of the book has been settled, the author should prepare two or three chapters and a full outline or scheme for the rest of the book, and submit them to the publisher. In the case of a travel book, or any other which the author proposes to illustrate with drawings or photographs which he himself is supplying, he should submit a few of these as well. In this way the author and publisher collaborate in producing the most appropriate type of book for the market in view, and in addition the author enjoys a greater measure of security than he could have were he just writing " on spec."

The field of non-fiction, comprising every sort of book from biography and memoir to school text-books, offers many opportunities to the non-creative writer with specialised knowledge or unique experiences. It is, in general, less immediately remunerative than novel or short-story writing or than popular journalism, but in the long run it is likely to pay better than any of them. A book on fishing, for instance, or a French grammar may show few or no returns for five or six years, but after that period may quite well produce a steadily growing income for the rest of the author's lifetime.

THE BUSINESS SIDE OF BOOKS

THE selling of books entails more in the way of business arrangements than the selling of short stories. It is not merely that more money is involved, for frequently a successful magazine short story will bring in as much money as a first novel, but the system of payment is different. Instead of the full fee being paid outright, when a publisher buys a book— fiction or non-fiction—some form of contract is usually drawn up between the author and himself. What the author of a first book may expect from the most usual form of agreement is a payment on account of royalties made on publication—in the case of a novel probably about twenty-five to thirty pounds—and royalties above that amount at the rate of 10 or 15 per cent. per copy on the selling price after 5000 copies have been sold.

In the case of a non-fiction book, commissioned by the publishers, the author may get as much as fifty pounds advance or even more if the subject is one demanding specialised knowledge, such as music, geology, or philately. But publishers do not commission works of this kind from unknown writers : journalists who have concentrated on one subject, or experts who have taken to journalism, are those most likely to be approached.

If the first novel has been a moderate success, the second should bring an advance of seventy-five to a hundred pounds, with a royalty of 10 to 15 per cent. These terms are about the average ; some publishers, however, offer considerably better ones, while a few make them even lower.

The beginner should never have any dealings with a publisher who wishes him to pay anything towards the cost of publication, for no reputable publisher will ever consider publishing a book of general appeal which is not sufficiently promising to induce him to bear the costs. Highly technical or specialised books, of course, form a special case. Publishers sometimes offer an author a lump sum for all rights in his book, but generally speaking this procedure is not in the author's interest. The author is the first owner of the copyright of anything he writes, but if he has sold his book outright he can claim no share in the profits if it proves to be a great success, is dramatised, made into a film, translated, etc.

There remains the question of what sort of income a writer may hope to earn. Authors of non-fiction works do not as a rule depend solely upon writing ; for them, their pens produce a useful addition to a regular salary from some other profession. Novel-writing, however, is more often a full-time occupation. A really successful first novel might bring the author between one and two hundred pounds, but these are exceptional figures. A successful novel which sells over a number of years may be a profitable investment, producing a steady income from royalties and from the various rights : film, dramatic, and translation. An established writer of moderate reputation may earn five or six hundred pounds a year, while a first-class popular novelist, writing only two or three books a year, may reach an annual income of seven or eight thousand pounds. This includes, of course, proceeds from royalties, rights, etc., on previous novels.

It is in the interests of every author to join the Incorporated Society of Authors, Playwrights, and Composers, which acts as a kind of society for the prevention of cruelty to all of the writing fraternity. It will look into all contracts and agreements to see that its members obtain a fair deal, will act for them in any dispute, and give advice on any problem that arises in the course of selling written work. Moreover, if, as sometimes occurs, the author or his agent sells separate rights abroad in any short story, book, or play, the Society will collect fees or royalties and look after the member's interest where he himself would be unable to do so.

WHERE TO FIND HINTS ABOUT STORY-WRITING

WRITING a short story is a very technical task, and the shorter the story the more difficult does the task become. There is no question of making the short story, as the novel is often made, a mere rag-bag for personal prejudice and experience. The craft must be acquired ; we must go to the experts for lessons. If a practised short-story writer happens to be among your acquaintances, an hour or two's conversation would prove most valuable, but, failing the personal contact, one or two books may be recommended. *Short Stories and How to Write Them* (Harrap) is a detailed and practical guide ; it is written by a man who should possess as much experience of a certain type of short story as any one, for the author, Cecil Hunt, is the fiction editor of *The Daily Mail* and *The Evening News*. The composition of short stories for these markets requires a more definite technique than that for any weekly or monthly periodical. Other books on the same lines are R. Francis Foster's *How to Write and Sell Short Stories*, published by Allen & Unwin, and *The Commercial Side of Literature*, by Michael Joseph (Hutchinson). A book of another kind, which deals more with the literary graces, what might be called the æsthetic side of the subject, is Percy Lubbock's *The Craft of Fiction* (Traveller's Library).

When the general idea of how to write a short story has been grasped and a number of the best tales of all countries have been read, then you should begin to make a special study of how to write that kind of short story you feel most drawn towards. Detective stories make fascinating reading ; authors may perhaps tell you they are not so fascinating to write. However this may be, a masterly monograph on the *genre* has been written by Dorothy L. Sayers in her introduction to *Great Short Stories of Detection, Mystery, and Horror* (Gollancz).

As far as hard-and-fast rules can be formulated for novels, the same hold good for the long as for the short story. The great novelists themselves are the best guides, but they have wisely refrained from writing recipes for books. C. E. Montague's *A Writer's Notes on his Trade* may be consulted for profit and pleasure. The most painstaking novelist who ever lived was probably Gustave Flaubert, the French writer ; in his *Correspondence with George Sand* (Heinemann) is to be found nearly everything there is to be said about writing.

PRACTICAL JOURNALISM

by HOLT ST. JOHN

MOST people who wish to write as a whole or part-time occupation send their first efforts to a newspaper. The vast organisation of the modern daily press receives the article, tests it by the needs of the public, rejects it, or sends it on its way to publication—through the hands of the sub-editor, compositor, on to the rotary presses, and out again in print. The newspaper is in closer and more immediate touch with the public than any other publication; it aims to mirror the world's news and activities, to interest every one, every day. News-papers must always be innovating; the need of maintaining vast sales in the face of unflagging competition from other dailies ensures that no contribution is overlooked, nothing of promise rejected. Those who wish to embark on the adventure of journalism should first familiarise themselves with the editorial machinery through which their articles must pass, whether it is their intention ultimately to become a permanent part of that machinery, or whether they wish to use it as an occasional intermediary between themselves and the public. The first part of this article, therefore, deals with the subject from inside the office and is written by a working staff journalist. The second part is a guide to the free-lance over the arduous, but always interesting, ways of outside journalism, and is written by a practising free-lance journalist.

Practical journalism means getting your work into a news-paper and being paid for it, whether as a full-time professional journalist or as a spare-time occasional contributor. In neither case is it such easy money as it looks. Of all the ways to earn a living open to the man or woman with a knowledge of the English language for stock-in-trade, there is probably none which makes a wider or a more illusory appeal than journalism. One man envisages himself as a political leader-writer, swaying Empires with his pen; another is dazzled by the industriously sustained legend of the glamour of Fleet Street—the street of the crack descriptive writers and of world-beating " scoops." More, I think, are attracted by the idea of a life spent in writing. They are fond of books. They have felt the urge to write—have written, perhaps, short stories, poetry, essays, or reviews, and nothing seems more agreeable than the prospect of earning a living in the same way. Well, it is not all illusion. The jobs are there—all of them. There are influential leader-writers, there are " star " reporters, there are critics and reviewers, and generally literary men ; and theirs is a good life. But there are not many of them.

If ever you think of trying journalism, do a little arithmetic first. It is not a very big profession. There are no certain means of knowing how many journalists there are. I should say, at a guess, rather more than 8500 altogether. The National Union of Journalists has about 6000 members. The Institute of Journalists has about 2000 members, but some of these are also members of the N.U.J. too, and must not be counted twice. Then there are some, but not a great many, who belong to neither body. If you assume a total of 8500 you will not be far out.

Half of them work for local papers. For this job the main qualifications are good shorthand, local knowledge, and common sense. A profound knowledge of the English tongue is not an impediment, but some people seem able to get by without it, and a knowledge of the points of sheep is perhaps equally useful. The local papers have often been called the " backbone " of British journalism. This is very true—in a sense. Ask the big names in Fleet Street where they started their careers, and more than half will answer that they learned the basis of their craft from a country editor on a little obscure weekly, the circulation of which was not 2000.

But in a larger sense the weekly local papers cannot be called the backbone of journalism. Their excellences as a training-ground are often in inverse proportion to their virtues as newspapers. The national morning and evening papers and their great provincial rivals set the standard of British journalism.

HOW THE JOURNALISTS ARE DISTRIBUTED

THERE are nearly one hundred evening papers published outside London. These will employ in all about 1500 journalists. But there is a certain amount of doubling with the weekly paper men—that is, in some fairly big towns, the same firm brings out both a weekly and an evening paper,

and the same men work for both. Blackpool is a good
example ; *The Blackpool Weekly Gazette* and *The West
Lancashire Evening Gazette* are published from the same office
and produced by more or less the same staff. The evening
paper men are nearly all either reporters or sub-editors, in
the proportion of, say, three reporters to two " subs," the
latter being the " inside " men who prepare copy for the
compositors. And here, too, a specialist element begins to
come in—sports-writers, and " City Page " men, and a
leader-writer.

The morning daily papers published outside London are
about thirty in number and employ probably about a thousand
men. Most of them have larger staffs than the evening
papers, and use more specialists ; there may be three or more
leader-writers, full-time literary, dramatic, film, or music
critics. Moreover, the morning papers take more from
outside contributors and from regulars who write periodically
on particular topics—for instance, natural history, bridge,
or motoring.

The London newspapers—mostly produced in the Fleet
Street area—naturally provide the biggest field of employment for journalists, because all of them, except the evenings,
have at least pretensions to a national circulation.

There are four national text morning papers which publish
simultaneously in London and Manchester—*Daily Herald*,
Daily Mail, *News Chronicle*, and *Daily Express*. The last
is also printed and published simultaneously in Glasgow.
These four papers are all intense rivals, produced to attract
as wide and popular a public as possible. Next come the
three more sedate and old-established text dailies—*The
Times*, *Daily Telegraph*, and *Morning Post*. Two national
daily picture papers appear in London, the *Daily Mirror*
and *Daily Sketch*. In addition, specialist dailies such as the
Financial Times, *Financial News*, and *Sporting Life* flourish
actively.

There are three London evenings : the *Evening News*
(associated with the *Daily Mail*), the *Star* (tied to the *News
Chronicle*), and the *Evening Standard*, owned by the same
proprietor as the *Daily Express*. This is a great falling off
in numbers, though not in circulation or quality. Before
the War London had eight evenings.

Ten Sunday papers are published in London. The
Observer and *Sunday Times* (same proprietor as the *Telegraph*)

are in the staid *Times–Daily Telegraph* tradition. The *Sunday Express* (tied to the *Daily Express*) and the *Sunday Dispatch* (tied to the *Daily Mail*) have much the same character as their prototypes. The *Referee, People, News of the World, Sunday Graphic, Sunday Pictorial,* and *Reynolds* are the others.

All these papers together employ about 1000 men and women journalists, and naturally posts on them are eagerly sought, because to work in Fleet Street is every journalist's ambition.

There remain two groups—the trade papers and the periodicals. The trade papers are a large, wealthy, and important class. Nearly all of them are published in London, but there are a few exceptions. The textile weeklies, for instance, are published in Manchester, and there is a woollen trade weekly in Bradford. The staffs of these papers have, naturally, to be authorities on the particular industries with which they are concerned ; a general knowledge of journalistic work is not enough, though sometimes a trade paper takes on an experienced journalist with no knowledge of the trade, thinking it easier to teach him the rudiments of the business than to teach a technical man the rudiments of journalism. The " periodical " group includes widely varying publications, from *The Economist* and *The New Statesman and Nation* to *Tit-Bits* and *Betty's Paper*. Most of these papers have very small permanent staffs, and depend largely on outside contributions for their material.

I have made this preliminary survey rather long because, if you are thinking of going into journalism, in one form or another, it is just as well to know more or less what jobs there are to be had in each category. Generally speaking, the more attractive a job is to the literary-minded layman, the more difficult it is to obtain, not only because there are so many people after it, but because there are so few jobs of the kind.

FINDING A WAY INTO JOURNALISM

I SPOKE of " going into journalism." How do most people go into it ? There is no orthodox way of becoming a journalist. Taking the Press as a whole, there are probably as many people who have come in as telephonists as through any other channel ; but even they are not in a clear majority. All daily papers, morning and evening, employ telephonists; usually they begin as youths of eighteen to twenty—some of them rather older—to take down in short-hand the telephone messages of district correspondents or of reporters out of town and to transcribe them on the type-writer. After a man has worked for a few years in the telephone-room he has acquired two qualities which commend him as a reporter—shorthand and a good idea of how a news-paper office works. Until the slump years, 1930–33, a telephonist could be pretty sure to get a job on a provincial paper as a junior reporter and so work up.

If you can get a job on a county weekly straight from school, without going through the telephone-room, so much the better. Thence the boy can graduate after two or three years to a provincial morning or evening paper. From here, if he is made of the right stuff, he will make his own chance of breaking into Fleet Street.

There are various courses in journalism. That at London University commands respect with some editors. Other courses may or may not give useful instruction in writing, but they carry little weight with editors. They are more likely to be helpful to the casual contributor than to the man after a staff job.

As well as the newspapers, the News Agencies carry large staffs of reporters and also a certain number of sub-editors. The three big ones are the *Press Association*, *Exchange Telegraph*, and *Central News*. In addition there are two large agencies, *Reuters* and the *British United Press*, which circulate foreign news to London papers by tape machines. Conditions of work and pay on these agencies are equivalent to those on a London daily paper.

THE MAN WITH THE NOTE-BOOK

A REPORTER is, by definition, a man who " brings some-thing back." He goes out of the office and comes back bringing something with him which wasn't there before. That is what the word means, " re-port," " carry back." A man can sit in the office writing reams of descriptive stuff out of his head ; he can go out and walk about all day with his eyes half-shut and his ears half-closed and write pretty well the same stuff which he could have written if he had never stirred from his desk. There are plenty of people doing that, and getting their names at the top of the column.

But that isn't reporting, and a man who constantly does it is a bad reporter, whoever he works for, and however large his name is printed. Reporting is by no means so easy a matter.

It is essential for the reporter to get into immediate contact with life. The closer he can get to his material the better. The full impact of the facts must come upon him, and it is his work to transmute them into words which still carry in themselves, as far as possible, the lingering imprint of actuality. I don't mean that he should write what are commonly called " personal impressions," which are as a rule far too " personal " and have far too little " impression " about them—which are vitiated by a subjective attitude to things, while a reporter's attitude should always be objective. Nor, on the other hand, does the word " objective " imply any shade of aloofness or indifference. It is the reporter's duty to fling himself whole-heartedly into the pursuit of facts—whether these facts are, in the particular case, spoken words, or things seen, or statistics—and " bring 'em back alive."

THE VALUE OF REPORTING "WORD FOR WORD"

I THINK this general maxim is true of all kinds of reporting, from the descriptive " special " to the verbatim note. There is not so much verbatim reporting of speeches in the daily papers as there used to be, though of course it is still the stock-in-trade of the local weeklies. I suspect that in dropping it the dailies have lost something more than they know. The trouble is, of course, that it takes up so much space, and space is always precious. But a good speech reported verbatim usually makes much better reading than the same speech summarised, and is worth its place on occasion. Nobody would suggest going back to the style of the 1890's, when you would see four columns of solid minion (that is, a rather small type without spaces between the lines) with a single headline in small capitals—" Mr. Gladstone at York," or words to that effect, and not a cross-heading in the whole four columns. But there are times when a man who can speak really well visits a provincial town and makes a first-class speech there; and then the local morning paper, if there is one, rightly gives him a verbatim report. This is, however, a rare occasion.

But if the newspapers have lost something in the verbatim

report, I am sure that the craft of journalism has lost a good deal more. Verbatim reporting for a weekly paper is just a slog. One man goes on taking notes for an hour or more on end, and then goes on transcribing them for hours more. There is no fun to be got out of that. But a verbatim for a daily paper is a very different matter, especially if it is wanted for all editions. It is a rush job calling for a high degree of skill—something one can take a real pride in. This is how it is done.

You have a " ring." The orthodox " ring " is five men and a timekeeper. The five men are all expert shorthand writers. The speaker begins his speech, and one of the five (say A) begins to write. When he has been taking notes for, say, three minutes, the timekeeper signals to A to stop, and to B to begin taking notes ; A at once begins to transcribe what he has taken. After another three minutes C comes in, and B begins to transcribe, and so on, so that A has just finished transcribing and is ready to take notes again when E is finishing his " take." And so they continue until the speech is ended.

Meanwhile the timekeeper collects the transcriptions as they come, runs quickly through them to see that they are legible, and no words missing, and gets them—no small feat sometimes—into the right order ; and a relay of messengers carry the bundles of copy away to the office. With a good ring you may have the speaker's last words in the office ten minutes or so after he has sat down. That is a job worth doing—a job at very high pressure for a comparatively short time ; even the hardened old hands get excited over it. There was a famous Manchester reporter who used to say with zest : " We will report him verbatim, literatim, and punctuatim " (word for word, letter for letter, and stop for stop).

DO REPORTERS NEED SHORTHAND ?

I HAVE mentioned verbatim reporting because you so often hear it said nowadays : " Oh, you don't need shorthand to be a reporter." How far is this true ? Even on a daily paper, where verbatim reporting is comparatively rare, occasions often arise when you must be ready to take at least a paragraph or two verbatim, when the whole point of the story is in the precise words which the man used. This is particularly true if they are words which he might wish to deny afterwards.

But quite apart from this precautionary consideration, it makes all the difference to the life and style of your report of a speech if it incorporates as much as possible of the man's own words. Any one with a tolerably alert mind can summarise the content of a speech without taking a note of it at all, or just taking a few notes in longhand to aid his memory, and his report may be a perfectly fair representation of what the speaker said. But it will not have anything like the same liveliness and force as a report which, while summarising, retains the speaker's most telling phrases and turns of speech.

There are a few reporters whose other qualties are so remarkable that they are worth their place, without shorthand, on a daily paper. But they would be still better with it. For service on a weekly paper, of course, good shorthand is essential. Half the paper will consist of speeches or meetings reported at length.

THE ART OF TRANSMITTING IMPRESSIONS

To pass from the reporting of speeches to the art of descriptive reporting, we find that the fundamental principle of "bringing back" something applies even more closely. A descriptive report is not a "set-piece" designed to show the rhetorical powers of the writer. It is an account of an event, or series of events, by some one who has seen it; and the best account is that which brings in the most striking or interesting facts—facts which could only be known to an eye-witness. The more intelligent and alert the witness, the more interesting things he is likely to notice.

Descriptive reporting is the great opportunity for the use of what artists call "significant detail." It affords much more scope and freedom to the writer than any other form of reporting, because each man will observe and be impressed by different things. But many descriptive reports are spoiled by pushing this freedom too far, by obtruding irrelevant personal reflections, or distorting one's genuine impressions by a tortured seeking after some "new angle." Another common defect, especially in descriptions of important events, is a grandiose introductory paragraph, which could have been written at home a week in advance.

TELLING THE PUBLIC WHAT HAS HAPPENED

THE ordinary "news story" is distinct from the "descriptive story," because it is, in the main, not the first-hand product of an eye-witness. (There is, of course, a point at which they can hardly be distinguished from each other.) The term " news story " covers a very wide field—anything from a fire or a railway smash to a by-election may be said to fall within it. The essence of it is that something has happened, and people want to know what. It is no use relying on one's eyesight for a news story. The required quality is that of finding the right man to give information and asking the right questions, until the possibilities of the subject are exhausted ; you never know that the really significant fact is not just round the corner.

The actual writing of a news story is a knack which some people never seem to learn. The old saying, " Put the point of the story into the first paragraph " is an over-simplification ; it begs the question : " What is the point of the story ? " You are not even safe in saying : " A death, if there is one," though this is good enough in most cases. For instance, it is a sound lead to say :

> " Two men were killed, and three seriously injured, when a corporation bus crashed into a brewer's dray at —— yesterday."

But I would write :

> " The worst floods seen in Teesdale for twenty years drowned two men and swept away three bridges . . ."

because floods on a serious scale are even more uncommon than sudden deaths. Accidents to buses, on the other hand, are fairly common, and interesting therefore only in regard to their effects.

But it would be ridiculous to try and lay down any definite " rules of procedure," for one man may be struck with one point in the story, and one by another, and each will, quite properly, open in his own way. The one thing you must not do is to begin, " The sky was blue, and the fields a brilliant green, when . . .," unless the point of the story is to contrast the weather on this occasion with a previous thunderstorm, which is an unlikely topic ; or " Women wept and children cried when . . ."—a distressingly common opening. This is just as much as to say : " Look out for a bit of pathos here," as if the writer distrusted his own powers of " putting it across."

WHY A STORY SHOULD START ON "THE TOP NOTE"

THE maxim " first things first " does not apply only to the opening paragraph, but to the whole. Do not hold up your best line for the last paragraph. There is a technical reason for this. The news value of any story is relative ; it depends on the other news of the same day. The length which can be given to a story varies not only from day to day but from edition to edition, as further news comes in. It is often necessary to " cut " a story at the last minute. To cut odd words or lines, even if superfluous to the sense, involves re-setting the type, but to cut a whole paragraph from the middle probably breaks the continuity of the story. To knock off the last paragraph or two is technically the easiest way, and does the minimum damage to a rightly written story.

In reporting meetings, some papers like a striking sentence brought up to the top, as, for instance :

> " ' An ant-heap is the Socialist State, *in excelsis*, said Dean Inge, lecturing at Oxford yesterday."

This is not a bad idea, but only if the opening sentence strikes the keynote of the whole report. If it does not, the " bright " opening sentence is an irrelevant excrescence, which misleads the reader. Sometimes, too, it tempts the sub-editor to throw away the rest of the report which fails to live up to its introduction. The classic instance is the evening paper report of the local Diocesan Conference—

> " ' When eating herrings, I prefer hard roes to soft,' said the Bishop of ——, speaking yesterday at the —— Diocesan Conference "

—and that was all.

PERSUADING THE INFORMANT TO TALK

I WILL barely mention two of the most interesting forms of reporting—interviewing, and what I may call original investigation. It needs some skill to interview a man—not simply to take a statement from him on a given subject, but to get him talking freely and interestingly. It needs an acute and sympathetic personality, a knack of guiding the conversation in promising directions, while doing little of the actual talking, and an unusually accurate memory, for few people will talk freely while one is taking notes of their conversation.

By " original investigation " I mean this. An editor says : " They say that the water shortage is very bad in this part of the world. I want the truth, and what is going to be done about it, in three stories each about a column in length. Go along and get them." There are not many papers doing this kind of thing, which is a pity, because people will read it with great interest, especially if it has local application, conscious that they are getting the real stuff, the raw material of policy. One cannot exactly call it " news " because it does not turn on any specific event, and therefore those overridden with the " news " complex tend to overlook it. They are wrong, for it is one of the essential functions of a newspaper.

There is one more thing to be said before I leave reporting. Some people may assume from what I have written that it does not much matter whether a reporter can write good English or not. And indeed there are some authorities who say that a good reporter can be quite illiterate so long as he " gets the news," and they cite the case of American reporters who never go into the office to write a line, but stay out on their beat, and telephone what they get to a " re-write man " inside. This may pass muster for the small jobs, but it is fatal to a big story, because it means that the story as it finally appears is necessarily told at second-hand—it loses that touch of actuality which is the mark of all good reporting.

If a man is an incompetent writer, either some one else has to re-write his " copy," so that it is no longer a first-hand impression, or, if he writes it clumsily himself, the impression arrives blurred and distorted by his deficient expression.

IN THE SUB-EDITOR'S ROOM

THE sub-editor's room is the hub of a newspaper office. I must, therefore, say a little about it here, although, as a sub-editor's is not a " writing " job, it does not come so directly within the scope of this article as a reporter's.

Classifying copy by source and not by subject, one can distinguish five kinds. There is " supplied copy "—that is, copy sent in by the persons responsible for it, as, for instance, a Government Report. There is " staff copy," that is, copy written by members of the staff, and mostly in the office. There is " correspondents' copy," sent in by the

paper's regular correspondents in various towns and neigh-
bouring villages—probably men on the local weekly papers, or
free-lances established in a particular district—by wire,
telephone, or train parcel. There is " agency copy," sent in
by the great agencies—*The Press Association, Exchange Telegraph*, and *Central News*—and by the foreign agencies, like
Reuters and *British United Press*. And there is " contributor's copy," sent in by people who are not regular correspondents of the paper, but who are either experts in some
field, writing on their own subject, or casual contributors
to the " magazine " pages of the paper—the literary page,
woman's page, etc.

From all these sources there comes, every night, far more
material than would fill any paper that the machines could
print. Nor would any one want to read it. All this great
stream of copy is swallowed and digested by sub-editors.

The sub-editing staff in the largest newspaper offices, the
London papers, and a few of the big provincial dailies, is
organised as follows : At its head are the Chief Sub-Editor
and his right-hand man, the Copy-taster. In consultation
with the executive Editor on Duty the Chief Sub-Editor
will decide how the news is going to be distributed through
the paper—which stories, for example, shall go on the front
or main news page, and how they shall be handled.

As all copy reaches the paper it goes to the Copy-taster.
It is his duty to read it and assess its value, if that has not
already been decided. If the Copy-taster decides that any
item does not interest his paper he discards it straight away
—" spikes " it is the technical term. Therefore his responsibility is very great, because he may " spike " through a
moment's carelessness or wrong judgment some few lines
of copy containing the germ of a news story of world importance. Alertness of mind, wide information, and experience
are essential for a Copy-taster. It is nerve-racking but very
interesting work, and correspondingly well paid.

On the Chief Sub-Editor's instruction the Copy-taster
hands out stories to be " subbed " by the men sitting round
the sub-editor's table. One story may be made up from
copy from six or seven different sources—there may be three
agency versions, the paper's own reporter's story, and various
additional comments and pieces of information from local
correspondents, experts, and specialists.

From all these the Sub-Editor must produce a single

coherent story, using as much as possible of his own reporter's copy. He must check the accuracy of all names, dates, etc., from reference books, and guard against any possible libels.

Libels in newspapers arise from carelessness, because facts cannot always be sufficiently verified for lack of time, or through a sheer mistake. Most large offices keep a lawyer on the premises, who reads all proofs as a check on possible libels. But a heavy responsibility still rests on each Sub-Editor.

Finally, the Sub-Editor must mark on the copy the type and style in which it must be set in the composing-room and write headings to it of the sort indicated to him by the Copy-taster. When his story is finished, it is passed through the Chief Sub-Editor's hands, approved or sent back for amendment, and finally sent to the printer to be put into type.

The Chief Sub-Editor is responsible for everything which passes through the Sub-Editor's room and into the paper. He must see that a continuous flow of copy reaches the printer in good time to be set and made up in pages before edition time. He must watch the trend of each story to see that it is in line with the general policy of the paper; he must take care that headings and sub-editing are bright and up to standard.

A good " Chief-Sub " is a man of incalculable value to his paper. He keeps his staff happy and hard at work, however nerve-destroying the night's work may be. Under a bad " Chief-Sub " panic and hysteria can invade the Sub-Editorial staff of a paper, destroying all initiative and good work. Brilliant " Chief-Subs " are few and much sought after. Few journalists envy their responsibilities. Most journalists envy their salaries.

THE ARTIST WITH THE BLUE PENCIL

A SUB-EDITOR is a builder with other men's bricks. He may write very little—except a headline—all night. His work is to straighten out or summarise what cannot conveniently be cut. He works, in the main, by excision. It is he who puts the polish, as it were, on the paper. We have learned, from Eisenstein and Pudovkin particularly, the science of film cutting—giving to each " shot " the precise length of time which will compose it most effectively in the picture. It has been said that, in Eisenstein's pictures, the whole art is in the cutting ; the reels of negative are only so much raw material.

The sub-editor, like the film cutter, is creative in effect, though destructive in technique. He gives to things their relative importance, not only by the amount of space allotted to them, but by the devices of black type, bold headlines, inset pictures, ruled borders, etc. Some papers, especially " nationals," attach enormous importance to this form of display, and consider the visible appearance of the page quite as important as the emphasis put upon the various items of news, and even go so far as to design the " make-up " of the principal pages beforehand.

Writing headlines is an acquired art, for they must tell the reader what the story is about and attract in very few, telling words. The principle is, the shorter and simpler the line the larger type it can go in ; conversely, the larger the type determined upon, the shorter the label must be. This need has led to the reintroduction of many words which had fallen into disuse, such as " pact " and " ban," instead of " agreement " and " prohibit."

Some people may think that this is doing the English language good. The disadvantage is that short, convenient words get used too often when they do not quite fit the meaning—not that headlines are capable of fine shades at any time. It is hard enough to find words which fill the right space and convey the right sense, without refinement. The first half-dozen come easily, but try writing headlines every few minutes for four or five hours at a stretch ; unless you are a hard case, you will find it an exasperating business.

Do not confuse a sub-editor with an assistant editor (who is a " big shot "), or with the head of a department in a newspaper. Sub-editing is a job on its own. It is the most technical of all the newspaper jobs, and for that reason it is rare for a man to become a sub-editor without previous newspaper experience.

ENGLISH THE SUB-EDITOR'S FAITHFUL ALLY

WHAT knowledge of the English language does the sub-editor need ? He does not have to write, but he must be an expert at re-writing. Therefore he must have a thorough mastery of right usage. He must be able to spot at once an idiom which jars, or a sentence which the ordinary reader will find obscure or ambiguous, and it is his right and his duty to re-shape it. He must be able to snatch at once the essential point in a tangle of verbiage, and bring it out quickly and cleanly. If all reporters were perfect, there would be no need to re-write; but many reporters are far from perfect, and sometimes a sub-editor must re-write a story from beginning to end, trimming it of its superfluities and extravagances. Still more important, he must be able to write a continuous narrative from a number of different or fragmentary reports sent in. In short, I would say that there is no department in a newspaper office in which a real knowledge of and feeling for the English language will make more difference to the published paper. The most common fault with sub-editors is that they allow themselves to be overworked; that is, they work at too high pressure, and have not the time to think over what goes in.

THE REST OF THE STAFF : JOBS FOR THE SPECIALIST

AMONG the further staff of a newspaper office, one may consider leader-writers, critics of various kinds, and specialists in sport, finance, and so on. There are also editors; but these are a law unto themselves. They all work differently, and my own prejudice is that editors ought not to do anything at all, but confine themselves to seeing that other people work. But most of them feel lonely, and cannot resist putting an oar in sometimes; and nearly all of them contrive to work very hard indeed at something.

Perhaps I should mention also foreign correspondents in this section, although they are not actually " in the office." Theirs is a distinct and difficult job. There are not many of them; only the biggest papers, and the news agencies, employ full-time men even in the chief capitals. The American papers, as a rule, pay more attention to foreign news than ours do; they have, of course, more room for it, being bulkier than ours. American papers normally have much more news about England than English papers have about the U.S.A. There is a technical reason for this—the difference in time between London and New York. When it is 10 p.m. in London it is 4 p.m. in New York, and only 3 p.m. in Chicago; so news from America is usually either incomplete or late. On the other hand, when we in this country are going to bed, the American editor is just beginning to say : " What's the news to-night ? "

The art of foreign correspondence is to combine the reporter's flair for news and capacity for concise description with a solid understanding of the politics and economics of the country concerned. It is a delicate job, because one is dealing largely with people in important positions to whom it matters a great deal what is said about them in the papers ; it is occasionally a dangerous one, because one is bound sometimes to cut across that strangest and most inflammable of passions—nationalism.

THE LEADER HOLDS ITS OWN

SOME people say that the leader-writer has had his day, and indeed there are papers which relegate the expression of editorial policy to an obscure and ignoble corner of the page to which it gives its name. They are wrong. The leader was never as dead as they thought, and to-day, when the " national " papers are all highly political in outlook, it is established as a vital part of daily journalism.

With the big papers outside London, like *The Yorkshire Post*, *The Birmingham Post*, *The Manchester Guardian*, or *The Glasgow Herald*, what one may call the *Times* tradition has been followed throughout—that is, a " long leader " of about a thousand words as the principal topic, followed by one or more short leaders on less important events. In the smaller and less sedate papers, the long leader is reduced to about four hundred words, and the supporting " shorts " are mere footnotes. A few evening papers take great pains with their leaders, which are skilfully if not profoundly written, but many content themselves with a bald paraphrase of what has appeared that morning in some daily of repute. On the weekly papers leaders are usually written by the editor, and those on local subjects are often exceedingly acute and pithy.

The editor of a daily paper may, and sometimes does, write leaders. But in the nature of things he cannot write them all, and all dailies have one or more men whose principal work is writing leaders. Very few have enough leader-writers to make it possible for them to specialise—*The Times* and *The Manchester Guardian* probably go farther than any others in this respect. In most cases the leader is supposed to convey the opinion not of an expert, but of an intelligent and knowledgeable layman. who looks on the news from a given angle, determined by the policy of the paper. His duty is to size up the events of the day and see how they fit into the general framework of policy. He gives his readers the background which they need for the interpretation of the facts ; he draws the moral which the facts reinforce.

I do not suppose that many readers are actually converted to a change of view solely by the persuasion or the exhortation, as the case may be, of a leader-writer. But I do believe that the degree of conviction with which a man holds his views, and consequently the lengths to which he will go to uphold them, and his influence thereby among his fellow-men, are enormously enhanced by good leader-writing. It is the same with sermons ; not many men have been persuaded by sermons to become Christians, but many have been far better Christians for listening to good sermons. *The Morning Post*, for instance, is noted for its excellent leaders. They are not written to persuade. Far from converting opponents, they usually rouse to fury any one who is not already a confirmed Tory. But they succeed wonderfully well in their object of keeping the Tories in good heart.

HOW THE LEADER-WRITER SCORES HIS POINTS

OF the qualities required by a leader-writer, a mastery of English is paramount. He works in the vein of rhetoric —not the blowsy and overblown circumlocutions which were in fashion a century ago, but a curt, clear, incisive rhetoric which scores the maximum of points in the minimum of space.

He must be almost as quick-witted as a barrister, for he will have to write—and not only write but express a decided opinion without leaving any obvious loophole for contradiction—on subjects which are not always familiar. (Many eminent lawyers have been leader-writers in their time.) No doubt it would be better, from the social point of view, if leader-writers were leisurely persons who could take twenty-four hours to think over their subject and produce a considered and impartial verdict on it ; and some of the big American papers—such as *The New York Times* and *The Baltimore Sun*—arrange for this, and their leaders are mostly on the previous day's news. But in this country promptness is preferred to profundity.

Nevertheless, a leader-writer must have a pretty good general knowledge of politics and economics. There are not the same technical qualifications required as for reporting or sub-editing, and consequently one may be able, without previous experience, to get a position as a leader-writer which one could not get as a reporter, and certainly not as a sub-editor, on a paper of equal standing. But the qualities (as distinct from acquired qualifications) needed are such that there is never a superfluity of capable leader-writers.

THE SPORTS WRITER'S DOUBLE LIFE

SPORTS writers are reporters of a kind, but of a particular kind. They lead a double life, accommodating themselves to the weekly tides of sport. On Saturdays they are all out on the football or the cricket field ; on Sundays they are busy sub-editing and digesting the huge masses of Saturday's sport. Through the week, the jam is spread thinner ; one man will be working outside, one inside, and a third off duty. The great disadvantage of being a sporting journalist is that you are, inevitably, working all of every week-end.

When you read a report of a football match in most papers, you think : " This is very simple stuff. Almost any one could do this." And often indeed it is simple stuff, straightforwardly and even banally put. But it is not so easy as it looks. Sports reporting demands, even more than any other form of journalism, extreme accuracy in detail. This is extremely hard to get. Watch a football match, and write four or five hundred words about it ; then read it through and ask yourself if you are absolutely sure of everything in it. You are a rare bird if you are. To watch the game for an hour and miss nothing, not only to have seen the moves of the game but to have understood them, to remember not only who shot the winning goal but who started the movement which led up to it—this demands a degree of concentration which does not come without practice.

A good " inside " knowledge of the game helps, of course, especially with the more fast-moving games, like hockey or lacrosse ; and in this department alone, perhaps, of all journalism, a knowledge of the subject is more important than ability to write fluently about it. The sporting public wants facts raw ; no cooking can conceal the mistakes from them. There is a distinct opening, even on fairly big papers, for men who know the various sports well, even though they have no previous experience of journalism. That does not mean that they have nothing to learn ; but there is nothing which they cannot be taught pretty quickly. On the other hand, it is a gruelling job.

Besides those who describe sporting events, there is, of course, the legion of racing tipsters who, in their own opinion at any rate, do more to promote the circulation of their paper than the rest of the staff rolled into one.

HOW THE REVIEWERS WORK

THEN there is the army of reviewers, music critics, dramatic critics, film critics, art critics, radio critics, and so on. It is impossible to say what is a standard outfit of critics for the average newspaper, because every paper has a different arrangement. A provincial newspaper, for instance, for which theatrical " first nights " always fall, two or three together, on a Monday, must obviously have several men at the theatre that night, and doing something else for the rest of the week ; a London paper, on the other hand, can keep one man going all the time, because managers take great care to keep " first nights " from clashing. *The Times* has two full-time dramatic critics.

Music spreads itself out over the week, and is therefore more easily dealt with by one man, and many of the big provincial papers have a full-time music critic. A point of importance is that the music critic is writing primarily for readers who know a good deal about music, whereas a film critic, for instance, is writing primarily for people who do not know much about the business of producing films, and do not want to know. The trouble with film criticism is that it is too liable to develop into mere gossip, because a large section of the film-going public is more interested in the personalities of the players than in the art of the screen.

WHAT THE DRAMATIC CRITIC MUST KNOW

THE dramatic critic (I have never understood why one does not say " drama critic "—the critic himself is rarely dramatic) is in an intermediate position. His readers do take an interest in the play as distinct from the players. A dramatic critic who takes his job at all seriously has his work cut out. He has not simply to go to plays and write about them. Any reporter can do that, and do it well. He must be erudite in the history of the stage. He must be widely read in the dramatic literature of many ages and of many countries. He must keep abreast of, and understand if he cannot appreciate, the contemporary currents of theory and practice. He must have seen and remembered many players, and not allowed their glamour to dazzle him.

I have never seen Elizabeth Bergner act. I am ready to believe that she is an actress of the first rank. But I did admire the refusal of James Agate of *The Sunday Times* to call her a " great " actress after seeing her in one part specially written for her. It put him at odds with a whole host of his colleagues, who had proclaimed the " greatness " of Bergner without hesitation. Agate did not deny that Bergner was a great actress ; he said expressly that nothing in the one performance he had seen was incompatible with greatness. When he had seen her in a few more exacting parts—such as Lady Macbeth, Hedda Gabler, and Phèdre—he would be prepared to say whether he thought her a great actress or not.

I feel that he was absolutely right. He was not criticising Elizabeth Bergner ; he was criticising his fellow-critics. He, almost alone, was taking his profession with proper seriousness. I admire his stand the more because I myself have been guilty of this very fault—" plumping " for an actress on the strength of one performance. There was some excuse. It was Diana Wynyard, who was not so well known then. A reporter (which I was) naturally wants to cry up a discovery ; it means that one has obtained an " exclusive " story. But a dramatic critic is a judge, not a detective.

THE DIFFICULT TASK OF THE ART AND RADIO CRITICS

ART critics have a most difficult task. Many newspapers do not take art seriously at all ; they merely treat it as " news." But even with the papers which do pay some attention to painting and sculpture and so forth, the art critic is nearly always in the position of trying to explain what the painters are about to a public which does not know the first thing about it.

Most newspapers now devote a good deal of space to criticism of and news about wireless programmes, because the interest of their readers in " listening in " grows each year. But one cannot yet say that the job of radio critic has settled down and developed firm outlines. Few radio critics know as much of broadcasting technique as dramatic critics know about theatrical technique. (When I say broadcasting technique, I mean what corresponds to production in the theatre, not simply the physical mechanism of transmission and reception, though I think a radio critic ought to know a good deal about that too.) Besides, there is this air of unreality about it. There are real openings here for intelligent journalists who want to specialise and who will take the trouble to master the job from the technical side as well as from the entertainment point of view.

THREE WAYS OF DEALING WITH BOOKS

THERE are three ways of dealing with books. One can review them ; one can notice them ; or one can " gut " them. To " gut " a book is simply to choose a series of extracts, on their news value, for publication in the news columns. It does not call for the exercise of critical faculties. A review is a long and profound analysis of the book, such as one finds in the important weeklies, or in *The Observer* and *The Sunday Times*, or in learned periodicals. The daily papers have not this space to allot to books. Most of them have a " book page " once a week, and get in four columns or so of notices of at least a dozen books. *The Manchester Guardian* reviews more books than any other daily paper ; it notices on an average five or six books a day for five days of the week.

The bulk of book reviewing is done by people who are not on the staff of any newspaper. In most cases it is a sideline. The reviews of many important books (other than fiction) are done by people who are experts in the field concerned. There is, however, a lot of general reviewing, especially on economic and social topics, of which one may do enough to get a living out of it. The work is exacting, almost jading. The strain of reading and reviewing half a dozen books a week is very great.

SHOULD A PAPER HAVE A LITERARY POLICY ?

MANY papers have a reviewer of fiction, and send him all the novels which come out, and leave him to make his pick of them and write a weekly article on the lot. This plan has certain advantages ; it saves the Literary Editor a lot of time, and it makes a good readable article. But it has more than equivalent drawbacks. A man who honestly tries to get to the heart of six serious books a week would be a very exceptional person if he did not go mad in a month. Some books will, therefore, get more careful attention than others. Unless, again, the reviewer is an exceptional man, he cannot

15

but have personal prejudices which sway his decision on what books to read most attentively, so that he can hardly help committing the paper as a whole to the support of some particular school of writers.

THE ESSENCE OF CRITICISM

FOR all the work which has been touched on during the preceding section, a mastery of the English language is absolutely essential. It is not simply that, in reviewing books, the subject is a literary one; that is, perhaps, an irrelevant factor. One is trying all the time to convey a purely intellectual content—not a record of facts or impressions, but a comment upon some other man's record. It is more difficult to understand than to see, and what is harder to understand is harder to put into words; indeed, the two processes may really be the same thing, for thought itself is impossible without the use of words (except in mathematics), and the man who cannot explain a work of art to another has not explained it to himself.

Hence, if you are a person who has mastered this business of understanding and explaining to yourself in intelligible terms what other men have seen or thought, you will have no great difficulty in adjusting yourself to the particular field in which you wish to work, or in moving from one to another. You have, of course, to learn the technique of the art concerned, and that needs an effort of mind comparable to that needed in learning shorthand. But if you have not got the critical habit of mind you will never make a critic, either of books or of art or of music or of anything else.

THE CHANCE FOR THE OUTSIDE CONTRIBUTOR

ALL newspapers take a good deal of " copy " from outside contributors, mostly in the way of special articles which are not " news " (because they do not record an actual event which has just happened) though they may be " topical," in the sense that they are more appropriately used on one day than on another. Some papers have a particular " magazine page " or pages for such matter. Others habitually publish one or more special articles on the leader page. Nearly all have a " Woman's page " or " Home page " devoted to such domestic subjects as cooking, dress, gardening, babies. Some run columns of miscellaneous jottings, for which contributions are accepted and paid for, though not published in the contributor's name. The more popular weekly magazines are, of course, largely made up of articles of this kind, usually illustrated.

HOW TO AVOID THE "EDITOR'S REGRETS"

How can one place one's articles with success ? There are two well-known rules, which I need only repeat briefly, since they are the theme of every handbook on writing for profit that ever I read. The first is : *Study your market.* The second is : *Keep the article short and clear.*

With regard to the market, what I mean is this. It is no good sending in to a newspaper an article of a kind which they do not use. All papers have, especially on their " magazine page," a normal framework or design, and they are not going to remould their page one day a month to accommodate an article out of the usual form. If a paper normally publishes a special article, in a particular position, of 900 to 1200 words, it is no earthly use sending them one of 500 or of 2000 words. Yet it is astonishing how often people do this, though one would have thought it the most elementary thing to grasp.

The second warning is primarily for people inclined to fine writing, purple passages, or forced humour. " Short " is, of course, a relative term. There are some things which cannot be done in less than 800 words, and these are the only ones which should have 800 words.

I would add to these two rules a third, and from a practical point of view, a far more important one. *Have a subject.* Better still, have several subjects. I don't mean simply have a subject for some particular article in question. That goes without saying—though there are people who try to construct a humorous article out of nothing. I mean, get to know a great deal about something, and make that special knowledge your stock-in-trade. It doesn't matter much what it is. It may be birds or botany or motoring or foreign travel or economic history or cooking. What matters is that you should know more about it than the average person, or than the average journalist. Newspapers do not take from outside contributors what they could as easily get done in the office.

I know one man, for instance, who makes a speciality of

what one may call political anecdotes. I fancy that he does it on the card index system ; gets each new volume of political memoirs out of the library, extracts the most entertaining bits from it and files them for reference. Then out they come as occasion serves. Mr. Neville Chamberlain goes fishing ; he looks through his card index and finds a very amusing story about another Chancellor some forty years ago, who went fishing with unusual consequences. Whatever turns up, he has an apposite story, and his contributions are a frequent relief to the harassed compiler of a column of " daily jottings."

SOME FRUITFUL FIELDS FOR THE FREE-LANCE

BIRDS are a very good subject, because there is an infinite amount to be said about them, and most people are interested in birds. A fairly sure draw is a description of places visited in the course of foreign travel, because, *ex hypothesi*, the writer knows more about them than the reader who has not been there. A keen observer can always find matter for an article in some remote and unfamiliar place, even if it is in this country. A disadvantage is, of course, that one has to travel. Stuff dug out of guide-books is no use.

The domesticities are a profitable field for the specialist, because many papers find it hard to fill their " Woman's page " with fresh and interesting copy. It is a field in which women are specialists by second nature, and often write very well, if they can be brought to see that these things are worth writing about at all. I remember a lady once asked me to have a look at a sheaf of her copy, and tell her what it was worth. There were some humorous stories, which were pointless and over-written ; there was some literary criticism, commonplace and flat ; and there were a lot of short paragraphs about housework and cooking and what sort of flowers will go together in a vase, and so on, which were not only informative but quite well written, concise, lucid, with plenty of punch and with the points made in the right order. It was simply that she knew her subject and had something to say about it. But she showed me these paragraphs deprecatingly, saying : " Well, they got published, but that's all I can say for them." It was a lot more than she could say for the rest. They were not worth publishing.

In the last year or two there has been an outbreak of articles on walking, camping, scenery, and other delights of the open air. This market is not yet saturated, and the quality of some of the stuff published is not such that it would hold its own against all comers.

If you have not already got a subject, get one. Choose it primarily because you are interested in it yourself. If you study something solely in order to write about it and without being at all interested in it yourself you are unlikely to interest others. When you have had a number of articles on a special subject accepted, it may help to state on the front page of subsequent work that you " have contributed articles on . . . to the following publications. . . ."

I will wind up this section with two purely practical points : (1) You do not need an agent if you are writing for a particular market. If you are just writing what comes into your head, an agent may be able to place it to the best advantage. (2) See that you are properly paid. It is as well to belong to a protective organisation. A professional journalist naturally joins the union. If you are a whole-time journalist, join the Society of Authors, Playwrights, and Composers. They will take in part-time contributors, and are stalwart allies in case of need.

THE FREE-LANCE AT WORK

by F. M. WINTER, B.A.(Lond.)

BEFORE the young writer sets out to explore the possibilities of any particular markets he should have some fairly clear idea of what he is aiming at. His early efforts are usually scattered and sporadic. He tries an article, a short story, a few chapters of a novel, perhaps some verses for children or some hints on how to paint the bathroom. A certain amount of such experimenting is necessary in the beginner, if he is to discover where his best capacities lie ; and, indeed, what one might call a scrappiness of output continues to be a characteristic of some quite well-known and successful writers. In many cases such work pays, once one has made a name. But there is little doubt that the best way to make a name is to concentrate on one particular form.

But after a certain amount of preliminary experimenting it should be possible for the young writer to make up his mind on the subject of what form of literary or journalistic success is his ultimate aim, and on his best method of getting some kind of financial footing in the writing world. There must be numbers of writers aiming in vain at publications like *The Argosy* or *The Saturday Review* or at novels on morbid themes, who might succeed in making money in popular journalism. And it is certainly true that young writers of real gifts and imagination waste their time, energy, and money trying to sell popular material of the kind that they will never write really well. There are decisions here that the writer must make according to his circumstances, his temperament, and the opinion of those who matter on his work.

Has he any gift of imagination and creative vision that might justify him in aiming straight away at the markets for work of definite literary value ? Has he sufficient faith in his gift and sufficient staying power to keep him on what may prove a difficult and ill-paid path ? Or, not possessing these things, has he the sense and courage to admit it to himself and to start along the still difficult but better-paid path of popular journalism ? If he is sufficiently free and sufficiently wise to make the choice early, he will save himself much trouble and disappointment and discontent later.

REWARDS OFFERED FOR POETRY

LITERARY success must, at any rate, be well established before one dare abandon the more immediately remunerative work for its sake. If one has acquired the very difficult art of writing first-class magazine short stories, one may count on excellent payment for them. But the better story of a more subtle kind will only sell to magazines which pay low prices. Verse, that first love of so many people of literary ambition, does not, except in unusual circumstances, make money. But because it forms an important part of the secret output of so many very young writers, and because it is only with the greatest difficulty that these young people are persuaded of its comparative uselessness as a financial asset, it should receive a little attention.

Poets, even minor ones, are rare. But it is fairly common for people of imagination and sensitiveness and literary gifts to turn out some quite delightful verses somewhere between the ages of sixteen and twenty-five. The young writer who is tempted to pin much hope to them should make a point of going to libraries and looking through as many periodical publications as he can. He will find that an extraordinarily small amount of space is given to verse, even by those papers or magazines which publish it regularly. The *Observer*, for example, publishes a poem, or perhaps two, each week, but these are usually by established poets.

If the young writer has a gift for the lighter kind of verses with an easy human appeal, and can combine with this gift the capacity to illustrate the verses with really clever pen-and-ink or what are known as wash sketches, there is a more considerable market in the women's magazines, and some-times, also, in greeting cards of various kinds. But no one should hope to make money from serious verse. A man who has the making of a real poet will go on writing verse, and eventually poetry, in spite of any amount of discourage-ment, but otherwise this youthful verse-writing is only a symptom. It indicates the presence of mental qualities that may one day lead to the writing of good prose and perhaps of really imaginative literature.

A FEW FACTS ABOUT EDITORS

SOME kind of decision on what type of market one is aiming at should narrow and simplify the actual task of getting to know particular markets. But a general survey of one's own capacities and of the markets that do exist is an important preliminary step. Some knowledge of the ways of editors and publishers also is essential. For example, the free-lance must realise from the beginning that an editor does not exist to help him in the job of market research that he is capable of doing for himself. An editor's job is to bring out a publication. Comparatively little of his time is devoted to reading the contributions of outside writers. When a con-tribution is returned to the sender as unsuitable, it is accom-panied merely by a printed rejection slip which is the same for everybody.

The editor does not, except in a very few cases indeed, dictate a letter telling one *why* one's effort is considered unsuitable. He has little time to do so, and he knows by experience that a kindly intended note to an unknown author may result in much idle argument, protest, or explana-tion. It may be that the contribution sent in is not good enough ; it may be that it is good enough for some quite different kind of publication but useless to him, or it may be that the subject is suitable, but the article four times too long, or that it is suitable in every way but has arrived at a time when there is no prospect of there being room for it for months to come. Free-lances are apt to forget that editors are constantly up against the fact that the columns of newspapers and magazines are inelastic.

I have occasionally known an editor take the trouble to send a letter, sometimes containing the most helpful criticism, in returning a contribution that may have seemed to him particularly good, though unsuitable, or particularly promising, though immature. But neither editors nor publishers should be asked, in letters accompanying contributions, to do things like that. It is a writer's business to start with a certain knowledge of his markets, and to increase it as he goes on.

A GUIDE TO MARKETS

THE first step should be to consult a journalistic guide, such as *The Writers' and Artists' Year-Book.* This is brought up to date and republished every year very cheaply. It gives the most valuable preliminary survey of all kinds of publications, indicating whether they are published daily, weekly, monthly, or quarterly, the kind of material which each is prepared to consider from outside contributors, the rough limits of length that should be observed, and in many instances the rate and method of payment to be expected. It is best to go through such a guide carefully, marking the publications for which the kind of material one is writing appears to be suitable.

After studying these guides, the periodicals themselves must be bought and most carefully read. Only this kind of research will indicate the nature of the subjects preferred, and the treatment which appears to be acceptable. The guide may state, for example, that a certain newspaper will consider leader-page articles appealing to women readers. But only a study of that particular newspaper over a period of some weeks at least will make it clear if the women readers are to be appealed to on serious lines or with a lighter touch.

Perhaps the articles should be of a controversial type which a woman might discuss with her husband or her friends or which might induce her to write letters of disagreement to the editor. Perhaps a more successful line would be the sentimental type that will make her feel pleased and important, such as an article on the heroism of motherhood, or the practical type that will give her a little help in some of her many problems. The same course should be followed in

the difficult task of selling short stories. Even editors themselves find it difficult to explain just what kinds of story
they are most likely to choose. " Just watch the magazine,"
they will say. Publishers expect one to watch their lists and
catalogues, and, as far as fiction at least is concerned, to discover
what sort of books they bring out.

POINTS THAT MAY BE LEARNT FROM ACCEPTANCES

THE young writer must supplement his knowledge of
markets gained in these ways by a campaign of experiment—a campaign that must be conducted entirely by post.
It should not include calling at random at an editor's office
and asking to see him, nor even telephoning and asking for
an appointment. Rejections teach one little, but acceptances
teach one a great deal. The real significance of the first
acceptance does not lie in the cheque. It is important in
what it implies for the future. No writer should treat such
a portent merely as a reason for self-congratulation. He
should at once be up and doing. So far he has known only
what certain publications do not like by the contributions
which they return to him. Now he knows something at least
about what one particular publication does like, and is
prepared to buy.

After waiting for what he may judge to be a tactful interval,
the length of which must depend of course on the frequency
of publication, he should send in another contribution,
choosing his subject and his style in the light of what he has
learnt. Or in certain cases one acceptance, or perhaps two
or three from the same publication, can be followed up by
a letter giving several suggestions for further contributions.

The editor concerned knows now that the free-lance can
write. (It is sometimes as well to remind editors in an
accompanying note that they recently accepted certain contributions, for they have much to remember.) He will be
likely to give more attention to a further contribution or to
suggestions. After a number of acceptances he will sometimes be prepared to give one a short interview with the
object of discussing the kind of work one might continue
to do for him. But such interviews should not be suggested
too soon. In fact it is often best to keep well in the background while things go well. One must judge from the tone
of the editor's correspondence, if any, and take one's chance.
Any rare letters from editors or publishers giving kindly

criticism should be followed up by a further effort, **or at**
least by a letter of thanks.

SHOULD ARTICLES COME FIRST ?

MOST writers' first commercial efforts take the form of
articles. Indeed, unless the young writer has an
obvious gift for fiction, it is usually his best plan to begin
with articles of some kind, for they are easier to write and
easier to sell than short stories or books. The writer who is
young in experience is more likely to have good ideas in his
mind than he is to have good plots or good themes, or the
capacity to create people in whom his readers can believe.
Moreover, an inexperienced writer let loose on a short story
is apt to let his passion for description run away with him ;
and if he has plenty of ideas, he is apt to forget now and then
that he is writing a story, and to hold up the action while he
expresses them.

An experienced journalist once gave an excellent piece of
advice to a young writer who was doubtful which market to
explore first. It was : " Go on writing articles until you feel
you have expressed all the more important, forceful, tangible,
expressible, and *saleable* ideas in your mind. Take care to
write them well, for you will be learning all the time. Then,
when you are tempted to repeat yourself or to become a
little less confident of your opinions, when you begin to be
aware of subtleties that no amount of ' what I think ' will
express, that is the time to turn to short stories, or novels."
Such a method is better both for the articles one begins by
writing, and for the fiction one goes on to write ; and though,
of course, like other good advice, it should not be applied
to every case, in a majority it will be found to work well.

THE WIDER SCOPE OF ARTICLES

ARTICLES, whether practical or theoretical, need a less sustained effort to write than fiction, and they are easier to
sell for many reasons. They have, as one of their most
important markets, the daily newspaper press all over the
country, which can absorb a considerable number of such
contributions. The editor of a newspaper is frequently more
willing to consider contributions from new and unknown
writers than the editor of a magazine. The newspaper circu-
lates to a more varied public, and its editor can accept more
varied expressions of opinion and is less loth than the editor

of a magazine to publish views that will arouse disagreement and draw protesting letters. The narrower magazine public necessitates a narrower policy.

The saleable " leader-page " article should, in a majority of cases, be of the " what I think " controversial type. It should not express a view that is so generally held as to be taken for granted. On the other hand, it should not express views that will only gain support from about one per cent. of a newspaper's readers. An editor likes an article that is sufficiently controversial to cause a few readers to write him appraising letters and to provoke a few indignant protests.

One is sometimes justified in giving an article a more un-compromising title than the material warrants—one that will startle the majority of readers into paying attention to it. Good titles go a long way towards selling an article. It is of little use to send in an article that is startling and well written under a title that does not tempt any one to read it. It is always possible that the editor will change the title, but the free-lance must at least think of one that will induce some one in the editor's office to give the article con-sideration.

There is on many papers an opening for other kinds of article on the leader-page, as the young writer will soon discover. There are, however, a few things to remember in aiming at this very important page of a newspaper. The length of articles should generally be somewhere between five hundred and a thousand words, and, from an unknown writer, an article stands more chance of acceptance if it is nearer to the five hundred mark.

In choosing subjects it is always wise to avoid politics (there will be people on the editorial staff who know more of this than the free-lance), religion (discussions of this subject are seldom welcomed except from well-known people), or class disputes. The kind of article that describes a personal experience or adventure should not be attempted unless that experience is more or less unique. And it should be realised that whereas the opinions of the unknown writer may be of interest on a controversial topic such as : " Have women any sense of duty ? " or : " Why do we dislike the highbrow ? " they are of comparatively little importance on any subject on which a specialist of any kind is more entitled to write, and they are of absolutely no value at all on intimate matters of personal behaviour. A famous film star could sell an article on what she eats for breakfast. An unknown free-lance could not.

CHANCES OFFERED BY THE MAGAZINES

THE market for magazine articles is very varied, and the choice of subjects therefore wide. But it will be found that the material in any one magazine is generally narrower in scope than that in any one newspaper. This should simplify matters for the free-lance in many ways, and indeed the magazine market might profitably come in for more exploration than it generally receives from the beginner. The competition is not so keen as it is on a newspaper. The editorial staff is usually a little less busy. The editor is frequently more willing to consider series of articles, and a series is a great help and stand-by to the beginner. I remember one unusual series that was particularly successful. It was called " How to Lose." It was lightly satirical and entertaining, but full of wisdom. It contained articles on such subjects as " How to lose your Friends," " How to lose your Husband," " How to lose Money," " How to lose Heart." It succeeded in extending itself for some time beyond the original half-dozen articles that had been commissioned on the strength of a first experimental article.

WRITING FROM THE WOMAN'S POINT OF VIEW

PUBLICATIONS that appeal almost exclusively to women are so numerous and of such importance to the free-lance that it is worth his while to consider them separately. It is a mistake to suppose that contributors to women's magazines are exclusively women. Articles of the controversial type, in particular, are much in demand from men, provided that they deal with subjects of interest and importance to women, and provided also that, however critical or condemnatory they may be, they are not entirely lacking in sympathy with a woman's point of view. Informative articles of the right kind are welcome from anybody, and a few of the best writers on cookery and handicrafts are men. This kind of publication is, however, the special field of the woman writer, and she will find editors of such magazines as willing as anybody to consider suggestions for series, either on general or on practical subjects.

It should be remembered that women's magazines carry a very considerable number of illustrations, and as far as possible material should be schemed and written with this in mind. An article, either on a general subject or of any practical kind, stands considerably less chance of acceptance if it cannot easily be illustrated by sketches or photographs. The free-lance who can either sketch or take good photographs, or work in conjunction with an artist or a photographer, has an unquestionable advantage here, but the lack of it need deter no one, for some editors even prefer to have material illustrated by their own artists.

There are subjects which are best avoided in sending contributions to a woman's magazine, merely because they are of the kind that are covered by regular contributors. A study of the magazine will soon show what these are, but subjects such as society gossip, cookery, and baby welfare are almost always treated in this way, and beauty culture very frequently.

Advertising is an aspect of newspaper and magazine production with which the free-lance need concern himself very little. But he is to some extent brought into contact with it in contributing to women's magazines, because in such publications the editorial and advertisement departments work in much closer co-operation than on a daily newspaper or on a magazine like *Punch* or *The Strand*. This need only concern the free-lance when he expresses an opinion about any article which might be advertised in the kind of magazine for which he is planning his contribution.

The safest rule is never to condemn any commodity which might conceivably be advertised. Let us assume, for example, that the article is describing a certain kind of needlework. It is easy to fall into the mistake of saying that a certain material is useless for the purpose. The manufacturers of the material may be valued advertisers in that particular magazine, and the free-lance must remember that the revenue of a magazine comes largely from the selling of space for advertisements.

HOW TO SUCCEED WITH THE TRADE PAPER

THESE considerations are even more important in writing for a trade magazine. The market for free-lance contributions in these magazines is in any case very much restricted, but if the writer has sufficient knowledge of a trade to aim at a business publication, he will have to keep an eye open for any tendency to make statements against the advertising interests.

The trade magazine, though it needs a certain amount at least of specialised knowledge on the part of its contributors, is not a remunerative market. Most of its material is written by its editorial staff. There is a fairly steady but very small demand for articles by experts, but even these will seldom sell for more than three guineas and must be generally quite a thousand words in length. Moreover, from the point of view of a trade magazine, an expert is not some one with an active interest in and sketchy knowledge of the subject. He is, in the building trade for example, either an architect or a consulting engineer, or a well-known decoration artist, or a prominent member of a firm specialising in lighting or heating equipment.

WHERE THE BEGINNER MAY GET ADVICE

THERE will always be people who have ambition yet lack confidence in their ability to teach themselves. For these the school of journalism may in some cases prove a friend and counsellor. Its chief value to the beginner who does not need help with any language difficulties is its value as critic and adviser. To the free-lance who has no writer friend to give him an honest opinion on his work, the school of journalism may supply valuable criticism. It will suggest subjects, if those are his difficulty, and give advice on markets which can be supplemented by the writer's own experience.

There are several schools of journalism of good standing, which conscientiously try to teach pupils their craft and to forward their interests. Unfortunately there are also many almost bogus " schools," fee-snatching institutions which teach nothing, waste time, and absorb money that can generally be ill-afforded by the would-be free lance. Even worse are idle old journalists who take " pupils " at a handsome fee. The pupil generally devils for his master, who reaps all the benefits from his work and gives nothing in return except a little casual and airy advice. Of course there are honourable exceptions to this rule—but not, alas, very many.

Readers should satisfy themselves most carefully of the credentials and standing of any school or person who offers to teach them journalism before paying a fee of any kind. Experience remains the best school, unless one can be fortunate enough to obtain a staff job in the offices of a firm owning magazines. Two years spent in such a post, at however humble a salary, is the best preparation for a free-lance career. But, of course, there are not many openings in this direction.

The presentation of material is of great importance. Editors and publishers cannot be expected to recognise a masterpiece if it is presented to them like a badly-written school essay. All material should be typed or legibly written on quarto paper, on one side only, and a good margin should be allowed on the left-hand side of the page. Articles should be secured with a paper-clip, and it is as well to finish them with a plain piece of paper as a frontispiece, bearing only the title of the article, one's name and address, and the approximate number of words employed. It is an excellent plan to back them with a plain piece of paper as well. Th n, if one's article comes back from several offices looking a little the worse for wear, it need not be re-typed completely, but can merely be supplied with new frontispiece and backing.

Manuscripts should, if possible, be secured in a folder to keep them flat, and the longer ones should be divided into sections, with the author's name clearly shown on each separate section. Needless to say, all pages should be numbered. All material should be accompanied by a stamped addressed envelope with the correct amount of postage attached. If a letter is sent as well, this should also be typed, if possible.

HOW TO AVOID BREAKING THE LAW OF LIBEL

AUTHORS, and especially those who are tempted to indulge in highly controversial writing, should remember that there is a law of libel in England capable of very wide interpretation. A glance at almost any newspaper or magazine will show to what lengths publishers are driven in order to avoid a charge of libel. In any account of a crime, for instance, the word " alleged " will occur every two or three lines, even though there can be no reasonable doubt that the statement is true. Again, most short stories, especially those appearing in newspapers, carry a notice in small print, " All Characters fictitious," in order to forestall possible accusation by a prompt denial. The position as regards libel, is briefly this : any statement which can be held to be derogatory or harmful to a person, institution, business, etc., can be made the subject of a libel action. The statement need not be untrue for it to constitute a libel. If, for instance, a reporter states that some well-known and highly respected citizen once served three months' hard labour for theft, and proves conclusively the truth of this, his paper might nevertheless be called on to pay heavy damages.

A further point—one which is a danger to every author—is that it is possible to libel a person without intention and without any knowledge at all of the person libelled. If, for instance, a dramatist introduces a character with red hair, one eye, a stutter, and a limp, and makes him out a villain, and a man with these disabilities, thinking he recognises a caricature of himself, chooses to sue the dramatist for libel, he need only prove the play has injured his reputation and he stands a good chance of gaining damages.

From this it will be seen that libel is a very easy law to transgress, and that its observance necessarily muzzles the author to a considerable extent. Editors and sub-editors naturally keep a close watch for anything which might be construed into libel, but every one concerned in writing needs to train himself to avoid statements, remarks, or portraits which could be made to fit particular cases. A general attack on the modern girl, for instance, is less likely to cause trouble than a detailed, unfriendly description of a modern girl which might be thought to be aimed at some well-known but not very popular young woman.

MAKING THE MOST OF REJECTED MATERIAL

NEVER, unless storage space fails, should the writer throw away contributions which, for the time being, he cannot sell. He should devise some method of keeping and cataloguing them. Sooner or later he may think of some way of improving them, or some event may give them topicality. He should conscientiously keep cuttings of all the material he has had published. An idea that has sold once may sell again in a different form. Already, of course, in the process of learning how to write, he should have started an ideas' library of his own, consisting of cuttings of anything that strikes his fancy and of his own jottings of the germs and developments of ideas.

The market for free-lance contributions has, like other markets, been somewhat restricted during the last few years. The revenue of papers and magazines has gone down, the fees paid for outside work have to some extent suffered, and more subjects have been covered by members of the editorial staffs. The most usual rate of payment is from two to three guineas a thousand words. It has certainly become more difficult than it once was to rely on free-lance journalism for a living. But as the beginner is seldom rash enough to do that he need not be unduly depressed. Conditions are improving, and, as they improve, the writer can be quietly building up his technique and increasing his markets. He will himself be able to judge when the time comes for him to join the ranks of professional scribes.

WHAT JOURNALISTS HAVE WRITTEN ABOUT THEIR TRADE

ANY ONE interested in free-lancing will find, sooner or later, that an acquaintance with inside journalism is not only interesting in itself but is necessary to avoid needless labour. There are, however, remarkably few books worth reading on the subject. Sir Alfred Robbins did a book on *The Press*, but this is mostly historical, and however interesting the newspapers of the nineteenth century may have been, their history throws little light on journalism to-day. G. B. Dibblee has an excellent little book, *The Newspaper*, in the Home University Library ; but it was written some time ago.

A very informative book is W. Hutcheon's *Gentlemen of the Press* ; the author was a sub-editor on several big dailies, and night editor of *The Morning Post* for many years, and he knows what he is talking about. On the technical side, F. J. Mansfield's *Sub-editing* is important. But Mansfield is a *Times* man, and the sub-editorial staff of *The Times* is bigger than that of other papers and therefore does not work at quite such high pressure ; so the book contains some counsels of perfection. A useful little book is W. V. Noble's *Interviewing*, published by Isaac Pitman ; the author has worked for two big Northern evening papers, and knows all the tricks of his trade.

There are a considerable number of books which aim at helping the free-lance writer, apart from the acknowledged text-books such as *The Writers' and Artists' Year-Book*. These aim more generally at telling him how to write the kind of articles and stories which are likely to sell than at assisting him in the actual business of selling. But some of them are full of the most valuable advice from experienced journalists or publishers or literary agents who are in a position to judge the nature of the mistakes made by the beginner trying to get into print. Two very helpful and very readable books of this kind are written by Michael Joseph, one entitled *Short Story-Writing for Profit*, and the other *The Commercial Side of Literature*.

There is much indirect value to be obtained from any books by well-known journalists and writers about their careers and about the inner workings of great newspaper and publishing offices. The free-lance who has never had any experience of such an organisation lacks something which may be of great value to him in his work. He will approach the business of writing for the public in a different spirit after reading such a book, for example, as Tom Clarke's *My Northcliffe Diary*. Two weekly publications that every journalist should read are *The World's Press News* and *The Newspaper World*. They are intended to keep writers *au fait* with all that is going on in the various departments of journalism.

WRITING FOR STAGE, SCREEN, AND RADIO

by ALAN HOWLAND (of the " Saturday Review " and formerly of the British Broadcasting Corporation)

IT must be assumed in the first place that the author is a person who finds it more easy to express himself in dramatic form—that is to say, in the form of dialogue—than in the novel, short story, or essay form. He need not be a poet—a primrose by the river's brim may remain a simple primrose to him to the end of his days, but it must inspire in him the desire to create living and speaking characters rather than to write a novel about a professor of botany, or a poem " To a Primrose," or an essay on the flora of the riverside. This may sound a truism, but it is not. For every person who says, " I am going to write a play because I *must* write a play and nothing else," there are scores of people who say, " I am going to write a play because it is such fun to be a playwright." The person who takes the latter attitude will probably never write a satisfactory play.

THREE MODES OF EXPRESSION FOR THE PLAYWRIGHT

THERE are three ways in which the dramatist may express himself, through the stage, the screen, and through the radio, and his first task is to decide in which of these three moulds he is going to cast his material. He will be guided in this decision by certain personal considerations. For the sake of clarity let us look upon the theatre as the home of three-dimensional art, the cinema as the home of two-dimensional art, and the wireless as the home of one-dimensional art. Television must be ignored at the moment as it is impossible to say whether it will follow the technique of the theatre or the cinema, or whether it will in the course of time evolve a technique peculiar to itself. The three dimensions of the theatre are, as I see it, sight, sound, and the conscious or subconscious interplay between actor and audience. The two dimensions of the cinema are sound and image, and the one-dimensional radio relies on pure sound for its effect.

To take the three in their chronological order, let us deal with the theatre first of all. We have already assumed that the author is a person who finds his natural form of expression in a stage play. He must have more than this. He must have a love of the theatre and a love of dramatic literature. He must make himself familiar with the works of the great dramatists—Shakespeare, Sheridan, Congreve—and the contemporary dramatists—Shaw, Somerset Maugham, Coward, Londsale. It would be of considerable advantage if he could study the plays of Æschylus, Sophocles, and Euripides, if not in the original, at least in a good translation.

There is only one way to read a play and that is to read it, as it were, with one's eyes shut. The characters should pass across the mind's eye just as vividly as if they were actually strutting their fretful hour upon the stage. They should be clothed by the imagination in the very habiliments which they would be wearing. Their gestures, their facial expressions, their voices, their very inflections should be as vivid to the reader as though they were being enacted before him in the flesh. Just as a musician reading a full score can actually hear that entry for the wood-wind, that delicate passage for the horns, or that magnificent sweep of the strings, so the reader of a play must merge himself in the thing he is reading and become one with the dramatist himself.

Love of the theatre is every bit as important. The reading of a play is a fine thing, but it lacks that vital contact between the artist and the beholder, that intangible sympathy which only the theatre can give. There are two distinct ways of watching a play—for the sake of entertainment and for the sake of analysis. For this reason the student of the drama should endeavour to go at least twice to the same play. The first visit will tell him what the play is about, whether it is a good play, whether it is well acted, and whether the author has been well served by his producer. The second visit will enable him to discriminate between the respective shares taken by the author, the actors, and the producer in the finished performance and to concentrate on the play itself. It will be possible to discover how the author presented his plot, how he introduced his characters, how he developed his theme, and how he achieved his dénouement. It does not matter whether the play be a good one or a bad one, the lessons are there to be learnt.

THE FOLLOW-MY-LEADER TENDENCY

NEXT comes the choice of a subject and the selection of a suitable way to present the subject chosen. In other words, is it to be a tragedy, a drama, a comedy, a farce, or just a play? There has been a regrettable tendency on the London stage during recent years for authors to play an extremely unprofitable game of follow-my-leader! No sooner does Charlotte Brontë take the stage as the central character in a new play than the theatre is deluged with plays good, bad, and indifferent about the Brontë Sisters. Henry the Eighth has but to swagger before an audience in Shaftesbury Avenue and the town is full of Bluff King Hals. Somebody digs up the Œdipus complex from a decent obscurity and there is a spate of plays about mother fixations and maternal jealousy. This is the wrong way to write a play. It is all very well to be in the fashion, but if the clothes are not made of good material they will not last.

The only way, then, to choose the subject for a play is by intuition, or, as some people prefer to call it, inspiration. The author must have either the desire to write or something to say—preferably both. Shakespeare had nothing in particular to say about the sea-coast of Bohemia or the Forest of Arden, neither of which had any real existence, but his imaginative genius could not be suppressed and, because he had that desire to write, the theatre and, indeed, the English language has been enriched by *Twelfth Night* and *As You Like It*. Shaw, on the other hand, has much to say about doctors and politics, hence *The Doctor's Dilemma* and *The Apple Cart*. Shakespeare could produce a perfect play out of nothing; Shaw selects the dramatic form as being the most likely to propagate his ideas.

It would be an impertinence to imagine that one can teach a genius to write a play or a novel or how to compose a symphony or to paint a picture. Shakespeare probably did not read a treatise on authorship before he wrote *The Tempest*, and Mozart was able to compose without resorting to text-books. But there is, and always has been, a large body of people who, while they know that they have ideas to express, know too that they must be expressed through some particular medium ; they cannot proceed unless they know the kind of scaffolding which they must erect before the building can take shape. It is to people in this category that those tentative remarks are addressed.

THE PLAYWRIGHT SEES LIFE IN DRAMATIC FORM

THE author, then, has something to say, and he is convinced that it must be said in dramatic form. He is the type of man who, if he sees some one fall off a bus, thinks of the incident in terms of its dramatic quality. He does not go home and write a letter to *The Times* about the carelessness of citizens who rely on buses for transport, or the high-handed attitude of the London Transport Board in allowing vehicles from which it is possible to fall to ply for hire. He does not see the occurrence in the Hugh Walpole manner, and write a novel about the man's family unto the third and fourth generation, nor does he evolve a scintillating essay in the manner of G. K. Chesterton to prove that in this topsy-turvy world it should have been, by an immortal paradox, the stairs which fell down the man and not the man down the stairs. He sees merely the drama of it all, and according to his mentality he translates it into terms of farce, tragedy, or high comedy.

The English theatre has a tradition which decrees that there shall be at least two intervals during any given performance. The author has in consequence a ready-made scaffolding with the aid of which he can build his play. It must be in three parts—in other words, it must have a beginning, a middle, and an ending. More learned writers than I would prefer to say an exposition, a climax, and a dénouement, but the fact is there in both cases.

Before we proceed to analyse the method of evolving a play, let us say just one brief word about the central idea which has prompted the author to try his hand at this hazardous profession. Every plot must have in it the elements of conflict—conflict of theories, conflict of personalities, conflict of circumstances, but conflict there must be. *Hamlet* would be nothing without the mental conflict of the Prince of Denmark ; the mere fact that Sheridan called his play *The Rivals* is sufficient to prove the truth of the axiom ; hundreds of years before, Æschylus wrote a play called *Septem contra Thebas* in which " contra " is the operative word.

Even in farce the same statement is true. If it were his own bedroom in which the young husband found himself, there would be no play ; his wife could not conceivably be annoyed at that. It is the fact that he is discovered in the bedroom of a young woman, clad only in a bath-gown, which provides the essential conflict between him and his wife and which provides us—the audience—with our real enjoyment. We may think we are laughing at slamming doors and elderly men in bath towels, but it is chiefly the misunderstanding between the two central characters which is causing us amusement.

KEEPING THE AUDIENCE IN SUSPENSE

WHICH brings me to the question of dilemma. There must be one central point in every play at which it is impossible for the audience to foresee the ultimate solution. They may guess, they may in the case of a so-called " thriller " exercise their mental ingenuity, but they will not be absolutely certain. The dilemma in *Macbeth* emerges after the killing of Duncan, in *Hamlet* after that very painful interview with the ghost. The most obvious fault of the modern playwright is that he sees no necessity for that central point. Too many plays are written, and actually produced, which rely entirely on brisk dialogue or swift production for their effect. Too often one sees plays sprawling over the stage with either no climax at all or fourteen different climaxes at ten-minute intervals.

These amorphous products are mere literary weaklings. They mean nothing, and in consequence they retire into limbo after half-a-dozen performances. There is another type of play which, so far from sprawling, is spread very thin on very underdone toast. There may be a crisis somewhere, but if there is, it either passes unnoticed or comes at the wrong place. The brilliant dialogue is supposed to make up for the absence of plot and theme.

Conflict and dilemma, then, may be accepted as two of the essentials in a well-constructed play. There is still the dénouement, or ending, to be considered. Everybody must have experienced that feeling of disappointment at seeing a play which does not finish but merely stops. Unfortunately in these sophisticated days the tendency to write plays of this sort is becoming more marked. Author after author presents us with what he considers to be " a slice of life," but he usually cuts it with a very blunt knife. This is due to two psychological misconceptions, the first based on artistic, the second on financial, grounds.

The author says to himself, " I hate the conventional happy

ending in which the heroine falls into the hero's arms at precisely 11 p.m., because it is inartistic and banal. On the other hand, people will not pay to see a play in which the final curtain descends on a stage full of corpses or on the heroine weeping over her husband's bier. My play, therefore, will have no ending, happy or otherwise, it will merely stop in time for the pittites to catch their trains." Such an author is utterly wrong. He is shirking the issue, and his conscience is making a coward of him. He is not altogether to be blamed, since the same tendency is to be observed in other branches of art. The modern musician refuses to resolve his chords, he does not believe in cadence, he writes notes and not music. It is as though a man were to set out on a walk and make up his mind to stop at 11 p.m., wherever he might be, whereas the essence of a walk is that one should arrive somewhere, even if it be only one's own home. A symphony must end with a cadence, a play must end with a resolution of the conflicting elements which have been portrayed, just as a walk must end with a bed or a meal or a drink.

To sum up this portion of the argument, there are of necessity three parts to every good play from the structural point of view, and the three-act form suits the exigencies of the modern theatre very well. This does not mean that the beginning, middle, and ending of any given play must coincide with Act 1, Act 2, and Act 3, but it does mean that although the rule of three may puzzle me, the practice of it need not necessarily drive me mad. The end of the first act should leave the audience anticipating a climax, the end of the second act should leave it wondering what the solution of the climax is to be, and the final curtain should provide the answer to the problem.

ERECTING THE "SCAFFOLDING" ROUND THE PLAY

So much for the groundwork. The plot has been selected and the foundations well and truly laid. We know also that there are eventually going to be three storeys to our house. What of the scaffolding ? The characters are going to provide the scaffolding, with the help of which we can lay our bricks, in the form of dialogue. There are all sorts of scaffoldings available to the modern builder. There is the old-fashioned wooden type which painfully and laboriously adapts itself to the particular building which it is proposed to erect, and there is the up-to-date tubular type which can easily be adapted to any job which there may be on hand. The latter can, of course, be run up very cheaply and at a minimum cost.

So with plays. There are a number of stock characters which, with a little ingenuity, can fit any situation in any play. There are also plays which depend very largely on characterisation for their full effect. *Hamlet* is only completely successful because every character, down to the second grave-digger, is perfectly drawn. Menas and Thyreus are as essential to the structure of *Antony and Cleopatra* as the Queen herself. If it is permissible to mix metaphors, you cannot graft a tubular *Hamlet* on to the trees of Birnam Wood. Feste would be as much out of his element in Arden as would Touchstone on the sea-coast of Bohemia.

Stock characters make stock plays, and stock plays are, both from the artistic and financial point of view, absolutely worthless. This does not mean that it is in the least necessary to invent new and extraordinary characters in order to write a successful play. The stage need not be peopled with Calibans. What is essential is that the characters should fit the theme and the situations. Caliban, Bottom, and the witches in *Macbeth* are only permissible because they merge naturally into their surroundings. In other words, it is not sufficient to create characters, the author must create in-dividuals who react to and upon the plot which is being unfolded.

LETTING THE CHARACTERS SPEAK FOR THEMSELVES

THE question of dialogue is one about which it is possible to say but little. There are people who can write dialogue and other people who simply cannot, nor is there any golden rule for learning the art. If the play is to be a sincere piece of work the probability is that the characters themselves will take charge of the situation and speak for themselves. If it is to be merely an essay in stagecraft they will all speak in the same way and with the same voice, namely, the voice of the author. I once had the opportunity of studying the methods of the play-reader of one of the big London managements. It was new to me, but obviously sound. Having read and digested the list of characters on the front page, he covered over the names as they occurred in the actual script with a piece of paper, and read the dialogue without any guide except his own intelligence as to which person was speaking.

If the play were well-written, he had no difficulty in following the action, but if he had continually to refer to the margin the play was usually set on one side.

The only possible way for an author to write natural and convincing dialogue is for him to place himself in the position of each character in turn and to look at the situation through the eyes of the puppet he has created. It is true, of course, that thousands of people in real life do talk and behave in the same way, just as thousands of monkeys gibber in the same way and one ass brays very like another ass. But that is no excuse for filling the stage with characters who speak and behave in exactly the same way as each other. Nothing is more irritating than a play about bright young people who all use the same catch phrases and do the same outrageous things —unless it be the bright young people themselves.

SIMPLICITY THAT IS WELCOMED BY THE PRODUCER

THERE is hardly any necessity to speak at length of the unities of time and space, since in every case they depend on the theme which the author has selected. There is, however, a more practical side to this problem. Managements in these days are not anxious to undertake a production which involves the building of half-a-dozen or more " sets " and continual changing of scenery and furniture—that is, of course, unless it be the adaptation of a 1500-page novel or a translation from the Russian. *Grand Hotel* and *Magnolia Street* would never have seen the light of day had they been written originally as plays by unknown authors.

The same thing applies in a lesser degree to plays with twenty or more characters. It has got to be a very good play indeed which will persuade the shrewd theatrical manager to embark on its production if he knows that his salary list is going to be a long one. These are hard facts but they are true ones. The modern impresario generally looks first of all at the number of characters and the number of scenes before he starts to read the play. He is not to be blamed ; he is giving employment and he must be sure of his profits. Economy, then, is the watchword, economy of scene, economy of characters, and, equally important, economy of language.

Let us suppose that the play is written, and possibly re-written two or three times. What is to be done with it ? In the first place, it is absolutely necessary to have more than

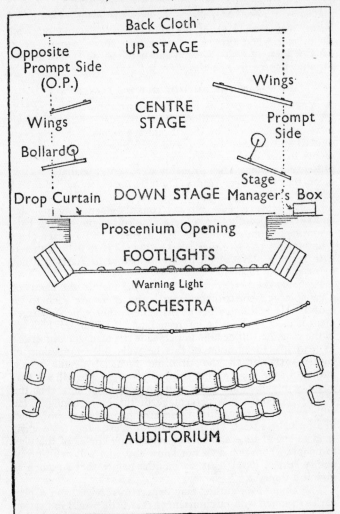

Back Cloth

UP STAGE

Opposite
Prompt Side
(O.P.)

Wings

CENTRE
STAGE

Wings

Prompt
Side

Bollard

Stage
Manager's Box

Drop Curtain   DOWN STAGE

Proscenium Opening

FOOTLIGHTS

Warning Light

ORCHESTRA

AUDITORIUM

A PLAN OF THE NORMAL STAGE.

*The playwright must visualise his characters in position on
the stage. This plan shows the various parts of the stage,
with the technical terms that are used in stage directions.*

one copy typed. Managements have an awkward habit of losing manuscripts or of not remembering having received them, and when the play does return to its owner—as it usually does—it is dog's-eared and battered, and quite useless for showing to any one else.

HOW CAN THE AUTHOR GET HIS PLAY READ ?

MARKETING a play is not the easiest thing in the world. One hears astonishing stories of plays which achieve instantaneous success on their London production having been sent to and rejected by fourteen or fifteen different managements before one has been found who will take the risk of presenting them. They probably were sent, but that does not mean that they were read. There is positively no means of making an impresario read any given play. He is a law unto himself. He may have already commissioned some popular and successful author to write a play round the leading lady whom he has under contract. He may have half-a-dozen plays " up his sleeve." In either case he does not wish to be bothered with reading plays which he knows before he starts will not be of any use to him.

Probably the best course is to put the play in the hands of a capable and trustworthy agent—and there are such to be found. He will know better than the author which management is most likely to be interested, and if he himself believes in the play, he will be able to persuade the manager concerned to read it. In addition to this he will—on commission, of course—arrange all the tiresome financial details which authors in the main shrink from discussing. He will see that advance royalties are paid, and he will make sure that the author receives a just percentage of the gross takings. He will, moreover, insist that these arrangements are embodied in a formal contract. It is far better to trust a reputable agent than to spend time and money registering copies of the play to people whom one does not know and who will in all probability keep it for at least six months before they so much as give it a thought.

The amount an author may expect to receive from a play varies so much with circumstances that little useful indication can be given. It is possible for a successful first play running for perhaps five or six months to bring its author more than a thousand pounds, and first plays have been known to make considerably more.

THE EMERGENCE OF THE CINEMA

FILMS were originally a form of one-dimensional entertainment. In the early days of moving pictures the action was explained, where explanation was necessary, by printed subtitles. The hero had to be identified, so had the villain : the heroine was usually identifiable by her golden locks or her general air of innocence. When comment was necessary for the better understanding of the film, flickering sub-titles were shown, bearing such legends as " Came the Dawn " or " And so into a world full of the hum of bees." These were the growing-pains so often suffered by the infant which is outgrowing its strength. The exciting thing in those days was that the picture was not merely a picture but a *moving* picture. It followed inevitably that the film which was most calculated to capture the imagination of the public was one in which horses galloped, motor-cars sped along the highways, and blonde heroines were borne off in aeroplanes. Speed was the essential factor and very little else mattered.

After a time the novelty of moving pictures began to wear off and something more was required to tickle the palate of the public who thronged the converted mission-halls which served for cinemas. Mr. and Mrs. Sidney Drew discovered that sheer acting could hold an audience as well or better than the sheriff and his posse. John Bunny and Flora Finch proved that the technique of the theatre could be equally well applied to this new and astonishing invention. Charlie Chaplin went a step further and, in an entirely different medium, brought the art of mime into its own again. Various people endeavoured to adapt themselves to the silent screen by using the technique which they already knew—Maurice Costello, Mary Fuller, Marc McDermott and, in the lighter vein, Ford Stirling and Chester Conklin.

All this time the exhibitors of the films had realised the necessity for giving the audience something to listen to as well as to watch. Consequently pianists were engaged to provide a dreamy waltz for the love passages, a rousing tune for the sheriff and his men, and a nice, slow, thumpy passage mostly in the bass clef and with plenty of wiggles in it for the villain. The cinema pianist foreshadowed the general application of sound to image and was also responsible for the development of the theme song and the signature tune.

Before we get on to the subject of " talkies " as such, there are one or two obvious points to consider. In the first place, it is clear that the rules which apply to the construction of a stage play apply with equal force to the writing of a film scenario. There must in each case be a beginning, a middle, and an end. This is rather more difficult in the case of a film, because there are no artificial pauses, in the form of acts and scenes, to aid the writer. Nevertheless the story must be built on a sure foundation. Instead of the curtain descending at the end of an act there must be a point at which the theme, as it were, changes direction. This is merely to say that as between the stage and the screen there is a distinction but not a difference.

The same is true of characterisation. Characters must be built up on exactly the same lines as though one were writing for the stage. They will have their exits and their entrances, and one man in his time will play many parts.

At this point it may be well for the prospective scenario writer to decide whether he is going to write for pleasure or for money. If he is going to hitch his wagon to the very distant star of creative film construction he may with advantage skip the next few sentences. If, on the contrary, he desires to make money out of the film racket he may, without any particular disadvantage, listen to a few words of wisdom.

STORIES WRITTEN TO "FIT THE STARS"

JUST as the theatre has cycles of plays on the same subject, so the cinema tends to circulate round a given idea or a given " star." It is only necessary for some one to produce a film about gangsters and the whole world is flooded with gangster films. *The Big House* is followed by *The Huge House* or *The Public House* before one has time to turn round. This is bad enough, but there is worse to follow. There are not only cycles of films but cycles of " stars." If Greta Garbo is holding the stage, it is no use writing a scenario which demands a Cicely Courtneidge as its leading character. If Wallace Beery is all the rage at the moment, it is hopeless to conceive a film in which the interest centres on a one-legged Welsh dentist. The story should fit the star. The star will never come down from its firmament to fit the story—at least under the present system.

THE ONLY WAY TO LEARN

As in the case of a would-be author of a stage play there is only one way to learn how to write a scenario. The written word can effect practically nothing. Every village in England has its cinema where it is possible to see almost every type of film. The person who is intent on becoming a scenarist should see any and every film at least twice. On the first visit he will probably be lucky if he can decide whether the film was well-constructed or not. But the second visit should leave him in no doubt as to where the climax came, how the suspense was sustained, and whether the dénouement was satisfactorily worked out.

A third visit, if funds will run to it, will enable him to study the scenarist's or producer's use of sound—that is to say, natural sound in the shape of aeroplane noises, waterfalls, and the like, as well as dialogue—and also the way in which the various sequences are built up into one composite whole. There are certain devices which he will be able to detect and recollect. He will see the camera " panning "—that is to say, moving around on its own axis in order to pick up an object or a character at some distance away. This is often used in news-films, when the camera " pans " from the goal-mouth to the applauding crowd after a winning goal has been scored. He will learn the value of " tracking " as when a camera follows a man walking along a street, keeping the one object in focus all the time.

He will realise that " cutting " from one scene to another creates a very different impression from " fading " from scene to scene, and he will notice that a quite legitimate effect can be produced from " dissolving." Perhaps " dissolving " needs a little explanation. Let us suppose that the heroine has to be in Carlisle by 11.20. She is on the train and it is now 11.10. The producer shows the close-up of a clock face with the hands pointing to 11.10 and " dissolves " it into an engine-wheel pounding along at full speed. He " dissolves " back to the clock face reading 11.15, and so on. All these devices, and many more besides, are perfectly sound, but they must be used with discretion. They must be necessary and vital to the unfolding of the plot. To use them as mere trimmings is as unpardonable as it would be to go to Covent Garden Opera-House in a top-hat and sand-shoes with a hollyhock in one's buttonhole. The temptation to juggle with all the exciting toys which the cinema and the microphone place in one's hands is well-nigh overwhelming, but it must be resisted at all costs. As Hamlet said in his famous advice to the players, it is necessary to " use all gently."

APPROACHING THE FILM MAGNATE

THE " placing " of a film scenario is, perhaps, a trifle easier than the " placing " of a stage play. Whether or not it may be due to the influence of American business methods on the film industry, film magnates are more easy of approach than theatrical managers and, generally speaking, their appreciation of the box-office qualities of a story is more sound. The proof of this, if proof is needed, can be seen from the fact that there are but few empty cinemas, while theatres both in London and the provinces have a habit of closing down for months at a time. To put this down to the unfair incidence of the Entertainment Tax is to take a biased view of the problem. Film magnates are business men who deliberately cater for the public taste ; too often theatrical managements consist of moneyed amateurs who trust their own judgment of popular taste even against professional advice in order to gratify their personal ambition.

When one is dealing with a business man it is as well to be as business-like as possible oneself. There is no need to go through the labour of writing a complete scenario with every sequence carefully modelled and every line of dialogue inserted. The story should be written in the first place in the form of a brief précis of five hundred words or so with an indication of how the author proposes to treat his theme should it be considered suitable. Only when the idea has been accepted need the story be elaborated into scenario form. Indeed, as often as not, the film company will prefer to pay for the idea and outlined story alone, and to leave the task of putting the material into scenario form to one of its trained staff of scenario w iters.

The scenario, when finished, should be easy to read, and to ensure this it is advisable to consider each page as divided vertically down the middle and to keep the camera instructions to the left-hand side of the page, with the dialogue on the right. Many a good play has failed to see the light of day because it was indifferently typed and because the stage directions were neither typed nor underlined in red, and the equivalent is true of a film scenario.

Fees for film stories vary considerably. The minimum paid by one British company for a useful idea is twenty-five pounds, and really first-class material has been known to command as much as five hundred pounds. In America, of course, remuneration is on a distinctly higher scale.

ENTERTAINING BY SOUND ALONE: THE RADIO PLAY

SINCE the wireless is the most recent invention by means of which entertainment can be given to the public, it may be pardonable to devote rather more space to radio plays than has been given to their two older relations.

In this one-dimensional art, we are dealing with pure sound, just as the silent film dealt with pure image. Sound in "talkies," whether it be natural sound or dialogue, is the background or scenery to the image, whereas in radio drama the natural sound, or " effects," is the background or scenery to the dialogue. To put it in another way, the picture of an aeroplane will be supported by a combination of the noise made by the propellers and the conversation of the pilot and the observer, while in the radio play the conversation of the pilot and the observer is the important thing and the noise of the propellers becomes the background. The author has to think—not in terms of pictures, but in terms of pure sound, and at the same time he has to realise that there are two different kinds of sound, namely, speech and " effects."

ONE OF THE FIRST RADIO THRILLERS

IN order to learn how to write for this difficult medium it may be well to consider how the sound drama has developed. One of the first plays to be written especially for broadcasting —if not the very first—came from the pen of Richard Hughes. It took place down a mine-shaft, and although it was written in the early days of broadcasting, it still remains one of the best little thrillers heard on the air. The main reason why it is interesting is that it marks the first stage in the development of a new art. Richard Hughes did not write his sketch because he had something vital to say about miners, but because a coal-mine gave him an excellent opportunity for the use of sound effects. He chose his background first and superimposed his dialogue.

This was followed by a series of programmes devised by

16

R. E. Jeffery and John Whitman, which were intended to exploit natural sound with the assistance of dialogue. Military tattoos and the like became the order of the day, not because either of the authors was in the least militaristic, but because that type of programme presented the opportunity to create a realistic background of machine-guns, bombs, shells, and shouted words of command. The background of sound was obtruding itself and becoming the foreground. It was inevitable that things should develop along these lines, and it is largely the result of the experiments of these two pioneers that the " effects " in the modern radio play are as good as they are.

The next development came when it was realised that the story was more important than the trimmings. The background became a background, and the dialogue started to take pride of place. The main difficulty was to find a suitable story, and as there were no suitable authors who had found it worth their while to devote their energies to this new game, it became necessary to take ready-made stories and adapt them for the microphone. Again, it was one of the earliest experiments which was the most successful. Cecil Lewis's adaptation of Conrad's *Lord Jim* remains one of the high-water marks of broadcasting. He used a form which, while it was more or less thrust upon him by the novel itself, continues to be the most satisfactory way of presenting a play to an unseen audience. The plot was unfolded by a narrator, and the action was supplied by interpolated scenes illustrating the events which the narrator was describing. This device was used in a modified form by Philip Wade in *Family Tree*, and is used continually in the Children's Hour in what are known as " Dialogue Stories."

THE RADIO AUTHOR'S HARD TASK

AFTER the adapted novel came the adapted stage play—which has remained with us ever since. It is much easier to take a play by Ibsen and turn it into a microphone play by putting the stage directions into the mouth of one or other of the characters than it is to condense a novel into an hour's dialogue. It is far easier to do either of these things than to write an original play in one dimension.

The author of a radio play has therefore a hard task before him. The adapted novel and the adapted play were first in the field, and he must write something really convincing in order to compete with these formidable rivals. That it is possible to do so has been proved again and again, and the fact that more " adaptations " than original plays are broadcast is due, not so much to lack of enthusiasm at headquarters as to the timidity of authors who are afraid to experiment in a new medium. Fortunately there were some brave spirits who determined to make themselves proficient at the game. They watched the gradual development of radio drama and were wise enough to see that the story, unlike the early experiments, must depend on dialogue for its success. The days of stunting were over by now, and the fact that the scene was laid at Niagara Falls or Brooklands was no longer likely to excite either the play-reader or the listener.

L. du Garde Peach was the first author to realise the importance of this fact. He has always something to say, and he invariably says it well. One of his best productions, *The Path of Glory*, depends almost entirely on its central theme and the briskness of its dialogue, and the sound effects do not obtrude themselves on the ear. Philip Wade, the most promising of the young radio dramatists, has developed along the same lines as L. du Garde Peach. He pays far more attention to his story and his dialogue than to the inclusion of pictures in pure sound. The effect of a situation is not always heightened by the noise of birds singing or waves beating on the shore. Something must be left to the imagination of the listener, and in many cases the producer is better able to judge what incidental sounds are essential than is the author himself.

CATERING FOR A UNIVERSAL AUDIENCE

THERE is one essential respect in which writing for the radio is different from writing stage plays or film scenarios, and that is in the matter of the potential audience. A playgoer who wishes to see a bedroom farce goes to the theatre where such a play is being staged and not to the one next door where Sybil Thorndike is playing in *Hecuba*. A film-fan does not go to *Mädchen in Uniform* if he wants to see the Four Marx Brothers. But the listener does not go to the radio drama at all ; the radio drama goes to him. Unless, therefore, the listening audience is to remain quite static, plays must have a majority rather than a minority appeal. This fact is not always realised by authors of wireless plays. The listening public is not a group of minorities, each of which has to be entertained in turn ; it is a wide and universal theatre, the audience of which is composed of people with hopes and fears, ambitions and aspirations, likes and dislikes, and no more peccadilloes than the best or the worst of us. It is, therefore, a mistake to pander to the tastes of minorities.

A radio play, to be successful, must be the type of entertainment which the ordinary person will welcome in his drawing-room. Nobody in these enlightened days is expected to shelter under his roof the kind of person for whom he has an aversion. He will close the door on tramps as well as on well-dressed cadgers. In the case of the radio he can soon close the door effectively by switching off. Radio drama, with its limited appeal, too often has the door shut in its face, but in reality there is not the slightest reason why plays should not be as eagerly listened to in the home as they are in the theatre or at the cinema.

SOUNDS WHICH TAKE THE PLACE OF DESCRIPTION

As in the case of the cinemas, there are no ready-made divisions into which a radio play will naturally fall. The beginning, middle, and ending do not coincide with any pauses in the presentation of the play. The transition, therefore, from each phase to the next must be definitely marked. It follows that radio plays should be written, not in three acts, but in scenes which correspond with the sequences in the film scenario. In the absence of scenery and vision, each scene must be " planted " in the ear of the listener by a distinctive sound. Thus, the noise of typewriters will convey to the hearer the imaginative background of a business office, just as the sound of an engine and the shouting of porters will suggest a railway station. If these and similar sound effects are utilised in an intelligent way there is no necessity for the narrator to describe the changes of scene.

Characterisation, too, takes on a slightly new complexion when it has to be created in one dimension. Characters must be simple and obvious. Listening at home, with all the distractions of daily life going on around one, is a vastly different thing from communal listening or watching in a theatre or cinema. Characters in a radio play, therefore, must be distinguished, not only by their behaviour, but by their voices. It is permissible, if not actually necessary, to have fourteen cowboys in any given cinema drama of the wide-open spaces, but fourteen cowboys in a radio play are a confusion and a nuisance. They will all speak with the same voice and in the same idiom, and there is no means of distinguishing one from another. Characters must, therefore, be as sharply differentiated from the purely vocal point of view as the incidental noises. There must be as much difference between the sound effect created by the hero and the villain as there is between the noise of a waterfall and a taxi-cab.

All this must seem fairly obvious but it cannot be sufficiently reiterated. Play after play is launched on the air in which it is impossible to follow the plot simply because the characterisation has been built up on the false assumption that pure sound can take the place of sound plus image. This is not the fault of the B.B.C., which has to take what it can get so long as authors are scarce. It is lack of enthusiasm on the part of the authors which is hampering the growth of this new art. All this will be changed provided sufficient authors interest themselves in writing for the microphone. Instead of adaptations and feature programmes there will arise a new and virile art which will appeal to the many instead of merely disappointing the few. Radio drama will give birth to its Shaws and its Galsworthys, its Maughams and its Cowards—who knows—perhaps even to its Shakespeares and its Sheridans. By this time the adapted stage play and the potted novel will, apart from certain exceptional masterpieces, be museum pieces. They have served their turn, and they will as a result have a place of honour in the memories of our grandchildren.

Radio drama has not arrived, it is still in its infancy and is a rather backward child at that. Sordid as it may seem, the real reason for this is that, in spite of the huge financial resources of the B.B.C., it is not possible to make as much money out of writing a radio play as it is by being a successful playwright or scenarist. An author who is receiving a percentage of the gross takings at a London theatre may make thousands of pounds if his play is a success ; a scenario writer may receive three hundred pounds or more for one film ; but the B.B.C. can only possibly pay its star writers about sixty guineas and the general level of remuneration is considerably less.

THE SMALL REWARDS FOR THE RADIO DRAMATIST

IT is only fair to admit that no author should expect to make as much out of a play which is only presented to the public for one, or at the most, two performances as he would from a play which would fill a theatre or a cinema for a number of months. The size of the audience is not the decisive factor—if it were, the B.B.C. would obviously pay higher fees than any other organisation—but it is the time element which must to a certain extent govern the size of the emoluments. In other words, the B.B.C. can present a play to five million people in the course of one hour, while it takes years to present the same play to the same number of people through the medium of the theatre or the cinema. A radio play is the May-fly of the arts. It is born, it makes its brief appearance on two different wave-lengths, and it dies. Some of the more successful radio plays have been repeated from time to time, but this does not benefit the author in the slightest degree, as he surrenders all broadcasting rights once his manuscript has been accepted.

This state of affairs cannot possibly last. The discrepancy between the financial returns from the Theatre, the Cinema, and the B.B.C. are so great that there is bound to be an adjustment in the near future. One of these days it will be as profitable to write a radio play as to write any other form of dramatic composition. It is bound to be a slow process. Fifteen years ago radio drama did not exist, in fact it was hardly thought of. It was sufficient in those days to hear a piano creeping through one's earphones out of the void. Nobody had realised the potentialities of broadcasting, let alone the possibility of grafting a new limb on to the oldest of all the arts. It was inevitable that payments should at first be small. They are improving by degrees, and there is no doubt that in the future the radio dramatist will be able to command as much for his services as the playwright and the scenarist.

The Drama Director is the final judge of whether a play is suitable for the vast listening public, and it is to him that all manuscripts should be sent. There is no need to employ an agent; he will charge at least 10 per cent., and that does not leave a great deal for the author.

THE MAGNIFICENT GAME OF MAKE-BELIEVE

WRITING plays, in whatever dimension, is a fascinating game. Generally speaking, the theme selects itself, but the characters sometimes take charge of the situation. They grow and develop before one's very eyes. They assume habits and mannerisms with which one had not the slightest intention of enduing them when the idea was first conceived. They give a twist to the plot which never existed in the mind of their creator. Whether one is thinking in terms of the Theatre, the Cinema, or the Wireless, they treat the author of their being in the most off-hand manner. It is sometimes as much as he can do to keep them within the bounds of his original concept. In the end, if the author is firm, they toe the line, and sometimes the result is a work of art.

The essential thing in this magnificent game of make-believe is to be sincere. The play, whether it be farce or comedy, tragedy or melodrama, must be true to itself and the author. The trivial performances one is sometimes condemned to see on the London stage, the idiotic shapeless films which occupy too many of our cinemas, and the pretentious nonsense which desecrates the ether from time to time only succeed in bringing the theatre, the films, and the radio into contempt. Sincerity in art is the only thing that matters. It is not given to everybody to be a genius, but those who believe that they have some natural gift stand every chance of success if they will write what is nearest to their hearts and not be led astray by the ambition to be considered clever. It is only the genius who can afford to disregard the rules of the game, the ordinary workman must master his craft with all its intricacies before he can hope to achieve recognition. The rewards are not always commensurate with the amount of labour expended, but to the true artist the knowledge of a piece of work well done is worth all the laurels which sometimes crown the brows of less deserving people.

WHAT TO READ NEXT ABOUT PLAY-WRITING

THOSE who are sufficiently interested to wish to pursue the subject further can supplement their visits to theatres and cinemas by reading various books that deal with the different aspects of play-writing. As already pointed out, there is no easy road to success, but a deeper study of the various problems involved may serve to increase the enthusiasm to overcome the obstacles which beset the path of the intending dramatist. In recommending certain books the writer does not necessarily subscribe to the conclusions at which their authors have arrived.

Publications of value on the drama are *How to Write a Play*, by St. John Ervine (Allen & Unwin), and *On Dramatic Method*, by Granville-Barker (Sidgwick & Jackson). Four books on scenario-writing which give the basic principles are

Films : the Way of the Cinema, by Andrew Buchanan (Pitman) ; *Film*, by Rudolf Arnheim (Faber & Faber) ; *Writing for the Screen*, by Jackson (A. & C. Black) ; and *Writing for the Films*, by L'Estrange Fawcett (Pitman).

No really classic work on radio plays had so far appeared, perhaps because broadcasting is such a comparatively recent factor in modern life. There are, however, several people who have set down their ideas on the subject and their views may be studied with advantage. The books referred to are *Shall I Listen ?*, by Filson Young (Constable) ; *Broadcasting*, by Hilda Matheson (Thornton Butterworth) ; *Learn to Write for Broadcasting*, by Claude Hulbert ; and *How to Write Broadcasting Plays*, by Val Gielgud (Hurst & Blackett). These four books, if they do not instruct, will at least stimulate.

In addition, the B.B.C. Drama Director issues a free pamphlet entitled *The Wireless Play*, which contains much useful first-hand information and gives authors an authoritative account of the type of play the B.B.C. requires.

Informative books on the subject of play-writing should, of course, be used in conjunction with, and not instead of, a study of plays and films at first hand, and the reader should not rely altogether on methods which other authors have found satisfactory.

CAREERS FOR THOSE WHO CAN WRITE GOOD ENGLISH

by F. M. WINTER, B.A.(Lond.).

JOURNALISM may be the career that most obviously opens itself to those with a gift for and a particular knowledge of English. There are, however, other careers in which it is equally necessary and valuable, though in a different way. Even in the business world, the use of that jargon which is still known as commercial English is slowly dying out. Much of the office drudgery that used to occupy the time and energy of the majority of those who entered business is now more efficiently performed by machinery, and there is an increasing demand for those who can freely develop and express ideas in speech and in writing, particularly in the higher posts. A greater number of occupations in the modern world are coming to need the easy expression of ideas, the clear delineation of policy, the stating of evidence and argument and the making of verbal or written reports. They all need the power of self-expression.

There are, however, careers which are more particularly the field of those who have achieved a facility of speech and writing. The teaching profession, for example, even though one may be teaching physics or mathematics or something else which has no direct connection with the subtleties of English language or the glories of English literature, clearly needs the capacity for easy and simple expression. Every career, however, needs various qualifications of temperament or training in addition to any natural gift for or acquired knowledge of the English language. It has already been indicated what additional qualifications are necessary for the journalist, particularly if he is working in an office. The free-lance may indulge in many peculiarities of temperament because he is a more or less solitary worker. There are no stipulations as to how he must have acquired his education. He may have left school at fourteen and acquired the most essential part of it after that age by his own efforts. No one will inquire or trouble about it.

But the teacher must fulfil certain conditions of training, and should, if he is to be a success, have certain qualifications of temperament that need not trouble the entrant to other professions. For elementary teaching, the minimum academic training essential consists of two years at an elementary training college, this period being devoted to further education and also to training in the practice of teaching. For secondary or high-school teaching, a good university degree is essential and in some cases a further year devoted to actual training, the whole preparation in this case taking four years.

The teacher should possess excellent physical and nervous health. He should be naturally fond of children, the not so bright ones as well as the bright ones, and have infinite patience and sympathy. He should remember that practically the whole of his working life will be spent in a room with about twenty other human beings, and that it should be possible for him to be constantly in command without constantly commanding. The beginner receives a salary varying from about £180 to £220 a year, and if he stays in the ranks and does not become a lecturer or headmaster or inspector, he may rise to something between £350 and £450 a year.

ADVERTISING : A CAREER FOR QUICK AND ORIGINAL MINDS

THERE are careers that are to some extent linked with journalism and with teaching, but which in many cases offer more attractive conditions or better financial prospects to people who are interested in the writing of English. Advertising, for example, offers almost as much opportunity for writing of a certain type as journalism, while it satisfies more adequately any business instincts and, given even moderate success, is frequently more remunerative.

It should be remembered that advertising has many branches, but it is safe to say that in all of these a special aptitude for English is necessary, a quick, original mind and facility of expression, and a capacity to judge the selling power of words. Those are the first essentials, but they are by no means all. In almost every case it will be found that the most successful people in the advertising world are those who have risen from the junior positions, a fact that illustrates the indispensability of practical training. Yet facilities for practical training in advertising are still to some extent limited and scattered. The best way to learn, even for those with an advanced education, is to take a junior post or even an apprenticeship in some kind of advertising office.

But what kind of advertising office ? There is, for example, the advertising department of a big business organisation. The work of the department consists in creating and planning all advertising campaigns for the firm concerned. Unless the work is done in conjunction with an advertising agency, it will entail the writing of copy, the lay-out of written matter, headlines, insets and illustrations, and the obtaining of such illustrations, either in the form of drawings from artists or of photographs specially taken to show the products or perhaps the process of production of the firm.

A knowledge of blocks, typography, lay-out, and printing must be acquired, a knowledge too, of how information about markets and prospects is acquired and of how different types of purchasers should be appealed to. A cursory glance at the advertisements issued by the same firm for publication in, for example, *The Daily Herald* and *The Daily Telegraph* will give a fair idea of how much is to be learned in the art of appealing to different classes of customers.

A different kind of advertising work embraces the selling instead of the buying of space in the press. A junior post in the advertisement department of a periodical publication is the best training for this. Here again a knowledge of typography, lay-out, and blocks must be acquired, but in this case a greater knowledge of the actual production of a periodical is necessary, of working in with editorial requirements, of proof-reading, and the placing of pages and spaces. For the actual selling of space, experience in canvassing must be acquired and the elusive art of establishing what the advertisement man calls " contacts " must be mastered.

INTERESTING PROBLEMS FOR THE ADVERTISING AGENT

SOME of the biggest jobs in the advertising world are those held by members of advertising agencies, contractors, and consultants. In fact many experienced men maintain that the very best preparation for a career in advertising is a junior post or an apprenticeship in a good advertising agency, for here the buying and the selling of space are both undertaken. The problems met with are of wide application and interest. One learns to buy space for a limitless variety of trades in an infinite variety of publications. One's knowledge of advertisement values and market exploration must of necessity be great. Moreover, one may meet tasks of the kind that no advertisement department of a magazine will need to tackle—the planning of sales campaigns, the putting of new products on the market, the compiling of statistics of demand gathered from house-to-house investigations or from questionnaires answered by retailers, the drawing up of all kinds of descriptive leaflets and catalogues.

MAGIC WORDS THAT SELL THE GOODS

THE branch of this work which frequently makes the most direct appeal to those interested in the writing of English is copywriting, and for this it is not absolutely essential to have experience in other branches, though such experience would be valuable. But it must be realised that the mere capacity to write good, expressive, or even literary English is not sufficient qualification for this most exacting work. It is absolutely necessary to be able to write the kind of copy that *sells* the article concerned. The only test of success is the record of sales statistics.

For the man or woman who aims at being a copywriter, the best preliminary training would be that in the advertising department of a commercial or industrial firm or organisation. Here, unless the advertising is managed by an agent, which it would be possible to discover before accepting a post—copy will have to be written, but it will only form part of the activities of the department and its staff, and it will, moreover, deal exclusively with the products or merchandise of that firm and so will be limited in range.

It should be possible to discover by such experience if one would be able to make a success as a copywriter alone. It is well-paid work, particularly in some of the larger advertisement agencies. One seldom earns less than £250 a year and may possibly rise to somewhere in the region of £750. But it must be remembered that such work entails little but writing, and writing always with a view to selling, and nearly always against time. In spite of the efforts of every one concerned in the business of advertising, it appears to be work that is always done in a rush. It should be clear that copywriting is not a resort for an unsuccessful journalist or for any one who imagines that money is easily earned. The kind of writing involved and the conditions would break the heart of many a man or woman who might be reasonably successful in ordinary journalism or indeed in some quite different profession that allowed a certain amount of leisure ime for writing.

There is one other point to remember in weighing the

advantages of advertising as a career. Its specialists will usually agree that it is a profession still in its youth, with its methods still in a more or less experimental stage. For those with adventurous minds, those who prefer to be in a job that may change or develop rapidly and are prepared to adapt themselves and their methods of work to such changes, rather than to settle down in comfort to work that is unlikely to be much altered in the space of a lifetime, advertising offers an inducement of ever-changing interest and excitement. It should be possible to decide whether or not one is suited to it by a year's experience, at the most.

HOW PUBLICITY DIFFERS FROM ADVERTISING

THE work of the publicity agent is sometimes confused with that of an advertising agent by people who are not very clear about the distinction between advertising and publicity. The object of the advertising agent is to get his client's products or activities known by means of buying space in the press and calling attention to them in the most direct and effective way. The object of the publicity agent is to achieve the same end, but, as far as the press is concerned, by editorial means. A capacity to write is essential and the necessary experience includes a knowledge both of journalism (from the inside of a newspaper office) and advertising.

The publicity agent must be able to assemble and to write the kind of material which interests and entertains the public and at the same time advances the interests of the person or organisation for whom he is acting. He must be able not only to turn out articles and paragraphs and choose and arrange for photographs or sketches, but to know exactly where to place them and by what means to make sure they are published. He must know what style each editor likes, and which is his press day. It is work at which one might aim after experience of the kind indicated, but not a career one can enter without such preliminaries. It is exceedingly well paid.

HOW TO BECOME A LITERARY AGENT

A CERTAIN amount of what has been said about the work of a publicity agent applies to that of a literary agent. While experience in an actual editorial office is not perhaps so absolutely indispensable as it is for publicity work, it is nevertheless of very great value and should be acquired as soon as possible after a very good education of the literary type. A knowledge of one or two modern languages should also be part of one's equipment, as it is frequently the agent's business to negotiate the sale of rights in other countries and to arrange for translations.

In some cases the work might be mastered as well by beginning in a junior post in the office of a literary agent, learning the ways of editors from the agent's point of view instead of from inside experience. But it must be realised that a capacity to judge literary value, resulting perhaps from familiarity with the classics of English literature during a university education, is not a sufficient qualification for this work. The agent must know everything there is to be known about markets in this country and abroad. He must know the peculiarities of taste of editors and publishers more intimately than the free-lance writer can possibly know them. He must have the kind of knowledge, as well as give the kind of service, that induces an author to employ him in the business of selling his output.

The literary agent's profits depend, like those of any other business man, on how much he sells. He is not employed by his clients, like the publicity agent, at so much a year. His income is derived entirely from a percentage of the prices he obtains for the work he sells. He should therefore combine the qualities of a salesman with those of a literary critic. He should be methodical, for he or his staff will be keeping elaborate records of a vast number of manuscripts. Even if he has the requisite capital and the requisite experience, he should not be tempted to set up in business on his own unless he has a considerable clientèle of authors who are likely to maintain a fairly regular supply of saleable manuscripts.

QUALITIES THAT MAKE FOR SUCCESS IN PUBLISHING

THE career of publishing, though apparently more closely connected with authorship than is advertising or publicity, bears less resemblance to it in that it less frequently involves actual writing work. No outstanding capacity for self-expression is necessary, though a never-failing interest in and knowledge of the writing of English is certainly required, in addition to an excellent education—preferably at a university. Moreover, it is essential for a publisher, even if he cannot himself write well, to be able to judge good writing—and also writing that will sell, though it may not be so good.

There is no recognised training for this work. The best thing to do is to take a junior post or an apprenticeship (a premium may be necessary) in a general publishing house that produces as wide a range of literature as possible. There is a tendency to overlook the fact that publishing is a highly skilled and technical profession, involving a thorough knowledge of typography, paper, block-making, binding, estimating, and costing. Infinite attention to detail is necessary, and an exceptionally good memory, for, however perfect the system of indexing publications and existing literature on every conceivable subject, a great deal will depend on how much of such information is immediately accessible in one's mind.

It is significant that the most successful publishers are those who have been right through the business and have mastered the technique of every branch of production. They are also the people who possess or can develop a sensitiveness to changes in public taste, not only in reading matter but in manner of presentation.

There are editorial posts in a publishing firm which require less journalistic experience than editorial posts on any kind of periodical, and at the same time less experience of production than most other forms of publishing work. It will be understood that the publishing of annuals, encyclopædias, or other books which are the result of garnering information or material from various sources needs a certain amount of editing as distinct from publishing work, and this means knowing where and how to get in touch with specialist writers on all kinds of subjects, and planning the book so that the ground is well covered yet no overlapping of material occurs. Journalistic experience should be supplemented by wide interests and comprehensive reading. Secretarial experience would also be useful, as there is much organisation involved.

A LESS STRENUOUS FORM OF TEACHING

THERE are a number of careers which, though they could not strictly be included in the profession of teaching, nevertheless need very similar education and training and involve very similar work, though in conditions which are generally less strenuous than those of actual teaching in schools. There is, for example, the work of lecturing in training colleges, either for elementary or secondary school teachers. A good honours degree is necessary, or, in some cases in elementary training colleges, a certificate of high standard in art, music, physical training, or handicrafts. A course of actual training in teaching work is frequently regarded as an essential also, and one must have had some years of successful teaching experience, preferably of a varied kind. There are, of course, a few exceptions to the rule, and occasionally a course of post-graduate research and a higher degree will be considered as sufficient qualification for a junior lecturer in a university college, provided always that the original degree was good.

In an elementary training college the lecturer will lecture on his own subject, not only in a direct way, but also from the teaching point of view. He will give demonstration lessons, followed by discussions. He must not be a mere specialist, as he has to train class teachers. In the day training department of a university or in a secondary training college, he will lecture on the teaching of his own subject, not on the subject itself. In a university college he will lecture solely on the subject itself. Salaries in elementary training colleges are based on the Burnham scale, but in any college connected with a university they are governed by the rules of that university.

The cost of training for elementary teaching, a training which may sometimes be regarded as a preliminary to a lecturing post in an elementary training college, is very considerably less than that for secondary teaching, for part of the cost is borne by the Board of Education. It is usually somewhere between £45 and £90 resident for the two years. On the other hand the cost of a university education is never less than £150 a year resident, though it is possible again to call on the help of the Board of Education for a non-residential course. It normally takes three years, and for certain subjects (chiefly scientific) four. The cost of a year of professional training following the three years at a university is considerably less.

PREPARING THE STUDENT FOR EXAMINATIONS

AN honours degree is also the one essential for a career in coaching. This, however, cannot be regarded as a full-time profession, for it is definitely precarious and indeed there is hardly any opening for it except in London or other large towns. It does, however, supply a great need, and is well worth doing by the man or woman who is not wholly dependent on earnings.

It is chiefly needed by people preparing for matriculation or for entrance or scholarship examinations for the universities, or for what is known as the higher schools examination. Matriculation is still regarded in a very great number of cases as a necessary educational qualification for all kinds of work, and there are an enormous number of young people who fail to pass it from school merely because they need extra coaching in certain subjects. In a case like this one must be prepared to tackle subjects which one has probably not studied since one's own schooldays or at least since one took the intermediate or higher schools examination. For university entrance or scholarship work, however, one would not be likely to take on a student except in one's own subject or in a closely allied subject, as the standard here is high and indeed the method of coaching rather different. It involves less actual teaching and very much more direction of reading and criticism of essay work.

Work for these higher examinations, though highly paid, cannot be very remunerative unless the tutor can establish a position where he can work in conjunction with a university or with one or more specific colleges who will send pupils to him. If he can do so, he is sure of a good, though not regular, income. Fees will vary from 7s. 6d. to 15s. an hour, according to the examination for which work is being done. The demand for tuition will be much heavier in vacation than in term time. It will very probably be found that examining work can be combined with coaching. This again is highly paid, though it must be remembered that it is work which is almost always very exacting and which must be done to time, whatever other work one is engaged in at the moment.

It must be remembered that coaching in connection with a university and examining are seldom given to people without a good degree and some teaching or lecturing experience, and are most frequently given to people who not only have these qualifications but whose work is well known to the university authorities. This kind of work, therefore, cannot be regarded as a career to be entered after education and training, however good, but only after experience in other work.

THE ART OF TEACHING BY POST

FOR the man or woman who has the instinct for teaching but not the natural aptitude for facing a class, there is work at correspondence schools and colleges. These are not so numerous as to provide any extensive openings for such a career, so that little need be said beyond pointing out that such work requires infinite patience and a genuine interest in the writing of English, for the work received will nearly all be written, and the lessons and criticisms sent out must be written well if they are to achieve their difficult purpose.

The kind of subjects taught will very largely determine the character of the teaching. It will be found, for example, that in many cases language courses mean standardised and rather mechanical work, and much the same is often true of courses which prepare students for a definite examination with a circumscribed curriculum, such as matriculation. Degree courses, however, would mean much more individual and therefore varied work, and correspondence teaching of journalism would also be less stereotyped, for very few students would be following exactly the same lines. For any one who aims at this type of work, it would be well to make a thorough preliminary investigation of the actual work involved in the correspondence teaching of the particular subject concerned.

WHAT IS EXPECTED OF THE IDEAL SECRETARY

THERE is a tendency in these days to apply the term "secretarial work" to almost anything which involves shorthand and typewriting. But the more serious secretarial job is definitely one for the man or woman (generally the woman) with an excellent education and a capacity to write flawless English. The secretary must be prepared to correct any serious faults of grammar which occur in letters dictated to her, for it is easy to make even elementary grammatical errors in dictating. She must write a large number of letters herself, prepare reports, record minutes of committee meetings. The best preparation is a degree course followed by secretarial training, including, if possible, elementary finance and the groundwork of economics and at least one foreign language. The cost of such training varies from £40 to about £80 for a six to nine months' course.

Much has been said about the temperamental qualifications of the ideal secretary, and there are few people of whom more virtues are expected. She should have a sympathetic personality and be able to deal with people of every rank. She should be prepared to take responsibility without fussing, and should have at least a certain amount of organising capacity. She should be clear-headed and accurate, adaptable and tactful and have common sense, initiative, and imagination in abundance. She should have had a first-class technical training. She will then be able to expect a salary of anything from £2, 10s. to £6 a week, or even more.

There are, then, a number of careers open to the man or woman with an excellent knowledge of English. If one has no natural or acquired gift for professional writing, there are, it is clear, opportunities to teach, help, check, and keep a generally well-educated eye on others who are trying to write English for all manner of workaday purposes.

INDEX AND PRONOUNCING GLOSSARY

Compiled by L. M. MONT-CLAR

How to use this Index.—In order to facilitate immediate reference to the principal entry on a particular subject, the page number for this entry is set in italics, thus : *258.* Subsidiary references to the subject which occur elsewhere in the book are indicated by numerals in roman type, thus : 387. References to illustrations are indicated by numerals in roman type surrounded by square brackets, thus : [156]. Cross references given in the index refer only to the index pages.

The pronouncing glossary.—Where the pronunciation of proper names and technical terms is not immediately understood from the spelling, or where the spelling may be misleading, a separate pronunciation is given after the first index entry. In simple cases a hint may be considered sufficient ; in all doubtful cases a complete phonetic re-spelling is given. The word is broken into syllables as it is spoken, and an accent mark (') follows the syllable on which the stress is placed. The notation used for the phonetic re-spelling is as follows :

ā	m*a*te	ė	th*e*re	th	*th*in
ē	m*e*te	à	f*a*ther	TH	*th*ine
ī	m*i*te	ẹ	h*e*r	zh	lei*s*ure
ō	m*o*te	aw	*aw*l	ch	*ch*urch
ū	m*u*te	oi	*oi*l	g	*g*et
ōō	b*oo*t	ow	*ow*l	j	*j*am

The French nasalised *n* is denoted by italicising the vowel and the nasal concerned, thus : *un*, b*on*, v*in*.